"An invaluable, lucid and practical guide to a crucial area of management."

Robert Heller, Founding Editor of *Management Today*

"An important book, taking a lead role in growing a new generation of professional project managers."

Oded Cohen, The Goldratt Institute

"This book provides an outstanding guide to success in navigating the project management currents, tides and obstacles. It complements the available theory by providing practical examples through case studies. This book draws on the author's extensive corporate and project management experience to provide an excellent practitioner's aide memoire to ensure your projects are successful."

John Pelton MBE, Global Lead for Project, Programme and Commercial Management, Mott MacDonald

The Project Workout

Projects are an important strategic management tool and a way of life in every business. But how do you get started and ensure you realize the benefits you need? Now in its 5th edition, *The Project Workout* is the definitive book on business-led project management. It is a valuable companion for every executive and project manager as well as a comprehensive resource for students of project management.

The Project Workout provides practical advice and techniques to direct and manage a project. Aimed at both project sponsors and project managers, it works through the life cycle of a project from initial idea to successful result. The practical approach is enhanced throughout with a series of "Workouts": exercises, techniques and checklists to help you put the book's advice into practice. The Workouts are supported by an on-line resource of tools, including MS project views, project logs and templates.

This revised edition contains a wealth of new material on governance, monitoring and control, resource and information management and working with standards, such as ISO 21500, BS6079, PRINCE2®, APM Body of Knowledge and PMBOK® Guide. The companion to this book, *The Programme and Portfolio Workout*, deals with directing and managing whole portfolios of projects, making sure everyone in your organization is working towards the same goals; together these books give you what you need to ensure *all* your projects succeed.

Robert Buttrick has a successful track record for building project management excellence in major organizations and is a contributor to project management methods, best practice and international standards. He currently works as a consultant and is a Visiting Teaching Fellow at the University of Warwick.

The Project Workout

The Ultimate Guide to Directing and Managing Business-led Projects

Fifth Edition

Robert Buttrick

Routledge
Taylor & Francis Group

LONDON AND NEW YORK

Fifth edition published 2019
by Routledge
2 Park Square, Milton Park, Abingdon, Oxon, OX14 4RN

and by Routledge
711 Third Avenue, New York, NY 10017

Routledge is an imprint of the Taylor & Francis Group, an informa business

© 2019 Robert Buttrick

First edition published by Pearson FT 1997
Second edition published by Pearson FT 2000
Third edition published by Pearson FT 2005
Fourth edition published by Pearson FT 2009

British Library Cataloguing-in-Publication Data
A catalogue record for this book is available from the British Library

Library of Congress Cataloging-in-Publication Data
Names: Buttrick, Robert, author.
Title: The project workout : the ultimate guide to directing and
    managing business-led projects / Robert Buttrick.
Description: Fifth Edition. | New York : Routledge, 2018. | Revised edition of
    the author's | Includes bibliographical references and index.
Identifiers: LCCN 2017019721 (print) | LCCN 2017027264 (ebook) |
    ISBN 9781315194424 (eBook) | ISBN 9781138744493 (hardback : alk. paper) |
    ISBN 9781138721449 (pbk. : alk. paper) | ISBN 9781315194424 (ebk)
Subjects: LCSH: Project management.
Classification: LCC HD69.P75 (ebook) | LCC HD69.P75 B885 2018 (print) | DDC 658.4/04—dc23
LC record available at https://lccn.loc.gov/2017019721

ISBN: 9781138744493 (hbk)
ISBN: 9781138721449 (pbk)
ISBN: 9781315194424 (ebk)

Typeset in Myriad Pro
by Apex CoVantage, LLC

FOR MY WIFE

Contents

Project workouts

Foreword

The forward progress of organizations has always depended heavily on the management of projects. New plants, new products, new organizations, new methods, new ventures – all require dedicated teams working to strict timetables and separate budgets. But today there's a vital difference. The project management mode has broadened and evolved to the point where managers may spend as much time in interdisciplinary, cross-functional, interdepartmental project teams as they do in their normal posts.

Many factors have contributed to this unstoppable development – among them the increased complexity of all businesses, the closer inter-relationships within organizations and with customers and suppliers outside, and the mounting pressure for speed. The last demands synchronous working. Organizations can no longer afford to play pass the parcel, with each department or function waiting for the others to finish. There simply isn't enough time to waste.

That pressure demands not only speed but effective delivery, on time, on specification, and on budget. That will not happen by accident – and Robert Buttrick's book, based on his extensive corporate experience, is an invaluable, lucid, and practical guide to a crucial area of management which has been crying out for the treatment it receives in these pages. Unlike management in general, project management is self-contained and dedicated to clearly defined ends. The organizations and the managers who best master the methods and maxims in this book will not only achieve their specific objectives, they will win the whole game.

Robert Heller

Acknowledgements

This book is built on the experience and knowledge of many people I have worked with over the years in corporate life, as a consultant, and on the BSI and ISO working groups. If I named them all, the list would be as long as the credits at the end of an epic film . . . and we all walk out of the cinema before they've finished rolling, don't we? Here are a few mentions for those who have gone the extra mile with me.

I would like to thank my former colleagues at Gibb Ltd who took me on as a graduate and turned me into an engineer. Thanks, too, to those at PA Consulting who took on an engineer and gave me my grounding in business-led project management.

Unlike many books, this one was written by one of the "infantry": I am not an academic. I would like to thank Jim Reynolds, formerly the Products and Services Director at Cable and Wireless for giving me the opportunity to write the first edition of this book and to share my experiences with you. My thanks also to Richard Cahn and Grant Holdom at BT, for creating an environment in which the methods in this book can thrive, to Alan Fowler, of Isochron, for his stunning insights into benefits management, to the one and only Dr Eddie Obeng for introducing me to his frameworks and concepts relating to project types, to Oded Cohen of the Goldratt Institute who opened my eyes to the Theory of Constraints, to Chris Worseley at CITI for his work on project manager profiling, and to John Anderson for his insights into portfolio management.

Thank you also to the companies who took part in the benchmarking. I'd also like to thank those business leaders who, frankly never "got it" and just loved their corporate silos and hierarchies; without them, there would be no challenge . . . and no competitive advantage for those who do "get it"!

Most important of all, I would like to thank my wife, Sandra, for hours of proof-reading and the solid support she has given me to ensure this venture succeeds.

And after all this, am I satisfied with what has been achieved? No – there's always more to do!

Robert Buttrick, projectworkout.com

About the Author

Robert Buttrick is an international authority on business-led strategic programme and project management. He has a successful track record for building strategic project management centres of excellence in a wide variety of blue-chip companies, most recently as BT's PPM Method Director. Prior to that, he was accountable for creating and running a project-based framework for managing change for a global communication company, enabling the planning and development of new systems, products, services, and capabilities to meet ever growing customer needs. He was also a member of the management team responsible for managing the company's UK residential sector, acting as coach to sponsors and project managers, in a wide range of business projects.

Before taking up a corporate career in 1993, Robert worked for PA Consulting, a management and technology consultancy where he specialized in business-led project management. Clients included Lloyds TSB Bank, National Rivers Authority, Property Services Agency, Avon Industrial Polymers, NatWest Bank, and RHM.

Robert's early career was as a civil engineer. After graduating from the University of Liverpool with a first class honours engineering degree, he joined Gibb Ltd, who provided engineering consulting, design, and management services for infrastructure projects worldwide. He has lived in countries as diverse as Kenya, Mauritius, Yemen, Senegal, and Sudan, working on the evaluation, design and supervision of a number of marine and water resource projects. He has also worked with the World Bank in Washington DC on investment appraisals for major development projects.

Robert is an active contributor to programme and project management practice through his writing and at conferences. He a UK Principal Expert working on the development of national and international project management standards, for which he received a Distinguished Service Certificate from BSI. He was an author of the 2017 edition of PRINCE® and the lead developer for the UK government's project delivery standard. He is a Member of the Chartered Institute of Marketing, a Chartered Engineer and an Honorary Fellow of the Association for Project Management.

Robert is currently an independent author, a consultant and a Visiting Teaching Fellow at the Warwick Manufacturing Group at the University of Warwick.

Robert can be contacted via his website, projectworkout.com

Preface to the Fifth Edition

Long gone are the days when project management involved little more than mastering a schedule and monthly budget, delivered by technical experts who were assigned or assumed the role of "project manager" by dint of their specialist knowledge. Instead, today's project management environment is characterised by benefits realisation, challenging external pressures, complex organisations and often requires sophisticated analytic methods, evolving management tools and a wide range of people from many disciplines to be involved.

The internal project environment is set within an external context, such that, in addition to the traditional pressures around time, cost and quality, we now need to consider other factors, including risk, productivity, continuous improvement, innovation, digitisation, collaboration and a range of 'softer' themes. Projects are driven by the need for organizations to adapt to their new environment or by the demands of clients; some are driven by societal changes. In response, the practice of project management has become increasingly agnostic to sectors and industries and become established as a profession in its own right. The range of accredited skills that must now be mastered has correspondingly increased both for those sponsoring projects and those managing them. All of this provides opportunity to the wise but a potential threat to the unwary.

In response to this seemingly intimidating context, there is a wide range of theory, doctrine and guidance available. Whilst there are some common, and often core, themes, there is also much contradiction and incoherence between the recommendations of the theoreticians. So where is the aspiring project sponsor or manager to turn in this chaotic and confusing world? Fortunately, there are some practitioners with the experience to be able to provide straightforward and pragmatic advice, both to the newcomer and to the experienced hand. Robert Buttrick is one of those practitioners and an exponent in the field.

This book provides an outstanding guide to success in navigating the project management currents, tides and obstacles. It complements the available theory by providing practical examples through case studies. It tackles the new and emerging trends head on, setting out the ways and means for managing them. It also provides tools for working with the differing guidance and managing the tensions that will inevitably arise between the contradictory pressures on the project team. This book draws on the author's extensive corporate and project management experience to provide an excellent practitioner's aide memoire to ensure your projects are successful.

John Pelton MBE
Global Lead for Project, Programme and
Commercial Management
Mott MacDonald

M
M
MOTT
MACDONALD

Introduction

This book is about driving change in your organization by directing and managing the right projects in the right way. The approach is to keep to some basic principles supported by only a few "rules". In this way, the likelihood of success is increased dramatically, giving the executive or director the freedom to direct projects and the project manager the freedom to manage projects to suit the circumstances and their own style.

In the mid-1990s, Sir Ian Gibson, then president of Nissan Europe, said:

> *"As organizations we must become increasingly able to change quickly and easily. This means building on and around people's abilities rather than limiting them for the convenience of recognizable roles."*

He recognized the need for a new way of working within our businesses; one that is flexible and not tied to specific departments and job titles; one where people can be used to the best effect; where what they do (their role) counts more than the department or function they come from (their job). In such organizations, reporting structures are flat, job titles are secondary and most personnel moves are sideways. This applies from top to bottom and no one should ever say, "I won't do that, it's not my job!" Change is built into the way they work.

Today, the term "corporate agility" is often advocated, not least by McKinsey & Company. In this context, McKinsey argues that being "agile" is all about "adhocracy" rather than bureaucracy. In an adhocracy, action and decisions are focused on objectives and purpose across functional boundaries. Some organizations have attained this vision but many have not. *The Project Workout* looks at one aspect of this, the part which relates to managing a change to your business and those of your clients. A "new way" of doing this has been with us for a long time, buried within the bowels of our technical and engineering departments and is now being recognized by business and governments alike as a discipline which is useful in any management context where change is needed. It is **project management**.

In fact, since the first edition of this book was published in 1997, there is evidence of many more organizations taking deliberate steps to use project methods. Yet, in some organizations, the support and training given to those sponsoring or managing a project is pitifully small and all too frequently the projects are more targeted at delivering "things" in separate departments than ensuring the achievement of specific business objectives. Managers are often given a project to sponsor or manage because it is "good for their development". True, but not if they have to invent how to "do it" for themselves with no grounding whatsoever. I have never heard of an accountant who was expected to do his job "from first principles". Newcomers to project management are often termed "accidental", be they project managers or project sponsors. Billions of pounds, euros and dollars rest on their shoulders and yet it is still a cause for concern that many major organizations do not provide these essential people with the training, methods, or tool kit to undertake their role.

The discipline of project management is often made to look too complicated, is frequently misunderstood and poorly practised. Consequently, some people seek to avoid it and its inferred bureaucracy, as their real-life experience has shown them that it does not always realize the promised rewards. They haven't grasped that uninformed and unskilled people cannot perform well. Whether you are a senior executive, manager, project manager, or "one of the infantry", I aim to make the "art of project management" clearer to you in this book by:

- explaining the challenges faced by many companies;
- outlining some lessons and advice from leading companies;
- proposing a staged framework for managing individual projects;
- explaining the key roles which need to be fulfilled;
- providing best practice techniques for managing projects.

Reading this book will benefit you as:

- having read it, you can really start doing it!
- the "mystique" of projects is exposed, making it simple to understand and accessible to finance, sales, marketing, customer services, administrators, engineers, scientists, and technologists alike;
- the content is not tied to any formally published "methods" but is positioned as "common sense" which overrides them all and will help you perform in your project role.

Part I covers the challenges and lessons. Part II looks at a typical project life cycle. Part III proposes a control framework for your projects. Part IV contains some thoughts on how to make sure project management works for you, personally.

Many of the key points will be restated in different sections throughout the book. This is intentional, both as reinforcement and to enable you to dip into separate sections without the need to follow up multiple cross-references simply to understand the basic message. It also emphasizes that in the "real world", life is not divided into a series of discrete topics with labels tagged on to them, but rather comprises an ever-changing mix of topics, each affecting the other. Successful project management is a complete system and to describe elements of it in isolation would be deficient.

If much of the book seems to be "mere common sense", then I have succeeded in relaying an important message – it *is* common sense. However, while it is obvious common sense to state it, the common sense of doing it is rarer.

If much of the book seems simple, I have succeeded in relaying it to you in a form that can be understood by anyone in your organization. Every manager involved in a project, from the top executive to the line supervisor, needs to understand the basics of project working. If they don't, you shouldn't be surprised if things go wrong.

Project management is an "art". To be effective, it requires both structured management skills (hard skills) and powerful interpersonal skills (soft skills). I have concentrated on the former as this is where the myth of project management most needs exploding. I do, however, refer throughout to the essential soft skills needed if a project is to be successful.

When the first edition of this book was published in 1997, the term "project" was not always understood in the same way as it is now. Most people saw a project as a delivery vehicle for technical or engineering outputs. Few saw it

> *Project management is an "art". To be effective it requires both powerful interpersonal skills (soft skills) and structured management skills (hard skills).*

as a means to achieve business outcomes. I was one of a few advocates of business-led project management. The practice of project management has moved on to incorporate the "business-led" project, perhaps not as fast as I would have liked, but many methods and standards now recognize this more powerful use of the discipline. Back in 1997, there was no consensus on the meaning of the words "programme" and "portfolio". Often the words "project" and "programme" were interchangeable and for some people, they still are. Whilst many still argue this point, the various standards bodies, including ISO, professional bodies, such as Association for Project Management (APM), International Project Management Association (IPMA) and PMI®, and method providers (like AXELOS for PRINCE2®, MSP®, MoP®) are beginning to use a common language.

In the first four editions of the book, I covered running one project at a time and running many projects at once in a single volume. Now, however, I have made *The Project Workout* into two volumes as it was getting rather fat:

The Project Workout is all about directing and managing a single project; the essential techniques and winning behaviours.

The Programme and Portfolio Workout looks at how to deal with many projects at once, together with all the other work done in an organization in order be successful in your business. It includes what much of the project management literature now refers to as "programmes", "portfolios" and "organizational project management", even if mainstream organizations still use the words differently!

To make each book self-sufficient, there is some overlap and reinforcement of key principles and I have included cross-references to help relate the detailed content which builds to create a whole approach. Whilst a great programme manager or business manager needn't be a great project manager, they do need to understand the principles to be effective in their roles. Similarly a great project sponsor or project manager should understand the needs of programme or business portfolio managers and why they are essential to overall success.

The workouts

The book contains a number of exercises, problem posers, and techniques to help put the "book work" into practice. They will be both a stimulus and a practical help.

Case studies

The case studies are derived from real-life incidents, but some have been simplified to make them more concise to convey the particular message being illustrated.

"Change the name and it's about you, that story"

HORACE, 65–8BC

Points of interest

Throughout the book, I have included a number of points of interest relating to the core theme of each chapter. They will provide you with some greater understanding of the subject but may be passed over on first reading so that you are not diverted from the main message. If this book were a presentation, these would be the questions which interrupt the presenter or the anecdotes the presenter may use to help bring the story to life.

Definitions of all those important words

The way we use words is important. In the field of project management, there is a converging consensus on what words mean but there are still instances where people have very different opinions; my work on international standards hit this problem time and again. Someone else's definition of a word or phrase is not necessarily wrong, but may simply be "differently right". What is important is any terminology you adopt must be used consistently in your project or confusion will reign. In this book, you will find a number of words which may be new to you or old words which have been used in a new way. I have therefore included a jargon-busting glossary in Appendix A. It also includes commonly used alternatives. So, if you come across a new word, look it up.

"How often misused words generate misleading thoughts"

HERBERT SPENCER

Principles

- These are the basic principles you need to apply if your projects are to succeed. You should ensure that any "rules" or procedures you develop and use within your organization are compatible with these.

Key points

- **Key points** are short checklists
- To keep you on track.

Cartoons

In many of the chapters I have used cartoons to emphasize a point. The cartoons are all set 2,000 years ago in the Roman Empire and show how, if the Romans had run their affairs as many modern organizations do, they would have failed miserably. This emphasizes the point that project management is essentially no more than applying the common sense that has been with us for a very long time.

The question "why" is very powerful

The web site and tools

Publisher's eResources – www.routledge.com\9781138721449

A number of the templates described in the book, including the health check, MS project views and project logs can be downloaded, ready for you to use, under the eResource tab here.

Author's web site – projectworkout.com

The author's web site, projectworkout.com, is where you can find:

- a "contact" form;
- my blog;
- articles;
- frequently asked questions;
- references and useful links;
- an outline of the services I provide.

Finally, when you come to Part IV of the book want to put project management in place in your organization, this web site might also give you an idea or two about the design of your own project management method, process and web site.

BusinessOptix evaluation system

Throughout this book, I have made use of flow charts to demonstrate the sequence of activities you need to go through to undertake some aspects of project management. Nowadays, processes are becoming a way of life in many organizations, particularly those moving up the maturity level and adopting models such as SEI's Capability Maturity Model Integrated (CMMI) for Development. Unfortunately there are very few "easy to use" business modelling tools on the market but one I have come across and use very effectively in my day-to-day corporate life is BusinessOptix. All the flow charts in this book were created using it and you can see a real example on the projectworkout.com web site.

Every owner of *The Project Workout* can obtain an evaluation copy of Business-Optix Author. For more details see process.projectworkout.com

PART I
CHALLENGES TO BE FACED

"Minds are like parachutes; they only work when open"

LORD DEWAR

In this part of the book I set out the challenges many organizations face in driving through the changes they need to make in pursuit of their strategic objectives. This is followed by a review of good practice used by some of the world's leading companies.

How to use Part I

Part I is for you to read and learn from. When first reading it, you should forget about your own situation and the problems in your organization. Open your mind to what others are saying and doing. If you find yourself saying "but we don't do it like that, we are different!" pull yourself back. You *are* different. So is everyone else. But other people's experience, even from other industries or sectors, may give you a clue to dealing with the issues confronting you.

The workouts in Part I are designed to help you think about your "project" and to prompt action or discussion on the parts you feel will benefit you.

You can share your own experience with the author on **projectworkout.com**.

Challenges we need to face

Problems, more problems

Initiatives fail, are cancelled, or never get started – why?

In our new world of the twenty-first century no organization is immune from "shut down" if it fails to perform.

"Facts do not cease to exist because they are ignored"

ALDOUS HUXLEY

Problems, more problems

All organizations have problems with the way they undertake their work and tackle change. Problems may be related to any aspect, be it technology, people, processes, systems, or structure. There is always something, somewhere that needs to be created, dropped, or improved. Over the past few decades, a variety of techniques and offerings have been available to business leaders to enable them to do this, including:

- Management by Objectives
- Added Value Analysis
- Total Quality Management
- Business Process Reengineering
- LEAN and Agile
- Six Sigma
- Value Management.

All these, and many more, have contributed greatly to the performance of a significant number of organizations but it is a sad fact that many organizations have failed (and continue to fail) to secure the enduring benefits initially promised. Something has gone wrong. It would seem that we are not all as good as we should be at managing and controlling change in order to achieve sustained benefits from such initiatives.

"Grand" initiatives of the kind just mentioned are not the only ones that can fail; organizations must continually strive to solve particular problems or achieve specific objectives. For example:

- new products and services are developed, old ones are enhanced or withdrawn;
- supply chains are changed;
- manufacturing processes are altered to take account of new methods and technologies;
- sales channels are developed;
- new plant and offices are opened, old ones are closed;
- key business functions are out sourced;
- businesses are disposed of;
- acquisitions are integrated into the mainstream business;
- information systems are built to give greater efficiency and add to the overall effectiveness of the operation.

Again, many of these initiatives fail. Either they:

- cost too much;
- take too long;
- are inadequately scoped and specified;
- don't work as needed;
- or simply don't realize the expected benefits.

This amounts to failure on a scale which costs billions every year and for some organizations results in their demise. It happens in the private, public and charitable sectors, small undertakings, and major multinational enterprises. In our new world of the twenty-first century no organization is immune from "shut down" if it fails to perform.

It would seem that we are not all as good as we should be at managing and controlling change in order to achieve sustained benefits from such initiatives.

Initiatives fail, are cancelled or never get started – why?

A review of a representative cross-section of large companies reveals a common pattern of cause and effect. Figure 1.1 shows the fundamental reasons are twofold:

- Organizations don't know HOW to control change. There is no "organization-wide" way of undertaking business change initiatives and so management and team members act to different and even conflicting rules and norms of behaviour.
- Organizations don't know WHAT they should be doing. There is no clear strategy driving requirements and decision making and consequently an organization may waste money on the wrong projects.

This book concentrates on how to solve the first of these root causes (how to do it) but, as Figure 1.1 shows, successful projects also rely heavily on the latter (what to do) being in place. You will, therefore, see frequent references to business strategy throughout the book.

Notice how most of the issues in Figure 1.1 can't be solved by the project manager; they require a change in the way the organization, as a whole, is directed and managed. Some organizations are so poor at providing the right enterprise-wide support, they are condemning their project managers to inevitable failure and only the rare "heroic" project manager will succeed and only then despite of the organization, not because of it.

A review of a representative cross-section of large companies reveals a common pattern of cause and effect.

If any of the problems identified in this chapter or drawn out from Figure 1.1 are familiar to you and recognizable in your organization, there is clearly scope for improving your performance:

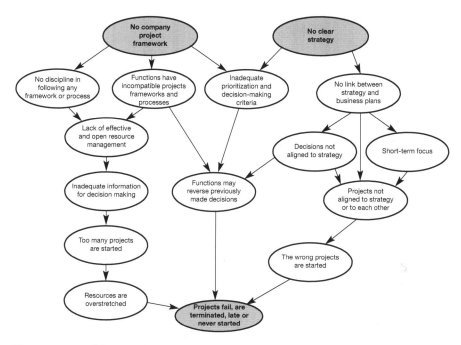

Figure 1.1 Problem analysis

A cause and effect analysis of the reasons for the failure of business change projects shows two fundamental reasons: (i) a lack of clear strategy, (ii) a lack of a rational way of managing the required changes. If your projects fail, then ultimately so will your business. Note how many of the problems can't be solved by a project manager but require a shift in how the organization, as a whole, is managed.

- The solution to issues relating to single initiatives in isolation, I refer to as **project management**; this is covered in this book, *The Project Workout*.
- The solution to issues relating to groups of closely connected projects, I refer to as **programme management**; this is covered in *The Programme and Portfolio Workout*.
- The solution to issues relating to the undertaking of a large number of programmes and projects, I refer to as **business portfolio management**; this is also covered in *The Programme and Portfolio Workout*.

If an organization is to reap the full benefits, it must be competent at all three management approaches. Further, those management approaches must be implemented in a mutually consistent way if the organization's people are to work together effectively and efficiently.

Workout 1.1 – Self-diagnosis

This workout is best done by a project sponsor with the project manager and key team members.

1   Use the following questions as prompts to help establish the areas of competence you may need to address.

- Can you establish a clear link between your organization's business strategy and your project?
- Is it clear why you are undertaking this project?
- Do you find upper and middle management communicate and pass on instructions accurately?
- Do you find it easy to get decisions made?
- Does your organization have any documented criteria against which decisions on whether or not to undertake initiatives are tested?
- If so, are they applied to your project?
- Is there a disciplined method or way of managing initiatives and projects across your organization?
- Is there always enough time to do those things which must be done?
- Do your managers and employees commit themselves to and meet the targets set for them?

2   Do you really KNOW, and can you prove:

- Who benefits from your project?
- Who is the project sponsor?
- Who makes the decisions on your project?
- Who is the project manager?
- Who will be adversely impacted by your project?
- The cost and benefits of your project to date?
- The total costs and benefits when it's finished?
- What activities your resources are committed to?
- When your resources have free or slack time?

3   Build a cause and effect diagram similar to Figure 1.1 for your organization. Start with "Projects fail, are terminated, late, or never started" written on a Post-it Note at the bottom of a flip chart. Ask yourself why this happens. Write each possible reason on a Post-It Note and place these on the flip chart. Again, for each Post-It Note, ask the reason why, writing these on more Post-It Notes. Eventually, if you are honest, you will discover a core reason(s), picking up many symptoms on the way.

2

Advice the best organizations give us

The study

The lessons and their implications

But we're different!: organization context

Using a staged project framework increases the likelihood of success

The advice in this chapter is based on a benchmarking exercise undertaken by the author, coupled with his own experience of working within a number of major organizations.

"Example moves the world more than doctrine"

HENRY MILLER

The study

The problems outlined in the previous chapter are significant and far-reaching. Finding solutions you can trust and have confidence in is difficult. The advice in this chapter is based on a study undertaken by the author, coupled with his own experience of working within several major organizations across a number of industries.

The study questions were not explicitly related to project management, and so avoided preconceptions on the part of those involved on what a "project" is. Rather, the questions related to "product development" as the development and launching of products

In a business context, a project is a project, regardless of whether it is technology based, for cultural change, complex change, or whatever.

or services touches almost every part of every organization. This field is an excellent medium for learning about complex, cross-functional projects and how organizations address them. If an organization cannot develop their products and services efficiently, it is probable that it cannot tackle any other form of cross-functional project effectively either. In a business context, a project is a project, regardless of whether it is technology-based, for cultural change, complex change, or whatever. The study had the following characteristics:

- The survey was undertaken through face-to-face interviews, thereby ensuring both the questions and answers were properly understood.
- It was predominantly qualitative with only a few quantitative questions added to obtain such "hard data" as were available. It was considered more important to find out how people worked rather than collect statistics which, in all likelihood, were not cross-comparable. Even today, obtaining statistics which are truly comparable across different organizations and sectors is very difficult.

The objective was to "learn from the best", hence the inclusion of a number of industries, in both growing and mature markets, in the study:

- aerospace
- construction
- computer hardware
- telecommunications
- manufacturing
- management consulting
- systems integrators.

The organizations chosen for the study had clearly demonstrated success in their own fields and markets. Despite the diverse industries, there was a marked similarity in approach taken by all those organizations interviewed. They are all using or currently implementing a "staged," "cross-functional" framework within which to manage their product development projects (Figure 2.1). The number of stages may differ from organization to organization, but all have the characteristic of investing a certain amount of the organization's resources to obtain more information across the full range of activities which impact a project and its outcome, namely:

- market
- operational
- technical
- commercial and financial

An additional finding was that some of the organizations did not confine their approach to product development but also applied it to business change projects, i.e. to everything they did which created change in the organization. In other words, they had a common business-led project framework for managing change generally.

There, however, the similarities between organizations end and the individual culture and the nature of the different industries take over. Figure 2.2 illustrates how any process (including project management) sits within a context of culture, systems and organization structure; alter any one and it will affect the others.

The organizations did not confine their approach to product development only, but applied it to business change projects generally, i.e. to everything they did which created change in the organization.

This single observation means that although project management processes in

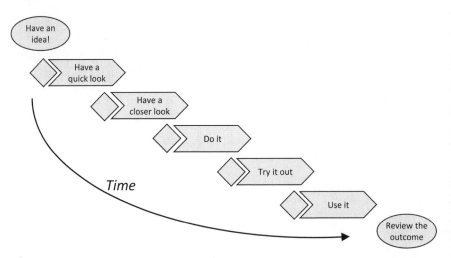

Figure 2.1 A typical staged project framework

A staged approach to projects starts with a preliminary look at the objectives and possible solutions and results, via more detailed investigation, development and trial stages, in the release of the outputs into the operational environment. You should not start any stage without meeting the prescribed criteria at the preceding gate. This includes checks on strategic fit and "do ability" as well as financial considerations.

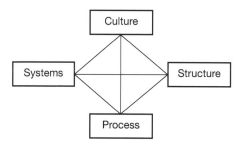

Figure 2.2 The organizational context for project management and other processes

No process sits in isolation. How you are organized, the systems you use to support the process, and the prevailing culture of the organization all affect how well any process works.

many organizations may be similar in principle, the culture and behaviours which make them work are different. Logically, if a proven process appears to break down, the fault may lie outside the process itself in one of the other aspects of the organization. This observation also means that a process which works fine in one organization will not necessarily work in every organization. One CEO told me: "We know our process is logical and has worked well; if it stops working, assuming it's not an IT failure, we look first at the people trying to make it work rather than at the process itself." This company had a well-established project management process in which it had a very high degree of confidence. It still, however, maintained the good practice of continually improving its processes by promoting feedback and having quarterly performance reviews. Another organization had a very effective gating process (see Chapter 4), which totally failed when a new management team took over the work.

It was also notable that certain industries were excellent in particular aspects of managing projects as a result of the nature of their business. Often, they took this for granted. For example:

"*Concentrate on the early stages*" was a message which came across loud and clear, but it was the organizations that relied on bids or tenders for their business which really put the effort in up front as the effect of failure was obvious: they won unprofitable work.

"*Manage risks*" was another message. The only company to tell me, unprompted, that it was excellent in risk management was in avionics. Interestingly enough, the company did not claim to use very sophisticated risk-management techniques, but rather designed its whole approach with a risk-management bias. It cites its staged process as a key part of this: you will hear a lot about this as you work through this book.

"*Measure everything you do*". Organizations which need to keep a track of man-hours in order to bill their customers (e.g. consultants, system development houses) also have the most comprehensive cost and resource planning and monitoring systems. These provide not only a view of each individual project, but also enable them to collate and summarize the current status for all their projects giving them a quantum leap in management information which most other organizations do not have.

The lessons and their implications

The lessons are summarized below and are described more fully on the following pages. Notice some of these apply to a single project, whilst others apply to all projects in an organization. This book addresses the lessons on a single project basis; *The Programme and Portfolio Workout* will revisit the lessons from an enterprise-wide basis. The quotations are taken from the study notes.

The first seven lessons apply throughout the life of a project:

1 Make sure your projects are driven by benefits which support your strategy.
2 Use a simple and well-defined framework, with a staged approach, for all projects in all circumstances.
3 Address and revalidate the marketing, commercial, operational, and technical viability of the project throughout its life.
4 Incorporate selected users and customers into the project to understand their current and future needs.
5 Build excellence in project management techniques and controls across the organization.
6 Break down functional boundaries by using cross-functional teams.
7 Use dedicated resources for each category of development and prioritize within each category.

The next three lessons apply to particular stages in the project:

8 The start
Place high emphasis on the early stages of the project.
9 The middle
Build the business case into the company's forward plan as soon as the project has been formally approved.
10 The end
Close the project formally to build a bridge to the future, to learn any lessons and to ensure a clean handover.

1. Make sure your projects are driven by benefits which support your strategy

"If you don't know why you want to do a project, don't do it!"

All the organizations were able to demonstrate explicitly how each project they undertook fitted their business strategy. The screening out of unwanted projects as soon as possible was key. At the start, there is usually insufficient information of a financial nature to make a decision regarding the viability of the project. However, strategic fit should be assessable from the beginning. Not surprisingly, those organizations which had clear strategies were able to screen more effectively than those which didn't. Strategic fit was often assessed by using simple questions such as:

- Will this product ensure we maintain our leadership position?
- Will the results promote a long-term relationship with our customers?

The less clear the strategy, the more likely projects are to pass the initial screening: so there will be more projects competing for scarce resources resulting in the company losing focus and jeopardizing its overall performance.

The less clear the strategy, the more likely projects are to pass the initial screening: resulting in the organization losing focus.

2. Use a simple and well-defined framework, with a staged approach, for all projects in all circumstances

"Our usual process is our fast-track process"

As discussed earlier, use of a staged framework was found to be well established. Rarely is it possible to plan a project in its entirety from start to finish; there are simply too many unknowns. By using a number of defined project stages, it is possible to plan the next stage in detail, with the remaining stages planned in summary. As you progress through the project from stage to stage, the end-point becomes clearer and your confidence in delivery increases. It was apparent that organizations were striving to make their project frameworks as simple as possible, minimizing the number of stages and cutting down the weight of supporting documentation. Further, the same generic stages were used for all types of project (e.g. for a new plastic bottle and for a new manufacturing line; for a project of £1,000 cost to one of £10m cost).

This makes the use and understanding of the framework very much easier and avoids the need for learning different frameworks and processes for different types of project. This is particularly important for those sponsoring projects or who are infrequently involved in projects. By having one basic framework they are able to understand their role within it and do not have to learn a new language and approach for each situation.

What differs is the work content of each project, the level of activity, the nature of the activity, the degree of risk, the resources required and the stakeholders and decision makers needed.

A common criticism is that a staged approach slows projects down. This was explored in the interviewing and found not to be the case. In contrast, a staged approach was believed, by those interviewed, to speed up **desirable** projects. One relevant point is the nature of the decision to start a new stage of a project, often called **gates**. Some organizations used them as "entry" points to the next project stage rather than the more traditionally accepted "exit" point from a previous stage. This simple principle has the effect of allowing a stage to start before the previous stage has been completed. In this way, stages can overlap without increasing the risk to the business, provided the gate criteria are met.

The existence of so-called "fast-track" processes to speed up projects was also investigated. In all cases, the organizations said that their "usual process" was the

A common criticism is that a staged approach slows projects down. This was explored in the interviewing and found not to be the case. In contrast, a staged approach was believed to speed up desirable projects.

fast track. Doing anything else, such as skipping stages or going ahead without fully preparing for each stage, increases the risk of the project failing. The message from the more experienced organizations was that "going fast" by missing essential work actually slowed the project down; the amount of rework required was nearly always much greater than the effort saved. When people talk of fast-tracking, what they usually mean is raising the priority of a project so it is not slowed down by lack of resources.

What's the point of speeding if you're on the wrong road?

Copyright © 1997 Robert Buttrick

3. Address and revalidate the marketing, commercial, operational and technical viability of the project throughout its life

"We are very good at slamming on the brakes very quickly if we see we cannot achieve our goals"

All the organizations addressed all aspects throughout the life of a project. No single facet is allowed to proceed at a greater pace than the others as, for example, there is little point in:

*   having an excellent technological product which has no adequate market rationale relating to it and cannot be economically produced;
*   developing a superb new staff appraisal system if there are no processes to administer it and make it happen.

As the project moves forward, the level of knowledge increases and hence the level of risk should decrease. The only exception is where there is a particularly large area of risk and this work may be brought forward in order to understand the problems and manage the consequences as part of a planned risk-management strategy.

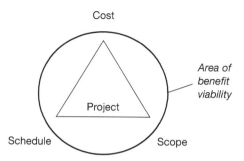

Figure 2.3 The project balance

A project comprises a defined scope, to be delivered in an agreed timescale, at an agreed cost. These must be combined in such a way to ensure that the project is always viable and will realize the expected benefits. If any one of these falls outside the area of benefit viability, the others should be changed to bring the project back on target. If this cannot be done, the project should be terminated.

Coupled with this, the ability of organizations to stop (terminate) projects was seen to be important. Some expressed themselves to be experts at this. A problem in any one aspect of the project (e.g. market, operations, technology, and finance) can lead to termination. For example, one company, which has a product leadership strategy, killed a new product just prior to launch as a competitor had just released a superior product. It was better to abort the launch and work on the next generation product, than to proceed with releasing a new product which could be seen, by the market, as inferior. If the company had done so, its strategy of product leadership would have been compromised, with the technical press rubbing their hands with glee!

Naturally, the gates prior to each stage are the key checkpoints for revalidating a project. The best organizations also monitor the validity of the project between gates and are prepared to stop it if their business objectives are not likely to be met. At all times, the project timescale, cost, scope, and benefits must be kept in balance (see Figure 2.3 above).

4. Incorporate stakeholders into the project to understand their current and future needs

"The front line customer interface has been and is our primary focus"

The involvement of stakeholders, such as users and customers, in projects was seen to add considerable value in all stages of a project. Usually, the earlier the involvement, the better the result.

The more "consultancy-oriented" organizations must, by the nature of their business, talk to customers to ascertain their needs. Yet, even these organizations said they often misinterpreted the real needs of the customer, despite great efforts to avoid this. Where project teams are more removed from their users or customers, there is even greater scope for error.

Many innovative ways have been used to obtain this involvement including:

- focus groups
- facilitated workshops
- early prototyping
- simulations.

Involving the stakeholders is a powerful mover for change, while ignoring them can lead to failure. When viewed from a stakeholder's perspective, your project may be just one more that the stakeholder has to cope with as well as fulfilling his or her usual duties; it may even appear irrelevant or regressive. If the stakeholders' consent is required to make things happen, ignore them at your peril!

5. Build excellence in project management techniques and controls across the organization

"Never see project management as an overhead"

All the organizations I interviewed saw good project management techniques and controls as prerequisites to effecting change. Project management skills are still most obvious in the engineering-based organizations, particularly those with a project/line matrix management structure. However, other organizations had taken, or were taking, active steps to improve this discipline across all parts of the business.

There must be project management guidance, training, and support for all staff connected with the projects, including senior managers who sponsor projects or make project-related decisions. Core control techniques identified in the organizations included planning and managing risk, issues, scope changes, schedule, costs, and reviews.

Planning as a discipline was seen as essential. If you have no definition of the project and no plan, you are unlikely to be successful. It is virtually impossible to communicate your intentions to the project team and stakeholders. Further, if there is no plan, phrases such as "early", "late", and "within budget" have no real meaning. Planning should be seen to be holistic, encompassing schedule, cost, scope, and benefits refined in the light of resource constraints and business risk (Figure 2.4).

Risk was particularly mentioned: using a staged approach is itself a risk-management technique with the gates acting as formal review points where risk is put in the context of the business benefits and cost of delivery. Projects are risky and it is essential to analyse the project, determine which are the inherently risky parts and take action to reduce, avoid or, in some cases, insure against those risks.

Despite good planning things will not always go smoothly. Unforeseen issues do arise which, if not resolved, threaten the success of the project. Monitoring and forecasting against the agreed plan is a discipline which ensures events do not take those involved in the project by surprise. This is illustrated by the "project control cycle" in Figure 2.5. The appropriate frequency for the cycle depends on the project, its stage of development and inherent risk. Monthly is considered the most appropriate by many of the organizations, although in certain circumstances this is increased to weekly.

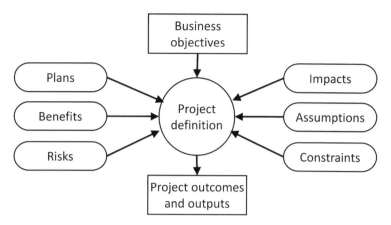

Figure 2.4 Planning

Planning should be seen to be holistic, encompassing schedule, cost, scope, and benefits refined in the light of resource constraints and business risk.

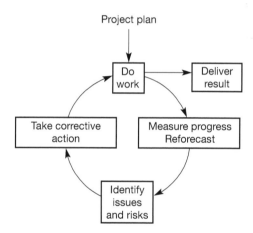

Figure 2.5 Project control cycle

The project control cycle comprises doing the work as set out in your plan, measuring progress against that plan, identifying any risks, opportunities or issues and taking corrective action to keep the project on track. From time to time, results, in the form of deliverables, are generated (copyright © PA Consulting Group, London).

Such monitoring should focus more on future benefits and performance than on what has actually been completed. Completion of activities is evidence of progress but is not sufficient to predict that milestones will continue to be met. The project manager should be continually checking to ensure the plan is still fit for its purpose and likely to realize the business benefits on time. Here, the future is more important than the past.

Completion of activities is evidence of progress but not sufficient to predict that milestones will continue to be met.

It is a sad fact that many projects are late, or never reach completion. One of the reasons for this is "scope creep". More and more ideas are incorporated into the project resulting in higher costs and late delivery. Controlling change is critical to ensuring the benefits are achieved and the project is not derailed by "good ideas" or "good intentions". Changes are a fact of life and cannot be avoided. Good planning and a staged approach reduce the potential for major change but cannot prevent it. Changes, even beneficial ones, must be controlled to ensure that only those enabling the project benefits to be realized are accepted. Contracting industries are particularly good at controlling change as their income is directly derived from projects – doing "that bit more" without checking its impact on their contractual obligations is not good business. Why should it be any less so when dealing with "internal projects"?

The full project environment

Lesson 5 says use "good project management tools and techniques", BUT it is only one of ten findings which provide the full environment for projects to work. Is this why some organizations say "we do project management, but it doesn't work for us"?

6. Break down functional boundaries by using cross-functional teams

"No one in this company can consider themselves outside the scope and influence of projects"

The need for many projects to draw on people from a range of functions means that a cross-functional team approach is essential. Running "projects" in functional parts with coordination between them always slows down progress, produces less satisfactory results, and increases the likelihood of errors. All the organizations in the study recognized this and have working practices to encourage lateral cooperation and communication rather than hierarchical (Figure 2.6). In some cases, this goes as far as removing staff from their own departmental locations and grouping them in project team work spaces. In others, departments which frequently work together are located as close as practical in the company's premises. Generally, the closer people work, the better they perform. Although this is not always practical, closeness can be compensated for by frequent meetings and good communication.

Cross-functional team working, however, is not the only facet. It was also seen that decision making has to be on a cross-functional basis. Decision making and the associated processes were an area where some of the organizations were less than satisfied with their current position. Either decision makers took too narrow a view or insufficient information was available.

Another requirement of cross-functional working is to ensure both corporate and individual objectives are not placed in conflict. For example, one company found

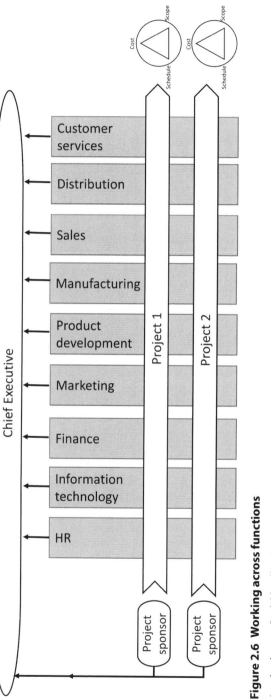

Figure 2.6 Working across functions

A project is a set of activities aligned to achieve a defined result. It draws in people from across the organization who provide their particular expertise and knowledge.

that team members on the same project received different levels of bonuses merely because they belonged to different departments.

The more functionally structured a company is, the more difficult it is to implement effective project management. This is because project management, by its nature, crosses functional boundaries. To make projects succeed, the balance of power usually needs to be tipped toward the project and away from line management (see Figure 2.10). For a "traditional", functionally led company, this is often a sacrifice its leaders refuse to make . . . at the expense of overall business performance.

The more functionally structured an organization is, the more difficult it is to implement effective project management.

7. Use dedicated resources for each category of development and prioritize within each category

"We thought long and hard about ring fencing (dedicating) resources and decided, for us, it was the best way to minimize internal conflict"

The management and allocation of resources was acknowledged by many organizations to be a problem. There is often continual competition for scarce resources between projects. One company said that at one time this had reached such a level that it was proving destructive. The impact was often that too many projects were started and few were finished.

I discovered that this problem was dealt with in two separate ways, both of which have their merits.

The first (Figure 2.7) is to apply dedicated (separate) resources for each category of project (say, aligned around a business unit) and take this principle as deep as possible into the company. In this way, potential conflicts are limited while decisions and choices are more localized. In fact, the more separate and dedicated you make your resources, the more local your decision making can be, providing a project only needs to draw resources from that single pool. The downside of such an approach is that you will have to continually reorganize and resize your resource pools to meet demand. In a fast-moving industry, this can mean you may have the right number of people but they may be deployed in the wrong places. It can lead to continuous, expensive reorganizations. Most traditional, functionally organized organizations follow this approach.

The second extreme is to have all staff in a single pool (shared) and use effective matrix management support tools for resource allocation and forecasting (Figure 2.8). This method was adopted by the consulting and engineering organizations. In one case, a person may work on up to ten projects in a week and there may be 300 projects in progress at any one time. It is very effective, conceptually simple and totally flexible. Major reorganizations are less frequent but it is also the most difficult to implement in a company with a strong functional management bias.

In practice, a hybrid between the two extremes provides the simplicity of purely functionally based organizations with the flexibility of full matrix-managed organizations.

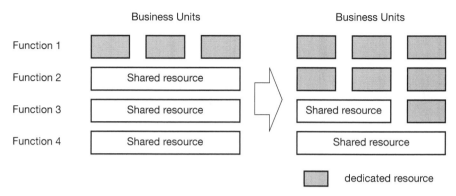

Figure 2.7 Apply dedicated resource to each project portfolio (e.g. by strategic business unit, market sector) as deeply as possible

Some organizations, as a result of their organizational structure, share most of their resources across a number of categories. This allows them to deploy the most appropriate people to any project regardless of where they are in the organization. It also minimizes duplication of functions within the organization. Other organizations separate their resource to a greater extent and confine it to working on a single business unit's projects. This allows quicker and more localized resource management but can lead to duplication of functional capabilities.

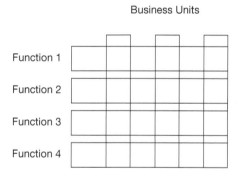

Figure 2.8 Resources from all functions are applied anywhere, to best effect

In this model, anyone from any function can work on any project. It is the most flexible way of organizing but, without good control systems, is the most complex.

The implication is, however, that the resource management and accounting systems must be able to view the company in a consistent way from both perspectives.

8. Place high emphasis on the early stages of the project

"Skipping the first stage is a driver for failure"

All organizations see the early stages of a project as fundamental to success. Some could not stress this enough. High emphasis for some meant that 30–50 per cent of the project life is spent on the investigative stages before any final deliverable is physically built. One American company had research data explicitly demonstrating how this emphasis significantly decreased time to completion. Good investigative work means clearer objectives and plans; work spent on this is rarely wasted. Decisions taken in the early stages of a project have a far-reaching effect and set the tone for the remainder of the project. In the early stages, creative solutions can slash delivery times in half and cut costs dramatically. Once development is under way, however, it is rarely possible to effect savings of anything but a few per cent. Good upfront work also reduces the likelihood of change later, as most changes to projects are actually reactive to misunderstandings over scope and approach rather than proactive decisions to change the project for the better. The further you are into the project, the more costly change becomes.

All organizations see the early stages of a project as fundamental to success.

Despite this, there is often pressure, for what appear to be all the right commercial reasons, to skip the investigative stages and "get on with the real work" as soon as possible (so-called fast-tracking, see Lesson 2). Two organizations interviewed had found through bitter experience that you can't go any faster by missing out essential work. One told me, "Skipping the investigative stages led to failure"; the other, "Whenever we've tried to leave a bit out for the sake of speed, we've always failed and had to do more extensive rework later which cost us far in excess of anything we might have saved."

9. Build the business case into the organization's forward plan as soon as the project has been formally approved

"Once it is authorized, pin it down!"

Projects are the vehicles for implementing future strategic change and revenue generation for a company. The best organizations are always sure the projects they are undertaking will produce what they need and fit the company's wider objectives. In all cases, organizations had far more proposals for projects than they could handle. It is, therefore, essential to know what future resources (cash, manpower, etc.) have already been committed and what benefits (revenues, cost savings, etc.) are expected. Unless this is done the "gap" between where the company is now and where it wants to be is not known, making the choice of projects to fill the gap more difficult (Figure 2.9).

Organizations handle this by having set points in the project life cycle at which cost and benefit streams are built into the business plan usually at the development gate (see Figures 4.6 and 4.7).

Clearly, financial planning and resource systems must be able to be updated at any time as projects may not recognize fiscal quarters as relevant to start or finish dates. Also, any such project systems must be seen as a part of the business and not an "add-on" outside the usual pattern of planning, forecasting and accounting.

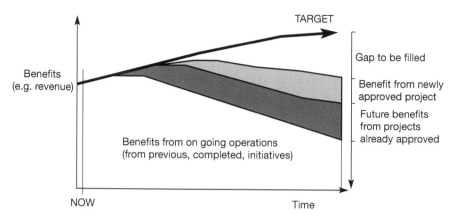

Figure 2.9 Build the project into your business plan as soon as it is authorized

The figure shows the revenue generated by the organization if no new projects are started. It then shows
the revenue which will be generated by projects which are currently in progress. The gap between the sum
of these and the target revenue needs to be filled. This can be by starting off new projects which will
cause this to be generated or/and by starting initiatives in the line which will deliver the extra revenue to
fill the gap.

10.   Close the project formally to build a bridge to the future, to learn any lessons and to ensure a clean handover

"We close projects quickly to prevent any left-over budget from being wasted."

Closing projects formally is essential for some organizations. For example, low-margin
organizations must close the project accounts down to ensure no more time is spent
working on completed projects, no matter how interesting! Their tight profit margins
simply won't allow this luxury. Similarly, component products in an aircraft can be in
service long after the project team has dispersed or even well after some team members have retired! Not to have full records (resurrection documents) on these critical
components for times of need is unthinkable.

All organizations interviewed either had a formal closure procedure or were
actively implementing one. This usually takes the form of a closure report which
highlights any outstanding issues, ensures explicit handover of accountabilities and
makes it clear to those who need to know that the project is finished.

Another key reason given for formal closure was the provision of an opportunity
for learning lessons and improving the processes and workings of the company. One
company left "closure" out of its process in the original design, but soon realized it was
vital and added it in. It simply found that if it did not close projects, the list of projects
it was doing was just growing by the day.

Workout 2.1 – Review of the ten lessons on your project

1   As a project sponsor or project manager, supported by your core team, review the ten lessons given in this chapter and ask yourself how well you apply them on your project at present. Agree a mark out of 10 and mark the relevant column with an "X". 10 = we currently apply this lesson fully on our project and can demonstrate this with ease.

   0 = this is not applied at all.

2   Discuss, as a team, your responses. Did you all agree or were there differences of opinion? If so, why do you think this is? Which lessons are not being applied? Why not?

3   What do you propose to do about this?

Table 2.1 Review of the ten lessons

Lesson	POOR							EXCELLENT			
	0	1	2	3	4	5	6	7	8	9	10
1 My project is driven by benefits which support the organization's business strategy.											
2 We use a defined project framework (life cycle), with a staged approach.											
3 We address and revalidate the marketing, commercial, operational and technical viability of the project throughout its life.											
4 We engage stakeholders to understand their current and future needs.											
5 We promote excellence in project management techniques and controls across the project.											
6 We use a cross-functional team.											
7 We always have the resources we need, when we need them.											
8 We place(d) high emphasis on the early stages of the project.											
9 We build (or will build) the business case into the organization's forward plan as soon as the project is formally approved.											
10 At project closure we will learn any lessons and ensure a clean handover with an explicit project "end" point.											

But we're different!: organization context

Project processes only work if supported by compatible accountabilities, culture, and systems (as shown in Figure 2.2). The previous sections of this chapter described how many organizations use or are moving toward a staged project framework, even though the environments in which they operate are entirely different. So, when you hear the plaintive cry of, "This won't work here, we're different!" you can confidently answer, "Yes, we are different but we can make it work if we really want to."

The following sections describe some of the wide range of approaches taken by different organizations.

Structure and accountabilities

Organization structures vary from pure project to pure functional; this impacts the ease of cross-functional working and project management. Figure 2.10 shows the range of organization shapes and the effect they tend to have on project management. In heavily functionally driven organizations, project managers are generally very weak, disempowered, and at the mercy of the functional heads of department. They are often called "project coordinators" which is very apt. In full project organizations, the project managers have greater power and influence over and above heads of department. In the middle is matrix management. This is a much maligned

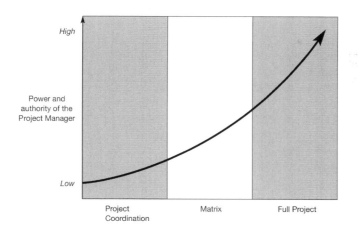

Figure 2.10 Project organizations

Organizations can be structured with differing emphasis on line and project management authority. When the most power is invested in line management, project managers are reduced to a "coordination" role. In full project structures, the project manager has greater power than the line manager. The line manager is there to satisfy the resourcing needs of the projects and business as usual processes only. The mid-point between these extremes is the "matrix," where there is a balance of power which is derived from the role someone takes as well as their position in the line.

structure but one which can be very effective in organizations which require a relatively stable functional structure but still need to have the advantages of a cross-functional project approach. It has often been said "matrix organizations don't work, they just confuse people". Yes, that may be true if they are implemented in an environment with no suitable controls and incompatible line and project accountabilities and processes. Generally, those organizations which have moved the balance of power away from the line and towards the project, have found project management and cross-functional working more effective and reap greater rewards. Another reason why matrix organizations fail is because they have been set up on a false premise. Sometimes a matrix is described as a structure where power and authority is **shared** between the line manager and project manager; if that's what people are working to, no wonder matrices don't work. The role of a line manager and that of a project manager are different. Two people cannot be accountable for the same work or decision. Generally, in a matrix:

- Line managers are accountable for deploying the right people on projects; the methods and processes used for the specialist work undertaken by their people, including quality assurance and control; ensuring their people are trained and skilled as needed; day-to-day human resource tasks (such as career planning, training, absence monitoring; adherence to organization-wide policies and procedures);
- Project managers are accountable to the project sponsor for delivering a successful project; fostering a project team approach, ensuring the work undertaken is on time, to proven quality and within the cost constraints; ensuing the team members understand their role on the project and what others need from them for the project to succeed.

The acceptance of clear definitions of roles, accountabilities and relationships for the key players are most apparent with those organizations comfortable with their processes. Further, the separation of "role" from job description is seen as crucial to maintaining simplicity as, in cross-functional, project environments, the role a person takes (e.g. as project sponsor or project manager or team manager) is more important than their job title or position in the functional hierarchy.

Some organizations set up cross-functional groups to undertake particular tasks on an on going basis. The most obvious are those groups which undertake the screening of proposals prior to starting the project. In this way, the structures created match the process (rather than leading or following the process). This must also apply to any review or decision-making bodies which are created. The one most commonly found to be adrift is that relating to financial authorizations. Many organizations have almost parallel financial processes shadowing their project processes, demanding similar but different justifications and descriptions of projects. This is usually found where finance functions have disproportionate power and act as controllers rather than in an assurance

You need your best people to create your future organization, not the "leftovers" from running yesterday's organization.

or business partner mode. The better organizations ensured that there was little divergence between decisions required for finance and those relating to strategy. They make certain that financial expertise is built into the project in the same way as any other discipline, with finance people being included on the project team.

Projects are "temporary" and cease to exist once completed. Clear accountability for on going management of the outputs in the line ensures that the right people are involved in the project and the handover is clean and explicit. Career progression and continuity of employment for people involved in projects must be a top consideration. Projects are about change and the future of your organization. Good organizations ensure the people who create these changes are retained, while projects are not seen as career limiting or the fast track to redundancy. You need your best people to create your future organization.

A large, global company was having difficulty ensuring its people worked cooperatively across department and functional boundaries (typical silo behaviour). This had been raised on a number of occasions at senior team level. One day, the chief executive officer told me he had fixed the problem. "How?" I asked. "I've put all problem functions under Andy," he replied. "How does an extra management tier and the creation of an even bigger silo solve the problem?" I asked. There was silence lasting for a full minute. "Well, that's what I've done," he eventually said.

Clearly, this chief executive officer had not fully understood the problem and was merely offloading it onto someone else. Further, he was using a structural solution in an attempt to solve a cultural problem. (You will recall Figure 2.2.)

Culture

Culture is probably the least reproducible facet of an organization and the most intangible. It does, however, have a very significant impact on how projects are carried out and project management is implemented. Unfortunately many cultural factors are outside a project manager's ability to influence and need to be addressed at programme, portfolio, or corporate level. Nevertheless, understanding this can help a project manager cope with it and plan accordingly.

For example, the corporate attitude to risk and the way an organization behaves if high-risk projects have to be stopped will have far-reaching effects on the quality of the outputs produced. In avionics, the "least risk" approach is generally preferred to the "least cost", despite being within an industry in which accepting the lowest tender is a primary driver.

One company interviewed explicitly strives to make its own products obsolete as it clearly sees itself as a product leader. It is forever initiating new projects to build better products, quicker and more frequently than the competition. This same company focuses its rewards on teams, not individuals, and takes great care to ensure its performance measurement systems avoid internal conflict. Another company admitted that its bonus schemes were all based on functional performance and not team performance despite 60 per cent of the staff working cross-functionally. An example was given of a staff member who received no bonus for his year's work while all his colleagues on the same project (in a different department!) had large bonuses. This was not seen as "fair", and was the result of basing bonuses on something that could be counted easily rather than on something that actually counted!

Another company had no bonus scheme below senior management level but provided "Well Done" awards (financial) for individuals whom they consider merit them. These are given almost immediately after the event which prompted the award and are well appreciated. This same company also has 100 per cent employee ownership and salesmen who are not commissioned.

Most of the organizations interviewed encouraged direct access to decision makers as it improved the quality of decisions. Project roles, rather than "job descriptions", promote this. Functional hierarchies tend to have a greater "power distance" and decision makers become remote from the effects of their actions or the issues involved.

As a paradox, those organizations which have the most comprehensive control systems (project accounting, resource management, time sheeting, etc.) are able to delegate decision making lower in the organization. Senior management does not lose sight of what is happening and always knows who is accountable.

A major producer of project-scheduling software confided in me that when it came to managing its own internal business projects, all the good practice and advice the company advocated as essential to its customers was ignored. The culture of the company's management simply does not fit the product it sells. Organizations can be very successful without any rational approach to business projects but are unlikely to remain successful for long.

Systems and tools

A number of those interviewed stated that the accounting systems must serve to integrate process, project, and line management. Projects must not be seen as an "add-on".

Resource management and allocation was found to be a problem for many organizations. Those which had least difficulty centrally managed their entire resource across all their departments and the departments and the projects used the same core system; only the reporting emphasis was different.

Other organizations had developed systems to cope with what they saw as their particular needs, for example risk management or action tracking.

The American organizations had acquired the practice of constantly validating their processes and systems through benchmarking.

Workout 2.2 – What happens to project managers in your organization when the project is finished?

(a) They are kept on the payroll and assigned to a manager for "pay and rations" until a new project or suitable alternative work is found.
(b) They are put on a redeployment list and then made redundant if no suitable opening is found for them within x months.
(c) They leave the organization straightaway if no suitable opening is found for them.
(d) They leave the organization.
(e) I don't have this problem as they are all contracted in when needed.

If you answered (b) to (d) you are probably very functionally driven and projects tend to be difficult to undertake.

If you answered (e) you may be in a very fortunate position to be able to source such key people OR you are in the same situation as (b) to (d).

If you answered (a) you are probably in a good position to reap the rewards of project working or are already doing so!

Debate with your colleagues: what motivates your staff to work on projects?

If you answered (b) to (d), do you really expect to have your best people volunteering to work on projects?

Using a staged project framework increases the likelihood of success

The study confirmed that:

- The staged framework is widely used for business change projects and is delivering better value than more traditional functionally based project processes. This is discussed further in Part II of this book.
- A cross-functional, project management-based approach is essential. This is discussed further in Part III of this book.

What is apparent is the that infrastructure which makes the projects work varies considerably, in particular the level of information decision makers have to support them. For example, it is usually relatively easy to decide if a project in isolation is viable or not. If you need to decide which of a number of projects should go ahead based on relative benefits, answers to the following questions are needed:

- What overall business objectives is the project driving toward?
- On what other projects does this project depend?
- What other projects depend on this project?
- When will we have the capacity to undertake the project (in terms of people and other resources)?

- Can the business, suppliers, and customers accept this change together with all the other changes being imposed? If so, when?
- Do we have enough cash to carry out the project?
- After what length of time will the project cease to be viable?
- How big is the overall risk of the full project portfolio with and without this project?

The challenge lies in having processes, systems, accountabilities and a culture which address these, both at a working level and at the decision-making level. If this is not addressed, the result will be:

- the wrong projects being undertaken;
- late delivery;
- failure to realize the expected benefits.

This will be in spite of having excellent processes and tools at an individual project level. These questions are discussed in *The Programme and Portfolio Workout*.

In one company, it was not unusual to find directors reporting to graduates on projects. The directors are on the project teams to add their particular knowledge and skills and not to lead the project. This company saw nothing strange about this arrangement. The most appropriate people were being used in the most appropriate way.

Reorganizing isn't always the answer!

Quotation from Gaius Petronius Arbiter, AD66

Copyright © 1997 Robert Buttrick

Enemies within

Running a project is difficult enough, but we often make it more arduous than need be by creating problems for ourselves. Here are a few examples:

Reorganizing – either the company or a part of it. Tinkering with your structure is usually NOT the solution to your problems, it just confuses people. The Romans realized this 2,000 years ago (see cartoon). If, however, you are a senior executive, this is a great way to hide non-delivery!

Functional thinking – not taking the helicopter, the organization-wide, view. This often happens when executives' or individuals' bonuses are based on targets which are at odds with the organization's needs e.g. sales bonus rewarded on revenue, regardless of profit or contribution.

Having too many rules – the more rules you have, the more sinners you create and the less happy your people become. Have you ever met a happy bureaucrat?

Disappearing and changing sponsors – without a sponsor there should be no project. Continual changing of the "driver" will cause you to lose focus and forget WHY you are undertaking the project. Consider terminating such a project to see who really wants it!

Ignoring the risks – risks don't go away, so acknowledge them and manage them. If I said that a certain airplane is likely to crash, would you fly on it? And yet, every day executives approve projects when a simple risk analysis shows they are highly likely to fail.

Dash in and get on with it! – if a project is that important, you haven't the time NOT to plan your way ahead. High activity levels do not necessarily mean action or progress.

Analysis paralysis – you need to investigate, but only enough to gain the confidence to move on. This is the opposite to dash in and ignore the risks. It is also a ploy used to delay projects: "I haven't quite enough information to make a decision, just do some more study work."

Untested assumptions – all assumptions are risks; treat them as such.

Forgetting what the project is for – if this happens terminate the project. If it is that useful, someone will scream and remember why it is being done.

Executive's "pet projects" – have no exceptions. If an executive's idea is really so good, it should stand up to the scrutiny that all the others go through. He or she may have a helicopter view, but he might also have his head in the clouds.

3

Projects in the context of businesses, portfolios and programmes

Whose project is it?

Business-led and enabling projects

Projects within a programme or portfolio

Putting it all together

Understanding the context of your project is vital as it is the context which provides the drive for the project and also determines how project governance dovetails into higher-level governance.

"If you're not confused, you're not paying attention"

TOM PETERS

Whose project is it?

Go to any other organization and you'll find there are "projects" but what they call a "project" may differ from your own perception. Sometimes the words "programme" and "project" are used interchangeably, just to add to the fun. Don't think of this as wrong, just accept it for now, as you are unlikely to change anything overnight. What matters is that chunks of change are identified with someone who wants it (a sponsor) and someone who makes it happen (a manager). Project management is a set of techniques for managing work in a way that increases the likelihood of a successful outcome. So, where is project management commonly used?

Typically, an organization uses project management to change its own operations, such as developing a new product or service, improving its manufacturing or operational systems, launching a market initiative, taking over another company, or building its infrastructure. Organizations undertake projects to further their business objectives and realize certain benefits. Let's call this an **internal project**, as it is done internally, within the organization.

Additionally, many organizations use project management to control work they are doing for their customers. The primary benefit gained is revenue as payment for the services provided. For example, a building contractor would undertake the construction of a house as a project but may have no interest in the house once it is handed over to the customer and paid for. Let's call this a **customer project** because it is done for a customer. Conversely, initiating an internal project is a company's own decision. Even if the project is intended to implement a new legal or regulatory requirement, the organization has a choice. If they want to stay in that business, they must comply . . . but no one is compelling them to stay in that business. A bid is an internal project, as it is the company itself that decides whether to bid for the work; there is no compulsion. Once, however, a bid has been won and a contract signed, then a "customer project" is created and the organization has an obligation to undertake the work, within the terms of a legal agreement or contract.

From the above, it follows that there are primarily two reasons for undertaking a project:

1   to develop your own organization: **promoting**
2   to provide services to another organization: **contracting**

Promoting organizations identify a business, strategic or political need, translate this into a set of objectives and, using a project as the vehicle of change, create the outputs and business changes needed to ensure those objectives are met. A promoting organization may undertake all the work themselves or sublet part to a contracting organization or supplier.

Internal and customer projects

A large communications and media organization had a well-defined project management method, tailored for their business. They identified a number of categories of "internal" and "customer" projects. The internal projects were those to build the company's operational environment, such as HR and finance, build service platforms and develop products and services. "Bids" were also classified as internal projects. Customer projects related to bespoke products or services for larger customers and included projects for transitioning services as part of taking on an outsource and transforming services to improve customer experience and add new services.

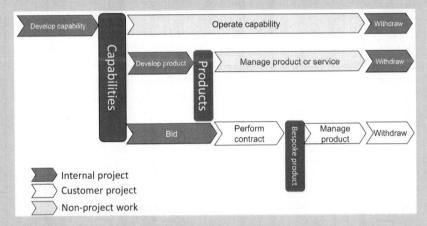

Figure 3.1 Internal and customer projects

As a business approach, project management is suited to undertaking business change activities, such as developing business capabilities, products and services to achieve strategic objectives. Projects may be internal to the organization, being changes which the organization "does to itself" and for which there is no binding contract obliging them to undertake them. Internal projects are undertaken by an organization and its suppliers to achieve the organization's defined goals rather than to meet externally driven requirements. Alternatively, customer projects are vehicles to provide and deliver complex services to customers, drawing on the organization's existing capabilities and products to provide a bespoke service to the customer. These projects are governed by a binding contract between a customer and the organization providing the product or service.

Contracting organizations identify an opportunity through market analysis, or an invitation to tender, prepare a response and then, if successful, undertake the work as a project. The relationship between the contractor and customer is defined by a formal contract. In most cases, the work the contractor does forms only part of the work needed by their customer (a promoter) to gain the full benefits they need.

Note: sublet work within a promoting organization's internal project would be a contracting organization's "customer project".

Figure 3.2 illustrates this. In the top diagram, Company X is the promoting organization and has an internal project, let's call it "Atlas", comprising four work packages, WP1 to WP4. Company X is doing all the work internally. The middle diagram illustrates the same situation, with Company X promoting an internal project, but work package WP4 is contracted to Company Y to fulfil. Company Y would see work package WP4 as a customer project undertaken for Company X. The relationship between Company X and Company Y would be determined by a contract. In the lower diagram, Company Y has sublet part of their contracted work, work package WP4.2, to Company Z. Company Z might then see work package WP4.2 as a customer project. The relationship between Company Y and Company Z is determined by the subcontract, which may itself be determined by the terms of the contract between Company X and Company Y.

A person in Company X would say that Atlas is "their project" and the project sponsor is accountable for the whole of it, looking after Company X's business interests. A person in company Y would say that WP4 is "their Atlas project" and the person accountable in that company would look after the business interests of Company Y within the constraints of the contract they have signed. Similarly, a person in Company Z would say that WP 4.2 is "their Atlas project" and would look after the business interests of Company Z within the constraints of their subcontract. So, if you asked who the project manager for Atlas is, three different people would put up their hands. Looking at this from the individual perspectives, it is easy to see how this happened but, without an understanding of the breakdown of the work, the situation could become confused and have serious consequences on governance. The case studies illustrate this further.

So far, we have looked at different companies having their own perspectives on a project. Even within a single organization, however, there can be several perspectives and scope for confusion, if the organization is not taking a business-led projects approach. This is most commonly found in relation to IT departments. It is not at all unusual to find two projects, with the same name, one led by IT and the other by the part of the business which is to use the IT system. Colloquially, the words "IT project" and "business project" are used. A person in an IT department sees their job as developing the new system, using money from their annual budget and expects the "business" to deploy the system and put it to work, as their "business project". The IT department will often sponsor the technical work and develop a business case, requiring the "business" to estimate the benefits. A separate business

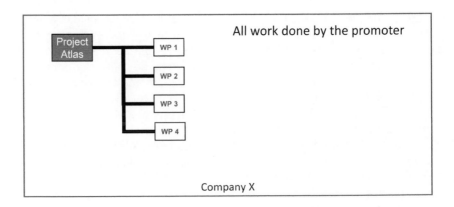

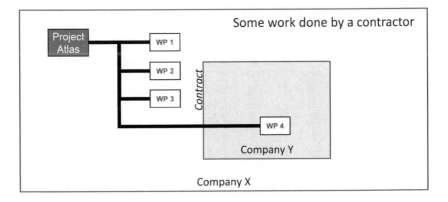

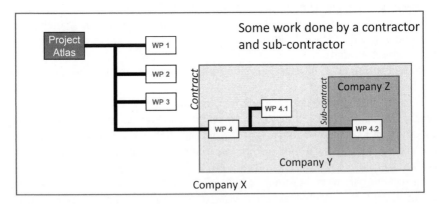

Figure 3.2 Projects from different perspectives

Company X owns Project A, but has contracted part of the work, WP 4, to Company Y, who sees this as "their project". Similarly, Company Y sublets part of their work, WP4.2, to Company Z, who in turn, sees this as "their project". To understand whose project is whose, you need to understand both the scope and the context.

Whose owns the Hodeidah Port project?

In the early 1980s, I designed and supervised part of a harbour complex built in Hodeidah, North Yemen. The overall project was owned by Yemen's Ports and Marine Affairs Corporation. The company I worked for, Sir Alexander Gibb & Partners, had a contract for the design and site supervision. Mitsubishi (from Japan) won the construction contract and sublet it to the Rinkai Corporation (also from Japan), who undertook the marine works themselves and sublet the building works to an Indian company. There were numerous specialist subcontractors for different aspects, such as piling, painting, roads, dredging and electro-mechanical equipment. The Chinese Civil Engineering Company provided most of the specialist tradesmen on the marine works. Each party had its own "Hodeidah Port project", with its own scope; each company had their own business interests to attend to but all were linked by a web of contracts which kept them aligned.

case is then needed for the "business project" as the money is coming from their budget. It can get messy. Through reading this book you will come to realize that in mature organizations, the "IT project" and "business project" should be part of a single project, with one business case, sponsored by the senior manager who needs the new capability to further their strategic objectives. The IT department is simply engaged on developing some crucial deliverables, but not necessarily all the deliverables, needed to ensure success.

As you will probably realize from what you have read so far, the distinction between promoting and contracting organizations is not always immediately obvious, especially in the case of a contractor undertaking the operation of any outputs from the projects as part of an extended project life cycle (see Figure 13.9), or where the project is undertaken to improve the operations within an outsource. Further, some large organizations implement internal trading arrangements, resulting in quasi-contracts between departments or divisions within the company; sometimes these are formalized for tax reduction reasons. It is not essential that you use terms like "internal project", "customer project", "promotor" and "contractor"; I have simply used these words to explain the different situations; use your own words if you want to. What is important, however, is that you understand the context for any project you work on:

1 Who will benefit from the project? In what way?
2 What is the scope of the work?
3 Who is accountable?
4 What is the relationship between various parties? What is their interest in the project?

Whose Olympic Games is it?

I was at a conference where BT's Olympic 2012 programme director presented their Olympic 2012 project but it wasn't the same person I expected and knew as the Olympic 2012 programme director. It seemed there were two Olympic 2012 projects in BT. One project was for the telecommunications and media infrastructure run out of BT Global Services. The other was for the local connectivity, run by BT Openreach. The Openreach work was a part of BT Global Services, but under the regulatory environment in the UK, they were usually run as separate organizations. This prompted me to think about who owned the London 2012 Olympic Games as a whole? The London Organising Committee of the Olympic and Paralympic Games (LOCOG) was the organization responsible for overseeing the planning and development of the games. It was jointly established by the UK Government's Department for Culture, Media and Sport, the Mayor of London and the British Olympic Association and structured as a private company limited by guarantee. LOCOG worked closely with the publicly funded Olympic Delivery Authority (ODA), which was responsible for the planning and construction of new venues and infrastructure. So in answer to the question, whose project was it? It depends on which bit you are talking about.

If you understand this, you can answer the question "whose project is it?" Without such understanding you will not have effective governance (we'll look at governance further in Chapter 16).

Business-led and enabling projects

Business-led projects

In this book, I advocate that all projects should be driven by a business need and result in benefits for the sponsoring organization. As we saw in the first part of this chapter, the organization may be a promoter or a contractor. For a promoter, the benefits can be wide-ranging; we'll look at benefits in Chapter 19. A contractor primarily realizes benefit from payments received for the services provided. There may be, however, other reasons, such as accepting a lower margin on a contract to provide an entry into a new market, or to develop experience in a new target sector. The test of any business-led project is that of financial viability: will the benefits outweigh the costs over a defined time period? This is usually justified in a business case which not only demonstrates the viability but also the associated risks. In short, business projects have business cases and are relatively self-contained as their scope covers all the work necessary to drive the business changes (outcomes) to realize the benefits.

Enabling projects

You will find, however, some projects which do not seem to have a business case, nor seem complete in themselves. Does this mean they are not projects? Let's put aside the possibility that the project is not really a "project" at all, but the word has been applied in a different way, such as in a child's school project. There are situations when an individual project may not need a business case and does not have to be viable on its own, but it does enable something else to happen. For this reason, such projects are often called **enabling projects**. An enabling project should be managed through the project life cycle, using all the principles, tools and techniques of project management, except that when completed, there may be no benefit for the sponsor. We see this classically in IT projects, which create a new code for a system which is then picked up within another project to be deployed and implemented; only when the new system starts to be used will benefits start to flow. But, you say, surely every project should be justified, otherwise there will be anarchy? You are right. Even though an enabling project can't have its own business case, it should be incorporated within the scope of a higher-level business case, which includes the other projects and work required. Writing a business case on a marginal basis would not help, as the case study on the next page demonstrates. So, a single business case may be used to justify and define a few closely related projects; we'll look at these in Chapter 14.

Projects within a programme or portfolio

Projects within a programme

Instead of running a few projects together, sometimes called multi-project management, you can run them as a programme. Although there is no universal definition of the term programme, there is a growing consensus that a programme must deliver a business change (outcome) and may comprise any number of projects and other work required to achieve this. A programme is a tightly coupled and tightly aligned grouping of projects and other related work. This puts another level of management between the host organization and the project but is worthwhile if the scale and complexity of the work warrants it. If you have a stand-alone project within an organization, the project sponsor is accountable to someone or some sponsoring group within the host organization. If, however, the project is part of a programme, the project sponsor would report to a person on the programme team. This might be to the programme sponsor or the programme manager. It may even be that the programme manager also takes on the role of project sponsor for that project. Whichever way this is done, the project would be encompassed within the programme's business case and the project manager would receive direction from the programme team. *The Programme and Portfolio Workout* goes into detail on programme management.

Ensure your business case scope makes sense

Some years ago, a major communications company was expanding its network to gain access to potential new customers. The finance department prided itself on having a good handle on cost management, especially capex. Each department knew exactly how much they could spend each year and it was tracked weekly, even holding weekly Capital Approval Board meetings to control the release of the funds.

Then, along came a project team and asked for lots of money to buy a telecoms switch to handle the traffic from potentially 5 million new customers. The revenue projections were good and the return promised to be enormous . . . and the wise men on the Capital Approval Board approved the project.

The following week, another project team came along and said, "You know that new switch you approved? It doesn't like getting wet, so here is a business case to construct a building to keep it dry." The revenue figure was the same as before as, without this building, the switch wouldn't work and no customer revenue would flow . . . and the wise men on the Capital Approval Board approved the project.

A week later, another team arrived. "You know that lovely building and switch? Well, it won't work without electricity, so here is the business case for the uninterrupted power supply systems" . . . and the wise men on the Capital Approval Board, nervously, approved this third project.

A week or two later, yet another team arrived. "You know that switch and powered building you approved? Well, switches don't like getting hot, so we need you to approve the air conditioning system to keep it cool. If you don't, you won't get any revenue" . . . the wise men on the Capital Approval Board were getting a little annoyed, but approved it as they really wanted all that revenue.

The final straw came a month later. "You know that lovely switch in its cool, dry environment with lots of power? Well, it's useless unless it is connected to the core network; the calls and data will have nowhere to go. If you really want the revenue (which we have attributed to this project's business case), you have to approve this business case as well." The CEO (who was chairing the Capital Approval Board that day) exploded.

This simplified tale led to the company radically changing its approach to funding projects. Following the changes, funding was no longer assigned to departments but directly to projects. In another words, business-led project management was adopted.

Projects within a business portfolio

In other cases, the sponsoring organization may be so large and the projects so numerous they are clustered into business portfolios. For example one large organization I worked in had over 2,000 projects, consuming £4bn a year and so they created business portfolios focused on their market sectors, infrastructure and support. A project sponsor of a project within one of these business portfolios took direction from the portfolio management team; in effect, the business portfolio team became the sponsoring group. Being a business management vehicle, business portfolios are managed to a **business plan** and each project undertaken had to be justified by a business case. To deal with the issue concerning enabling projects, business portfolios can also contain programmes, as described above.

We look at business portfolio management in *The Programme and Portfolio Workout*.

Putting it together

Putting all this together, we can see how a project can sit in a variety of contexts and may be:

1   undertaken for internal purposes, or to serve a customer;
2   business led with its own business case or an enabling project, under the umbrella of a higher level business case;
3   part of a programme or business portfolio.

Figure 3.3 illustrates some possible structures, showing:

- a stand-alone project with an organization;
- a project as part of a programme;
- a project as part of a business portfolio, and
- a project as part of a programme within a business portfolio.

In each case, the project sponsor would take direction from the higher level element to which the project is attached. There are other possibilities, not shown in the figure such as a project being fully stand-alone and set up as its own legal entity (due to the size and complexity of such undertakings they are usually better run as programmes) or the organization may be split into divisions, each with some degree of autonomy. In addition, business portfolios may comprise "sub-portfolios" and programmes may have sub-programmes, also not shown, but you'll read more about these in *The Programme and Portfolio Workout*.

Understanding the context of your project is vital, as it is the context which provides the drive for the project and also determines how project governance dovetails into higher-level governance. We will look at governance in more detail in Chapter 16.

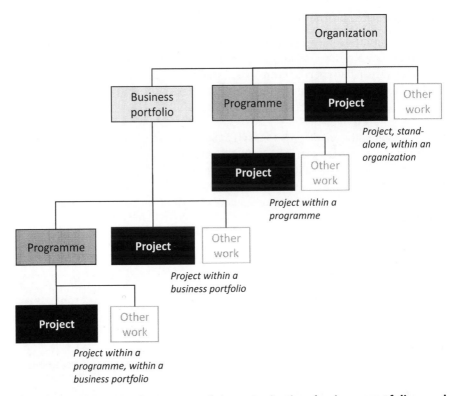

Figure 3.3 Projects in the context of the organization, business portfolios, and programmes

A project may be stand-alone within an organization, part of a programme, part of a business portfolio, or part of a programme within a business portfolio. Each project sponsor would take direction from the higher level element to which their project is attached, therefore defining the line of direction, reporting and escalation.

Figure 3.4 shows the activities for managing portfolios, programmes and projects and hence defines the flow of information between them. This shows that if you are a project sponsor, depending on the way the business is organized, you could take direction either directly from the host organization (as in the top diagram), or from a programme sponsor (as in the lower diagram) if your project is part of that programme, which is itself part of a business portfolio. Downward arrows denote the managers at the respective levels, providing direction, advice, and information on the context and risk at their level to the lower-level manager; upward arrows depict reporting, escalation, and requests for advice or direction from the lower-level manager to the higher-level manager. A manager should not bypass any levels as this could result in individuals getting conflicting direction. For example, in the lower diagram, the business portfolio sponsor should provide instructions directly to the project sponsor.

When developing a method or process, you must take into account whatever combinations you are likely to have in your organization.

A stand-alone project

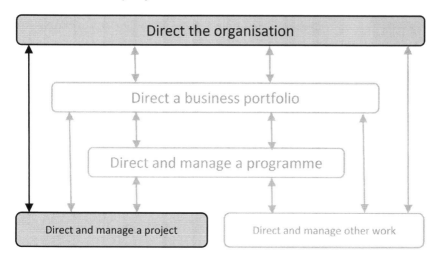

A project, within a programme, within a business portfolio

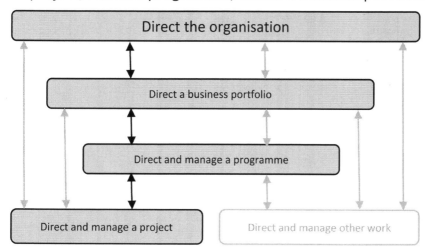

Figure 3.4 Organization, portfolio, programme, and project management activities

The activities, and therefore methods or processes, for managing business portfolios, programmes, projects, and other work, define the flow of information and should reflect the hierarchy of the elements. For example, in the top diagram, the project is directed from the host organization, whilst in the lower diagram, the project is being directed within a programme, which is itself part of a business portfolio. Downward arrows denote providing direction and advice and information on the higher-level context and risk; upward arrows show denote reporting, escalation, and requests for advice or direction.

Workout 3.1 – Putting your project in context

Consider your project and answer the following questions:

1   Why are you undertaking the project?

- is it internal, to improve your business?
- are you providing a service to another organization, as a customer project?

2   If your project business-led or "enabling":

- does, or should, it have its own business case, in which case it is business-led?
- does it only add value to the organization when combined with other work, in which case it is an enabling project?

3   Identify what level, within your organization, the project sponsor takes their direction from:

- the top level in the organization?
- the top level of a division in the organization?
- a business portfolio level?
- a programme level?
- other – if so, define it.

From the information you have from question 3, draw a structure, like Figure 3.3, to show your project in the context of other management elements. Consider who is accountable for each box you draw. We'll pick this up again in Workout 16.2.

PART II
A WALK THROUGH THE PROJECT LIFE CYCLE

"How narrow is the line which separates an adventure from an ordeal"

HAROLD NICOLSON

In this part, I will explain the management framework for a single project, taking it from an idea, through the various life cycle stages, until benefits start being realized in your organization.

Principles

- Make sure that your projects are driven by benefits supporting your strategy.
- Manage your projects within a staged framework.
- Place high emphasis on the early stages.
- Treat gates as "entry" points to stages, not "exit" points.
- Address and revalidate the business aspects of the project throughout its life.

How to use Part II

Chapters 4 and 5 are for you to read and understand. They explain the fundamental aspects of a project framework or life cycle and the roles of those needed to make it work. The workouts are designed to help you place the project framework in the context of the type of projects undertaken in your organization.

Chapters 6 to 12 comprise a skeleton project management framework. In these chapters, I explain what happens during each stage of a project and who is accountable. You can use these directly or tailor them to meet the particular needs and language of your organization. Each chapter describes a set of "control documents" for that stage: the content is given on the book's web site and in Appendix B. Each chapter concludes with a project workout to review any projects you currently have: choose the workout which matches most closely the life cycle stage of your project.

In the final chapters (13 and 14), I take this basic framework and show how you can apply the principles of the staged approach to match a wide range of different business situations.

4

The project framework

An overview of its gates and stages

Projects as vehicles of change

Stages and gates

The project framework

Some key questions

How can I apply the framework?

Project management is still seen as a specialist discipline, requiring special people who are difficult to find and to retain. While this is to a certain extent true, a scarcity of "project managers" should not be a barrier to any organization starting to develop a "projects" approach to managing its own future.

"The Golden Rule is that there is no golden rule"

GEORGE BERNARD SHAW

Projects as vehicles of change

Rosabeth Moss Cantor, former editor of the *Harvard Business Review*, once said, "The middle of everything looks like a mistake; the middle of every successful project looks like a disaster." Well, perhaps not so, if you follow the advice in this book. "Projects" are rapidly becoming the way organizations manage change and apply not only to work we have always associated with projects, such as large construction projects, but also to any change initiative aimed at putting a part of your business strategy in place. Projects, in the modern sense, are strategic management tools and you ignore the reborn discipline of enterprise-wide project management at your peril. It is fast becoming a core competence which many organizations require their leaders and employees to have. It is no longer just the preserve of the engineering sector, but an activity every executive and manager should be familiar with. The problem is that most people simply do not have the right skills; project management is still seen as a specialist discipline requiring specialized people who are difficult to find and to retain. While this is to an extent true, a scarcity of "project managers" should not be a barrier to any organization's leaders starting to develop a "projects" approach and making the future of their organizations more predictable. Project management is simply applied common sense. All executives say that their most important asset is their people (although the shareholders may be more interested in the balance sheet), but no organization, however excellent, has a monopoly on "good people"; some organizations are simply much better at getting "ordinary" people to perform in an extraordinary way and their few "extraordinary" people to perform beyond expectations. Such high-performing organizations provide an environment which enables this to happen. Add to this a few, well-chosen project experts and you have a sound foundation for generating successful projects and a successful business. Well directed and managed projects will enable you to react and adapt speedily to meet the challenges of your competitive environment, ensuring you drive toward an attainable, visible goal.

Most organizations are never short of ideas for improvement, and your own is probably no exception. Ideas can come from anywhere within the organization or even outside it: from competitors, customers, or suppliers. However, deciding which of these good ideas

> *Projects, in the modern sense, are strategic management tools and you ignore the reborn discipline of project management at your peril. It is fast becoming a core competence which many organizations require their leaders and employees to have. It is no longer the preserve of the engineering sector, but an activity every executive and manager should be familiar with.*

the business leaders should actually spend time and money on is not easy. They must take care in choosing which projects to do, as:

- they probably don't have enough money, manpower, or management energy to pursue all of the ideas;
- undertaking projects which cannot easily reconcile with the organization's strategy will, almost certainly, create internal conflicts between senior managers, confuse the direction of the business and ultimately, reduce the return on the company's investment.

Business leaders should consider for selection only those projects which:

- have a firm root in the the organization's strategy;
- meet defined business needs;
- will realize real benefits;
- are derived from gaps identified in business plans;
- and are achievable.

Having created a shortlist of "possible projects", it is important to work on them in the right order, recognizing interdependencies, sharing scarce resources and bringing the benefits forward whenever possible.

Figure 4.1 illustrates this. Selecting the right projects will help to achieve the business objectives by realizing benefits to support the business strategy. Two key roles are associated with projects:

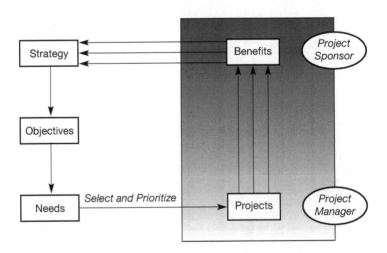

Figure 4.1 Select the right projects to support your strategy

Selecting the right projects will help you achieve your objectives by realizing benefits which support your strategy. (Copyright © PA Consulting Group, London. Adapted with kind permission.)

The project sponsor is the person who wants the benefits the project will provide.

The project manager is the person who manages the project on a day-to-day basis, ensuring its deliverables are presented on time, at the right quality and to budget.

A simple illustration of these key project roles is that you may want to build an extension to your house to give you a fully equipped home office. You want the benefits this will accrue. You and your family do not want all the dust, debris and inconvenience the construction will entail, but you accept this as the price (together with the monetary cost) you are willing to pay to obtain the benefits you seek. By the same token, the architect is more interested in designing an appropriate solution to meet your needs. As project manager, he is not fundamentally interested in the benefits you seek, but rather in the benefits he receives for carrying out the work (his fee). He must, however, understand your needs fully so that he can deliver an appropriate solution. In a good partnership, sponsorship and management are mutually compatible. Thus:

- the **project sponsor** is primarily "benefits focused"; he or she **directs** the project;
- the **project manager** is primarily "action focused" towards the achievement of the benefits. He or she **manages** the project.

The framework for managing business-led projects is aimed at making the results of projects more predictable by:

- being benefits-focused;
- building in quality;
- managing risks and exposure;
- exploiting the skill base of the entire organization.

The cost of getting the scope wrong

The technology development team in a major organization created a stunning service platform, years ahead of the completion. By bolting a super-fast computer onto a standard telecommunications switch they were able to make what became known as "the intelligent network" a reality. By calling a single number, from anywhere in the country, your call could be directed to the local branch of, say, a shop or other business. Unfortunately that was all that was developed. The missing element was how to provide such services to their customers and how to bill the customers. That took another three years to work out, by which time the rest of the industry had caught up. If the development of the "intelligent switch" had been seen as just one part of a service-development project, with service management and billing as part of the scope, these enabling systems would have been ready years earlier.

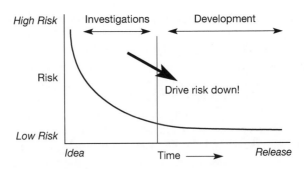

Figure 4.2 Managing the risk

The investigative stages are crucial and you should hold back any development work until your investigations show you know what you are doing and have proved that the risks are acceptable.

As a project proceeds over time, the amount of money invested increases. If none of this money is spent on reducing the risks associated with the project, then it is poorly spent. Your objective, whether you are a business leader, project sponsor, or project manager, is to ensure that risks are driven down as the project moves from being an idea to becoming a reality.

Figure 4.2 demonstrates this. The investigative stages are crucial and you should hold back significant development work until your investigations show you know what you are doing and have proved that the risks are acceptable.

You do this by using a staged approach, where each stage serves as a launch pad for the subsequent stage. In this book I have used five stages, but other models are equally acceptable if they suit the environment and culture of your organization. I will tell you about how you can do this later in this chapter.

Gates and stages

Stages

Stages are specific time periods during which work on the project takes place. These are when information is collected and outputs created and outcomes recognized.

For each stage of the project, you should carry out the full range of work covering the entire scope of functional inputs required (Figure 4.3). These functions should not work on the project in isolation but as a team, in a continuous dialogue with each other, thus enabling the best overall solution to be developed. In this way, your knowledge develops and increases on all fronts at a similar pace and solutions are designed, built and tested in an integrated way. No one area of work should advance ahead of the others. Your solution will not be what is merely optimal for one function alone but will be a pragmatic solution which is best for your organization as a whole. This has the benefits of shortcutting the functional hierarchies, enabling the flat, lean structures we all seek to attain to work in practice as it forces people with different perspectives to work together, rather than apart. Further, you should limit the work undertaken in any stage to that which is needed at the next gate: there is little point in spending effort and money until you need to.

Your solution will not be what is merely optimal for one function alone but will be a pragmatic solution which is best for your organization as a whole.

During each stage, it is essential for the project manager to continually forecast and reforecast the benefits likely to be gained and the time, resources and costs needed to complete the project. He/she should always keep the relevant function managers informed and check, on behalf of the sponsor, that the project still makes sound business sense. This is illustrated by the "project control cycle" in Figure 4.4 which is the heartbeat of every project stage.

Runaway horses and cattle drives

A project is not a horse race, with individual departments and functions competing to see who can finish first. Projects are more like a cattle drive where all of the cattle must get to market in tip-top condition. Some cattle will be faster and stronger (better resourced), other cattle are yoked together (by process and functional hierarchy). As drovers, we must ensure that some cattle do not get too far ahead and others do not lag behind. We must also ensure the cattle aren't pounced upon by wolves (other projects) and scattered. But *please* don't take the analogy too far and treat your people like animals!

Stage

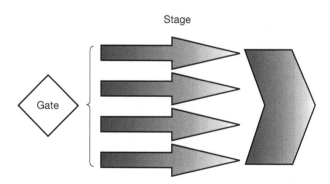

Gate

Figure 4.3 Address all aspects of the project in parallel

For each stage in the project, you should carry out the full range of work covering the entire scope of functional inputs required. In this way your knowledge develops and increases on all fronts at a similar pace and solutions are designed, built and tested in an integrated way.

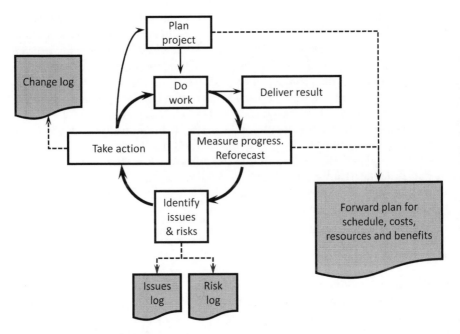

Figure 4.4 A typical stage

A stage may be represented by the project control cycle together with the plan and key control tools you need to manage it (these are described in Part III).

Before you start work on any stage, you should always know what you are going to do next in order to increase your confidence and decrease risks; you should have a detailed project plan for at least the next stage and an outline plan for the full project.

Gates

Gates are the decision points preceding every stage. Unless specific criteria have been met, as evidenced by certain approved deliverables, the subsequent stage should not be started. Being a decision "point", gates are special milestones on the project. Gates serve as points to:

- check the project is still required and the risks are acceptable;
- confirm its priority relative to other projects;
- agree the plans for the remainder of the project;
- make a go/no go decision regarding continuing the project.

You should not regard gates as "end of term exams," but rather the culmination of a period of continual assessment, with the gates acting as formal review and decision points.

Gate criteria are often reinforced in consecutive gates to ensure the same strands of the project are followed through as the project progresses. The further into the project you move, the more confidence you should have in the responses to the criteria.

At each gate, you will need to answer three distinct questions (Figure 4.5):

- Is there a real need for this project and is it viable in its own right?
- What is its priority relative to other projects?
- Do you have the funding to continue the project?

It is convenient to think in terms of these questions because, in many organizations, distinct people or groups are needed to address each of them.

The first question concerns the viability of the project, assuming no other constraints. Does it fit your strategy? Does it make business sense? Are the risks acceptable? Have you the resources to undertake the work and operate its outputs? You will see later on that this question is addressed by the "project sponsor".

The second question (priority) concerns the project in its context. It may be a very worthy project *but* how does it measure against all the other projects you want to do or are currently doing? Are there more worthwhile projects to spend your time and money on? Is it "a risk too far", bearing in mind what you are already committed to? This question is dealt with in *The Programme and Portfolio Workout* where I will show you a method of managing such decisions.

The third question involves funding. Traditionally, businesses have discrete and very formal rules concerning the allocation of funds and which are generally managed by a finance function. So, you might have a viable project, it may be the best of those proposed BUT have you the working capital to finance it? This question is also dealt with in *The Programme and Portfolio Workout*. If your finance function is less dominant, the funding question(s) may come before the question of priority (question 2).

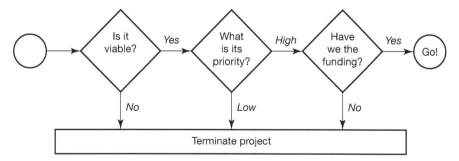

Figure 4.5 The three decisions required at each gate

Gates – an end or a beginning?

Gates have traditionally been defined as end-points to the preceding stage. The logic is that the work in the stage culminates in a review (that is, the end of stage assessment) where a check is done to ensure everything is complete before starting the next stage. This viewpoint has come about as people have confused system or software development **processes** with project **life cycles**. An IT development process, rightly, concentrates on quality and hence the need for completeness before moving on. Project management, however, is based on business risk. Due to time pressures, it is often necessary to start the next stage before everything in the previous stage has been fully finalized. For example, in the typical project framework in Figure 4.6, we see it is sound sense to undertake a trial operation of any new output before all the process, training and communication work is completed. What is essential is to have sufficient work done to enable to start the next stage with confidence. So, if you treat a gate as the end of a stage, this gives rise to the difficulty of having a traditional "rule" that common sense encourages us to break.

The solution to this dilemma is to treat gates as entry points to the next stage. In this way, you can start the next stage as soon as you are ready, regardless of whether or not the full work scope of the previous stage has been completed. You simply need to ensure the risks are acceptable and you have the resources and time built into your plan to complete the unfinished work. In this way, stages can overlap, reducing timescales, without increasing the risk associated with the project.

Treat gates as entry points to the next stage. In this way you can start as soon as you are ready, regardless of whether or not the previous stage has been completed.

This approach also opens another powerful characteristic of the staged framework. Gates are compulsory, stages are not. In other words, provided you have done the work needed to pass into a stage, how you arrived there is immaterial. This allows you to follow the strict principles of the staged framework, even if a stage is omitted. In Chapter 13, I will introduce the concept of "simple" projects and show how this principle enables them to be accommodated.

If you still aren't convinced, think of this from a senior executive's point of view. How many executives like to make decisions on what has already happened? Senior executives make decisions about what they are going to do next; this fits in with the "entry gate" approach perfectly. They like to announce they are investing untold millions over the next six months into the next stage of the company's development.

Personally, I have never met an executive who led by looking backwards.

The project framework

As we have learned, projects draw on many resources from a wide range of functions within an organization. Ensuring these are focused on achieving specific, identified benefits for the organization is your key management challenge. You can increase the likelihood of success for your projects, and hence of the business as a whole, by following a project framework which:

- is benefit driven;
- is user and customer focused;
- capitalizes on the skills and resources in the organization;
- builds "quality" into the project deliverables;
- helps manage risk;
- allows many activities to proceed in parallel (hence greater velocity).

As we have already seen in Part I, sound approaches to tackling projects achieve all these objectives by breaking each project into series of generic stages and gates, forming a framework within which every project in the organization can be referenced.

If business leaders were to take the above approach, together with a project framework approach on every project across the whole organization, it would enable them to gain control of two key aspects of their business:

1   They would know that each project is being undertaken in a rational way with the correct level of checks and balances at key points in its life.
2   They would be able to view the entire portfolio of projects at a summary level and, by using the generic stage descriptions, know where each project is and the implication this has on risk and commitment.

The remainder of this part of the book concentrates on the "single" project (point 1) and takes you step by step through a framework you can use on your projects. The second point will be investigated further in *The Programme and Portfolio Workout*, but note, unless each project is directed and managed in an effective way, the leadership team cannot hope to have visibility and control over the entire range of work undertaken within the business.

The project framework is shown in Figure 4.6 as a bar chart and in Figure 4.7 as a diagrammatic overview. The stages are, briefly, as follows:

Identify the need – Proposal: a need is first formally recognized by describing it (i.e. say *why* you want to initiate a project in terms of business outcome you need/ want to achieve). If known, you should also describe what you believe the project will produce (i.e. its output but don't jump to conclusions too soon).

Have a quick look – Initial investigation stage: the first stage in the project – a quick study of the proposal, to outline the scope and make a rough assessment of the possible ways of meeting the need, benefits, resources and costs needed to complete it. At the end of this stage you should be sure of why you are doing it. You may also know what you are doing, although this may comprise a range of defined options. You should know how to go about at least the next stage, even if not for the full project.

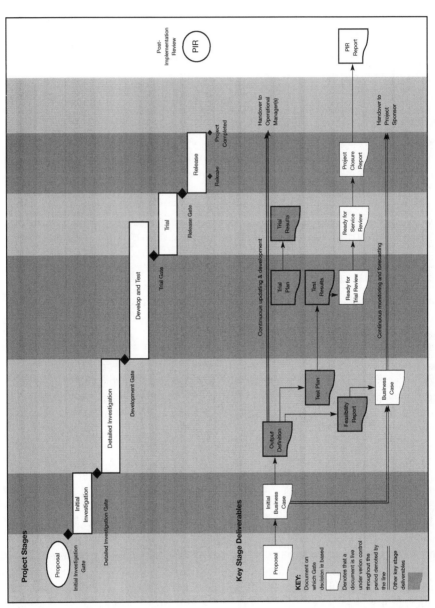

Figure 4.6 The project framework as a bar chart

The project framework is shown here in "bar chart format" at the top, with the document deliverables for each stage shown below. These are described more fully in

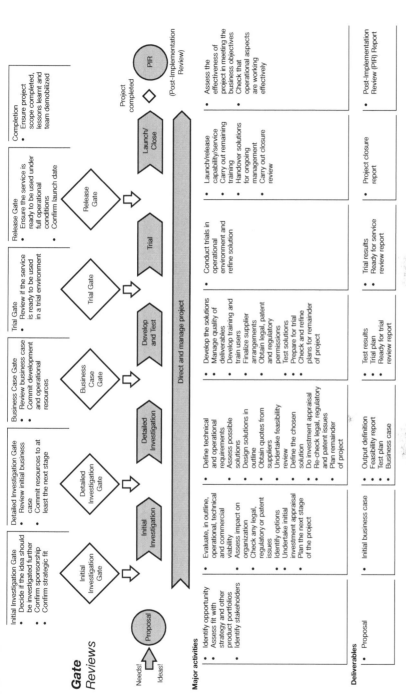

Figure 4.7 The project framework in diagrammatic form

The project framework is shown here in a format which clearly distinguishes between the gates and the stages. It also shows the activities and deliverables which relate to each stage.

Q   **Have a closer look – Detailed investigation stage:** a feasibility study, definition and full investment appraisal, culminating in a decision to proceed with development work. At the end of this stage, you will have high confidence in all aspects of the project and, if authorized at the next gate, "What you want to do" becomes "What you are going to do!"

Q   **Do it! – Develop and test stage:** the actual development and implementation work.

Q   **Try it – Trial stage:** a trial of all aspects of the development in the users' or customers' operational and working environment. What has been created may work very well under "test conditions", but does it work under normal operational conditions?

Q   **Use it – Release stage:** the last stage in the project when you unleash your creation on the world! This is when products are launched, new computer systems used, new manufacturing plant goes into production, new organization units start operating to the "new rules," new processes are invoked, acquisitions sealed, and disposals shed. The ongoing operational aspects are embedded in the organization to make sure the required business changes have been absorbed and, finally, the project is formally recognized as complete.

Q   About three to six months after completion, a check, known as a **Post-implementation review**, is done to see if the project is achieving its business objectives, the business changes have been absorbed into usual practice and the outputs are performing to the standards expected.

Some key questions

How many gates and stages should I have?

Firstly, as a gate is the decision point for starting a stage, you should always have the same number of gates as you have stages, plus a "project completion" gate at the end of the project. To decide what the right number of stages is, consider the types of project undertaken in your organization. Do they fit the generic stages described earlier? Are there some modifications you would like to make? Some organizations have only four stages in their projects, others six or more. Generally, the fewer the better, but they must be meaningful to you and fit every project you are likely to do. My experience is that three is too few and five will fit most purposes, so if in doubt try five. Of the five stages used in this book, it is the trial stage which is often either left out (see "Is a trial really needed" later in this chapter) or merged in with the develop and test stage. I prefer to have the trial as a distinct stage to differentiate it from testing. Testing is very much an internal, "private" activity. A trial, on the other hand, is "public", involving real users and customers. You are therefore open to poor press comment or to hostile reactions from employees and suppliers. Making the trial a distinct stage forces people to focus on whether they really are ready. There have been enough high profile cases of failure of beta tests on software and of premium automobiles receiving very poor press due to a poor state of market readiness to act as a warning to us all.

Portfolios, programmes, phases, stages, and gates

In this book I refer to stages and gates as convenient descriptions for the periods when work is done and for the points in time when a check is made on the project prior to starting the next stage. Alternative terminology often found in practice includes:

For Stage: Phase;

For Gate: Tollgate; Gateway; Quality Gate; Checkpoint; Assessment; Review

The word "programme" is problematic, much used and abused to the extent that it is often meaningless. For example I had a job title of "programme manager", but I did not use it on my business cards as it did not tell anyone what I did; indeed it might even have misled them. Programmes are introduced in Chapter 14 as a tightly aligned and tightly coupled set of projects and other related work. In this book, I reserve the use of the word "phase" to describe a part of a programme that is to be introduced or built with benefits designed to arrive in different time frames. An alternative word for phase is "tranche". For example, major roads are frequently constructed in phases so motorists can benefit from the first 30 miles built and do not have to wait for the full 180-mile stretch to be completed. Each phase is often a project in its own right and comprises a number of stages.

The word "programme" is frequently used to bundle any projects together for the convenience of reporting purpose. In this book I refer to these as a "portfolio" and discuss further in *The Programme and Portfolio Workout* in relation to what I term "business portfolios". In this book I define a programme as a tightly aligned and tightly coupled set of projects and other related work.

In hierarchical terms the relationship, as used in *The Project Workout*, is:

- business portfolio;
- programme;
- project;
- stage;
- work package.

This hierarchy mirrors the emerging consensus appearing in standards and publicly available methods. Nevertheless, the above terms can look confusing to some people, mainly because, despite an emerging consensus, there is not yet universally accepted definitions for each, not least because the way people use the terms in day-to-day life isn't changing as fast. Senior executives are hardly likely to adopt what they perceive as jargon from any discipline until it makes them look up to date and informed! Research at the University of Oxford in 2015 showed that the terms "project" and "programme" were used interchangeably but, even more interesting "project" is more associated with failure than "programme". The point therefore is for you, in your organization, to choose what suits you and visibly define the terms as you want them used and then use them consistently. And please, don't get into arguments over people using the "wrong" word; just think of it a "differently right".

You may find instances of organizations with anything up to a dozen stages. This usually happens because the industry and project type requires a more granular approach. For example, in regulated industries, like aerospace, the gating often reflects mandatory regulatory approvals. I found this from one of the study participants from Chapter 2 who was in avionics. In the rail industry in the UK, Network Rail has a project life cycle called GRIP (Guide to Rail Investment Process) which has eight stages; like aerospace, the rail industry is also regulated, as safety is paramount.

What should I call the stages and gates?

The stage and gate names I have chosen and used throughout this book have evolved over a number of years and are based on my experience of working in several organizations on different business projects. What you choose to call them is up to you but that decision is not trivial. Words are emotive and hence can be both very powerful movers for change or inhibitors of change. In all organizations there are words which:

- mean something particular to everyone;
- mean different things to different people.

You can build on the former by exploiting them in your project framework, provided the meaning is compatible with what you wish to achieve when using the words.

You should avoid the latter and choose different words, even making up new words if the dictionary cannot help you. For example, working in one company I found the word "concept" problematic. "Concept" to some people, was a high-level statement of an idea (the meaning I wanted to convey), but to others it meant a detailed assessment of what has been decided should be done (this was not what I wanted). Rather than try to re-educate people in their everyday language, I used a different word (proposal) which had no strong linkages to current use of language. There were similar problems with the word "implement": it has so many preconceived meanings that it is better not to use it at all! Implement to some people means implement the plan and get on with the meaty part of the project, whilst to others it means put whatever you created into beneficial use. "Execute" is another interesting word but to some people it is more associated with capital punishment than undertaking projects! For this reason, the International Standards Organization's committee on project management avoided the use of the word and its derivatives, despite many "hard-nosed" business people liberally using it to show how effective they are.

If you look at the list of possible names in Table 4.1, you will notice that certain words appear in more than one place: this is a sure sign that they might be misunderstood, but not necessarily in your organization.

The same issues apply to the naming of the gates (see Table 4.2 on page 68). For these, however, it is better to name each one according to the stage it precedes. This emphasizes the "gate as an entry point" concept. An alternative approach is to name the gate after the document which is used as the control on the gate. You will see I have mixed these. Again, this is your choice, but make the same terminology apply across the whole organization.

I do, however, strongly advise you not to refer to the stages and gates by a number or letter. It will cause difficulties later (including significant cost) if you need to revise your framework. You will not believe the number of times a "Gate 0" or "Stage 0" has had to be added to the front of a framework. Using proper names is simpler, more obvious and will not box you in for the future if you do not get it right at the start or there are real pressures to change.

Table 4.1 A list of alternative stage names

Stage names used in this book	Possible alternatives
Proposal "Identify the need"	Concept Start up Initiation Ideation Idea generation Identification Brief
Initial Investigation "Have a quick look"	Pre-feasibility Initial assessment Initial planning Preliminary investigation Evaluation/Evaluate Research Justification/Justify Incubation
Detailed Investigation "Have a closer look"	Feasibility Appraisal/Appraise Definition/Define Planning/Plan Scope Specification/Specify Design Business case Evaluation/Evaluate Authorization
Develop and Test "Do it"	Implementation/Implement Execution/Execute Realization/Realize Development/Develop Production Construction/Construct Build Do

(Continued)

Table 4.1 (continued)

Stage names used in this book	Possible alternatives
Trial "Try it"	Beta test Validation/Validate Commissioning
Release and operate "Use it"	Initial operation Finalization/Finalize Launch Completion Implementation/Implement Handover Acceptance/Accept Closure/closedown/Close
Post-implementation review "How did it work out?"	Business review Project audit Post-project review Post-project evaluation Post-investment review

Table 4.2 A list of alternative gate names

Gate names used in this book	Possible alternatives
Initial investigation gate	Concept gate Proposal gate Initiation gate
Detailed investigation gate	Feasibility gate Evaluation gate Design gate
Development gate	Business case gate Authorization gate Implementation gate Execution gate
Trial gate	Beta gate Validation gate Commissioning gate
Release gate	Ready for Service gate Operation gate Implementation gate Handover gate
Project completed	Closure gate Project end gate

How do I decide what work is done in the investigative stages?

The investigative stages exist in order to reduce risk (see Figure 4.2). Therefore everything you do should have that aim. If any proposed activity does not reduce risk, you should consider postponing it to a later stage.

What is the best way to depict a project framework?

If your project framework is to be understood, you need to communicate it in an unambiguous way, making sure it is clear that stages and gates serve different purposes. In *The Project Workout*, I use circle, arrow and diamond icons:

- a circle depicts activities which happen before a project starts or after it is completed;
- a diamond represents a gate;
- an arrow represents a stage.

This approach is used in Figure 4.7 and has withstood the test of use in many diverse organizations and is now incorporated in the British Standard on project management (BS6079 Part 1).

Gates are shown and labelled separately from stages. The gates are described with the key questions which should be asked by the decision makers. The stages are described by the activities which are undertaken during the stage with a list of deliverables which are generated within the stage.

Where do people go wrong?

In designing their frameworks, I have found people make mistakes in two key areas: at the very start and at the end.

All too often, I see frameworks with minimal start-up activity, immediately followed by the develop and test stage. They have in effect gone from "idea" to "do it" in one small step. In all but the simplest projects, such a leap is naive and may account for why so many projects are ill-defined and doomed to failure. By all means, make it easy to start the project off (i.e. pass through the initial investigation gate), but do ensure there is rigour in the actual investigations themselves. A project comprises both investigation and implementation.

> *I have found people make mistakes in two key areas: at the very start and at the end*

At the end, people often confuse project closure with post-implementation review. The former looks at project efficiency and delivery, whilst the latter looks at benefits realization and operational effectiveness. These two views cannot be combined as the measurement points are separated by time. Also, note that "Proposal" and "Post-implementation review" are not stages of the project. They are activities which happen *before* and *after* the project, respectively; that is why they are shown as a circle and not an arrow in Figures 4.6 and 4.7.

Isn't this just a "stage-gate"?

Have you come across people using the term "stage-gate"? When I come across it, I wonder if they really understand what they are talking about. Do they understand what this term means and where it comes from? All too often, I find people use as the term as yet another piece of management jargon. Figure 4.8 shows some examples of this and how it can confuse people.

Example A starts well, in that there are a number of stages depicted. Unfortunately we know nothing about where the decision points are. Where does the project start or end?

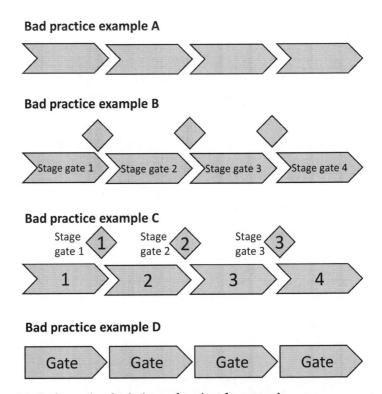

Figure 4.8 Bad practice depictions of project frameworks

How you depict the project framework is crucial if you want it to be understood. This figure shows four examples of badly defined life cycles where it is not at all clear what the author's intentions are. None of the examples makes it clear when a project starts or finishes nor the nature of the gates themselves (entry or exit?).

Example B has the same issues as example A except that a number of decision points have been added. This, however, doesn't clarify matters much, for example, is stage-gate 1 the first stage of the project or the activity before the project starts?

Example C has all the issues raised in examples A and B, except in this case it seems the decision points (gates) are labelled as "stage-gates". I wonder what the stages are called – gate-stages? Notice the numbering, which implies that the "gates" are decisions at the end of a stage, rather than decisions to start a new stage.

Example D shows the gates as if they were periods of time, with no clue as to what happens between them.

So, if you are designing a project life cycle for your project, don't fall into the real-life traps highlighted in the bad examples above; make sure you understand the difference between a gate and a stage; avoid using the term "stage-gate" and make sure your depiction of the life cycle is clear and unambiguous.

Stage-gate: don't use it!

Where did the term "stage-gate" come from? "Stage-gate" is a registered trademark devised by Robert Cooper, to describe his stage-gate approach for new product development. If you do a web search for R G Cooper or "stage-gate" you'll find lots of good articles. He never applies the term "stage-gate" to a gate or to a stage; it is simply the name he gave to his new product development approach. Like my own work on project management, he talks about "gates" and "stages" as being different but related. There is no reason to use the term and every reason not to use it.

Is a trial really needed?

"I have already tested this rigorously. Surely I don't really need to trial it as well? Won't this just delay the benefits?"

This is a very valid question. The answer, as always, is "yes and no". Assume you have a choice of strategy from:

- product leadership;
- operational efficiency;
- customer intimacy.

1 Under "product leadership" you are developing and delivering innovative, new products and services; you must be sure they really work as intended. You are aiming to be first and best in your market;

2 Under "operational efficiency" you deliver what others deliver but more efficiently and at lower cost;

3 Under "customer intimacy" you provide an experience for your customers such that they want to do business with you.

Thus, if your strategy is to have any practical meaning you must be sure that anything you do does not compromise it. The choice of "to trial or not to trial" comes down to risk. What is the likely impact on your business if this goes wrong? How confident are you that it won't go wrong? With this in mind, you may choose to subject certain aspects to a trial more rigorously than others – balancing the speed to benefits realization with the risks.

Always assume you need a trial. Omit it only if you have proved to yourself and your stakeholders that it will not add any value to your project. Never skip the trial because you are in a hurry! If in doubt, try it out.

How can I apply the framework?

The staged approach is the framework for the management of any type of project, for any purpose. It is not concerned with the technicalities of how specialist deliverables are created. As such, it is flexible and provides project managers with the opportunity to tailor it to suit the requirements of their individual projects. This ensures an optimum path through the generic project framework, rather than one which is tied by bureaucracy. Any such tailoring of the project must, however, be recorded as part of the project definition (see chapter 17). Particular types of project require their own methods and steps but provided you know how they match the overall high level framework, they can be used with confidence and in an environment where the business also knows what is happening. A common project framework in an organization will ensure alignment between different parts of the organization with clearer communication and understanding. Table 4.3 shows how a range of different projects and their key activities can fit into the framework.

Chapters 6 to 12 of this book describe the key actions, deliverables and decisions for each stage and gate of the framework. Chapter 13 looks at tailoring the framework further to deal with simple, complex, phased, agile, and other types of project.

Table 4.3 How the different projects and activities fit in with the framework

	Initial investigation	Detailed investigation	Develop and test	Trial	Release
Product development	Concept	Alternatives and feasibility	Develop and test	Market validation	Market launch
Product withdrawal	Initial investigation	Detailed investigation	Develop and test	Pilot withdrawal	Close operations
Information systems	Analysis	Logical and outline physical design	Detailed design, build and test	Pilot	Cutover
Bid or tender	Receive request and evaluate	Prepare detailed tender	Develop, build, internal test	Commissioning trials	Handover
Construction	Inception study	Feasibility study, tender design	Detailed design and construction	Commissioning trials	Handover
Publishing	Proposal	Prepare manuscript	Edit, typeset	Final proof	Launch
IT waterfall	Requirements review	Analysis and design	Build	Beta test	Cutover
DSDM/agile	Feasibility	Foundation	Evolutionary development	Deployment	Deployment

Talking the stages

A product marketing manager is accosted in the corridor by an engineer:

Engineer: I just heard from Bill that you've got plans to muck about with my installation. You ignore me as usual. Why on earth wasn't told? It looks like a real big change!

Product Manager: But, Leigh, we only decided to start the initial investigation two days ago. I've told no one yet: the proposal goes out tomorrow.

Engineer: Sorry Bill. From what I heard, I assumed it was more advanced than that. I look forward to getting the proposal.

In this scenario, an interdepartmental conflict was diffused because, despite having totally different business backgrounds, they both understood the project framework for the organization they worked in. If they had each talked in their own jargon (e.g. marketing concepts, pre-feasibility studies, inception reports) they would as likely as not have been none the wiser and continued their argument.

Workout 4.1 – Tailor your own project framework

Consider the list in Table 4.3 of different types of project. Do you recognize any from your own organization? Can you add to the list? If so, reproduce Figure 4.7 with modified activities, deliverables, and gate review criteria. You'll find a blank template for this on the web site.

Workout 4.2 – Your current business projects

List the business projects you are undertaking at present in your organization in Table 4.4.

1   Based on the descriptions for the stages just given, decide which stage of the project life cycle each project is currently in. If you have completed Project Workout 4.1, use your own stage names; if not, use those in Figure 4.7.

2   Now consider where in the project life cycle, the project was last approved. This would be a gate. Again, if you have already defined your own gate names, use those, if not use those in Figure 4.7.

3   Now consider whether the stages and gates you have selected match. Does the gate immediately precede the stage or has the project moved through the life cycle without any approval beyond the initial authorization? How long ago was the last approval made?

4   Chapters 6 to 12 include workouts at each gate. You can use these to confirm whether each of your projects has "legitimately" progressed to its current stage or whether it might just be proceeding on the basis of "hoping it all turns out right in the end".

Table 4.4 Sample check list

Project name	Current stage	Last gate approval was given at:	
		Name of gate	Date of approval

If in doubt, try it out

Who does what?

In simple a project needs people who come up with the idea (the originator), wants the benefits (project sponsor), who manages the project (project manager) and who undertake the work (the project team).

"Even emperors can't do it all by themselves"

BERTOLT BRECHT

The players

Chapter 2 showed that a process or method is nothing without the culture, systems and organization supporting it (see Figure 2.2). Those related to projects are no exception. Hence, to understand "projects", you need to have a firm grasp of who the players are and what is expected of them. The roles described here are relevant to a single project (see Figure 5.1). Roles required for running a programme or a portfolio are described in *The Programme and Portfolio Workout*.

In simple terms, a project needs people:

- who come up with the idea – the originator;
- who want the project benefits – project sponsor, often supported by a project board;
- who manage the project – the project manager;
- who undertake the work – the team managers and members.

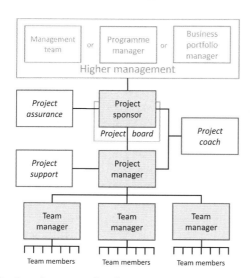

Figure 5.1 A typical project organization structure

The project sponsor who requires the benefits is accountable to, depending on the context, either a management team, programme manager or sponsor, or to a business portfolio sponsor. The project manager reports to the project sponsor and is accountable for the day-to-day running of the project. Team managers, accountable for particular work report to the project manager. Each team manager may have a team of people, team members, who actually undertake the specialist work. A project coach supports these key roles. The project sponsor may be supported by a project board. Project assurance aids the sponsor in making sure the project will achieve its objectives. The project manager may be supported by project support.

The originator

He/she is the person who identifies the "need" for a project and publishes it in the form of a proposal. This person can come from any function or level inside or outside the organization. Ideally, if the idea comes directly from the strategy, the originator will become the sponsor.

The project sponsor

The **project sponsor** is an essential role on a project and is accountable either to higher management, such as a programme sponsor (if part of a programme), for the overall success of the project. The project sponsor is accountable for championing the project's business objectives, engaging senior stakeholders, making key decisions and intervening in high-priority issues involving all benefiting units (using a project board if appropriate), approving key deliverables and making decisions or recommendations at critical points in the project's life. The project sponsor is usually a director, executive or senior manager.

Project sponsor

The project sponsor is accountable for realizing the benefits for the organization. He/she will:

- ensure a real business need is being addressed by the project;
- define and communicate the business objectives in a concise and unambiguous way(see Chapter 20);
- ensure the project remains a viable business proposition;
- initiate project reviews (see Chapter 26);
- ensure the delivered solution matches the needs of the business;
- represent the business in key project decisions;
- sign off key project deliverables and project closure;
- resolve project issues that are outside the control of the project manager;
- chair the project board (if one is required);
- appoint the project manager and facilitate the appointment of team members;
- engage and manage key stakeholders.

The project sponsor is ultimately accountable to the chief executive/ president via a project board (where required) or to an intermediate management team or board.

An underlying principle of project management is that of "single point accountability". This is meant to stop things "falling down the cracks" and applies not only to the management of projects and the constituent work packages, but also to the direction of a project; there should be only one project sponsor per project. In this respect, the term "sponsorship" should not be used in the same sense as "sponsoring Chris to run a marathon," where the objective is to have as many sponsors as possible. If a project sponsor is to be effective, rather than just someone who gives out money, he/she will need to be:

- a business leader;
- a change agent;
- a decision maker.

The project sponsor as a business leader

Project sponsorship is not merely a "figurehead" role. A sponsor is fundamentally accountable for ensuring "why" the organization is spending time and resources on a particular project. He/she must ensure the business objectives are clearly articulated, that whatever is being created is really needed and this need is fulfilled in a viable way. The project team will have their **heads down**, developing whatever outputs and deliverables are needed. The sponsor has to keep his/her **head up**, making sure the need still exists and the capabilities being produced fit the need. This cannot be over-emphasized; current research indicates that a prime cause of project failure is the lack of effective sponsorship and stakeholder engagement (we will come to stakeholders later, in Chapter 26).

The project sponsor as a change agent

Some may see the role of change agent and leader as synonymous. If so, that is good. For others, I have separated these out so it can be related to what many consultants and academics often refer to as "the management of change". Every project will create some change in the organization, otherwise there is no point in undertaking it! However, some changes are "easier" to effect than others as they align with the status quo and do not cross any politically sensitive boundaries. In essence, most of the people carry on as they always have done. Other changes, however, are fundamental and will result in shifts in power bases internal to the organization or even external, such as in unions, suppliers, or customers.

All organizations are "political" to some extent and the greater a project's scope to change the status quo, the more those involved will need to be tuned in. Whilst

Every project will create some change in the organization, otherwise there is no point in undertaking it!

projects create change, that change may not necessarily be beneficial to everyone it touches and this will trigger a political dimension to the sponsor's role. People's attitudes to "corporate politics" differ, ranging from believing it is unnecessary through to seeing it as an opportunity. Suffice to say, you must acknowledge the political aspects, understand the sources and motivations of the key players and then develop an appropriate approach to them.

The project sponsor as a decision maker

The decisions a sponsor will need to make fall into two broad types:

- decisions which steer the project in a certain direction;
- approval of certain deliverables.

The first type relates to go/no go decisions at the gates, decisions regarding how to react to issues and changes and decisions on when to close the project. The second type relates to particular outputs or outcomes from the project.

If a person is unable to make decisions, the project sponsor is not likely to be a role they will be comfortable with. Most of the decisions which have to be made will be predictable (in terms of timing, if not outcome!) and backed up by evidence. The project documentation, such as business cases and closure reports, are designed to provide the sponsor with the information he/she needs.

Attributes of a good project sponsor

If being a leader, change agent and decision maker are what is required of a project sponsor, then what sort of personal attributes does a good project sponsor need to have? There is nothing magic in the answer; as sponsorship is essentially a business role, the attributes are what you would expect for any good business executive. The exception is that, in a project managed context, business leadership is highly likely to cross departmental boundaries (See Chapter 2, lesson 6) and hence the sponsor cannot rely solely on "position power" get his or her way.

Performance in a role can be looked at as a combination of four factors: knowledge, experience, skill, and behaviours and the key ones are shown in Table 5.1. At such

Table 5.1 Attributes of a good project sponsor

Knowledge	Skills
Strategic perspective	Ability to inspire and motivate
Market and customer	Communication
Supplier and supply chain	Relationship building
Professional and technical	Analysis and problem solving
Business law	Creativity and innovation
Financial	Learning
Behaviours	**Experience factors**
Honesty	Evidence of business change leadership
Ability to delegate	Evidence of endurance and perseverance
Confidence	Evidence of adaptability
Commitment	Evidence of intuition
Positive attitude	

a leadership level, however, it is the behavioural attributes which should be paramount. Gaps in knowledge and skills may be compensated for by building a team to ensure completeness, or by appointing project board members for their particular skills.

Table 5.1 shows those attributes which have been shown to be essential to good project sponsor performance. Basically, they need to be sound business leaders who understand how to work across the organization and not just in departmental hierarchies or silos.

Project sponsor working with the project manager

The key relationships for a project sponsor is between them and:

- higher management;
- the project manager.

As far as the project manager is concerned, he or she should expect the following from the project sponsor:

- take an interest in their project – it is, after all, their project;
- communicate their vision for what the project should achieve;
- be clear on what outcomes they need;
- agree the governance arrangements;
- keep the project manager informed of the business context and risks;
- challenge the project manager in a constructive way;
- be realistic;
- make decisions and give the necessary direction and respond to requests for advice;
- accept that all risks are their risks!

Unfortunately, project sponsors are not usually selected for the role but implicitly "self-appointed" through the job they have. In which case, it is the organization's overall attitude to project management and the role of the project sponsor that will have the most effect on their performance, in other words, organizational maturity, which is looked at more deeply in *The Programme and Portfolio Workout*. Nevertheless, an executive with the right sponsor attributes in a poor organization will perform better than a poor sponsor in a good, or mature, organization. As far as the project manager is concerned, he or she will need to work with whoever they are told to. If they are unfortunate enough to have a sponsor who displays the wrong behaviours, they should not give up. The project manager should always remember it's "the sponsor's project" and their risk. Sometimes a sponsor may make what look like bizarre decisions but this may be because they have information which cannot be released. I remember a chief executive of a top UK company once saying, "I will never lie to you, except when the rules of disclosure from the City require me to." A project manager needs to make "personal contract" with the sponsor; this is, after all, a person-to-person relationship, where the success of one relies on the other. If the sponsor isn't performing as expected, assume they want to undertake their role and coach them (sensitively!): make requests for direction and decisions. Most project sponsors will not be trained project managers and will be uninterested in the minutiae of project management techniques; don't assume or expect them to understand the "jargon"; look at the world through their eyes – think about benefits and risk. Similarly, report the world through their eyes but don't try to take over their role.

Is project sponsorship really so important?

Publicly available research continually points out that organizations with active sponsors are more likely to have better project outcomes, leading to better overall business performance. Standish believes "The most important person in the project is the executive sponsor. The executive sponsor is ultimately responsible for the success and failure of the project." I agree. BUT most business leaders spend less than 5 per cent of their time on sponsor related activity. Yet surely, their role is all about leadership and making change happen – leading change . . . and mismanaging change is the commonest reason CEOs get fired. If you look at project failure, six reasons are commonly cited and four, possibly five, of those come under the accountability of the sponsor:

- unrealistic goals – set by the sponsor;

The inadvertently poor sponsor

I was a project manager for a financial systems project, with the divisional CFO acting as sponsor. I met up with him prior to the project starting and we agreed I would report, face to face, every two weeks or, in exceptional circumstances, as needed. The project was going well until the supplier started taking people off the work and deadlines were threatened. I flagged this up in the report and at my face-to-face meeting. He was pleased to find out about this and was able to rectify this through executive level contact with the suppliers' senior management team. On leaving his office, he remarked, "Why don't other project managers come to me in plenty of time?" The answer I gave was that they were scared of him as he had a reputation for balling anyone out who came with bad news. There was silence, followed by a simple, "Do I really?" This particular executive had a reputation for being difficult to work with as a project sponsor and so most project managers did not take the time to build a working approach with him, that both found workable within his busy schedule. His frustration stemmed from there being no personal relationship with the managers and that if he did happen to hear from them, it was always bad news. True, he could have made more of an effort to build the relationship himself, but a project manager should know how to fill the vacuum and make the essential first approach if necessary.

- poor alignment of project and organization objectives – decided by the sponsor;
- inadequate human resources – influenced by the sponsor;
- lack of strong leadership – led by the sponsor;
- unwillingness of team members to identify issues – influenced by sponsor behaviour;
- ineffective risk management – set by the sponsor.

If you do a web search on project failure, you will find a plethora of reasons derived from as many research projects as you care to look at and all of them contain elements of wisdom pointing to failure being determined at an organizational level above the project manager. Despite this wealth of research and learning, many business leaders continue to ignore the issue or treat it informally. Everyone says they believe it is critical to project success and yet sponsors:

- are not "trained" to be effective;
- do not make the "time" to be effective;
- are just expected to "know" how to do the job.

The project sponsor's trooper – the project champion

Often a project requires high-level sponsorship from either a vice president or even the company president him/herself. Unfortunately, senior ranks do not always have enough time to carry out all the duties being a project sponsor entails. Here, it is best if they delegate the role and name someone else as sponsor. Half-hearted sponsorship can be very demotivating for the team and may even lead to the failure of the project. Alternatively, another manager may be assigned to act on their behalf. This person is often a "project champion" who is as committed to the benefits as the sponsor himself. In all practical terms, the project champion acts on a day-to-day basis as the project sponsor, only referring decisions upwards as required.

The project board

A **project board** is usually required for projects spanning a number of processes or functional boundaries and/or where the benefits are directed to more than one market segment or function. Alternatively, the role can be undertaken by a programme board or management team. Unfortunately, bodies such as project boards are often ineffective, adding little value for the project sponsor. It is the responsibility of the chairman to keep board members focused on the key aspects of the project where their experience can be used to best effect. Bearing in mind the political nature of some projects, project boards are often essential as a way of formally engaging senior stakeholders, without whose help, the project may not achieve its aims. Be very careful, however, as boards solely created for stakeholder engagement purposes rarely perform effectively.

In the example structure in Figure 5.1, a project board is there to support the project sponsor role and chaired by the project sponsor. In some cases, the project board may be at a higher level to which a project sponsor is accountable. In other cases, a project board may not even be necessary. There is no wrong or right approach, but if a project board is created, it must be clear what its purpose is, the line of accountability and the limits of authority (including decision making), especially in relation to the accountability and authority of the project sponsor. Such accountabilities and authorities should be defined in a terms of reference.

A project board is often called a steering committee, steering group, or steering board.

The project board

The role of the project board (if required) is to support the project sponsor in realizing the project benefits and in particular:

- to set direction, review progress, manage key issues and risks (as escalated) and agree any actions which are necessary to keep the project on track to meeting its objectives;
- to monitor the project progress and ensure that the interests of your organization are best served;
- to provide a forum for taking strategic, cross-functional decisions, removing obstacles and for resolving issues.

 ### Who's running this organization?

Do you often find people in your organization hunting around for someone to "sponsor their project?" If so, who do you think is running the organization? Surely, it is the accountability of the business leaders (i.e. sponsors) to set the direction and identify the needs that must be met. They should be the ones looking for people to manage their projects, not the other way round. Is your organization led by its generals or by its troops? Is your project framework going to be a vehicle for change or merely an elaborate organization suggestion scheme?

The project manager

The **project manager** is accountable to the project sponsor for the day-to-day management of the project, involving the project team across all necessary functions and
engaging stakeholders as necessary. Depending on the size of the project, the project
manager may be supported by a project administrator, or office support team.

Project manager

The project manager is accountable for managing the project on a day-to-day basis.
He/she will:

- assemble the project team, with the agreement of appropriate line managers;
- prepare the business case, project definition and detailed plans;
- define the accountabilities, work scope and targets for each team member;
- monitor and manage project progress;
- monitor and manage risk and opportunities;
- manage the resolution of project issues;
- manage the scope of the project and control changes;
- forecast likely business benefits;
- deliver the project deliverables on time, to budget, at agreed quality;
- monitor and manage supplier performance;
- communicate with stakeholders;
- manage the closure of the project.

The bodies of knowledge of various associations, such as the Association for Project Management or the Project Management Institute, seek to define the attributes
or competencies of project managers. They are, however, not always easy to apply in
practice. To put them in context, consider three levels of project manager competence:

- **Intuitive** project managers are capable of managing a small or simple project
  very effectively with a small team. They rely on their own acquired common
  sense, much of which is inherent good practice in project management. They
  intuitively engage stakeholders, seek solutions, plan ahead, allocate work and
  check progress. Many "accidental" project managers fall into this category.
- **Methodical** project managers are capable of managing larger, more complex
  projects where it is not possible to keep the whole venture on track using simple
  tools and memory. Formal methods, procedures and practices are put in place to
  ensure the project is managed effectively.
- **Judgemental** project managers can cope with highly complex and often difficult
  projects. They can apply methods creatively to build a project approach and plan
  which is both flexible and effective, whilst keeping true to all the principles of
  good project management.

Performance in a role can be looked at as a combination of four factors: knowledge, experience, skill, and behaviours.

- Knowledge comprises learning a set of tools and techniques which are necessary for effective project management.
- Skills are the application of tools and techniques.
- Behaviours represent the attitude and style used by the project manager towards team members, sponsor, board, and stakeholders.
- Experience measures the depth to which any knowledge, skills, or behaviours have been applied.

Table 5.2 comprises a summary of these and shows those attributes which have been shown to be essential to good project manager performance. The extent to which a person complies very much depends on their level of attainment. You would expect an intuitive project manager to have far less project experience than a judgemental one. (Source: CITI Limited.)

The preceding paragraphs give the dimensions to look for when selecting a project manager and are sufficient for you to discuss a brief either with other managers or your Human Resources department. When it comes down to it, however, how would you distinguish between people with similar skill sets? What should you look for or avoid?

Table 5.2 Attributes of a good project manager

Knowledge	Skills
Project definition	Team building
Project planning	Facilitation and coaching
Benefits management	Conflict resolution
Schedule management	Analytical thinking and problem solving
Financial management	Organization
Risk and opportunity management	Administration
Issues management	Technical expertise
Change control	Communication (verbal; written and active listening)
Behaviours	**Experience factors**
Integrity	Evidence of delivery
Self-motivated – proactive	Evidence of problem solving
Comfortable with ambiguity	Size and complexity of teams managed
Open	Number of projects managed
Even-handed	Complexity of projects managed
Approachable	Evidence of effective leadership

Good reasons for selecting a particular project manager include the following:

- **Inherent enthusiasm.** They need to understand the role and what it entails or be willing to learn and have the aptitude to cope. Look for the spark that tells you they really want this to succeed.
- **High tolerance of uncertainty.** They need to be able to work effectively across the organization, without formal line authority or rank authority. They need to be able, especially in the investigative stages, to deal with the many potentially conflicting needs and signals as the project hunts its way towards a solution.
- **Excellent coalition and team-building skills.** People are at the heart of projects, both as team members and stakeholders. If the project manager doesn't have the necessary "people" skills, the project is unlikely to be a success.
- **Client orientation.** This means they need to understand the expectations and differing success criteria of the various stakeholders, especially the project sponsor.

Poor reasons for selecting a project manager, if taken in isolation, include the following:

- **Availability.** The worst reason to appoint a person is simply because he or she is available. Why are they available? What aptitude do they have? This tends to happen in organizations with a low level of maturity in project management, as "project staff" are often not seen as part of the normal work of the organization and having them "do something", rather than "nothing" is seen as more important.
- **Technical skill.** This can be useful on a project but not essential. The project manager can draw on technical experts as part of the core team. The danger when the project manager is also the technical expert is that he or she will concentrate on the technical area of interest to the exclusion of everything else. For example, a good systems engineer may ignore the roll-out, training, and usability of a new system as they are more interested in the technical architectures and features.
- **Toughness.** The "macho" project manager who closely supervises every aspect of the project, placing demand upon demand upon the team (or else!) is the way to demoralize a team. Add to this the likelihood that many of the team may be working part-time, it may be a fast way of losing the very people who are vital to a successful outcome. Yes, a project manager needs to be emotionally tough and resilient but this should not translate into being a bully.
- **Age.** Grey hairs do not necessarily indicate a more experienced project manager. Maturity in project management comes from exposure to a wide range of different situations and projects, not just length of service. Managing a single project over five years is quite different to managing ten projects, each of a six-month duration. Length of time alone is not an indicator of experience.

The team managers and members

The team managers are the "doers" who report to the project manager and are accountable for prescribed work packages and deliverables. This may range from a complete subproject to a single deliverable. It is essential that the full experience of the team be brought to bear on any problems or solutions from the start. In the case of large projects, the project manager may choose to have a small core team, each member of which manages his or her own subsidiary teams, either as work packages or subprojects. Project teams often comprise two parts:

- The **core team** – those members working full time on the project and report directly to the project manager. A core team size of six to ten people is about right.
- The **extended team** – those members who report to the core team (team managers) and who may be part-or full-time.

The team managers

Team managers are accountable to the project manager. The role of team members is to:

- be accountable for such deliverables as are delegated to them by the project manager, ensuring they are planned and completed on time and to budget;
- liaise and work with other team managers and members in the carrying out of their work;
- contribute to and review key project documentation;
- monitor and manage progress on their delegated work scope;
- manage the resolution of issues, escalating any which they cannot deal with to the project manager;
- monitor changes to their work scope, informing the project manager of any which require approval;
- monitor risk associated with their work scope;
- be responsible for advising the appropriate team managers and/or project manager of potential issues, risks, or opportunities they have noticed;
- be accountable for directing and supervising the individual members of the team.

Team managers form the bedrock of a successful project. Not only do they have to be competent in the specialist work relating to their assigned deliverables, but also need to be competent in a range of project management techniques. If you look at the accountabilities above, you will notice that many aspects including planning, reporting, risk and issues management, change control, and stakeholder management are the same as those required by a project manager. It is not unusual to find that work scopes for some team managers' work packages dwarf other project manager's projects in terms of team size and spend. It is for this reason many organizations include project management techniques as a core part of every manager's training and development. If team managers are not competent at the management aspect of their role, as part of a project team, it is the project manager's accountability to brief them on what is needed and, if necessary, tailor the techniques to suit the competence levels of those who need to use them.

It is essential that each member of staff working on your project has a clearly defined:

- role and reporting line to the project manager when working on the project (he/she may maintain their normal reporting line for other activities);
- scope of work and list of deliverables (both final and intermediate deliverables);
- level of authority (i.e. directions on what decisions he/she can and cannot take on behalf of his/her line function).

All groups or individuals associated with the project and which make up the team should be identified and listed with their role, scope and accountabilities.

Project assurance

Assurance covers all interests of sponsorship, including business, user, and supplier needs. It should be independent of the project manager. Assurance should be focused on the project's business objectives and whether they will be achieved. As such assurance is inextricably related to the project sponsor role.

Project assurance

Specific responsibilities include assuring:

- fit with the overall business strategy;
- the project is still needed and viable;
- focus on the business need is maintained;
- risks are being controlled;
- user needs and expectations are being met or managed;
- constant reassessment of the value-for-money solution;
- the right people are being involved;
- an acceptable solution is being developed;
- the scope of the project is not "creeping upwards" unnoticed;
- internal and external communications are working;
- applicable standards are being used;
- any legislative, regulatory, or contractual constraints are being observed.

Everything relating to assurance is the accountability of the project sponsor. Thus, in the absence of project assurance, the sponsor is accountable for the activities. The most common reason for creating a project assurance function is simply because a sponsor may not have the time or competence to undertake the sponsor role effectively. By having a project assurance function, the time pressure can be relieved and more experienced people used when needed.

Those undertaking assurance roles need to be able to take an independent view to enable them to challenge and confront any issues they come across. Often the major issues are well known within a project team, but political or other constraints prevent those involved from speaking up about the "elephant in the room" which everyone can see but no one acknowledges is present; or to point out the facts behind the "emperor's new clothes" where some aspect of the project is exposed, whilst all those involved pretend it is well covered. Those undertaking assurance must have the gravitas and management style to be trusted by the project team and stakeholders and need to provide constructive and practical views based on insight and experience. Assurance undertaken on the basis of scoring points off the project team or doggedly sticking to checklists will not be beneficial to anyone. Finally, don't confuse "project assurance" with "quality assurance"; the former is about ensuring every aspect of the project is run to ensure the business objectives will be met, whilst the latter is focused on the processes, procedures, and practices which ensure quality is built into the deliverables.

Remember, in many business-oriented projects, the participants are likely not to be fully trained and capable project managers. They may need to have someone who can give them the confidence to work in a way which may be alien to them.

Project coach/facilitator

 The project coach or facilitator is accountable for supporting the project manager, project sponsor, and project board. This may be by pure coaching or by giving advice, facilitation, and guidance on project management. Both approaches will help project teams, experienced and inexperienced, to perform beyond their own expectations. It is a role which is found infrequently but can prove extremely effective.

Remember, in many business-oriented projects, the participants are likely not to be fully trained and capable project managers. They may need to have someone who can give them the confidence to work in a way which may be alien to them.

The power of coaching and facilitation

A cross-functional team was put together with the aim of reducing the delivery time for a telecommunications product from ten days to less than two hours. The team comprised people drawn from line and operational roles who had little project management experience. A project coach was employed to facilitate the setup stages of the project and provide ongoing guidance throughout the execution. Setup was hard work and many of the team complained that it was wasting valuable time which could be better spent doing "real work". Perseverance and a commitment on behalf of the coach to seeing the team succeed got the team through the early stages. Once the development stage was underway, all of them understood the project fully. At the end, a marketing manager on the project commented to the coach, "I wondered what you were doing to us; I now see it was key to have the hassle at the start if we were to achieve our objectives." Things did go wrong on the project but, as all the core team members knew their own role and that of the others, changes could be more easily, speedily, and effectively implemented so that the overall objective was met. In fact the delivery time was reduced to an average of twenty minutes.

Project support

At its most basic, **project support** provides support and administrative services to the project manager on activities such as filing, planning, project monitoring, and control. The services provided by project support can, however be very specialist, and go far beyond mere, though essential, administration.

Project support

Specific responsibilities may include the following:

- define and establish governance arrangements;
- specify, set up and maintain project information managemen systems;
- establish document control procedures on the project;
- compile, copy, and distribute all project management deliverables;
- collect actuals data and forecasts and update plans;
- assist with the compilation and analysis of reports;
- administer project meetings;
- monitor and administer risks, issues, changes, and defects;
- provide specialist knowledge (for example, estimating, risk management);
- provide specialist tool expertise (for example, planning and control tools, risk analysis);
- undertake reviews.

Project support can provide expertise, support services, specialist advice, and guidance on any aspect of project management. They are often given names such as project office, project management office, or project support office.

Working with the programme or project manager, project support establishes the most appropriate governance strategy and implements planning and control mechanisms, methods, processes, and tools. The provision of any support on a formal basis is optional and in some cases (where the project is relatively straight forward), the project manager provides their own support. Where set up as a specific service, project support can act as the focal point for lessons learned and as a central source of expertise and advice using any methods and specialist support tools.

Specialist roles

All the above roles are related to directing and managing the project; they are agnostic to the type of work being undertaken. In fact, what people sometimes refer to as "the real work" is all directly undertaken by the team manager and team members; the work is whatever the scope of the work package defines it to be. Calling everyone a "team manager" on an organization chart is not very useful, so you will often see team manager's roles defined by the specialist work they do, whether communications, sales, design, development, engineering, manufacturing, or whatever. The team manager and team members should be skilled and competent to undertake the work assigned to them, often using specialist processes or methods specifically for that work. For example, for a system engineering project, the team manager may be called the "System Engineer" or "System Architect" and they may follow the organization's prescribed engineering method when developing the specialist deliverable for the project. As they are accountable for those deliverables in terms of quality, time and costs, they will also act as the "team manager". As you have already read, above, the team manager role defines what management approach they should take and their interactions with other roles, such as the project manager and team members; a person managing a team on a project must be competent at both their specialism and the project management techniques needed for the management of their work package. Unfortunately, you often see people taking the opposite approach, saying, wrongly, that the project manager is accountable for time and cost and the specialist manager for the quality of the deliverable. Projects run in that way can rarely succeed. It is true that the project manager is accountable for time and cost but this is for the entire project; a project manager relies on the plans developed by the team managers and risks perceived by them, drawing everything together to ensure a complete solution with a robust plan.

Workout 5.1 – Understanding your roles and accountabilities

This workout is best done with the project team, but may be done by the project manager or sponsor.

1   Take any one of your projects and identify who (both individuals and teams) is involved in it. List them, one per Post-It Note. Place these on a flip chart.
2   Against each name, write in your own words what that person's needs or accountabilities are regarding the project.
3   On the left-hand side of a separate flip chart, list the roles described in Chapter 5.
4   Match, as best you can, the names from step 2 to the key project roles described above.
5   For those names listed against "team member," divide them into "core team member" and "extended team member".
6   If you cannot allocate a person to one of the defined roles, put him/her in a separate cluster called "stakeholders".

Look at the role descriptions described in the chapter again. Do the individuals have the knowledge, skills and competences to perform the roles? You should have only one name against project sponsor and one against project manager. If not, your roles and account-abilities are likely to be confused. Further, the sponsor and manager should not be the same person.

Project sponsor

*   Can this person articulate a vision of the business changes and outcomes which will result from the project?
*   Can this person articulate the benefits the project will provide?
*   Are they proactively leading and giving direction, when needed?

Project board

*   As a group, does it have all the facets of the project covered?
*   Have its members ever met as a group?
*   Could they all describe the project's business objectives and its current status consistently?

Team managers

*   Do the team managers cover the required work scope between them?
*   Are they supported with adequate resources and expertise?

- Do they ever meet with the project manager as a group?
- Could they all describe the project's objectives and its current status consistently?

Team members

- Do the team members know whom they are accountable to on the project and what they have to deliver and when?
- Do they know who is relying on their outputs in order to complete their work?
- Could they all describe the project objectives and its current status consistently?

6

The proposal

Identify the need!

Overview

Key deliverable

Process steps

The gate prior to the initial investigation is the first decision point when resources are committed to working on the project; it is also the point at which the potential project is first formally recognized.

"One of the greatest pains to human nature is the pain of a new idea"

WALTER BAGEHOT, 1826–1877

Overview

The proposal describes the business need (i.e. it focuses on **why** you want a project) and, if known, what you want to do. You should document the proposal formally and have it reviewed by potential stakeholders prior to a go/no go decision for starting an initial investigation. The proposal document is used as the key deliverable at the initial investigation gate. This gate, just prior to the initial investigation stage, is the first decision point when resources are committed to working on the project; it is also the point at which the potential project is first formally recognized. The gate is unique in that it is the only one in the project life cycle which does not require you to have a plan for how you undertake the work which follows.

The proposal describes the business need (i.e. it focusses on why you want a project).

It is important for you to document the proposal as:

- it acts as the brief for the team undertaking the initial investigation stage;
- the mere fact of writing the proposal down serves to clarify your thinking and ensures clear communication of your intentions;
- if you can't be bothered to write it down, why should you expect anyone to work on it?

Key deliverable

The proposal is a very brief document (one to five pages), outlining the need the project will meet, its intended outcome, likely benefits, and how it fits with current strategy. If known, the impact on the organization (market, technology, and operational), broad estimates of benefits and cost and required time to completion can also be included.

Table 6.1 The proposal

Deliverable	Prepared by	Reviewed by	Approved by
Proposal	Originator	Likely stakeholders, including, functions or business units likely to be impacted by or to benefit from the proposal	Sponsor

Process steps

1   The need (or idea!) for a project should result directly from your business strategies and plans. This is not always the case as, for example, opportunities may be spotted as the result of technical innovation, operational experience or feedback from suppliers or customers.

2   The originator of the "idea" should identify a senior executive in the company who is likely to benefit most from the idea. (If the project comes directly from the business plan, that person will be obvious, or may even be the originator!)

3   The senior executive first checks that a similar idea has not been proposed before. If it has, the "idea" should not be pursued further unless different circumstances now exist (market, technology, etc.). He/she should determine who else in the company has a stake in the idea in terms of benefit, impact, and/or contribution, and then appoint a potential project sponsor. In the case of large projects or small companies, the senior executive may become the project sponsor.

4   The potential project sponsor should write up the idea in the form of a proposal. The draft proposal is reviewed with any other stakeholders identified in point 3. If necessary, it is amended. This review should look not only at the proposal in question but also at any other related proposals and projects. It is essential to screen out any duplicate proposals and those which do not form part of a coherent programme of change related to the business strategy and plan.

5   The potential project sponsor should identify a project manager who will be accountable for managing the initial investigation stage, complete the registration of the proposal and file a reference copy.

The proposal is submitted for gate authorization.

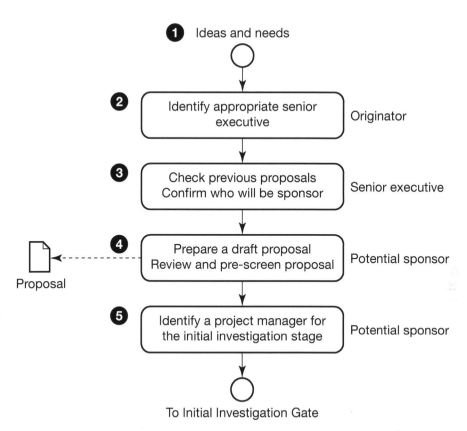

Figure 6.1 Steps prior to the initial investigation stage

Workout 6.1 – Checklist for starting the initial investigation stage

Business need and strategic fit

- Is it clear that the project fits the strategy?
- Is the opportunity attractive (size, share, cost saving, contribution, etc.) relative to alternative proposals?
- Is the proposal likely to be acceptable to the customers and users?
- Do any competitors have capabilities similar to this? If so, will this proposal provide you with any competitive advantage?

Health check!

- Has a project "health check" been done to identify areas which need to be covered (see Workout 27.1)?

Accountabilities

- Has a project sponsor been identified?
- Has a project manager been identified for the initial investigation stage?
- Can resources be committed to do the initial investigation?

Operational and technical

- Is the organization likely to be able to develop or acquire the required capabilities to support this proposal, if they don't yet exist?
- Is it technically feasible with current technology?
- Has the organization operational capability to support it? If not, can it acquire this?

Health check scores

P	R	O	J	E	C	T	Total
☐	☐	☐	☐	☐	☐	☐	☐

Risk

☐ Low ☐ Medium ☐ High ☐ Impossible

Issues

Risk

Executive action

The initial investigation stage

Have a quick look at it!

Overview

Key deliverables

Process steps

The goal of the initial investigation stage is to examine the proposal as quickly as possible (say, within one to six weeks) and evaluate it against the existing business plans of the company to determine if what is intended is likely to be viable in financial, operational, technical, and customer terms.

"To have begun is half the job: be bold and be sensible"

HORACE, 65–8BC

Overview

The goal of the initial investigation stage is to examine the proposal, as quickly as possible, (say, within one to six weeks) and evaluate it against the existing business plans of the company. You need to determine if what is intended is likely to be viable in financial, operational, technical, and customer terms. You will need to:

- make a preliminary assessment of the business opportunity, likely benefits, possible solutions, costs, technology needs, and the expected impact on the operational platforms and groups, infrastructure, and capabilities;
- check for overlap, synergy, or conflict with other projects in progress or capabilities in use;
- scope and plan the work content for the remaining stages of the project.

Remember, this is only an initial assessment; do not run ahead of yourself by working to too much detail. Think in ranges, rather than absolutes. For example, "this project will cost between £75,000 and £200,000, take four to eight months, with cost savings of the order of £100,000 to £200,000 per year".

Key deliverables

The **initial business case** contains the business rationale for the project. It is the docu- ment which outlines WHY you need the project, WHAT options you intend to work on, HOW you will do it, and WHO is needed to make it happen. It also answers the question HOW MUCH? and hence is used to authorize the funding for at least the next stage of the project. The initial business case does not comprise a full analysis, but only sufficient detail to enable you to decide if continuing the project is worthwhile. The full business case, which is completed in the next stage, will provide the definitive appraisal for the project. The initial business case includes:

- a preliminary assessment of the financial aspects of the proposed development;
- a definition of the project which would be required to meet these, including an outline of the requirement in terms of customer/user "feel", technology, commercial, market needs and desired outcomes. There may be a number of options at this point in time;
- a description of how the project will be organized in terms of roles and governance.

The initial business also enables the evaluation of the project against the existing strategies and goals of the company to confirm its fit and determine if it is likely to be viable in business, technical, operational, and customer terms.

The project plan is a key appendix to the initial business case and defines the schedule, cost and resource requirements for the project. This is defined in summary to completion of the project and in detail for the detailed investigation stage.

Table 7.1 Key deliverables plan

Deliverable	Prepared by	Review by	Approved, prior to gate, by
Initial business case	Project manager	Impacted stakeholders or benefiting functions and business units	Project sponsor
Project plan	Project manager	Impacted or benefiting functions and business units	Project sponsor

Note: These are minimum roles and deliverables only. Each project manager should define the full set prior to the start of the stage. At the discretion of the project sponsor or manager, a separate initial investigation report and/or blueprint may also be produced.

Process steps

Initial investigation gate. This gate is the point when a decision is made as to whether an initial investigation (business, technical, marketing, and operational) should be undertaken and if there are resources to do it. If the Proposal is authorized, the initial investigation stage is started. See checklist in Workout 6.1.

1   The appointed project manager engages the study team, registers the project, ensures a project account has been opened and informs all relevant stakeholders of stage entry (see Chapter 17).
2   The team, led by the project manager, undertakes the initial investigation, confirming the need for the project, objectives, and strategic fit. The team will also develop possible solutions to meeting the needs and requirements laid out in the proposal. The project manager agrees the outcome and recommendations with the project sponsor. You might find Workout 19.2 (Transfiguration) and Workout 24.1 (Resolving issues – from breakdown to breakthrough) helpful here.
3   The team defines the project and prepares the project plan, in detail for the next stage and in outline beyond. The potential resource needs should be discussed and agreed with the relevant function managers.
4   The project manager, with the team members, prepares the initial business case.
5   The initial business case, including the project plan, is reviewed by the project sponsor and any other relevant stakeholders. It is either accepted, rejected, deferred, or amendments are requested.

The initial business case is submitted for gate authorization for the detailed investigation gate.

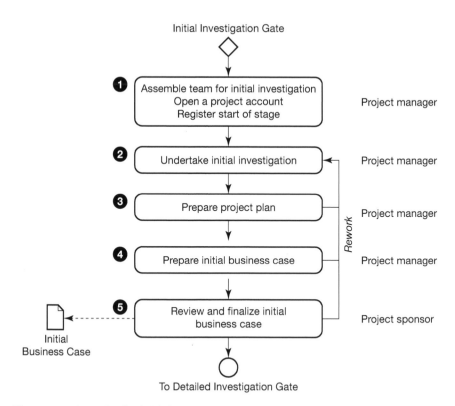

Figure 7.1 Steps in the initial investigation stage

Workout 7.1 – Checklist for starting the detailed investigation stage

Business need and strategic fit

- Does the project fit the strategy?
- Is the business opportunity attractive?
- Are the risks acceptable?

Deliverables

- Is the initial business case and investment appraisal acceptable?
- Is there a detailed schedule, resource, and cost plan for the Detailed Investigation Stage?
- Is there an outline schedule, resource, and cost plan for the full project?
- Have all the relevant business units and functions been involved in creating and reviewing the deliverables?

Health check!

- Has a project "health check" been done and been found acceptable (see Workout 27.1)?

Accountabilities

- Has a project sponsor been identified for the project?
- Has a project manager been identified for the project?
- Do you have the resources to undertake the detailed investigation stage?

Operational and technical

- On current knowledge, is it technically feasible with existing technology, or is there a likely technical development path to provide the capability or service?
- Does the organization currently have the operational capability to support it? If not, is it likely this can be put in place?

Health check scores

P	R	O	J	E	C	T	Total
☐	☐	☐	☐	☐	☐	☐	☐

Risk

☐	Low	☐	Medium	☐	High	☐	Impossible

Issues

Risk

Executive action

The detailed investigation stage

That looks promising ... let's have a closer look

Overview

Key deliverables

Process steps

During the Detailed investigation stage you will identify the optimum solution and commercial proposition.

"Understanding is the beginning of approving"

ANDRÉ GIDE. *The Immoralist*, 1869–1951

Overview

During the detailed investigation stage, you will identify and define the optimum solution and commercial proposition. You will need to:

- evaluate possible options and identify a preferred solution;
- ensure the preferred solution will meet the defined needs;
- define process, technical and operational requirements where appropriate;
- test/research the concept with the target users and/or customers;
- check any legal or regulatory issues;
- evaluate possible suppliers and partners.

The next gate, for which this stage prepares you, is critical as it is the last point at which you can stop the project before substantial financial commitments are made.

Key deliverables

The **blueprint** is the fundamental document (or set of documents) describing the outcome and output of the project in terms of operating model, process, organization, systems, technology and culture. This document integrates all the individual system, process, and platform requirements and specifies how they will work together. The document will continue to develop as the project proceeds and will be handed over to the manager(s) of any operational parts before the project is completed.

The **feasibility report** builds on the initial business case. It includes the recommendation for which option should be adopted as the solution, comparing it against rejected solutions in financial and non-financial terms.

The **business case** contains the business rationale. It is derived from the initial business case and feasibility report, together with the outputs from other investigative work. It is the document on which the decision is made to authorize funding for the remainder of the project and the building in of costs and benefits to the business plan. The document is "live" and under strict version control for the remainder of the project.

The **project plan** includes the detailed schedule, resource, and cost plans for the develop and test stage, with the remaining stages in summary.

The **test plan** documents the tests required to verify performance of any outputs from the project, both in isolation and working as a complete system.

Table 8.1 Key deliverables plan

Deliverable	Prepared by	Review by	Approved, prior to gate, by
Blueprint	Project manager	Team managers and experts	Project sponsor
Feasibility report	Project manager	Team managers and experts	Project sponsor
Business case	Project manager	Team managers and key functional managers	Project sponsor
Project plan	Project manager	as above	Project sponsor
Test plan	Project manager	as above	Proposed owners of deliverable

Note: These are minimum review roles and deliverables only. Each project manager should define the full set prior to the start of the stage.

Process steps

Detailed investigation gate. This gate determines whether further effort and resources should be invested in undertaking a detailed investigation. If the initial business case is authorized, the detailed investigation stage is started. See checklist in Workout 7.1.

The initial business case and project plan now come under formal version control.

1 The project manager informs the stakeholders and key team members that authority to start the stage has been given.
2 The project manager ensures the start of the stage has been registered, assembles the team and briefs them on the scope of this stage (see Chapter 17).
3 The detailed investigation work is carried out (within the project control cycle, see Chapter 18) to assess possible solutions and a preferred option is recommended, bearing in mind the risks and benefits. A feasibility report is prepared.
4 The feasibility report is reviewed, amended if necessary, then agreed by the project sponsor who decides which option should be chosen and refined further.
5 Work on defining the chosen option is carried out. This may involve refining the blueprint, the operational aspects, change management and training plans, business processes, market plans and system designs.

The blueprint now comes under formal version control.

6 The project manager, with the team, prepares the detailed plan for the develop and test stage and finalizes the business case. These are reviewed with the team and stakeholders and, if necessary, are amended.

7   The detailed plan and business case are reviewed by the project sponsor and the relevant stakeholders. It is either accepted, rejected, deferred, or amendments are requested.

The business case is submitted for gate authorization.

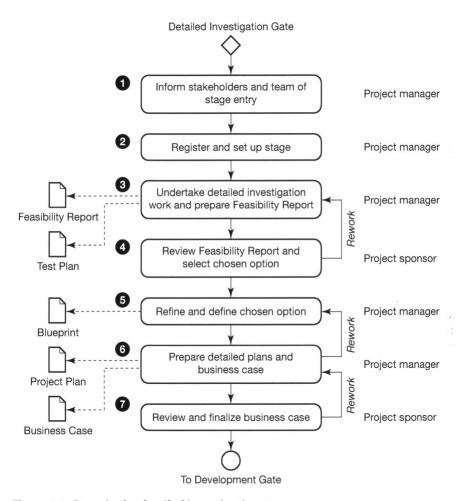

Figure 8.1 Steps in the detailed investigation stage

Workout 8.1 – Checklist for starting the develop and test stage

Business need and strategic fit

- Does the project still fit the strategy?
- Have the development concepts (e.g. marketing) been researched and tested on target segments and the need reaffirmed?
- Is the business case acceptable and compelling?
- Have the key sensitivities and scenarios for the recommended option been checked and confirmed as acceptable?
- Is the business case ready to be built into the overall business plan?

Project plan

- Is there a detailed schedule, resource, and cost plan for the develop and test stage?
- Is there an outline schedule, resource, and cost plan for the full project?
- Are there sufficient review points in the plan (see Ch. 27)?
- Has the project been designed to eliminate known high risks (see Ch. 23)?

Accountabilities

- Are there resources to undertake the develop and test stage?
- Have formal commitments been made by the relevant line managers?

Operational and technical

- Is it technically feasible with current technology?
- Does the organization have the operational capability to support it?

Deliverables

- Is the blueprint complete?
- Is it clear how the output will be tested?

Health check!

- Has a project health check been done and been found acceptable (see Workout 27.1)?

Health check scores

P	R	O	J	E	C	T	Total
☐	☐	☐	☐	☐	☐	☐	☐

Risk

☐ Low ☐ Medium ☐ High ☐ Impossible

Issues

Risk

Executive action

The develop and test stage

Do it!

Overview

Key deliverables

Process steps

The Develop and Test Stage is when you spend the bulk of the costs relating to the project.

"The world can only be grasped by action, not contemplation"

JACOB BRONOWSKI

Overview

The develop and test stage is when you usually spend the bulk of the costs relating to the project. It comprises the outstanding design, development, creation, building, and implementation of the chosen solution, with the supporting systems, manuals, business processes, organization, and training. It concludes with a full test in a controlled environment to verify the deliverables have been "built right" and work together, as expected. If this stage is of long duration (more than four months), it is essential to build review points into the plan to ensure its ongoing viability is assessed (see "Reviews during a project", Chapter 27). It is also wise to have additional review points prior to letting any major supplier contracts relating to the project.

During this stage you will need to make a decision to start the trial stage, when you validate, with customers and users, that what you have produced is the "right thing". This decision can be taken prior to completion of the full work scope for the stage because only activities required for the trial need be completed.

Key deliverables

The **test results** verify that any testing has been completed in accordance with the test plans and acceptance criteria, prior to preparing for the trial review. Any outstanding issues are noted.

The **trial plan** documents the way in which the output will be piloted in order to validate that the expected outcomes will be realized. It includes the criteria for determining whether the trial is successful.

The **ready for trial review report** is a short report confirming all deliverables, resources, and prerequisites across all functions required for starting the trial are in place.

The **business case:** the business case should be updated to demonstrate the project is still needed and viable.

The **project plan:** the schedule, resource, and cost plan for the trial stage should be fully detailed with the remainder of the project in outline.

Table 9.1 Key deliverables plan

Deliverable	Prepared by	Review by	Approval, prior to gate, by
Test results	Project manager	Team managers and experts	Project sponsor
Trial plan	Project manager	Team managers Operational staff	Project sponsor
Ready for trial review report	Project manager	Team managers Operational staff	Project sponsor
The following are reviewed and updated as needed:			
Blueprint	Project manager	Team managers and experts	Project sponsor
Business case	Project manager	Team managers and key functional managers	Project sponsor
Project plan	Project manager	Team managers	Project sponsor

Note: These are minimum review roles and deliverables only. Each project should define its full set prior to the start of the stage.

Process steps

Development gate. This gate determines whether the development and testing work should start. If the business case is authorized, the develop and test stage begins and the benefits, revenues and costs are built into the organization's business plan. See checklist in Workout 8.1.

1   The project manager informs the stakeholders and key team members that authorization to start development has been given (see Figure 9.1).
2   The project manager assembles the team (including suppliers) and confirms the project controls, roles, and accountabilities for each individual. The plan (as produced at the end of the previous stage) should be reviewed to ensure it is still valid.
3   The work, as defined in the business case and laid out in the project plan, is carried out within the project control cycle (see Chapter 18). Work is done, progress is measured, issues and variances noted, and corrections made. As deliverables are produced, they are reviewed, amended, and finally accepted. These comprise the deliverables required prior to:

  •   starting testing;
  •   starting the trial stage (if one is required);
  •   the release gate.

4   The tests are carried out, the results are reviewed and any modification or retesting done. Some deliverables and the blueprint may need to be amended in the light of the tests.

5 A review is done to check that all activities have been completed and deliverables are ready for the following stage(s) to start. All project documentation (including the project plan, blueprint, and business case) is updated.

If a trial stage is required, submit the ready for trial report for gate authorization.
If a trial is not required, submit the ready for service report for gate authorization.

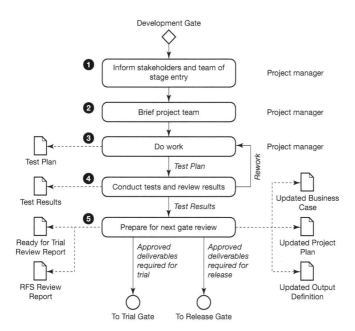

Figure 9.1 Steps in the develop and test stage

Workout 9.1 – Checklist for starting the trial stage

Business need and strategic fit

- Is the project still a good business proposition?
- Is the project still correctly reflected in the overall business plan?
- Have all high risks been eliminated?

Project plan

- Is the project plan up to date, full, and complete?
- Is there a detailed schedule, resource, and cost plan for the trial stage?
- Is there an outline plan for the remainder of the project?
- Do we have sufficient resources to undertake the trial?

Health check!

- Has a project "health check" been done and been found acceptable (see Workout 27.1)?

For the trial

- Have the tests been finished and the results accepted?
- Has the trial plan been prepared?
- Have checklists been prepared for the customers and users?
- Have customers/users been identified and trial agreements drafted?
- Have the business processes been finalized?
- Are all relevant functions and units ready for the trial?
- Is the communications material ready?
- Are results monitoring systems in place?
- Have the trial acceptance criteria been agreed?

Health check scores

P	R	O	J	E	C	T	Total
☐	☐	☐	☐	☐	☐	☐	☐

Risk

☐ Low   ☐ Medium   ☐ High   ☐ Impossible

Issues

Risk

Executive action

10

The trial stage

Try it out

Overview

Key deliverables

Process steps

The solution must be acceptable to the users, functionally correct and highly likely to meet the organization's business objectives.

"The full area of ignorance is not yet mapped. We are at present only exploring the fringes"

J D BERNARD

Overview

During this stage, your partially proven solution is validated in the operational environment with live users and/or customers. The purpose is to validate:

- the solution is acceptable to the users and customers;
- all the capabilities work, as needed, in a live environment, including the business processes and supporting infrastructure;
- the business objective is likely to be met.

In this respect, the solution must be acceptable to the users, functionally correct and highly likely to meet the organization's business objectives (see also p. 117 if you are not sure if you need a trial). The trial validates if you have "built the right thing" and not just built something that merely meets the specification.

Key deliverables

The **trial results** is a summary document confirming the trials have been completed in accordance with the trial plan, acceptance criteria. If validated, the developed solution is now ready to move to the release stage. Any outstanding risks and issues are also noted.

The **ready for service (RFS) review** is a short report confirming all deliverables and prerequisite activities required before starting the release stage have been completed.

The **business case:** the business case should be updated to demonstrate the project is still needed and viable.

The **project plan:** the schedule, resource, and cost plan for the release stage should be fully detailed.

Table 10.1 Key deliverables plan

Deliverable	Prepared by	Review by	Approved, prior to gate, by
Trial results	Project manager	Team managers and operational managers	Project sponsor
RFS review report	Project manager	Team managers and operational managers	Project sponsor
The following are reviewed and updated, as needed.			
Output definition	Project manager	Team managers and experts	Project sponsor
Business case	Project manager	Team managers and key functional managers	Project sponsor
The project plan	Project manager	Team managers	Project sponsor

Note: These above are minimum review roles and deliverables only. Each project manager should define the full set prior to the start of the stage.

Process steps

Trial gate. This gate determines whether you can start a trial of the proposed solution using real users or customers. If the ready for trial report is authorized, the trial stage is started. See checklist in Workout 9.1.

1   The project manager informs the relevant stakeholders and key team members that approval to start the trial stage has been given.
2   The project manager assembles the team and confirms the project controls, with the roles and accountabilities for each individual. The plan (as produced at the end of the previous stage) should be reviewed to ensure it is still valid.
3   The final preparations for the trial are carried out, as defined in the project plan.
4   The trial is carried out, the results are reviewed, and any modification and retrials done.

While the trial is being carried out, other activities and deliverables (such as training) are being delivered from the develop and test stage.

5   A review is done to check the trial was acceptable, all activities have been done and deliverables are ready for the release stage to start. All project documentation (including the project plan, output definition, and business case) is updated.

The ready for service report is submitted for gate authorization.

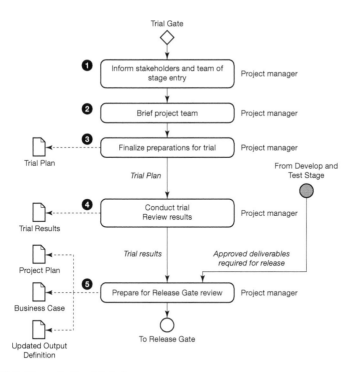

Figure 10.1 Steps in the trial stage

Workout 10.1 – Checklist for starting the release stage

Business need and strategic fit

- Is the project still a good business proposition?
- Have all high and medium risks been eliminated from the project?

Ready for service

- Are you absolutely sure, beyond reasonable doubt, that it will work? (Your reputation is at stake!)
- Have process designs across the organization (and to third parties if needed) been accepted and is all training completed?
- Are benefits/results monitoring systems in place?
- Have the costs and benefits been reforecast against the business plan?

Project plan

- Is the project plan updated, full, and complete?
- Is there a detailed schedule, resource, and cost plan for the release stage?
- Do we have the resources to undertake the release stage?

Health check!

- Has a project "health check" been done and been found acceptable (see Workout 27.1)?

Health check scores

P	R	O	J	E	C	T	Total
☐	☐	☐	☐	☐	☐	☐	☐

Risk

☐ Low ☐ Medium ☐ High ☐ Impossible

Issues

Risk

Executive action

The release stage

Let's get going!

Overview

Key deliverable

Process steps

This is the stage when the "rubber hits the road".

"What we call the beginning is often the end. And to make an end is to make a beginning"

T S ELIOT

Overview

This is the stage when "the rubber hits the road", you unleash your creation on the world and start to reap the benefits your project was set up to realize. It involves:

* releasing the validated solution into its operational environment;
* the start of all operational support;
* making sure the new "rubber sticks" and people really absorb the changes and do not just revert to the "old way" of doing things;
* the handover of the solution from the project manager to the functions and business units for ongoing operation and assurance.

In addition, work is carried out post-release to ensure the environment left by the project is "clean".

The stage finishes with a project closure review, at which the project is formally shut down, performance against the project plan assessed and the project outcome checked against what was intended. The review should also include a "lessons learned" session. What worked well on the project? What didn't? Were all the controls effective and useful? What would we use again? What would we do differently next time? Closure is discussed in more detail in Chapter 29.

Key deliverable

The **project closure report** contains the notes of the solution handover and project closure, including "lessons learned" from the project in terms of how the processes, organization, systems, and team worked (i.e. the efficiency of the project). A terms of reference for the post-implementation review is also included. A table of contents can be found on the web site.

Table 11.1 Key deliverable plan

Deliverable	Review by	Approval, prior to gate, by
Project closure report	Involved key team members and operational managers	Project sponsor

Note: These are minimum review roles and deliverables only. Each project should define its full set prior to the start of the stage.

Process steps

Release for service (RFS) gate. This gate determines whether you can start using the proposed solution in a full operational environment. If the ready for service report is authorized, the release stage is started. See checklist in Workout 10.1.

1 The project manager informs the stakeholders and key team members that approval to start the release stage has been given.
2 The project manager assembles the team and confirms the project controls, roles and accountabilities for each individual. The plan (as produced at the end of the previous stage) should be reviewed to ensure it is still valid.
3 Final release activities and preparations are carried out (e.g. major print runs, manufacturing, final training), ensuring all operations staff are ready to take over.
4 The decision on the launch date is confirmed and communicated to all who need to know. If there are any snags, then release may be put "on hold" until they are sorted out.
5 The launch/release takes place.
6 Monitor initial operations, tune and adjust as needed.
7 Any outstanding work to complete the scope of the project is carried out. This may include removing redundant data from systems, withdrawing old manuals and literature, or shutting down redundant capabilities.
8 Preparations for project closure are made.
9 Handover to day to operations is confirmed as having been completed. The project closure review is held and the project sponsor declares the project formally completed:

   • the project accounts are closed;
   • the development(s) (with specifications) handed over to the line for ongoing management;
   • the terms of reference, accountabilities, and timing for the post-implementation review are agreed (see Chapter 12);
   • lessons on the efficacy of the project approach are recorded and fed back to the relevant capability, method, or process owner(s);
   • people are reassigned, resources, and facilities are demobilized and released.

The project is now completed and is closed.

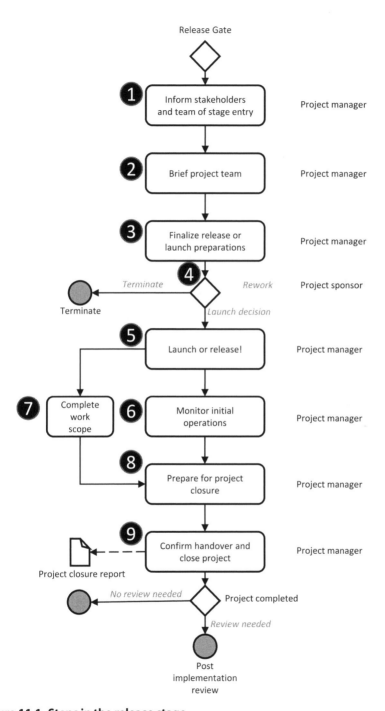

Figure 11.1 Steps in the release stage

Workout 11.1 – Checklist at project closure

Business need and strategic fit

- Has the business forecast been updated to take into account the benefits arising from the project?
- Has someone agreed to be accountable for monitoring the benefits?
- Have review points and metrics for measuring the benefits been defined?
- Has the project account been closed so no more costs can be incurred?

Risks and issues

- Have all issues been resolved?
- Has ownership of each outstanding risk and issue been accepted by a NAMED person in the line or in another project?

Post-implementation review (PIR)

- Have the timing, accountabilities, and terms of reference for the PIR been agreed?

Team/stakeholders

- Have all who need to know about the closure of the project been informed?
- Have team appraisals relating to the project been completed?
- Have those who deserve special thanks been acknowledged?

Lessons learned

- Have all lessons learned been recorded and communicated to the relevant process and documentation owners?
- Handed over risks, issues, and actions.
- Lessons learned.
- Executive action.

12

The post-implementation review

How did we do?

Overview

Key deliverable

To be effective, the review must not be used as a "witch hunt". If you use it in this way, you'll never have the truth presented to you again!

"You can do anything in this world if you are prepared to take the consequences"

W SOMERSET MAUGHAM

Overview

You should carry out a post-implementation review after sufficient time has elapsed for the benefits of the project to be assessable. The review cannot cover every aspect but it should establish whether:

- the predicted benefits were delivered;
- the most effective operational processes were designed;
- the solution really met the business needs, both for users and customers;
- the changes have been sustained and are likely to remain so; sometimes referred to as being "sticky".

As the project sponsor is the one who wants the benefits and for whom the project is undertaken, it is in his/her interest to initiate the review. This review should result in action plans for improvement, where necessary and hence help in the achievement of the benefits. For major projects, this review might be carried out by an independent "audit" function. In all cases, it is better if it is conducted by someone independent of the project team or those who are operating or benefiting from the output. To be effective, the review must not be used as a "witch hunt". If you use it in this way, you'll never have the truth presented to you again! (See also Chapter 27.)

Key deliverable

The **post-implementation review (PIR)** report assesses the success of the project against predefined success criteria given in the business case and confirmed in the terms of reference for the review. It assesses how effective the project was in meeting its objectives and includes recommendations for improvements.

Table 12.1 Key deliverable plan

Deliverable	Review by	Approved by
Post-implementation review report	Independent reviewer or internal audit	Project sponsor

Note: Minimum review and approval criteria: the terms of reference should define all those who need to be involved.

Workout 12.1 – Checklist for the post-implementation review

Business need

- Are the benefits being realized as expected?
- Are there any unexpected dis-benefits or additional costs?

Operational aspects

- Are all aspects of the solution working as envisaged?
- Are there any unwanted side effects which weren't envisaged?
- Are changes being sustained?

Actions

- Create a corrective action plan to address any shortfall in expected benefits.
- Create a corrective action plan to address any shortfall in operational aspects.
- Record all lessons learned and communicate them to the relevant stakeholders.

13

Tailoring the staged framework

Tailoring – making it work for everyone

Four types of project

Fitting into the staged framework

Small stuff, or "simple" projects

"Just do it" projects: loose cannons

Agile or rapid "projects"

Concurrent engineering

Projects which impact a lot of people

Big stuff, or projects, subprojects and work packages

The extended project life cycle

The staged approach requires that, by the time you reach the development gate, you know, with a reasonable level of confidence, what you are going to do, how you are going to do it and who is accountable for seeing it is done.

"Through the unknown remembered gate"

T S ELIOT

Tailoring – making it work for everyone

The previous chapters have taken you through a project management framework you can use for each of your projects. This framework leads the project sponsor and project manager on a journey to ensure quality and purpose are built into the project from the start and developed further as you proceed to your end-point. If your organization also has a common life cycle, then all projects undertaken in your organization can be referenced to the same, defined, and known set of stages; it makes managing a lot of projects much easier and simplifies the associated information systems. You may have wondered, as you read this book, whether this implied "one size fits all" approach is practical. Can you really direct and manage a small internal project using the same methods and life cycle as you would for a major multi-million pound endeavour? Common sense tells you this cannot be right . . . and usually common sense is right! All organizations are different, with an emphasis on different types of project but the principles and building blocks in the book are applicable to all.

In Chapter 4, you learnt how to tailor the life cycle in terms of deciding the number of stages you need and what to call them. In this chapter we will look at how we can adapt the standard project framework to suit different circumstances; we will "tailor" the approach for specific needs. I can't tell you what every circumstance is likely to be but, by looking at a range of different examples, I can help you develop the mind-set to enable you to do this for yourself.

In this chapter we will look at how we can adapt the standard project framework to suit different circumstances.

Four types of project

In his book, *All Change! The Project Leader's Secret Handbook*, Eddie Obeng describes four types of projects, each of which deals with a different kind of change. I have shown these in Figure 13.1. You should know *why* you want to do the project in the first place but, depending on circumstances, you may or may not know *what* you want or *how* to achieve it.

Painting by numbers

What are often termed as "traditional projects" tend to be of this kind. These projects have clear outputs and a clearly defined set of activities to be carried out. You know *what* you want to achieve and *how* you will achieve it.

This project is often formally called a **closed project**.

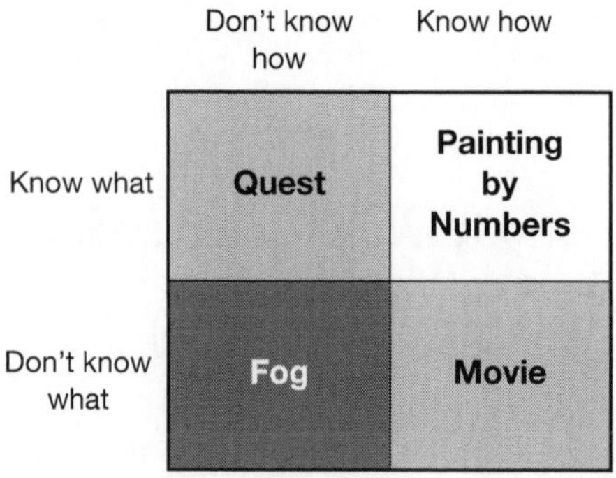

Figure 13.1 Different types of change project

If you know what you are doing and how you are going to do it, you have a "painting by numbers" project. If you know how but not what, you have a "movie". A "quest" is when you know what you want, but not how you will achieve it. Finally a "fog" is when you don't know what you want, nor how to achieve it.

Going on a quest

You are clear on *what* is to be done but clueless as to the means (*how*) to achieve it. It is named after the famous quest for the Holy Grail. The secret of this type of project is get your "knights" fired up to seek for solutions in different places at the same time and ensure that they all return to report progress and share their findings on a fixed date. You can then continue to send them out, again and again until you have sufficient knowledge of how you can achieve your objectives.

Quests are invaluable as they give "permission" for your people to explore "out of the box" possibilities. Be warned, if you don't keep very strict control over costs and timescales they are notorious for overspending, being very late, or simply delivering nothing of benefit, hence you have to bring your "knights" back regularly to see how they are getting along.

This project is formally called a **semi-closed project**.

Making movies

In this type of project, you are very sure of *how* you will do something but have no idea *what* to do. Typically, your organization has built up significant expertise and capability and you are looking for ways to apply it. There must be several people committed to the methods you will use.

This project is formally called a **semi-open project**.

Walking in the fog

This type of project is one where you have no idea *what* to do or *how* to do it. It is often prompted as a reaction to a change in circumstances (e.g. political, competitive,

Table 13.1 Project types

Project type	Type of change it helps create or man	Application
Painting by numbers	Evolutionary	Improving your continuing business operations
Going on a quest	Revolutionary	Proactively exploring outside current operations and ways of working (recipe)
Making a movie	Evolutionary	Leveraging existing capabilities
Lost in a fog	Revolutionary	Solving a problem or exploring areas outside your current operations and ways of working (recipe)

Source: Adapted from Eddie Obeng *Putting Strategy to Work* (London: Pitman Publishing, 1996).

social), although it can be set off proactively. You know you have to change and do something different; you simply can't stay still; you also may need to act quickly. This project needs, in some ways, to be managed like a quest. You need to have very tight control over costs and timescale; you need to investigate many options and possible solutions in parallel. Like a quest, these projects can end up in delivering nothing of benefit unless firmly controlled.

This project is formally called an **open project.**

Each of these project types has different characteristics and requires different leadership styles. They are also suited for different purposes (as shown in Table 13.1 above).

Fitting into the staged framework

The staged framework requires that, by the time you reach the development gate, you know, with a reasonable level of confidence, *what* you are going to do and *how* you are going to do it. That is to say, at the development gate you will have a painting by numbers project (see Figure 13.2). The investigative stages are there to give you the time, resources, and money to discover an appropriate solution to your problem and finalize your plan. The proposal should have stated *why* you need the project, however, your level of background knowledge will differ for each proposal you want to address. This will have a considerable impact on the way you undertake the investigative stages and the level of risk associated with the project at the start. Painting by numbers projects tend to be less risky than the other types, but not always. Figure 13.3 shows this in a different way: a "normal" project (if there is such a thing!) can change from being a quest, movie, or fog to painting by numbers as it moves through the project life cycle. The clarity of your scope, timescale, costs, and benefits will improve as you gain more knowledge. In addition, as we earlier learned (Figure 4.2), the level of risk should decrease as you progress through the project.

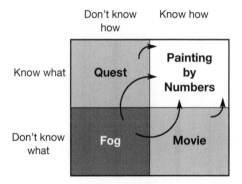

Figure 13.2 Creating a project you can implement

The staged framework requires, by the time you reach the development gate, that you know what you are going to do and how. That is to say, at the development gate, you will have a painting by numbers project. You may, however, start off as any of the project types – the investigative stages are the means by which you define your solution.

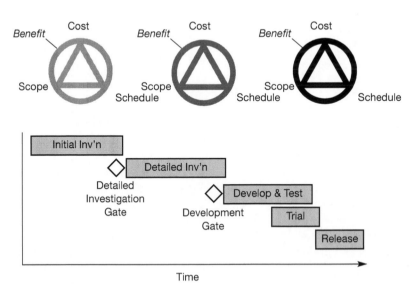

Figure 13.3 Getting to paint by numbers

A "normal" project can change from being a "quest", "movie," or "fog" to "painting by numbers" as it moves through the project life cycle. The clarity of your scope, timescale, costs, and benefits will improve as you gain more knowledge.

Just to make your day, there are circumstances when you would allow a project to continue past the development gate as a fog, movie, or quest. For example, when the risks of not proceeding outweigh the risks of proceeding. The level of risk would be higher than under normal circumstances but that is your choice. The "game" of projects has principles but few rules. Directors have to direct and managers have to manage; that is your role. If an action makes common sense, do it and do it openly, keeping the risk firmly in mind.

Rules and exceptions

Some companies tie themselves up in process-driven rules bound neatly in files with quality assurance and control labels. These rules often go to great levels of detail covering every conceivable scenario.

I would argue that this is a fruitless exercise. It is better to have a few basic principles and make sure your people understand why you need them and how they help them do their jobs. You can then handle the odd "exception" using "exception management," dealing with it on its own merits within the principles you have laid out. In other words, give the managers and supervisors the freedom to do their jobs and exercise the very skills you are paying them for.

If you write rules at a micro-level:

- you might get them wrong;
- they might be used in way you never conceived and contrary to what you wanted;
- you will spend a long time writing them thus diverting your attention from the real issues;
- people will look for "legitimate" ways round them, playing with words in a legalistic game;
- you will cause people to break them (perhaps through ignorance) and then risk making them feel bad about it;
- you risk employing an army of policemen to check that the rules are being adhered to.

Remember, you are trying to run a project, not create a penal code.

Small stuff, or "simple" projects

"I now understand gates and stages," you may say, "but isn't it all a bit too much for smaller, simple projects?" Let us take the example of what I would term a "simple" project differs from the type of project normally associated with staged approaches and how you can deal with them using the same management framework.

A normal project may start off as painting by numbers, a fog, a quest, or a movie. The investigative stages are worked through until you are confident (say, around 85 to 95 per cent) the required benefits can be achieved. At the detailed investigation gate you will have narrowed your options down and have approval and funding to complete the detailed investigation stage. At the development gate you would have approval to complete the project as a whole – it has become a painting by numbers project.

With a simple project, you may know a great deal about it before you even start. By the time you finish the initial investigation stage you might have fully defined the project outputs and your plan; your confidence level will be as high as it is normally for a more complex project at the development gate (Figure 13.4), so undertaking the detailed investigation stage is either trivial or unnecessary.

Full authorization to complete the project can therefore be given at the detailed investigation gate (see Figure 13.5). This doesn't mean you can bypass the remaining gates, you still need to have reviews and checks to ensure ongoing viability. If you omit the detailed investigation stage you must meet the full criteria of the development gate before you start the develop and test stage.

In this way, you have used the principles of the framework, checking at every gate but you have avoided doing any unnecessary work. Making the key control documents, initial business case and business case have identical content enables this to happen without the need to duplicate any documentation.

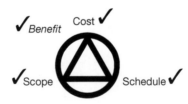

Figure 13.4 Simple project

A simple project can be defined very rigorously by the end of the initial investigation stage.

"Just do it" projects: loose cannons

There are cases when senior management will issue an edict to finish a project by a certain time, whatever the cost. In certain circumstances, this is a valid thing to do, especially when the survival of the organization requires it. Such projects must be treated with extreme caution as often they come about as an executive's "pet project" and may have little proven foundation in business strategy. I have found that there are very few

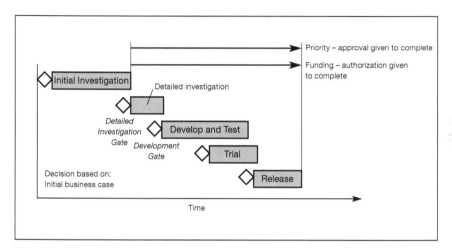

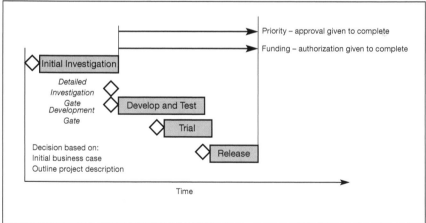

Figure 13.5 The stages for a simple project

The top diagram represents a project where some detailed investigation work still needs to be done. Nevertheless, the level of confidence is high enough to authorize and fund the project to completion.

The lower diagram represents an even simpler case where no further investigative work needs to be done. The project is checked against the criteria for the development gate and, if acceptable, moves straight into the develop and test stage.

instances in companies where something needs to be done regardless of the costs and consequences. These projects invariably start off being optimistic and end up bouncing around the organization demanding more and more resources are assigned to it without delay. Consequently, there can be considerable impact on day-to-day operations as well as significant delays to other projects. Remember, delayed projects lead to delayed benefits. They also tend to be very stressful for those associated with them. The damage left in the wake of such projects can be awesome even if they appear to succeed!

Most organizations can cope with one of these kinds of projects – occasionally. Most organizations cope better if there aren't any. If you believe one is necessary, it should still be aligned into the project framework as closely as possible and managed as an "exception". Before starting, consider:

- Why am I doing this?
- Is it really far more important than everything else?
- Am I really sure what I am doing?

There must be very compelling reasons to allow a loose cannon project to start. Responding to a problem by panicking is not usually a good enough reason! Using the issue breakthrough technique is a better starting point (see Workout 24.1).

You must be absolutely clear what other activities and projects it can be allowed to disrupt. You can create more problems, for yourself and for others, than you will solve. You must consider the real "cost/benefit" and take into consideration the inefficiencies and lost or delayed benefits from the disrupted projects. After all that, if you really must do it then:

1 undertake an initial investigation first so you can make an informed decision;
2 keep the project as short as possible (say, three months maximum). If you need longer, chunk the project up into smaller pieces.

- **No matter what project you want to undertake, always carry out an initial investigation to help you decide, on an informed basis, the most appropriate way to take the project forward (e.g. normal, simple, or other approach);**
- **Having decided your approach, record it in your initial business case.**

Agile or rapid "projects"

Harnessing agile concepts

Let's now consider the concept of "agile", or what used to be commonly called "rapid" projects. Agile delivery techniques involve iterative requirements definition, design and delivery, using either a prototype platform or the actual operational platform, where work is undertaken within a fixed budget and timescale, but where the scope is varied to suit (see Figure 13.6). If a team runs out of time or money, the scope is reduced in order to meet the time/cost targets. Provided a predefined, minimum scope is delivered, the work should remain within its area of benefit viability. In many ways, it is like a "simple" project, except the scope is variable within known limits. You are, therefore, able to assign resources to it with confidence, knowing when they will become available for other projects. In this respect, agile approaches are a way to deal with "Quest" projects, with the sprints representing the periods of time the knights are out hunting for the Holy Grail. They also apply to "Foggy" projects, where the knights are simply looking something, but they are not sure what it is until they find it.

Agile project management?

Be very careful about how you relate "agile delivery" to "project management". Often people talk about traditional project management being "waterfall" and advocating agile project management instead. If you are a software developer, this perception can make sense; software developers tend to equate what they term as traditional project management with "big design up front" and "waterfall" methods for developing the code, moving sequentially from requirements definition, system architecture, software design, build, testing and deployment. Software developers are, however, only concerned with building code and often see this work as "their project". Their view is other activities, such as building and deploying the hardware, developing processes and training, rolling out the new tools to users and ensuring their use are somebody else's problem, outside "their project". If the software developers are from a supplier or contractor, then the coding may indeed be the limit of the scope for "their project"; they develop code for a fee, which represents the benefits they gain.

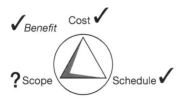

Figure 13.6 "Agile" project

A project using agile techniques has fixed timescale, cost, and minimum benefits. Scope varies to suit these constraints.

In an organization, with its own development resources, such a limited view can be damaging to the business and you should start worrying if you hear people talk about the "IT project" and the "business project" as separate. In this book, I advocate all projects should be business-driven and the scope of a project should include everything needed to change a business and start realizing the benefits. From this viewpoint, developing code is simply an essential package of work which, combined with the rest of the work, forms a complete, business-led project. Agile is a delivery or development approach used for the software outputs and its activities can take place in any of *The Project Workout's* life cycle stages. The other outputs, such as training, would be developed using whatever processes or methods are appropriate. Do not try to map agile steps to project stages; agile steps can happen within any project stage so there is no definitive mapping, just as any other specialist work may not have unique mapping. For example, staying with the IT enabled projects, usually, user training cannot be designed until after the code has been tested and training design activities, follow after software test activities; "design activities" do not all happen at the same time, nor within the same project stage.

- Don't think in terms of "agile project management", but rather "agile delivery";
- Consider "agile techniques" as applying to work packages, not to whole projects;
- Don't try to map agile steps into specific project life cycle stages; put your agile managed work packages in whatever life cycle stage makes sense, bearing in mind risk and dependencies on other work.

The CIO of a global company was trying to improve the productivity of his developers, who had to work on a number of separate service platforms. After careful thought, he decided agile was the answer to all his concerns and set about creating an environment in which agile would thrive. This included redesigning office spaces, furniture and equipment for the agile teams, developing a reference web site with guidance on good practice, behavioural training and setting up a network of coaches to help each team adopt and use the methods correctly. It was all well thought through, properly funded and done correctly. Unfortunately:

- as part of the communication he asserted, "From now on, traditional project management is dead and all projects will now be run using agile." The construction and infrastructure project teams were bemused and joked: "It's all very well for the IT mob, but you can't design and build a building infrastructure iteratively; once the foundations are in, you are stuck with them";
- customers wanted to get what they had contracted to get and did not like the idea of signing a contract for a fixed sum with scope being flexible.

Thus, a great intention failed to get the traction needed to succeed. In the first instance, the CIO only considered the type of work which was his immediate concern, in his silo of the business, namely software. In the second instance, he failed to consider the wider stakeholders who were essential to success. This included both internal and "real" customers, who also had to play an active and continuous role in agile delivery as the "agile customer".

- If he had framed his initiative as agile delivery, the first problem would not have happened.
- If he had taken a "whole project" perspective and defined who would undertake each role agile delivery required, he could have ensured buy-in from the internal "customer".

Whether he could have addressed the external customer is a moot point; contracts relying on agile do exist but rely on trust; not many contract lawyers will bet their jobs solely on that.

The lessons taught us that there is no "fast track". If there were, it would become the usual approach (see lesson 2 in Chapter 2). "Agile" or "Rapid" are development methods

The lessons taught us that there is no "fast track". If there were, it would become the usual approach.

or techniques to enable you to develop your deliverables faster *within* the overall project framework. A correctly designed and applied staged framework should not slow any projects down, unless they need to be.

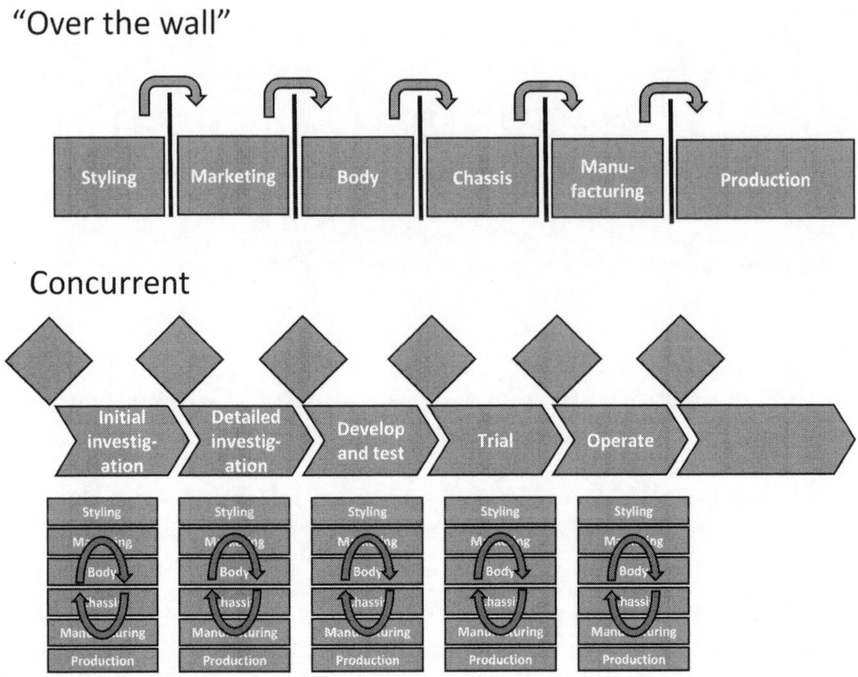

"Over the wall"

Concurrent

Figure 13.7 Concurrent engineering

The top diagram shows the "over the wall" approach, in which each department works on its own aspects in isolation. When they are finished, the work passes on to the next department. The lower diagram shows a concurrent engineering approach, in which the various departments work on all aspects of the product together. This can easily be mapped to the project framework.

Agile techniques should be used when they suit the particular circumstances. If you use them merely because you are "in a hurry," you risk reducing your project to chaos, i.e. it will become "rabid" rather than rapid!

Concurrent engineering

Concurrent engineering, also known as simultaneous engineering, is a method of designing and developing products in which the different development steps run simultaneously rather than consecutively (see Figure 13.7 above). It decreases product development time and hence the time to market, leading to improved productivity and reduced costs. The approach was developed in the late 1980s with the aim of improving the prevailing "over-the-wall" approach in which the various departments work, in isolation, on their part of the development before handing off to the next department to work on. The over-the-wall method resulted in a large number of unresolved issues being built up as time progressed making the final period before launching the product very lengthy, expensive, and fraught. By contrast, in concurrent engineering the number of issues reduces as time progresses as all interested parties are able to work together to resolve them as the project progresses.

The concurrent engineering approach is wholly compatible with the project management approach in *The Project Workout*, which also advocates cross-team working and progressing, in stages, to a final solution. Concurrent engineering is also compatible with "system engineering" approaches, which also advocate a multi-disciplinary approach. The only differences are likely to be in the terminology used.

A common mistake many people make when considering how to align engineering approaches and project management is to confuse project life cycles and engineering processes. In the beginning there were sequential development processes, which we now know as waterfall or "over the wall". When project management was applied, the names of each process activity became the names of the project stages. It was a simple and obvious one-to-one mapping; for example, the "design" process activity became the "Design Stage"; the test activity became the "Test Stage". When, however, concurrency emerged and processes became iterative, as in agile, concurrent engineering and system engineering, people stuck to the familiar life cycle stages and invented a plethora of spiral, circular, and curvy diagrams to show the iteration and concurrent working. Unfortunately, projects are driven by the immutable laws of physics and "time" and so we cannot go back in time and rework yesterday what we did wrong yesterday; we need to rework today, what we did wrong yesterday. Processes, however, are logical and iterative and not bound by time, but happen in time. In other words, processes can be cycled through as many times as you need during any period of time, such as in a project stage.

If you make this distinction between process and stage, you'll find the project to process relationship easier to understand. There are, however, a number of definitions in the public domain which use "process" and "stage" interchangeably thus adding to the confusion. During my international work I even came across project life cycles which were deemed to be "logical" and not time bound . . . in other works, what was being talked about was a process and not a project life cycle which could be mapped to a Gantt chart.

Projects which impact a lot of people – the two stage trial

People are central to everything we do and the more you try to change an organization, the more people you need to engage as stakeholders, and move them towards behaving in a way you would like them to. Let's keep this grounded and consider a major change in a hypothetical company, such as putting in place a new procurement system. The business objective is to reduce the costs of procurement by reducing the number of procurement managers and enabling business managers to initiate and manage this for themselves. Naturally, such a complex initiative requires thorough investigation and, even then, it may be uncertain as to how it will work in practice with the full range of scenarios it has to cater for. There is a trial stage in the project life cycle to cover this risk. Whilst testing will verify the system has been built and configured as per the design, the trial will validate that it was the right design in the first place. Trials of this type are often undertaken using a selected group of users who are monitored by the developers to see how they use the system. The intention is to make sure the system's functionality covers the full extent of the goods and services needed, both in terms of selecting suppliers and gaining approval for the spend. The system can then be re-tuned depending on the findings of the trial. Unfortunately, even this won't guarantee the system will meet the needs of the whole organization. Users selected for trials often have a degree of knowledge and aptitude greater than that of the overall user base. Even if this is not the case, as the trial is monitored, the users have a higher level of access to help than is normally the case, often being personally coached in using the system. Users are often more aware of what they are doing/expected to do, as they are briefed and are being watched. Finally, as the trial only covers a small proportion of users, the response time shouldn't be a problem. Such a trial is usually adequate for making sure the system has the required features, but not necessarily that it can be used by everyone who needs to, or that it is usable in terms of performance. For this reason, where risks are considered high enough, it may be better to have two parts to the trial or even two trial stages:

- the first looks at whether the system has the right features for the job;
- the second looks at whether the use of the system is scalable, bearing in mind the range of users with different abilities and needs, as well as the impact on system performance of a large user base.

There are other approaches you can take to reduce risks, for example, building the system using agile methods, releasing it for specific types of procurement and then, in each release, adding more features. You would, however, still need to consider the form of your trials, depending on the extent of user involvement in the development. Agile delivery merely delivers working code to an operational environment, which may be for a trial or full-scale operations. For this reason, you need to design your overall project life cycle to ensure it helps you manage the risks associated with the project and is compatible with the delivering methods used within the project.

Moving the costs around

Have you noticed the trend for management "self-service", where the corporate functions, like HR and finance load more work on the general managers, justifying it with reductions of costs in their own departments? How often do you think they consider the cumulative impact on the managers of having to do more and more for themselves? Do they actually check the managers have the time? Do they ensure the managers have the right skills and experience to do the job themselves? If they don't consider these aspects then, despite their being able to show a reduction in their headcount and budget, the company as whole may actually perform worse. They have simply moved a visible overhead cost into the front line where it becomes invisible. By taking a holistic, benefits-led, project managed approach, such issues can be exposed and explored, resulting in a solution that is best for the whole organization, not just one department.

Big stuff, or projects, subprojects and work packages

Defining the scope and boundaries of a project is often problematic. The term "project," like its cousin "programme," is often used so loosely that it has very little meaning. Research at the University of Oxford in 2015 found that the two terms are used by senior managers interchangeably. Bearing in mind that organizations have run for decades with no concept of "programmes" as we now define them, the loose use of the terms is not surprising. We just need to be aware that what one person calls a project, another might call a programme.

Nine times out of ten it doesn't matter what you call things as long as you are consistent but, if you are to understand business projects fully, you need to be able to see the distinction. It might be that the configuration of your support systems will determine the terminology you use.

If you are to have clarity of communication regarding your project, you must decide on the definitions which suit you best and stick to them.

A **project**, in a business environment, is:

- a finite piece of work (it has a beginning and an end) undertaken in stages;
- within defined cost and time constraints;
- *directed at achieving a stated business benefit.*

In other words, the key elements of benefit, scope, time and cost are all present. The only place where all this is recorded is in the business case, which serves as the key document for approving and authorizing the project in initial form at the detailed investigation gate and in full at the development gate. As a working assumption, therefore, we can say a project is only a project if it has a business case. Business cases are attached to business projects!

It, therefore, follows that . . . any piece of work, which is finite, time and cost constrained but does not realize business benefit, is not in fact a business project. It may be managed using project techniques, or it may be a subproject or work package within a project. On its own, however, it has no direct value. Only when combined with other elements of work does it have any value. For this reason, you need to consider carefully how to handle what are often called "enabling projects". Enabling projects are undertaken to create a capability or platform which a later project will use as part of the solution. Enabling projects do not create any value on their own and cannot have a business case, merely a cost. For this reason, enabling projects cannot be "stand-alone" but must be considered as part of a wider business project. They can be treated as work packages or as a subproject.

Any piece of work, which is finite, time and cost constrained but does not deliver business benefit, is not a business project. It may be managed using project techniques or it may be a subproject or work package within a project.

In any project, the project manager delegates accountability for parts of the work to members of the core team. This is done by breaking up the project into work packages, usually centred on deliverables. Each work package has a person accountable for it. This work package can be decomposed again and again, down to activity or task level. This structure is called a "work breakdown structure" (WBS) and is a fundamental control tool for a project.

The first level of the breakdown structure is the project itself. The second level comprises the life cycle stages (initial investigation, detailed investigation, etc.). Below this are the more detailed work packages which, in turn, comprise more work packages and, ultimately, activities.

The top diagram in Figure 13.8 shows this: the development and test stage comprises three work packages (XX, YY and ZZ). Of these, package YY is divided into three more packages (Y1, Y2 and Y3). The whole structure of the project flows logically from project to stage to work package and ultimately to activity. Each work package has its own defined time, cost, scope, and person accountable. It will *not* have its own discrete benefit. This is the way to structure your projects. It provides good control as no part of the project can proceed into the next stage without all preconditions being met.

The bottom diagram in Figure 13.8 shows an alternative structure for exactly the same project. In this case, however, the project manager has chosen to treat work YY as a subproject. In other words, it has a single identifiable work package, which is itself divided into stages and then into the lower-level work packages (Y1, Y2 and Y3).

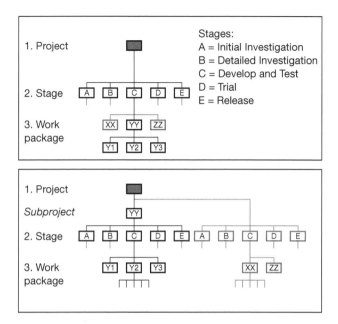

Figure 13.8 Explaining work packages and subprojects

The top diagram shows a project divided into the five stages of the project framework. Each stage can then be divided into a number of work packages (e.g. C is divided into XX, YY and ZZ). In the bottom diagram the same project has been restructured to have YY managed as a subproject.

The remainder of the project is dealt with in the preferred way. It is a more complex structure for the same work scope and so there are risks in using it:

- you might have a timing misalignment between subproject YY and the rest of the project as there are two separate life cycles and gating might not be aligned;
- interdependencies between the subprojects and project might be missed as it might be assumed "the other end" is dealing with it.

These risks require a greater level of coordination by the project manager.

From this we are able to define subprojects more exactly:

Subprojects are tightly coupled and tightly aligned parts of a project which are undertaken in stages.

The conditions under which you would choose to set up subprojects depend on the degree of delegation you want to effect – it is akin to subcontracting the work. You find this type of structure happens as a result of systems and process limitations or reporting requirements. It may be more convenient to represent and report a completely delegated piece of work as a subproject as it may relate to work which has been let externally, under a contract or internal agreement. Many companies treat their internal software development in this way, hence the common use of the terms "business project" and "IT project". Such companies generally have no enterprise-wide project accounting capability and hence give the development budget to the IT department at the start of the year, which it then spends on IT projects until the money runs out, whilst the other departments involved have to absorb their costs into their day-to-day budgets. Such an approach is not "wrong" but it can be managed better. When projects become fragmented across an organization in this way, they can become unmanageable and the reasons for doing them can be lost. I have even seen organizations where each department writes their own business case for their part of the project and that part of the project goes through a departmental form of gating. No wonder so much corporate money and time is wasted on projects which are never completed. If you are a project sponsor or manager of a project in such circumstances, my advice is to try and get it managed as one business project, with one life cycle and one business case, but, if not, then make sure your project structure, accountabilities and interdependencies are clear, cover the whole scope and justify it in a single business case. It will be slightly more work, but sometimes it is necessary to flex your approach to fit the host organization, its culture and level of maturity.

The extended project life cycle

Many projects are undertaken not only to create products, services or capabilities, but also to operate the outcomes of the project. For example, a contractor may not only build a road, but also maintain it throughout its useful life. In such situations, the classic project life cycle, described in Chapter 4, is extended to cover the full operation of the service (sometimes this is referred to as a product life cycle as shown in Figure 13.9), as opposed just an initial operational period. Here, the stages of the project may cover:

- the **investigative and development stages**: a new capability is developed using a project as the delivery vehicle, taking into account the "whole life" needs of the organization, with respect to the use of the outputs, cost of creation and cost of operation. The last stage of the project (release stage) should overlap the early operation of the new capability in order to facilitate knowledge transfer and to be able to react to any operational issues uncovered. In a contracting situation, this is often defined in the contract (for example in construction's "Maintenance Period");
- the **operational stages**: the capability is used and minor upgrades are done as work packages;
- **upgrade stages**: more significant upgrades are undertaken to extend the product life, often using a project as the delivery vehicle;
- **retirement or withdrawal stages**: the capability is withdrawn, retired or de-commissioned when it is no longer needed. This is often complex and also requires a project approach.

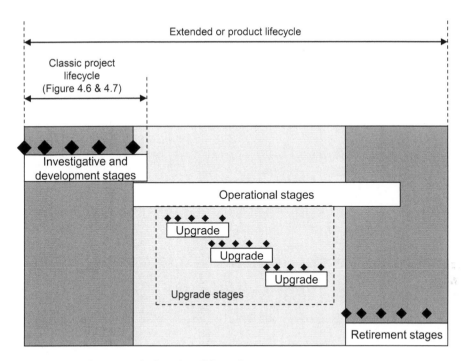

Figure 13.9 The extended project life cycle

The project framework in Chapter 4 can be extended to include the operation of the outputs, but such situations are usually better treated as a programme if the revisions are too complex to be managed as work packages.

The "extended" or "product life cycle" is being seen more frequently, particularly in government work. Except in the simplest cases, it is taking the project concept too far to treat all the above as a "single project". It is better to treat such situations as a programme and provide a greater degree of flexibility in how they are directed, managed, and structured. This is looked at in more detail in *The Programme and Portfolio Workout*.

14

A few related projects

Simple programmes

Simple programmes

Sharing project deliverables: interdependencies

Phased programmes

Simple programme organizations

Some projects are simply too large to manage as a single entity.

"Adventure is just bad planning"

ROALD AMUNDSEN, 1872–1928

Simple programmes

We have seen how the staged project framework can be applied to any type of project, for any purpose. It is a tool you can adopt and adapt to suit your needs. Nevertheless, a simple string of activities, passing through five defined stages, may not give you the full flexibility you require. We saw in Figure 13.8 how to manage the subparts of a project using the work breakdown structure. This is how the project manager delegates work to the managers within the core team.

Some projects, however, are simply too large to manage as a single entity. It is often more convenient and effective to define the work in a series of closely related and linked projects, each of which is managed by a project manager, reporting to a programme manager (Figure 14.1). The role of the programme manager in this respect, is identical to that of a project manager (as described in Chapter 5), except that detailed management of parts of the project would be delegated, as is the associated administration. He or she will have a core team of project managers, rather than team managers. Such a programme would have a single business case as the projects are inextricably linked and add no value on their own.

Sharing project deliverables: interdependencies

A project comprises all the work required to ensure you put the changes in place to enable the benefits to be realized. On occasions, however, the deliverable you require may be produced by another project's team, often within the same programme, but

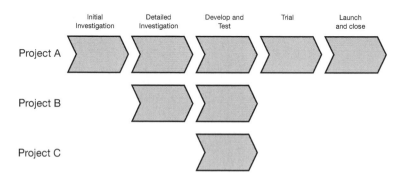

Figure 14.1 A simple programme

A simple programme where each constituent project is used to manage a substantial work scope.

not necessarily so. In this scenario, your project is said to be *dependent* on the other project. Such interdependencies should be noted explicitly in the business case in the "scope, impacts, and interdependencies" section (see also Chapter 17), stating:

- the deliverable;
- the project and work package which creates the deliverable;
- the project and work package which needs to use the deliverable.

Sharing of work between projects in this way:

- adds to the efficient use of resources on your projects;
- ensures consistency between developments;
- reduces costs of projects for your business.

In all, it sounds like a "good thing". With most companies relying heavily on platform-based information systems to enable them to run the business, software development, whether in-house or out sourced, is frequently required as part of business change and is "shared" between projects. From the point of view of the systems developer, it is preferable to batch requirements from new projects and deliver them as a new software release. It makes life easier for the development team, configuration management, implementation, and training. In many cases, this is sound practice but bundling requirements into a single release needs to be considered more widely. If you take this approach, a number of projects, serving different needs and under different programmes, may be bundled together. If this one software delivery is delayed by a single problematic part of the development, relating to one project only, the whole bundle slips. In other words, the full set of interdependent projects is tied to the one with the greatest risk. In fact, the slippage may be caused by the features required by the lowest priority project in the bundle. It is hardly surprising that software delivery is invariably "blamed" for making projects late. (While I have made an example of software, the same principle applies to any type of deliverable which is shared between projects.)

If this one software delivery is delayed by a single problematic part of the development, relating to one project only, the whole bundle slips. In other words, the full set of interdependent projects is tied to the one with the greatest risk.

From a risk-management viewpoint, it is often preferable to separate out the discrete high-priority developments and carry them out in separate releases. Don't build in risk from the start by bundling things together that need not be bundled. The loss of efficiency may be paid many times over by the benefits flowing from having projects delivered on time.

The interdependency needs to be able to be traced both ways. The manager of the creating project must know who needs a particular deliverable and when, while the manager of the receiving project must know who is creating the deliverable and when it is likely to be delivered.

Interdependencies represent a risk and must be explicitly shown in any plans and managed carefully if the project is not to be derailed. We will look at interdependencies again in Chapter 20.

Don't build in risk from the start by bundling things together that need not be bundled.

Phased programmes

Whilst some projects are complex in terms of scope, other projects are so extended in time it is beneficial to phase the development and delivery of the solutions. This ensures the organization starts benefiting as early as possible and also increases the likelihood of success (Figure 14.2). It also gives the organization a "get-out" if the need the programme was set up to fill either evaporates or the chosen solution is not meeting it. The start-point for each new phase acts as just such a review point. This type of programme should have an over-arching business case to prove the viability of the complete set of projects. Further, as each project in the programme leads to a "release", and hence a new stream of incremental benefits, each project could have its own business case to check the viability of that particular stream of work. Notice that the projects in Figure 14.2 don't all have five stages, as the preceding project may have already done the ground work normally covered in an initial investigation.

The permutations beyond this are endless. For example, you may have a phased programme where each phase is itself a programme such as that described in Figure 14.1. There are no rules, you just have to make it very clear what you are doing and who is accountable. The staged framework is very useful in this respect as it provides an overview of a programme in terms of known stages such that any person in the organization can understand it.

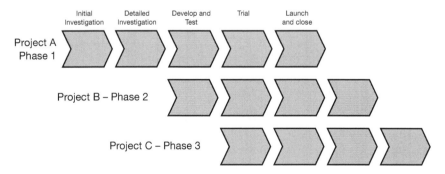

Figure 14.2 A phased programme

A phased programme comprising a number (in this case three) of phased outputs, each managed as a project, with its own life cycle.

Simple programme organizations

Organization structures for simple programmes are many and varied. In principle, however, they are very similar to those described in Chapter 5 for a project. The key difference is that instead of the structure comprising a project manager supported by team managers and members, it comprises a programme manager supported by project managers, all of whom have their own teams. An example is shown in Figure 14.3. The accountabilities of a programme manager in other respects are the same as those of a project manager. The scale of most programmes is such that the experience and skill set required to carry out the accountabilities are quite different. Note, in this structure, the programme manager might take on the "project sponsor" role for each project within the programme. It is, however, perfectly acceptable for the sponsorship role to be undertaken directly by the programme sponsor or another person appointed by him/her.

The Programme and Portfolio Workout picks up the themes in this chapter and develops the concept of programme management as a distinct discipline from project management. The boundary between project management and programme management is not always clear cut and unless you are trying to pass a particular exam on the topics, no defined boundary is necessary. What matters is that the work

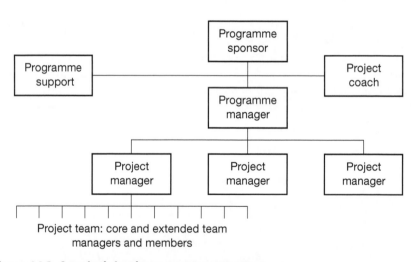

Figure 14.3 A typical simple programme structure

A programme structure comprises a programme manager supported by project managers. In addition, there is often a programme support group to undertake the essential coordination, administration and to implement common standards. The project sponsor role for each project may be undertaken by the programme manager or assigned by the programme sponsor to others.

is defined, has a viable business case and the team has the management capability and skills to undertake the work. It is a matter of applying the right tools and techniques in a given situation.

Programmes

As discussed in Chapter 4, words such as "programme" can be used in many different ways. Although, through standards organizations and methodology writers, there is a gradual consensus emerging, in my view it will take a long time for any common definitions to be fully accepted, if at all. Three different uses of the term "programme" are given below to show the range of possible interpretations:

- **Portfolio**: a set of related projects and other work aimed at meeting fulfilling a business plan (or part of). These are dealt with in *The Programme and Portfolio Workout*.
- **Goal directed**: a set of closely related projects aimed at creating a new capability (as described in this chapter). This is typically outside the usual routine of the organization. They are a way of effecting one-off, major change. In this book, I simply call them "programmes".
- **Heartbeat**: a set of activities managed around platform based service delivery e.g. regular releases for a large IT system or from agile developments. This is a very "functional" view and not really much to do with business-led project management, although its work content may represent work packages or interdependencies.

These are shown below:

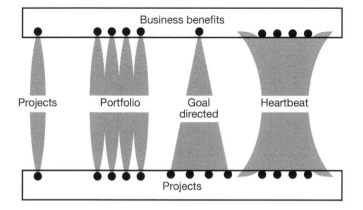

Table 14.1 Portfolio, goal directed, and heartbeat

	Portfolio	Goal directed	Heartbeat
Programme's control of projects	Coordinate to extract synergy benefits	Definition and direction of all projects within the programme	Integration of identified changes into a cohesive programme
Planning organization	Programme overlays project roles: project and project manager retain strong relationship	Programme acts as sponsor client for all projects	Programme arbitrates between multiple client needs
Planning horizon	Indeterminate: as long as it adds value	Until the goal is achieved	Until the "system" is withdrawn
Programme relationship with the line	Draws on line resources and complements line management with business leadership	Draws resources from line management	Takes on traditional line management role of functions (e.g. operational performance)

Source: Pellegrinelli, S. (1997) "Programme management: organising project-based change", International Journal of Project Management.

Workout 14.1 – Questioning your programmes

1 Choose any programme in your organization and identify the component projects.

2 Split each project into the five project stages, one stage per Post-It Note, using a different colour for each project.

3 Prepare a large sheet of paper or a white board, indicating a timescale on the horizontal axis sufficient to include the entire programme timescale. Draw a vertical "time now" line.

4 Place each project onto the board, with each stage aligned to the appropriate date. Can you actually do this? If not, question how you really know what is going on and how you can direct the programme with any degree of confidence or knowledge.

5 Identify any interdependencies and mark them with an arrow from the delivering project to the receiving project. Check for multiple two-way dependencies – this could indicate poor project scoping. Remember, interdependencies are potential weak points which can be forgotten or where accountability is abdicated. Good programme definition minimizes dependencies!

6 Look for any very long stages – can you shorten these? Be very wary of any prolonged investigative stages.

7 Look for when outcomes become apparent and when benefits start to flow – can you redesign the programme to achieve any benefits earlier than this?

8 Look at where your key review and decision points are (they should map onto your gates) – have you sufficient of these to ensure control? Be very wary if it has all been authorized in one lump.

PART III
THE ESSENTIALS YOU NEED TO KNOW

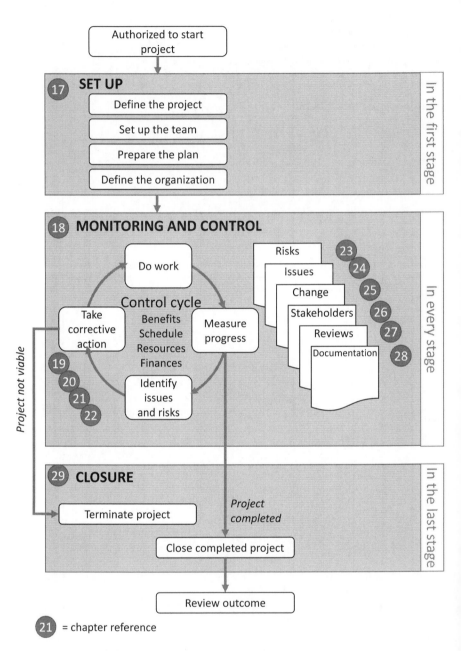

Figure 15.1 The full project control environment

The project control environment can be represented in three sections, starting with "set up" and ending in "closure". Between these are the tools and techniques for monitoring and controlling every stage of the project.

"People love chopping wood. In this activity one immediately sees results."

ALBERT EINSTEIN

In Part II, I explained the management framework for a single project, taking it from an idea, through the various life cycle stages until benefits are realized for your organization.

In this part, I will explain the approaches, tools and techniques you can apply to ensure your project is kept under control and likely to realize the promised benefits. Figure 15.1 shows the full project control environment, starting with "set up" and ending in "closure". Between these are the techniques for monitoring progress and handling risks, issues, opportunities, and reviews. At the heart is the project control cycle. These factors apply throughout the life of the project, regardless of which stage you are currently working within.

The project control environment can be represented in three sections, starting with "set up" and ending in "closure". Between these are the tools and techniques for monitoring and controlling every stage of the project.

Principles

- Encourage team work and commitment.
- Practise single-point accountability.
- Break down functional barriers by using a cross-functional team.
- Manage your stakeholders' expectations.
- Build excellence in project management techniques and controls across your organization.
- Ensure success by planning for it.
- Monitor and control against the agreed plan.
- Manage changes to the plan actively.
- Close the project formally.

How to use Part III

The sections in Part III are written as working guides either to apply directly or to adapt to include in your own control framework. Many of the chapters include workouts to help you apply the guides in practice.

15

Project teams and style

Culture: the way we do things around here

Project teams

Leadership and influence

I thought you were doing that!: accountability

RACI tables

An environment in which energy is expended on blame and fault finding, rather than looking for solutions to problems, will damage morale and hinder the performance of any team.

"I must follow them. I am their leader!"

ANDREW BONAR LAW

- **Encourage team work and commitment.**
- **Practise single-point accountability.**
- **Break down functional barriers by using a cross-functional team.**

Culture: the way we do things around here

Culture has two fundamental elements:

- the norms and behaviours of a group;
- unconscious programming of the mind, leading to a set of similar collective habits, behaviours, and mind-sets.

While this book is not primarily aimed at culture, interpersonal skills and the often named "soft" aspects of project management, it would be negligent not to include key aspects of behaviour and culture which have been shown to encourage success in a projects environment.

As Obeng has pointed out, "People create change and people constrain change", and culture is what people are about. Let us remind ourselves of the fundamental differences between working in a project, as opposed to a line environment.

Line management is about maintaining the existing processes and business operations. It is performed in a relatively stable environment. It often abhors change which often affects the ever increasing drive for efficiency. People work in defined jobs, in a fixed hierarchy with prescribed work to carry out. It is often (but not always!) predictable.

Project management is about change. Projects are one-off initiatives, carried out over a finite time period. They often break new ground and step into the unknown. Thus, projects require management that can adapt to conflicting pressures, changing requirements, and unfamiliar situations. Projects are often staffed by groups of people from disparate functions and locations.

The managers involved do not necessarily share the same skills and competences. Nevertheless, an organizational environment must be set up such that the two aspects of management (steady state and change) can coexist.

Project teams

In line management, the manager or the supervisor has the power and authority to instruct a person in his/her duties. In many organizations, however, the project managers have little authority of this nature, although ideally they should. Often, they have to deliver the project's outputs and outcomes using a less visible power base, more rooted in the shared commitment of the team than in directives. No matter how good a project proposal is, or how thoroughly the investigative stages have been undertaken, the bottom line is that success is rarely achieved by a poorly led, ill-motivated group of individuals. (Notice, I have not used the word "team".) It is widely recognized that team work and team spirit in line roles leads to better results than sticks and sanctions. In projects, team working is even more crucial. A project team has a short time to form, normalize its behaviours and start performing. In addition:

- a team might be dispersed geographically;
- its members might have other duties to attend to;
- the most appropriate people might not be available.

This can place demands on individuals, particularly those new to projects as it can set the stage for conflicts of loyalties which the project manager and others must recognize and try to avoid. The project manager must be the leading player in creating and fostering a team spirit and enrolling the commitment of those associated with the project. The project sponsor and line managers of the project team members have a similar responsibility. Their behaviour can derail a project just as drastically, or even more so, than any action of the project manager. Clear reporting lines, good information flow, realistic work plans, and defined project roles will also help "ease" the pathway.

Leadership style and team values are also important. An open, even-handed approach encouraging good communication and giving individuals the confidence to raise potential problems, tends to be the most effective. An environment where energy is expended on blame and fault finding, rather than looking for solutions to problems, will damage morale and hinder the performance

Success is rarely achieved by a poorly led, ill-motivated group of individuals.

of any team. This approach must be present in fact as well as theory. For example, most project-scheduling software shows which activities were late. What is the point of reporting on them if you can't do anything about it? What is important is know which are likely to be late in the future and taking preventative action to ensure they will not be late.

When dealing with your team, or indeed any other stakeholders, assume they will act to avoid pain and seek pleasure. Be a role model and display the behaviours you wish all the team to emulate. For example, if you:

- concentrate on inconsequential trivia and absolute adherence to process, so will they;
- thump the desk when things go wrong, so will they;
- shout at them when they bring bad news, they'll avoid telling you.

Publicly reward the behaviours you want to encourage.

Publicly reward the behaviours you want to encourage. Success depends on the commitment and willingness of each team member to succeed.

> *"He that complies against his will is of his own opinion still"*
>
> SAMUEL BUTLER, 1835–1902

Encouraging open communication

A team progress meeting had just finished and the participants were talking as they left the room. One was overheard by the project manager saying to a colleague that a deliverable he is accountable for was going to be nine months late. This had major implications on the project and yet had not been raised at the progress meeting. The project manager was understandably annoyed, not about the delay, but that it had not been reported. He took the view that he needed to know about delays in sufficient time to deal with them. He believed he made a point of encouraging the reporting of bad news, being careful not to harangue the messenger for delays or whatever. This did not mean he was soft on people not delivering to plan but rather showed his focus on recognizing problems and achieving the objectives in spite of them . . . and yet a person did hold back the "bad news".

Leadership and influence

There are probably more books and seminars on effective personal style than any other management topic and yet time and time again projects go wrong for very human reasons. During the 1990s, it was estimated ten academic papers a day were published on the subject and nowadays virtually every organization includes leadership as a topic within their management or executive development courses. Few, however, include "project sponsorship" in those courses. Project management roles are interesting in this respect as they challenge many of the traditional assumptions associated with power and leadership. Prime amongst these is the likelihood of the following:

- you may be leading or managing across the organization, impacting people and capabilities outside your traditional line management remit and even from other organizations; further, these people may be from different disciplines with different ways of working, language, and values;
- traditional hierarchy and ranks may be side-stepped, thereby making senior line managers accountable to managers they perceive to be more junior;
- you may have no direct authority over the team you are accountable for from a line management perspective. As such, the normal disciplinary sanctions for non-performance of individuals might not exist – you have no "big stick".

In such situations, certain aspects of "pushy", "blue", or "hard" styles, such as assertion and persuasion, can be ineffective.

- **Persuasion** is only useful if the issue is open to rational debate and you are perceived as being competent in the topic under discussion. It is notoriously poor if used in a highly charged emotional environment.

- **Assertiveness** can be powerful if your needs are legitimate and you stand to lose if those needs are not met. The list of accountabilities associated with your role gives you legitimacy but do check what incentives you can offer or sanctions you can impose to gain agreement or compliance with your wishes. If you can provide neither, assertion can be fruitless. Most line managers rely on assertion as their primary leadership style.

"Pull", "green", or "soft" styles such as bridging and attraction might be more effective.

- **Bridging** involves gaining others' commitment and is most valuable if it is seen that you are open to influence and value their opinions. Look at your key stakeholders and you will probably find this form of influence is appropriate for many situations involving them.
- **Attraction** or envisioning is all about generating enthusiasm and excitement, taking people beyond the everyday to new possibilities. It is often seen as totally irrational, but is no less effective for that. If shared values and trust are what you need to achieve your aims, this is a good influencing style.

In summary, the "best style" to use depends on the situation you find yourself in and the person you want to influence. If you find yourself saying the following, think again:

- "Don't come to me with problems, come with solutions."
- "I only accept 'can do' as an option."
- "Don't come moaning to me; just do it."
- "I want action NOW!"

All these expressions may lead to over-optimistic reports of progress, the truth being hidden and blame being cast on others for failure to deliver. It is more powerful for a leader to surround himself with "constructive dissenters" prepared to tell the truth or ask awkward questions than with "yes men" who merely repeat what the leader wants to hear.

The "best style" to use depends on the situation you find yourself in and the person you want to influence.

Remember, the benefits from whatever the project produces will only start to flow once the deliverables have been put into use in an operational environment. If those leading the project have not obtained the consent of the senior managers who will actually operate the "new order", their efforts and that of the team will come to nothing. It would have been more cost effective to send the team and their families on holiday to Spain for three months than to create something which is never used.

The examples given above are based on Western culture and behaviours. If your team members come from a number of different countries and traditions, you need to be aware of how your behaviour will be seen by them; like you, their behaviour is influenced by their own cultural norms. If not taken into account, a leader's behaviours may reflect back on them and solicit a response from the team which is counter-productive in terms of project performance, but very predictable on a human level. Leadership style needs to reflect the situation; assertion in one culture may be seen as bullying, whilst in another culture it may simply be a sign of strong leadership.

Are you a sunny or cloudy person?

In Iran, where the skies are a boring blue day after day, clouds bring happy relief and are welcomed. In the UK, clouds represent gloom and the people long for the blue skies and sun.

I thought you were doing that!: accountability

How many times have you been in a meeting, with your colleagues and the following has happened:

Chairman: Right. That's agreed then. Kim and Leigh, you sort that one out and let us know next week.

Next week . . .

Chairman: Kim, what happened?
Kim: I don't know. I thought Leigh was doing something on this.
Leigh: Oh! I was waiting for you to phone me.

Some clarity on who was actually accountable was needed. Kim and Leigh might both have been necessary, as skilled, knowledgeable resources, to carry out the action, but only one of them should have been accountable. This is called "single-point accountability".

The person who is accountable is not necessarily the person who does the work, but the one who sees that it is done. This is not only useful in a meeting environment but also in planning projects. We have already introduced the accountabilities of the project sponsor and project manager. The project manager is accountable for managing the work on a day-to-day basis, ensuring the deliverables are in place at the required time, quality and cost. He or she cannot do it all, or in many cases manage it all. We have also seen how a project is decomposed into life cycle stages (see p. 154). This decomposition can be followed through with major packages of work being made the accountability of a particular, named, core team member. These work packages may be divided into smaller packages and, ultimately, into individual activities and tasks. This decomposition is called a work breakdown structure (see Chapter 4).

In practice, single point accountability means every work package at any level in the work breakdown structure has a person named as accountable for it.

In practice, single-point accountability means every task, activity, and work package at any level in the work breakdown structure has a named person accountable for it. This has four advantages:

- it is clear what is expected of each person;
- overlaps should be eliminated as no deliverable can be created within two different work packages (which is why we have interdependencies);
- if a gap in accountability appears (due to loss of a team member, for example), the next person **up** the tree is accountable to fix it;
- if scope, cost, or time proves to be inadequate to create the deliverables, it is clear who is accountable for raising these issues.

In practice, accountability is shown in the way that project plans (bar charts) are designed. The schedule plan examples given in Chapter 20 clearly show accountability.

In a dictionary, the words "accountability" and "responsibility" are interchangeable but in a management context it is often helpful to draw a distinction.

Accountability: what you can count on a person to do. That person and only that person can be called to account if something he/she has accountability for is not done.

Responsibility: what a person is, or feels, responsible for. It assumes commitment on the part of that person, beyond his/her own accountabilities, to act responsibly to ensure the project objectives are met.

You may be *accountable* for ensuring a computer system functions correctly. I would be acting *responsibly* if I told you of any defects I observed.

In projects it is essential that accountabilities are clearly stated and are unambiguous so everyone knows what they are accountable for and who they are accountable to. Similarly, team commitment should be fostered which promotes a responsible attitude by all team members.

"The business of everybody is the business of nobody"

LORD MACAULAY, 1800–1859

Ideally a project team should be selected for their skills, competences, and ability to work together; any weaknesses in some individuals should be compensated for by strengths in others. There are a wide range of team-profiling tools available, many of which are used as a part of executive development programmes and are suitable for use in a project context. The most commonly used tool is Belbin's team roles. It was originally developed as a self-assessment tool for individuals to gain greater insight into their own team styles but was later applied more widely in businesses. Such tools can be controversial, especially regarding the degree of academic and research rigour applied; a practical management tool, designed to help a manager understand team dynamics and personal behaviour is very different to a formal psychometric analysis tool. A full discussion on team profiling is beyond the scope of this book and anyone using such approaches should ensure they have expert advice on which tools to use in particular circumstances and whether a trained facilitator should be used to apply them and interpret the results. Unfortunately, in business, many people haven't the luxury of selecting the "perfect team" and a project sponsor often has to work with the project manager they are given and vice versa. Similarly, a project manager may have little choice over who is assigned to their team. The larger and more autonomous the project, the more likely it is that people can be selected especially for the project. Note, however, even when profiling cannot be used to select a team it can be used on an incumbent team to understand the individual and group behaviours and enable the managers to compensate where necessary.

Encourage an open, even-handed style to encourage communications

Copyright © 1997 Robert Buttrick

RACI tables

If you are truly accountable, you must not only be accountable for an activity or out-come, but also be accountable to someone. If you are not accountable to anyone, there is no one to hold you to account; you can do what you like, with no consequences. In a project, the prime accountabilities can be treted and follow the work breakdown structure:

- the project sponsor is accountable to "higher management" for directing the project;
- the project manager is accountable to the project sponsor for managing to the project;
- the team managers are each accountable to the project manager for managing a specific work package(s);
- the team members are each accountable to the team manager for undertaking their assigned activities;
- project assurance is accountable to the project sponsor for their delegated assurance activities;
- project support is accountable to the project manager for providing the defined support services.

An "RACI table" seeks to summarize "who does what" in a table where:

- R denotes a person who is also involved, as a resource;
- A denotes the accountable person;
- C denotes a person is consulted;
- I denotes a person is informed.

You can make an RACI table clear by ensuring the "A" is against the actual activity a person is accountable for, at the level they are accountable, as in the examples in Tables 15.1 and 15.2.

Table 15.1 RACI table

Activity	R (accountable)	A (involved in)	C (consulted)	I (informed)
Direct project	Project sponsor	Project assurance	Higher management	Stakeholders
Manage project	Project manager	Team managers Project support	Project sponsor	Stakeholders
Manage work package	Team manager	Team members	Project manager	
Undertake activity	Team member		Team manager	

Table 15.2 Alternative RACI table

Role / Activity	Higher mang't	Project sponsor	Project manager	Team manager	Team member	Project assurance	Project support	Stakeholders
Direct project	C	A				R		I
Manage project		C	A	R			R	I
Manage work package			C	A	R			
Undertake activity				C	A			

In poorly constructed RACI tables, you see the most senior person listed as accountable for everything. In the examples in Tables 15.1 and 15.2 above, this would mean the project sponsor would be designated "A" for everything. As only one role can be accountable, everyone else would need to be designated "R" leading to a plethora of meaningless "R"s, making the table almost useless in practical terms. Tiering accountabilities, based on division of work and delegation leads to far clearer tables.

16

Project governance

*If you restrict your perception of "governance" to
being either a process or a structure, you are severely
limiting how other people perceive governance
and that will limit their behaviours and attitude.
The entirety of project management is project
governance, with each part affecting every other part.*

*"In modern business it is not the crook who is to be feared most,
it is the honest man who doesn't know what he is doing"*
WILLIAM WORDSWORTH, 1770–1850

- **Governance is not a structure, nor a process.**
- **Understand what influences and constrains governance on your project.**
- **Build governance into your plans.**
- **Harness the project framework to manage risk.**

So what is governance?

Corporate governance

This is what Dame Suzi Leather, Chair, Charity Commission said in the opening pages of *Good Governance, A Code for the Voluntary and Community Sector*:

> *The central importance of good governance to all sectors of the economy is now clearer than ever. The crisis which beset our financial system has highlighted how dangerous a tick-box approach can be. Truly good governance has to be lived. Each and every trustee and board member needs to embrace its values, and apply them to the particular needs and circumstances of their organization.*

So what is a book on project management doing talking about the voluntary and charitable sector? Throughout this book, I advocate that a "project" is not simply a delivery vehicle to create deliverables, but is a vehicle for creating strategic change. You manage your way to the future by using project management to make sure you achieve the outcomes you want and the benefits you need, when you want them. Further, project management can be used in any organization, in any sector. If the charitable sector sees the necessity of emphasizing good governance, then such demands must surely apply to project management generally. Different sectors express concepts and practices in different ways and it is often helpful to transfer their knowledge to other sectors, especially if they achieve the same result in a simpler way.

The OECD defines corporate governance in the *Principles of Corporate Governance*, as

> *Corporate governance involves a set of relationships between a company's management, its board, its shareholders and other stakeholders. Corporate governance also provides the structure through which the objectives of the company are set, and the means of attaining those objectives and monitoring performance are determined.*

Since its publication in 2004, the OECD has added six more guides on governance to supplement it. You will also find countless references to governance in the public sector, both at national and international level. Clearly, "governance" is a hot topic and as all corporate and public sector organizations have projects, this is relevant to project management as a project is directed and managed in the context of a higher level organization (see Chapter 3).

The Oxford Dictionary's definition of governance is somewhat simpler:

1 conduct the policy, actions, and affairs of (a state, organization, or people) with authority;
2 control, influence, or regulate (a person, action, or course of events).

Making governance work

From the above examples, you should now have a feel for what governance is about, although I am sure people will argue the subtleties of definition for a very long time. What is important is how governance is applied on the ground and, for us, how it applies to projects. In very simple terms, a board sets the long-term vision and protects the reputation and values of its organization. To do this, the board needs to ensure the organization has proper policies and processes in place. A board will be effective if its members:

1 work effectively, both as individuals and a team;
2 understand their role;
3 ensure delivery of organizational purpose;
4 exercise effective control;
5 behave with integrity;
6 are open and accountable.

Central to this is also a focus on risk; you will always see the terms "governance" and "risk" closely associated. The characteristics for effective governance are a mix of:

- **knowledge**: an understanding the business of the organization and context it operates within;
- **behaviour**: in terms of ethics, reputation and integrity;
- **purpose**: to set the vision, values, and objectives, which are compelling and achievable;
- **process**: to enable the right level of control, delegation, operational efficiency, and effectiveness.

This leads us to challenge some misconceptions about governance:

- **governance is NOT a structure, although structure is a vital element;**
- **governance is NOT a process, although processes are a vital element;**
- **governance is NOT just about decision making, although decision making is a vital activity within governance.**

If you restrict your perception of "governance" to any one of these, you are severely limiting how other people perceive governance, thereby limiting their behaviours and attitude.

The term "structure" can be interpreted as "organization" or "arrangement" and I believe that is what the OECD meant when it used the term in its definition of corporate governance. Unfortunately, the word structure is so interlinked with "organization structure" in the business world it is easily misinterpreted. All too often, I have heard "governance structure" described as simply the reporting line of senior management and boards within the company; necessary, but not enough.

Similarly, the term "process" can simply mean activities, but in a management context it frequently refers to the formal management of activities where an input is converted to an output.

If governance is restricted to be concerned solely with decision making, that could lead to the right decisions being implemented in an illegal or unethical way.

Make sure governance is clear and unambiguous

* Victor was a common name for a horse in ancient Rome.

Project governance and governance of project management

What then is project governance? As a project is an activity undertaken within an organization, its sponsor, manager, and team are subservient to the governance of the overall organization. The entirety of project management is project governance, with each part affecting every other part, as we saw in Figure 2.2. **Project governance** covers how a project is directed and controlled through its structures, processes, roles, systems, standards, values, and the behaviours of the people involved. If someone asks you to explain your project's governance approach, you need to ask them what aspect they are interested in as their view on governance may not be the same as yours.

The **governance of project management** differs from project governance as it is aimed at how the organization, as a whole, is set up to direct and manage its projects. As such it sets the context for how each project is managed, usually through policy, methods and processes. The UK's Association for Project Management (APM) provides advice to board members on the governance of project management, which has eleven principles (shown in Table 16.1), supported by questions on four themes or components, which are:

- **Portfolio direction**: this seeks to ensure all projects are identified within the one portfolio (we'll look at this in *The Programme and Portfolio Workout*).
- **Project sponsorship**: this seeks to ensure project sponsorship is the effective link between the organization's senior executive body and the management of the project (see Chapter 5).
- **Project management effectiveness and efficiency**: this seeks to ensure the teams responsible for projects are capable of achieving the objectives defined at project approval points (gates).
- **Disclosure and reporting**: this seeks to ensure the content of project reports will provide timely, relevant and reliable information that supports the organization's decision making processes, without fostering a culture of micro-management.

Table 16.1 Governance of project management principles

1	The board has overall responsibility for governance of project management.
2	The roles, responsibilities, and performance criteria for the governance of project management are clearly defined.
3	Disciplined governance arrangements, supported by appropriate methods and controls, are applied throughout the project life cycle.
4	A coherent and supportive relationship is demonstrated between the overall business strategy and the project portfolio.
5	All projects have an approved plan containing authorization points at which the business case is reviewed and approved. Decisions made at authorization points are recorded and communicated.
6	Members of delegated authorization bodies have sufficient representation, competence, authority, and resources to enable them to make appropriate decisions.
7	The project business case is supported by relevant and realistic information that provides a reliable basis for making authorization decisions.
8	The board or its delegated agents decide when independent scrutiny of projects and project management systems is required, and implement such scrutiny accordingly.
9	There are clearly defined criteria for reporting project status and for the escalation of risks and issues to the levels required by the organization.
10	The organization fosters a culture of improvement and of frank internal disclosure of project information.
11	Project stakeholders are engaged at a level that is commensurate with their importance to the organization and in a manner that fosters trust.

Source: Association for Project Management (APM), *Directing Change, A guide to governance of project management*, 2004.

The APM's governance principles are aimed at managing all the projects within an organization. Principles 5, 7, and 9, however, can be sensibly applied to a single project; they relate to reporting and escalation and to having a plan and a business case. Many of the questions in the supporting components can also be applied to a single project. The governance of project management is covered in *The Programme and Portfolio Workout*.

Constraints on project governance

Having now understood what project governance is, you should also realize that you do not have total freedom to apply governance on your particular project. Constraints are imposed by external factors, as well as the organization itself. Organizational constraints should not be looked on as "bad". The more consistent an organization is in its approach to directing and managing its projects, the less time is wasted in deciding "who is accountable" when decisions are needed. This especially applies to an organization's most senior people: they simply haven't the time and energy to find out all the different nuances of naming and lines of authority on every project they are the sponsor for or stakeholders in. Consistent governance will lead to good governance. Also, remember your project is just one set of activities within a larger organization and the leaders of that organization have an obligation to apply effective governance to everything that organization does. Your project governance is actually a part of their corporate governance. You can therefore expect constraints to come from a number of sources such as:

- legal, regulatory and codes of practice;
- corporate polices;
- platform and technical conformance;
- processes and methods to be used;
- contracts with suppliers;
- contracts with clients and customers.

In any country, the legal and regulatory frameworks are paramount. All business activities must comply with both civil and criminal law. In many cases, there are also regulations and voluntary codes of practice which prescribe certain behaviours, processes and practices. Some industries, like telecommunications, finance, utilities, railways, and aviation, are more highly regulated than others.

In order to protect its reputation and operate within the law and other binding agreements, organizations have policies dictating the boundaries of governance for particular themes, covering a range of topics such as diversity, safety, environment and sustainability and well as the more routine human resource and technical topics. Policies determine the way processes are designed and which practices are used; they set the overall values and vision for each topic.

With the rise of platform based product, service and management systems, many organizations seek to promote "operational efficiencies" by ensuring the maximum reuse of standard solution capabilities. This may be a financial or ERP platform, like SAP or Oracle, or an automotive chassis which serves a number of car models or it could be that only certain components or "parts" are selected from specific preferred suppliers or from the organization's internally certified products or components.

Standard processes and methods dictate or advise how to undertake certain activities. Some (processes) are very rigid, which others (methods) looser, leaving a lot of discretion in how they are applied. Using consistent processes and methods creates the opportunity to learn and move faster and for people to work together more efficiently.

The contracts with the suppliers limit your degrees of freedom and may impose, on both parties, particular governance requirements, say for meetings, consultation, agreement, procedures and payment triggers.

The contract with the customer, if you are working in that context, like that for a supplier, limits your degrees of freedom and may impose, on both parties, particular requirements influencing how governance is applied. For example, it may dictate the roles of any joint boards and the contractual basis on which they take their authority; it may dictate that a supplier has to inform a customer as soon as they believe a delay or overspend is likely; it may define how changes to the contract scope are approved and paid for; it will always define how and when payments will be made.

Aspects of project governance

Fundamentally, an organization undertakes projects in order to realize benefits. As we learnt in Chapter 5, to achieve this, its people need to be effective at both management and doing the specialist work at the core of the business. There is little point in being in the "car business" if you haven't the capability to design, manufacture and distribute cars, no matter how good your managers are. Table 16.2 lists the scope of governance, and therefore points to decision rights, which need to be covered.

You will find all these aspects covered within this book but I'd like to draw out a few significant points to emphasize the breadth and interaction between them. For effective governance you need to:

- harness the project's work breakdown structure;
- build governance into your project plans;
- use baselines effectively;
- integrate the project roles;
- design project boards appropriately;
- clarify decision rights.

Table 16.2 Different aspects of governance

Roles	Ensuring people, from top to bottom know what they are accountable for and whom they are accountable to. Key in this is the "project sponsor" role, who is accountable for ensuring the organization's business interest are maintained.
Project assurance	Helping the project sponsor exercise their business leadership role.
Technical assurance	Ensuring platform and product strategies and standard are maintained and deliverables of the required quality.
Customer contracts	Ensuring we know and meet our obligations and that our customer does the same.
Supplier contract	Ensuring suppliers know and meet their obligations and that we do the same. Ensure we know explicitly who is accountable for each contractual obligation.
Meetings	Who meets whom, when, and why?
Prioritization	Determining who can make decisions when there is a conflict of priority. In business-led projects, the choice should relate to maximizing benefit to the organization, bearing in mind the associated risks.
Escalations	Ensuring accountabilities can be met, even when things fail.
Reporting	Ensuring the right people have the right information in order to undertake their accountabilities.
Controls	Monitoring the project's progress to be reassured everything is on track and to prompt action when things start going wrong. Key in this is the creation of a plan (baselined), the management of risks and issues and the introduction of changes to the plan in a controlled way, keeping focused on the required benefits. A key pillar of control is the work break-down structure.
Processes and procedures	Defining how a project is set up, managed, and its work controlled.
Project gating	Ensuring only those projects which should be started are started and only those which should continue, do continue.
Quality	Ensuring we achieve the quality of outputs that we need and that the specified quality really does meet the stakeholders' needs.

Harness the project's work breakdown structure

A proper and well-thought through work breakdown structure (such as shown in Figure 16.1) is the basis of good multi-level governance. It ensures every activity in the plan is directly traceable, through the various levels of accountability from the team member undertaking the work via the project manager to the project sponsor, who respectively manages and directs the entire project. Conversely, a poorly thought through work breakdown structure is a recipe for confusion, duplication, and omission. A properly constructed work breakdown structure provides:

- clear accountability, at every level in the project, for work in terms of scope, time, cost and schedule;
- obvious point of accountability when a "level manager" goes missing (upward accountability);

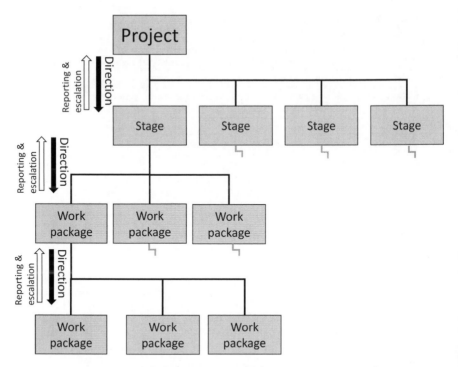

Figure 16.1 The work breakdown structure as an essential element of governance

A properly constructed work breakdown structure provides clear accountability, at every level in the project, for planning, delegation, escalation, reporting, and decision rights.

- clear escalation path, without the need to negotiate the corporate organization structure;
- clear line for management reporting and escalation;
- clear view of who has the decision right over whom.

Don't confuse a project's work breakdown structure with its organization structure. On the face of it, they might look similar, with team member reporting to team manager reporting to project manager (as in Figure 5.1). However, a single individual could work on a number of separate work packages, reporting to a different team manger on each and even be acting as a team manager on others.

Build time for governance into your project plans

Governance is not "free". It takes effort and it takes time. For this reason, when you develop your project plan, you need to take account of the time some aspects of governance can take. In particular, look at decision making. Certain deliverables may require extensive peer review before they can be approved. In system engineering, it is not unusual to have preliminary and critical design reviews, each lasting a week, when the subject matter experts look into every aspect of the design before making any recommendations. Gate decisions will usually require senior level approval and in many organizations, this will be a review board which might only meet on a monthly basis. Look at all the reviews, approvals and decisions required in your plan and check whether:

- any individuals are overloaded, having too many decision to make;
- you allowed enough time for reviews to take place;
- decisions are linked into regular (heart beat) boards or whether will you sometimes need extraordinary meetings to maintain momentum.

Figure 16.2 shows a real-life example of the number of decisions required each month on a transformation programme comprising nine projects. It peaks at about fifty-four decisions a month when the various project teams are completing their investigative stages; that is fifty-four decisions on top of the decisions the six directors have to make as a part of the day-to-day running of the business.

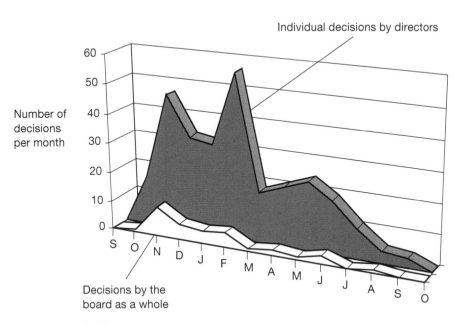

Figure 16.2 Decisions

In the planning stages of a complex change programme, the project managers identified each point which required either a board decision or the decision of one of the directors. In all, about 200 decisions were identified, spanning nine key change projects.

Use baselines effectively

The management of baselines is an essential part of governance. At any point in time you need to know three aspects:

- the plan baseline;
- the solution, comprising requirements, design, and product;
- contract baseline.

The project plan baseline tells you what the approved plan is, in terms of benefits, schedule, costs, resources, and scope, against which progress will be measured.

The solution baseline tells you everything about the output the project is going to create. This is made up of three parts. The requirements baseline is the definitive set of requirements driving the project. The design baseline provides the configuration of the various components of the solution and the detail for each part of the solution. The product baseline is the solution "as built" and handed over for steady state operation. You might not be familiar with this terminology, which is derived from system engineering but you are sure to have definitions or descriptions of your outputs in text or diagram form, electronically or in documents which are used in a similar way.

The contract baseline is the contract, as signed, together with any agreed variations (changes). This may apply to a customer or to suppliers.

Note, however, that these three baselines are not independent. It is vital that every requirement and solution component can be traced to the planned work being undertaken in relation to it. In addition, requirements should be traceable to any contract clauses (both up to the customer and down to a supplier – allocated requirements) to which they relate. Without this level of control, changes, an inevitable fact of life, cannot be adequately assessed and, if implemented, the effects cannot be adequately communicated to those who need to know. We will look at change control in Chapter 25.

The project roles are fundamental to good governance

We looked at the project roles in Chapter 5. Let's just revisit three of these roles and how they impact governance.

The project sponsor is ultimately accountable to higher management for the success of the project. This includes championing the business objectives, engaging senior stakeholders, making key decisions, and intervening in high-priority issues. The sponsor is the link from the organization to the project. A project only exists if the sponsor wants it to exist. The sponsor, as the owner of the business case, is the primary risk taker as you cannot separate a business case from risk. A project sponsor directs the project and is accountable for project governance.

The project manager is accountable to the sponsor for successful delivery of the required solutions, capabilities, and outcomes (as required). The role requires the effective coordination of the constituent work and interdependencies, taking into account any risks and other issues arising. The project is also accountable for the effective and efficient undertaking of the project and use of resources. The project manager is therefore accountable for defining and promoting the practices which form good governance, including encouraging the appropriate behaviours and mind-set.

The team manager is accountable to the project manager for undertaking the work. It is though the team manager, the "real work" happens and the practices impacting the quality and suitability of the outputs are actually carried out. Team managers also have management accountability for planning, monitoring, and control of the work against the baselines.

Without these roles, projects would be little more than loosely coordinated activities where alignment and success are elusive and often cannot even be defined.

Design project boards appropriately

Many projects have boards to ensure direction and decisions are in the best interest of the company. As we saw in Chapter 5, in some cases a board supports the project sponsor role, whilst in others, it is a higher-level entity to which the project sponsor is accountable. In all cases, a board's purpose must be clear and the limits of its authority (including decision making) set. These should be defined in a terms of reference. Board membership is a prime consideration as the mix of personalities and skills determines its effectiveness. Unless the role of the board is defined, you cannot decide its membership or way of working. If the board is there to support a project sponsor, you need to decide if it is purely advisory and can be overruled by the sponsor or if some decisions require a consensus or even a vote. The "rules" for a board will affect the behaviours of its members. Board members solely representing the interests of their own departments or divisions rarely make a good contribution as they will invariably place the needs of their departments over the needs of the wider organization. Beware also of having boards with too large a membership; a project board is not a stakeholder engagement device and treating it in this way leads to a lessening of its authority and it risks becoming a mere "talking shop".

Clarify decision rights

The setting of decision rights for a modern organization is very difficult and often controversial. For a bureaucratic hierarchy, it was simple: whoever "owned" that part of the business made the decisions. Modern organizations are more complex with many decisions impacting many parts of the business. Badly constructed decision rights can lead to an inefficient, sluggish and moribund organization. To optimize decision making, decisions need to be made as close as possible to where the work is done. Nick Pudar, director of planning and strategic initiatives at General Motors, said, "If I know someone in the organization's lower levels can make a tough call *that won't affect other parts of the company*, then it's their call." I have italicized what I believe are the most crucial words. Delegation is a good thing but the prime risk associated with placing decisions making at lower levels is that the lower-level manager's motivations and aims may not align with those of the organization's leaders. The way you allocate decisions, therefore, must take this into account, particularly in the way the hierarchy of decisions is structured.

Effective decision making relies on the person making the decision having enough information at the right time. To achieve this, processes and support systems need to be designed to enable the flow of information to the decision maker, with the right stakeholders being involved. I would argue that you cannot design a "decision making process", only ensure processes support the decision maker. The costs of this, however, have to be commensurate with of value of the information gained. Any gaps in knowledge require assumptions, which represent a risk. General wisdom in corporate governance is that single point accountability for each decision is essential (see Chapter 15).

In this context, good project management practice is already set up to promote good decision making, through its web of roles, work breakdown structure, processes and individual practices. The crucial part is ensuring decision making within a project dovetails into decision making at a higher level, such as programme, business portfolio or sponsoring organization. The failure to ensure a project fits into the wider organization is fundamental to why even well run projects fail and it is why, in the quest to ensure every project succeeds, more and more attention is directed at high-level management techniques; we'll go through these in *The Programme and Portfolio Workout*.

Before we leave the topic of governance, however, I would like to cover two situations in the next sections of this chapter, namely, where decisions are required, which are especially applicable to projects:

- at a macro level, decisions concerning whether a project should be started, should continue or be terminated. This was introduced in Chapter 4 and relates to project gating;
- at a more granular level, whether a particular document or deliverable should be approved.

 ## Workout 16.1 – Your project's governance

Consider the project you are sponsoring or managing.

1   Look at Table 16.2, which lists some common aspects of management. Use this table as the basis for defining what influences the governance of your project; discard any from Table 16.1 which don't apply and add any special ones you believe are missing.
2   Having listed the aspects of governance, amend the second column to say how they should be dealt with on your project.

Project gating

In Chapter 4, we learned how gates are the decision points preceding every stage. At each gate, three distinct questions need to be answered:

- is there a real need for this project and, in its own right, is it viable?
- what is its priority relative to other projects?
- is there sufficient funding to continue the project?

Unless specific criteria have been met, the subsequent stage should not be started. We saw examples of typical criteria in Chapters 6 to 11. These criteria set the parameters for any decision but do not define who can make the decision. Looking at the three questions, we notice that only the first question relates to the project; the other two questions look at the relationship to what else is going on. In other words, a decision to start or continue a project at a gate cannot be made in isolation unless the project is truly stand-alone and does not impact anyone else's resources or objectives. Who, then, can make the decision? Clearly, the project sponsor should be able to deal with the first question. The second question, on priority, must be dealt with at a higher level, at a point where resources are no longer shared. This may be at programme, business portfolio, or enterprise level. The important point to note is that the decision maker might not be the project sponsor and is very much influenced by the project's context (see Chapter 3). It is at this point project governance meets corporate governance.

You will have noticed in this chapter that the terms "risk" and "governance" are interlinked. The power of the project framework, and hence gating, as an essential element of project governance, is that the approach enables a sponsor to invest money a stage at a time, gathering more information until they determine the project is highly likely to be viable or should be terminated. Compare this with the approach where all the funds are allocated when the project is started, with the only control being on individual purchases or with the commonly found corporate model of all project funds being allocated to each department at the start of the financial year for them to spend when they want.

Recording agreement on deliverables

Obtaining agreement to key deliverables during the project is essential but it can often prove difficult to:

- identify those who need to be involved;
- engage them in taking time to address the review;
- be certain that a review has, in fact, been done.

You will need to use the stakeholder management approaches introduced in Chapter 17 and described in Chapter 26 to identify and engage the right people. In order to make their involvement clear, it is often useful to formalize the review and acceptance of project deliverables. Deliverables might be documents (see Chapter 28) or physical outputs. The same approach can also be used for verifying outcomes. This is key for final deliverables but applies as much to intermediate deliverables (i.e. those developed during the project) setting the "agenda" for the next stage of work. Unless this is done, there is a danger that work might proceed on a premise which does not have the support of critical stakeholders.

The following is a recommended approach where alternative formal "quality processes" have not been adopted.

Standard record for reviews and approvals

A standard form (such as given in Figure 16.3) can be used either as a stand-alone document or as content in an email, memo, letter, or within a process workflow. It provides a concise and instantly recognizable prompt which clearly states what is required of the recipient. For example, some individuals may receive a deliverable for comment on particular points only, while others will receive a "final" deliverable and will be required to accept (approve) it.

The project documentation should list the key deliverables from the project, stating who has responsibility for reviewing and accepting them. If a deliverable is not readily portable, alternative methods of review (inspection, demonstrations, tests, etc.) should be arranged.

Procedure

1 The originator of the deliverable (or project manager) sends the deliverable under cover of a request form to the reviewer.
2 The reviewer carries out the action noted under "criteria," completes their part of the form and returns it to the originator. It is not usually necessary to have a real signature, as email or electronic signatures are generally adequate in most organizations.

Review/Approval Request			
Project number and name: Work package:			
Request: < state what the request is, being very clear on whether it is for approval / for review / for informal comment or other purpose >			
To:	<name>	Requested by:	<name>
Issued:	<date>	To be returned by:	<date>
Deliverable:			
Criteria:			

Review/Approval Response			
Response	<state response to the request, such as "Approved", "Not approved", "Reviewed with critical findings", "Reviewed with significant findings" >		
Comment	< Add any comments to justify the response and to help the requestor to remedy any shortcomings. Refer to any appended information, such as a review record.>		
Name:	<name of responder>	Role:	<role>
Date:	<dd mmm yyyy>		

Figure 16.3 An example of an approval or review form

A form which can be used as a request for approval or review of a deliverable, which also includes the response. The deliverable may be a document, physical output or even a recognizable outcome.

Workout 16.2 – Chains of accountability

Pick up your results from Workout 3.1. If you haven't completed it, then finish it now!

1 Based on what you now know about the importance of roles and breakdown structures, verify on your project:

- Who, by name and role, is accountable to whom, within the project (team managers, team members, project manager, and project sponsor).
- Whom the project sponsor is accountable to (name and role).
- The governance of the project dovetails with higher-level organizational governance with no gaps or overlaps in accountability.

2 Does each individual, named on your structure, understand their accountabilities with respect to the project?

- Do they know whom they take direction from and report to?
- Do they know who is expecting direction from them?
- Do they understand what particular aspects of governance they are accountable for exercising?

3 Who is accountable for the following?

- Decisions at each project gate.
- Decisions on whether the project should be terminated.
- Decisions on which project takes priority over another.
- Decision on whether quality of deliverables is adequate.

4 If there are any answers to question 2 and 3 such as "unknown" or "not sure", or if you find two or more people seem to be accountable for the same thing, then, you need to clarify the accountabilities for any people reporting to you and ensure the individuals know what is expected of them. Similarly, having put your own house in order, you may need to ask for clarification from any person higher than you in the hierarchy so you understand what they are accountable for and what part you play in helping them undertake their role.

Note, in poorly defined matrix organizations and ones run primarily on departmental hierarchy, this will not be a simple exercise and it may be that you cannot get the clarification you need, If this is the case you need to ensure the risks associated with this situation are at least recognized.

17

Project setup

How to go about it

Set up the project team

Prepare a business case and definition

Prepare the project plan

Define your project organization

Define how you will manage the project

Identify and engage your stakeholders

This chapter explains the steps you need to take at the start of the initial investigation stage to set up a project and ensuring control is established from the very beginning.

"Mix a little foolishness with your serious plans; it's lovely to be silly at the right moment"

HORACE, 65–8BC

- **Understand the driving business need.**
- **Define the scope and boundaries for the project.**
- **Use your team to define and plan the project.**
- **Harness your stakeholders' influence.**

This chapter explains the steps you need to take at the start of the initial investigation stage to set up a project, ensuring control is established from the very beginning. For clarity these steps are described sequentially, but in practice you will find you need to do them in parallel, as each step may influence any of the others.

How to go about it

There are five key activities to undertake when setting up a project:

1 set up the project team;
2 prepare a business case and definition;
3 prepare a project plan;
4 define your project organization;
5 engage your stakeholders.

The purpose of formally setting up the project is for you to state explicitly the *business drivers*, *scope* and *objectives* for the project, namely:

- *why* you are doing the project;
- *what* you will produce in terms of outputs and outcomes;
- *how* you will approach and manage the project;
- *when* you will produce it;
- *how much* it will cost and benefit you;
- *who* will be involved.

This information is gathered in a document, or set of documents, providing the starting point (baseline) on which all subsequent project decisions will be taken and against which you can measure project performance. Different organizations have different sets of documents to support this, the common ones being:

- Project initiation documentation (PRINCE2®);
- Project plan (PRINCE2®, APM, PMBOK®);

- Project management plan (APM, PMBOK®);
- Business case (PRINCE2®, APM).

All these contain similar information; it is just the way they are assembled, the terminology used and names of the documents which change. For example, the project management plan is often made up of a series of subsidiary documents defining how each aspect of the project is managed, such as risk management plan, schedule management plan, change control plan, stakeholder management plan. Sometimes the term "management plan" is called a "management strategy" and so you might see "risk management strategy", for instance.

Some organizations combine the "business case", which justifies **why** you are doing a project and proves its viability, with the "definition and plan", which defines the scope, schedule, and costs. This is the approach I have taken in this book. I have found that often finance functions want a particular document, prescribed by them, on which to base the authorization of funds for the project (a business case), whilst the operational side of the business wants additional content to define the project and its associated plan. In such circumstances, the two documents often conflict, say, with different timescales or scope. By combining the two documents into a single document, duplication and conflicts can be avoided. It is, however, important for the different users of the document to find the sections they need easily. Accordingly, I have structured the document in three parts, each serving a different interest group. Good design of a key document, such as that outlined here, can avoid duplication that might occur if separate documents are used. It will reduce your workload and eliminate discrepancies which can appear if separate documents are drafted for different interest groups.

What a waste of time!

"But why do I need to write it all up? Isn't it just a waste of time?"

Writing up your project in a structured and thorough way helps to ensure all the important aspects are covered. The template is, in itself, a checklist for building quality into your projects.

Unless you are the only person involved in the project, you will need to communicate your intentions. You may know everything about the project, but if the others who need to be involved don't understand what you are trying to achieve, the project will fail. The document is your explicit form of communication and is your "memory aid" so you don't forget either.

Keep the document brief. Put in the minimum content to communicate the bare essentials. Ironically, the simpler the project, the more people tend to write, as they know so much about it. Larger, more complex projects are frequently ill defined and too brief.

Headings to define your project

The four parts of the business case and definition are:

Section 1 – Finance, which is primarily aimed at the finance function. They will be interested in this section as a priority and then in Section 2.1 to 2.4. The project sponsor will also be interested in this as it sets out the financial criteria to be met.

Section 2 – Project definition and plan is of interest to the project sponsor, stakeholders and project team. It is the meat of the document.

Section 3 – Project organization is of most interest to the project manager, team and line managers as it sets out how the project has been organized and who is accountable to whom.

Section 4 – Management plan describes the tools, processes, procedures and techniques used by the team to manage the project.

If an organization has an enterprise-wide project management method and the project manager is following it without any tailoring, there is no need to include Section 4 in the document; it would simply repeat the standard approach. If there is an enterprise approach which has been tailored, Section 4 would only include the tailored aspects. If there is no enterprise-wide approach, each project manager would have to define and document this for themselves and brief and train the project sponsor and team accordingly. In an organization undertaking a number of projects, this duplication of effort is a waste of time. Further, with each project manager deciding on their own approach and even their own terminology, this can represent a major risk and source of confusion. It is better to have an enterprise-wide project management method as the core management plan and for the project manager to define only the tailoring they have done to suit their project.

Table 17.1 overleaf includes my suggested headings for each part of the document.

The remainder of this chapter will help you to complete each part of this. Don't expect to complete it in numerical order, a section at a time. Setting up a project tends to be an iterative activity, where one part influences the other parts. By the time you have undertaken all the activities necessary for each part, the content for each section will become clearer and start to settle down. Also remember in the staged approach we looked at in Part II, the document does not have to be perfect when first created; it only needs to be good enough in relation to where you are in the project life cycle and can be improved as the project advances.

Table 17.1 Contents for a typical business case and definition document

Section	Section heading	Question answered
1	**FINANCE**	
1.1	Financial appraisal	HOW MUCH?
1.2	Sensitivity analysis	HOW MUCH?
2	**PROJECT DEFINITION AND PLAN**	
2.1	Background	WHY?
2.2	Business objectives and outcomes	WHY?
2.3	Benefits	WHY?
2.4	Output description	WHAT?
2.5	Scope, impacts and interdependencies	WHAT?
2.6	Deliverables	WHAT?
2.7	Schedule	WHEN?
2.8	Costs	HOW MUCH?
2.9	Risks	CONTEXT?
2.10	Prerequisites, assumptions and constraints	CONTEXT?
2.11	Project approach	HOW?
2.12	Analysis of options	HOW?
3	**PROJECT ORGANIZATION**	
3.1	Organization chart and roles	WHO?
3.2	Progress reporting	HOW?
3.3	Change control criteria	HOW?
3.4	Gating and review points	HOW?
3.5	Stakeholders	WHO?
4	**MANAGEMENT PLAN**	
4.1	Benefits realization management	HOW?
4.2	Reporting	HOW?
4.3	Planning	HOW?
4.4	Risks and issues	HOW?
4.5	Change control	HOW?
4.6	Document and information management	HOW?

Set up the project team

The typical "project structure" was described in Chapter 5 and is shown again in Figure 17.1.

Project teams are:

- short-term, established only for the duration of the project;
- cross-functional, to provide the necessary skill mix;
- often part-time, with team members fulfilling line and project tasks.

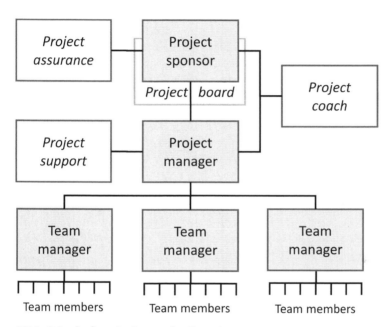

Figure 17.1 A typical project organization structure

The project sponsor requires the benefits, possibly supported by a project board and reports to higher level management. The project manager reports to the project sponsor and is accountable for the day-to-day running of the project. A project coach supports these key roles. All team managers and members report to the project manager.

Bearing this in mind, it is essential to agree the project roles from the start (e.g. project sponsor and project board membership, project manager, team managers) with the individuals concerned and their line managers (if appropriate). As some team members are likely to be part-time and have other daily duties, it is essential to agree with their line managers what their commitments are and how you should handle changes to this. If the line managers also have a quality assurance or control role to undertake, this must be agreed. If necessary, write and agree a role description, defining the individual's accountabilities. Even if these descriptions are never referred to again, the act of creating and agreeing them with the individuals, will clarify each person's role and lead to fewer misunderstandings. Finally, do ensure the accountability for any activity or work package in the project rests with a single person only. Shared accountabilities do not work; they lead to omission, duplication, and confusion. Summarize the key members' roles in Section 3.1 of the initial and full business case documents.

You should work with the team to create a set of values for the project to share and an agreed way of working together. Project Workout 17.1 provides some ideas for this. Fostering team spirit is the responsibility of all on the team, led by the project manager. The sooner the team can settle down to work together in an environment of openness and trust, the better it will be for the project. Project setup is the ideal time to do this but as the project proceeds, you may need to revisit this at the start of each stage; your project team is likely to change and you need to ensure the new joiners are engaged, feel part of the team and behave accordingly.

Preferably, the early days of the project should be spent as much as possible as a group, including the project sponsor, working in a creative environment. Project planning is an ideal vehicle for forming the team as well as being of vital importance to achieving results. Even if *you* know what to do on the project, sparing the time for the team to contribute will lead to greater commitment and better results. Projects designed and planned solely by one person usually lack the vitality and level of involvement necessary for achieving extraordinary results. They also risk having vital deliverables missing! Team forming and planning should be done face to face; it is very difficult to build good working methods and relationships over the telephone or a video link. Research repeatedly shows good teams create better outcomes and yet many organizations will risks millions of pounds of investment by not allowing teams members to come together for such a vital part of the project. If you are managing a project with a team that has never come together, you will find it more onerous, personally stressful and risky as you are likely to be the only person with enough knowledge to hold things together.

Projects designed and planned solely by one person usually lack the vitality and level of involvement necessary for achieving extraordinary results.

 ## Welcoming new team members

It is all well and good ensuring the team is bonded and aligned from the start but do not forget, as the project moves through its life cycle, team membership will change. Welcome new team members and ensure they have bought into the team values and the project objectives. If there are a number of new members, for instance, for a new project stage, treat it as if it is a new project. Project Workout 17.1 (The first team meeting) and those related to planning can easily be adapted for the start of each stage.

Workout 17.1 – The first team meeting

This is best done in a relaxed atmosphere without any tables acting as barriers between people. The "board room" arrangement is not recommended. Team meetings are best in rooms with space to move around and wall room for flip charts. Confined and cramped rooms confine and cramp thinking.

The first time team members gather is very important and can set the tone for the rest of the project. Some individuals may know each other (and you) well. Others may know no one. Some may have worked together before on other projects. Even if some have not met before, they may have preconceived ideas of others on the team based on gossip and rumour from other colleagues, which may or may not be accurate. It is you, as project manager, who must bond this disparate group into a committed team. One way of doing this is to:

- encourage the group members to respect each other;
- create a set of team rules which are seen, by all, as fair!

Respect each other

1   Ask all present to introduce themselves and say a little about their interests outside work. Ask them to tell the others something about themselves none of the others knows.
2   Ask each person to say what his/her commitments are to the project, why he/she would like to see it succeed and what that person will do to help success become a reality.
3   When the individual has finished, each of the other team members should build on what that individual has said about him/herself by saying what skills and competencies they know or feel the person has which they respect. Keep to positive and strong points only.

On receiving this acknowledgement, the individual should not be embarrassed. "Thank you" is all he or she needs to say.

4   Steps 1 to 3 should be gone through for every person in the group.

This may sound contrived, but it does work if treated seriously. It can remove or dispel rumour. It brings people onto a personal footing.

Create the team's values

Creating a set of "rules" that the team accept as fair and which each of them agrees to live by and uphold is also a powerful way of bonding:

1   Brainstorm a set of values or rules for the team to live by. Put these on a flip chart.
2   The team should then select those which it wants to live by.
3   Display the values prominently in the team's workroom and at every team meeting.

During the brainstorm, individuals will often shout out things that annoy them. For example, if someone really gets heated if meetings start late, he may want the rule/value "All meetings start on time". The brainstorm list, therefore, becomes a set of potential "hot buttons" which can turn each person from a likeable, rational soul into an angry unreasonable one. It's good to know what these are at the start! Some of the most powerful values can also appear very shallow. One senior team had "chocolate" as a value. At every meeting someone was accountable for bringing one or two chocolate treats, often from a country they recently visited on business. It became a symbol of "looking after each other" and something to joke about to lighten the tension when business issues were weighing heavily and the team could not agree a way forward. If one member became over-excited, another would simply offer him or her a chocolate as a reminder that the team had the same objectives and all its members are on the same side.

Prepare a project definition and plan

Part 2, the project definition section of the business case document, defines your project – why you are doing it, what you will produce and how you will go about it. The details for each section are as follows.

2 Project Definition

2.1 Background

Describe, briefly, the background to the project:

- Explain why the project has come about (e.g. as a result of a strategy study, as a result of findings from another project).
- Refer to any other associated projects or initiatives, business plans, or conclusions from previous studies.

2.2 Business objectives and outcomes

You should describe why you are doing the project. Explain:

- the business objectives the project will satisfy and how the project supports your business strategy;
- the needs the project fills and the outcomes (business changes) which will result.

Describe:

- the minimum conditions of satisfaction required in order to declare the project a success (e.g. achievement of a specific outcome, such as market share, revenue, cost saving by a specific date);
- the method for confirming the achievement of each condition of satisfaction.

2.3 Benefits

You should describe the benefits you hope to achieve from the project (see also Chapter 20). These may be in two forms:

- *Financial* – these should be stated in "money" terms (e.g. increased revenue, cost savings, etc.).
- *Non-financial* – changes in operational and key performance indicators should be quantified. If you are unable to quantify a particular benefit, describe it as best you can – just because you can't count it, doesn't mean to say it does not count.

Include a statement on what else the project will accomplish; for example, what new possibilities will be created operationally, commercially, or for new projects.

Answering the question "Why?" is very important

There are four basic reasons why you should want a project:

- to earn more revenue;
- to save costs;
- to reduce working capital;
- to enable you to remain in business.

All projects will ultimately be aiming for one or more of these. In a programme, individual projects might focus on different benefits, for example, improving performance and service quality. Other projects may be created as vehicles to learn about new markets, technologies, or approaches. Be honest when stating the business objective. If you pretend a "learning" project is a revenue generator, don't be surprised if it is cut in favour of projects which generate greater revenue.

In addition you should outline any possible events which, if they occur, will lead you to consider terminating the project.

2.4 Output description

You should describe, in one paragraph, the key output(s) the project is going to produce in order to achieve the outcomes from Section 2.2. The output may be a new product, a new culture, process, manufacturing line, computer system, etc. Section 2.6 will list the key deliverables and these need not be stated here. The blueprint will contain the detail.

2.5 Scope, impacts and interdependencies

Define the work necessary to meet the business objectives outlined in Section 2.2 and to create the outputs described in Section 2.4. Include:

- the areas impacted by the outcome of the project (boundaries of the project);
- any aspects specifically excluded from the project;
- key interdependencies with other projects (see Chapter 20).

You should also state, in broad terms:

- the impact the project will have on current business operations and existing projects;
- the functions or departments in your organization which will be affected.

Interdependency. If Project B requires a deliverable from Project A in order to achieve its objective, Project B is dependent on Project A, i.e., a deliverable is passed from one project to another.

For example, Project A builds a computer platform as one of its deliverables. Project B uses this platform to run software it has built as one of its deliverables. If Project A failed, Project B will fail as it is dependent on it.

A deliverable can be created by one project only. It may, however, be used by many subsequent projects.

Scope

The project scope must comprise everything needed to ensure that the benefits can be realized. There should be no assumptions that "others" are providing a key part. If other projects are providing deliverables, this must be stated explicitly as a dependency, not assumed.

2.6 Deliverables

List the major deliverables from your project which are needed to create the outputs described in Section 2.4. Deliverables may take two forms:

- **Final deliverables** – to be handed over by the project team to the users at the end of the project (e.g. hardware, software systems, brochures, product specifications, tariffs, business processes).
- **Temporary deliverables** – to be produced during the course of the project for review and sign-off (e.g. feasibility report, business case).

For each deliverable, specify:

- the format and content in which it is to be produced (e.g. a written report, TV advertisement);
- the named individual accountable for its production;
- the named individual(s) accountable for reviewing and/or approving it.

If the list is extensive, you should detail them in an appendix and list only the key ones in the main body of the document.

2.7 Schedule

Outline the overall project timescales by stating the target completion dates for key milestones. Include all the gates. Add any other significant milestones or events such as the letting of a major contract or significant reviews.

2.8 Costs

Outline the overall costs for each stage of the project and for each work package within each stage. Include a sum for scope reserve and contingency.

2.9 Risks

This section should contain:

- a list of the significant threats and opportunities with the potential to jeopardize or enhance the success of the project;
- actions to be taken at the outset to reduce the likelihood or impact of each risk identified;
- actions or contingency plans that may be implemented, should any risk happen.

You may conveniently present this in the form of a risk log. (See Chapter 23 for a full discussion of risks.)

2.10 Prerequisites, assumptions and constraints

Include:

- any circumstances outside your control which must be in place if your project is to be successful;
- key assumptions about the environment (e.g. economic factors, competitors, systems, people) in which your project is to be conducted;
- any constraints imposed on your project which may affect the outcome.

It is important to list all assumptions and constraints, even if they appear obvious to you; they may not be so obvious to others associated with the project or may even be forgotten as time moves on.

A contractor was using a major system engineering programme as a vehicle to break into a new market and build the expertise to grow the business in this more profitable line of work. The cost estimate for undertaking the work exceeded the bid price, generating a loss. This loss was assumed to be acceptable, bearing in mind the whole programme was an exercise in building a new business and more lucrative work would follow, either as variations on the existing contract or in new contracts. Within a few years and after a few changes of leadership, the planned loss was noted and the current team blamed for continuing with unprofitable work. By not keeping in mind the original business objectives, the overriding business objective for winning the work was forgotten and simple short-term profit objectives imposed. That organization never managed to build the capability to enter the lucrative system engineering sector and after a few more years dismantled the capabilities it had developed.

2.11 Project approach

Describe how the project will be undertaken and explain why you have chosen this particular approach. Include:

- the life cycle model to be applied and key activities undertaken in each project stage;
- how managerial (gating), technical (reviews), and quality aspects will be governed;
- what aspects of the project's outputs or work will be bespoke, undertaken by suppliers, or reuse of existing service or capability;
- the processes and methods to be used for specialist and technical work packages.

2.12 Analysis of options

Summarize the key points from the investigative studies, stating which options were investigated, which have been rejected and which have been carried forward for further analysis. Give your reasons for any choices made.

Workout 17.2 – Defining a project

Take any new project that you are associated with. With the project sponsor, project manager and key team members, create, in a workshop environment, the project definition part of the business case document. Use flip charts and base it on the template given in Table 17.1.

Ensure you answer every section fully – it all counts.

Note where there are gaps in the answers. Be honest. You will fool no one but yourself in the long term.

Work with the team to fill the gaps identified in this workout:

- if you don't know *why* you are doing the project, consider terminating it;
- if you don't know *what* you are delivering, regard your costs and timescales as unstable and your risk high;
- if you don't know *when* it will be done, carry out more investigations until you do know;
- if you don't know *how* you will approach the project, regard risk as high and investigate further.

Workout 17.3 – Project definition checklist

Use this checklist to review any projects currently in progress.

Criteria

- Has a project definition been written, reviewed by the stakeholders and approved by the project sponsor?
- Have the benefits been fully assessed and quantified wherever possible?
- Is the outcome clearly described? Would you recognize it if you saw it?
- Will the benefits you need lead from the outcomes?
- Are the outputs sufficient, taking into account interdependencies, to enable the desired outcomes?
- Have all significant risks been identified, categorized, and taken into account in the plan and business case?
- Has a comprehensive and satisfactory work breakdown been developed?
- Does the work breakdown reflect the deliverables to be produced?
- Are all key logical relationships between projects and activities clear?
- Has the plan been developed to minimize or offset the risks?

The only way a project can be delivered is by its deliverables. For each deliverable, check:

- Are the project deliverables relevant and are they feasible both to produce and use?
- Have quality criteria been established?
- Is it clear who is accountable for preparing each deliverable?
- Is it clear what resources are needed?
- Is it clear who will review the deliverable prior to signing off acceptance of each deliverable?
- Is it clear who will approve each deliverable?
- Has sufficient time been allowed for reviewing/amending each deliverable?

Project definitions which make a difference

A major food manufacturer was undertaking a radical reorganization of its processes and working methods. This involved warehousing, distribution, manufacturing, marketing, human resources, and sales. In all, there were seven projects within the complex change programme. A considerable amount of study work had been completed and some of the projects had actually started. The managing director asked his management team, each member of which was sponsoring one or more projects, to write up each project in a form similar to that given in this book. When asked how long it would take, they all said a week. The managing director gave them two weeks.

Seven weeks later the last project definition arrived. "What took you so long?" the managing director asked. One director said that as he was writing his, it dawned on him, he wasn't really sure what he was doing. Further, when they read each other's documents, they were surprised and often perturbed at how their colleagues had interpreted the same brief. The extra time was to work together on the gaps and to check that they all formed a coherent programme of work.

Testing if people are really working on their definitions or merely paying lip service

For the projects in the case study, I designed a front cover with a space for the name and signature of the project sponsor and project manager. No one was asked to sign anything. Of the seven documents, four came back, unprompted, with both signatures and the other three with only that of the project manager.

Guess which projects proceeded more smoothly and with fewer misunderstandings!

I do not advocate inky signatures on every piece of paper. It looks too much like bureaucracy but it can be used as a device to test commitment in a culture where a signature has value.

Prepare the project plan

A project plan is not simply a time line. A good plan tells the entire story of the project: who is accountable, who is involved, when things happen and how much it will cost. The sole purpose of the plan is to ensure you achieve the project's business objectives and keep the risks at an acceptable level. It acts as the baseline against which you can monitor progress and which makes terms such as "late", "early" and "overspent" meaningful. Figure 17.2 outlines the main steps to prepare a project plan, which are:

- **define the scope** – specify the high-level activities (work packages) which need to be performed to complete the project scope and the target dates for their completion; develop a work breakdown structure; identify an owner for each work package;
- **determine schedule** – identify activities, put them in sequence and estimate durations;
- **estimate resources** – identify the people and equipment needed to undertake the work to the defined schedule;
- **estimate costs** – calculate the cost of undertaking the work;
- **assess viability** – assess the benefit that will result together with the risks; check the plan, as a whole will meet the business objectives. If the plan is not viable, then rework it until it is. If no viable plan can be developed, there project should not proceed.

Earlier in this chapter we discovered that "projects designed solely by one person usually lack the quality and level of involvement necessary for achieving extraordinary results". I was illustrating the vital team-building benefits of working together at the start of the project. The benefits are, however, far more practical and tangible than that. If a team develops an approach to the project and plans it together, there will be debate and argument based on the differing perspectives of each team member. As a result of such discussions, each member will come to understand the needs and viewpoints of the others. Blind spots will be eliminated. Building a good plan is hard work but once done, it becomes embedded in the minds of those who created it. Each individual is less likely to make isolated decisions on his/her work scope which will have adverse effects on the work of others. Similarly, when things go wrong (as they probably will), the team members will know more instinctively the correct way to handle it. Team members will be more likely to concur on the method of resolution: they will have already cleared away all the interdisciplinary blockages in their minds when they created the original plan.

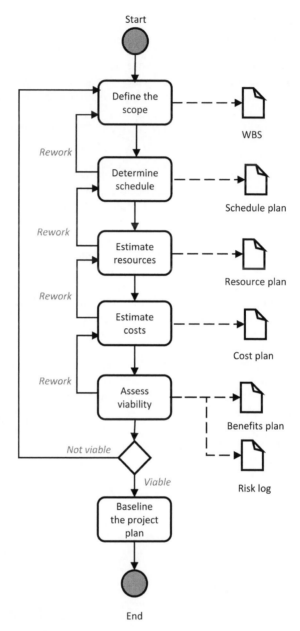

Figure 17.2 Developing a project plan

The project plan is developed in an iterative way, ensuring that the schedule, resources, and costs components of the plan are consistent and will achieve the project's business objectives at an acceptable level of risk.

If you have no plan, all roads lead there

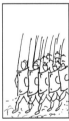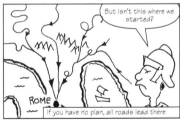

Copyright © 1997 Robert Buttrick

The project was one which comprised a number of related software changes to four interrelated systems. The owner of each system had planned their parts of the project, BUT no one had, as yet, put them all together. They spent two full days locked in a room listing what each needed from the others and eventually built a plan showing how the whole project fitted together. They had it on large sheets of paper with Post-It Notes joined by arrows. It was hard work. They didn't understand each other. Everyone else was unreasonable. They didn't know why the "others" had to do their work in such an inconvenient way (a way inconvenient to them).

Once completed, the plan looked obvious. The approach was clear and the team members were happy with each other. They had even agreed who would be accountable for end-to-end testing across the systems (previously missing from the plan). When the inevitable happened and one team member's part went wrong, there was no blame apportioned, only solutions offered. They didn't even need to consult the plan; they knew it well enough as it was theirs.
The project was completed successfully.

"Planning is everything – the plan is nothing"
DWIGHT D EISENHOWER

The core of the project plan

A good project plan should be made up of consistent plans for benefits, schedule, cost and resources, and would include:

- **Stages** – these represent the natural high-level break points in the project life cycle, looked at in Part II of this book (e.g. initial investigation, detailed investigation, develop and test, trial, release).

- **Work packages** – these represent the clusters of work within each stage, usually focused on a key deliverable. Work packages can be nested, that is to say, one work package may comprise a number of component work packages.
- **Activities** – these are the individual components of work within the work packages that must be undertaken to complete the project. They are the lowest level in the work breakdown structure.
- **Milestones** – these are the significant events which should be used to monitor progress at a summary level. They would include the gates at the start of each stage, the end-point of each stage, delivery of significant deliverables, realization of an outcome together with any other milestones which are considered significant and need to be tracked.
- **Deliverables** – each of the key deliverables defined in the project definition should be shown in the plan. Use milestones to represent their completion.
- **Reviews** – include reviews at key points throughout the project when qualty, progress and performance will be critically evaluated.
- **Interdependencies** – define all inputs from (and outputs to) other projects. These should include all those defined in the project definition.

You will rarely be able to plan a project in full at the very start but you should always be able to plan the next stage in detail, with an outline plan for the remainder.

Format of the project plan

Cost and resource plans are best shown in tabular format, perhaps summarized in a graphical format (S-curve) or histogram. See Chapters 21 and 22 for a fuller treatment of these topics.

Project schedule plans are most conveniently presented as bar charts, two forms of which are illustrated on the following pages:

- In detail – (Figure 17.3) a progress bar chart, used by the project manager and the team members to control their day-to-day work. This contains all the elements defined in the previous section.
- In summary – (Figure 17.4) a management summary used to present overall progress of the project to the project sponsor, project board, and other interested parties. This should show the stages, milestones, and other important activities necessary to give an overview of the project. (See Chapter 20 for a fuller treatment of schedule planning.)

Having developed the project plan, you should now be able to complete Sections 2.3 to 2.11 of the business case and definition defined in Table 17.1.

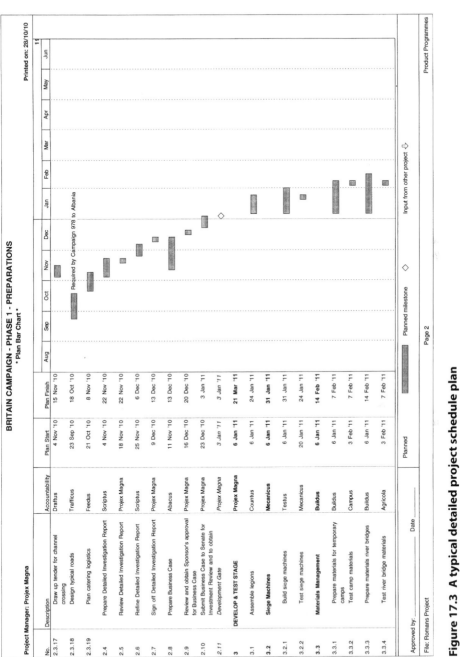

BRITAIN CAMPAIGN - PHASE 1 - PREPARATIONS
* Plan Bar Chart *

Project Manager: Projex Magna

Printed on: 28/10/10

No.	Description	Accountability	Plan Start	Plan Finish
2.3.17	Draw up tender for channel crossing	Draftus	4 Nov '10	15 Nov '10
2.3.18	Design typical roads	Trafficus	23 Sep '10	18 Oct '10
2.3.19	Plan catering logistics	Feedus	21 Oct '10	8 Nov '10
2.4	Prepare Detailed Investigation Report	Scriptus	4 Nov '10	22 Nov '10
2.5	Review Detailed Investigation Report	Projex Magna	18 Nov '10	22 Nov '10
2.6	Refine Detailed Investigation Report	Scriptus	25 Nov '10	6 Dec '10
2.7	Sign off Detailed Investigation Report	Projex Magna	9 Dec '10	13 Dec '10
2.8	Prepare Business Case	Abacus	11 Nov '10	13 Dec '10
2.9	Review and obtain Sponsor's approval for Business Case	Projex Magna	16 Dec '10	20 Dec '10
2.10	Submit Business Case to Senate for Investment Review and to obtain	Projex Magna	23 Dec '10	3 Jan '11
2.11	Development Gate	Projex Magna	3 Jan '11	3 Jan '11
3	DEVELOP & TEST STAGE	Projex Magna	6 Jan '11	21 Mar '11
3.1	Assemble legions	Countus	6 Jan '11	24 Jan '11
3.2	Siege Machines	Mecanicus	6 Jan '11	31 Jan '11
3.2.1	Build siege machines	Testus	6 Jan '11	31 Jan '11
3.2.2	Test siege machines	Mecanicus	20 Jan '11	24 Jan '11
3.3	Materials Management	Buildus	6 Jan '11	14 Feb '11
3.3.1	Prepare materials for temporary camps	Buildus	6 Jan '11	7 Feb '11
3.3.2	Test camp materials	Campus	3 Feb '11	7 Feb '11
3.3.3	Prepare materials river bridges	Buildus	6 Jan '11	14 Feb '11
3.3.4	Test river bridge materials	Agricola	3 Feb '11	7 Feb '11

Timeline months: Aug, Sep, Oct, Nov, Dec, Jan, Feb, Mar, Apr, May, Jun

Required by Campaign 978 to Albania

Approved by: _____ Date _____

Planned   Planned milestone ◇   Input from other project ⇨

File: Romans Project   Page 2   Product Programmes

Figure 17.3 A typical detailed project schedule plan

BRITAIN CAMPAIGN - PHASE 1 - PREPARATIONS

* Summary Plan Bar Chart *

Project Manager: Projex Magna | **Printed on: 28/10/10**

No.	Description	Accountability	Plan Start	Plan Finish
1	INITIAL INVESTIGATION	Projex Magna	1 Aug '10	6 Sep '10
2	DETAILED INVESTIGATION STAGE	Projex Magna	9 Sep '10	3 Jan '11
2.3	Undertake Detailed Investigation	Projex Magna	23 Sep '10	15 Nov '11
3	DEVELOP & TEST STAGE	Projex Magna	6 Jan '11	21 Mar '11
3.2	Siege Machines	Mecanicus	6 Jan '11	31 Jan '11
3.3	Materials Management	Buildus	6 Jan '11	14 Feb '11
3.4	Boats	Buildus	6 Jan '11	7 Mar '11
3.6	Training	Militus	27 Jan '11	21 Mar '11
3.7	Campaign catering	Feedus	6 Jan '11	7 Mar '11
4	TRIAL STAGE	Quintus Sextus	17 Feb '11	14 Mar '11
5	RELEASE STAGE	Projex Magna	17 Mar '11	14 Apr '11

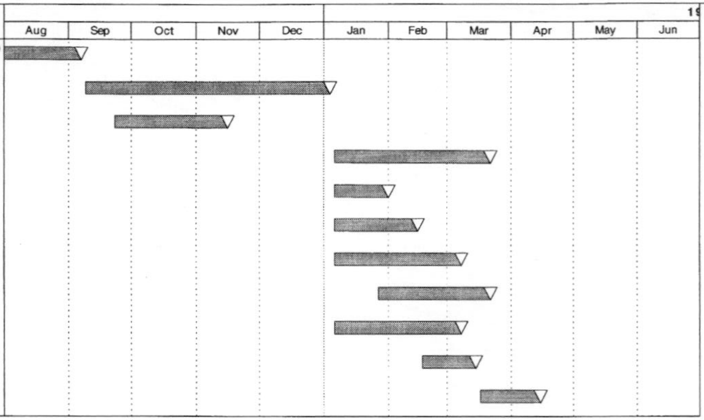

Approved by: ____________ Date: ________

Plan

File: Romans Project | Page 1 | Product Programmes

Figure 17.4 A typical summary project schedule plan

Define your project organization

Once you have planned a project, you should make sure the organizational and management aspects of the project are addressed, including defining:

- the organization structure and roles;
- project progress reporting needs;
- who can authorize changes to the project;
- who is accountable for gate decisions;
- what formal review points are required;
- project administration needs (information management and filing).

Project organization chart and roles

This should reflect the work you did when you set up the project team. Remember this is likely to evolve as the project progresses.

Set up your progress reporting

If you are the project manager, you are accountable for controlling the project and taking the necessary actions to ensure that it delivers the expected outputs and outcomes. You need to understand what is actually happening and identify problems while there is still time to correct them. We'll look at this in more detail in Chapter 18.

You should plan to gather your team together on a regular basis and check progress made against the plan and what progress is forecast. You should also assess the issues which have arisen and the risks looming on the horizon. Don't just focus on the near term, always look to the long term asking, "Will this project still deliver the outcomes needed?"

Progress should be recorded by updating the project benefits, schedule and cost forecasts to show:

- activities completed and milestones achieved;
- forecasts of completion dates for activities in progress (or not yet started) where these are known to differ from the agreed plan (e.g. slippage);
- costs spent to date;
- forecasts of costs to complete the current stage of the project and for completing the project in full.

Additionally you should prepare, for the project sponsor and other key stakeholders, a concise progress report to include the following information:

1   Business objectives;
2   Progress summary and outlook;
3   Financials;
4   Milestones;
5   Key issues;
6   Key risks – threats and opportunities;
7   Changes.

A description of the content of each of these sections follows. Progress reporting should be active, with you telling the stakeholders what they need to know in as concise a form as possible. If your organization has a single defined format for the report, then that is excellent. It helps make sure the reports are full and complete and aids the reader by providing a familiar, consistent format. Similarly, if you have a reporting system, use the same headings.

Make sure your reports:

- are forward-looking, focusing on the likelihood of the benefits being realized and objectives achieved;
- are honest, without undermining confidence; don't hide the bad news;
- are focused on key issues;
- are moderated by a realistic view on the risks;
- acknowledge the achievements of the team members.

Document how you intend reporting to be undertaken in Section 3.2 of the business case. This should list the reports which need to be produced, whom they are for, who prepares them and their content. As a minimum you are likely to have:

- reports from the team managers to the project manager;
- reports from the project manager to the project sponsor and board.

Contents of a project manager's progress report

1. Business objectives

As some stakeholders will not be familiar with your project, you should summarize:

- the business objectives the project will satisfy;
- how the project supports your business strategy.

This is taken from Section 2.2 of the business case. This repetition also means the reason the project was created in the first place is not forgotten in the hurly burly of delivery and a changing environment.

2. Progress summary and outlook

Briefly describe the progress of the project, both in terms of achievements to date and expected future performance. Will it achieve its objectives? For any significant schedule slippage or cost variance give:

- the reason;
- its impact;
- any corrective action being taken.

3. Financials

Provide a summary of the project finances in terms of expected benefits, spend to date and total expected spend compared to that planned. Keep scope reserve and contingency visible. See Table 17.2.

Table 17.2 Sample summary of project finances

	Actual this month £000	Actual to date £000	Previous to date £000	Estimate to completion £000	Forecast at completion £000	Budget £000
Benefits	200	3000	3200	2500	5700	6000
Time costs	20	920	900	370	1290	1180
Purchases	20	480	460	150	630	520
Scope reserve				0	0	100
Contingency				70	70	200
TOTAL COST	40	1400	1360	590	1790	2000
Contribution	160	1600	1840	1910	3910	4000

4. Milestones

List the major milestones. As shown in Table 17.3, these should at least include the gate milestones as defined in Part II. For each give:

- original and current baseline date;
- forecast date or actual date achieved;
- a confidence indicator (how confident a manager is in achieving the forecast date).

Table 17.3 Sample milestone record

	Original date	Current baseline date	Current forecast date	Date achieved	Confidence H/M/L
Initial investigation gate	31 Jul 2017	31 Jul 2017	31 Jul 2017	31 Jul 2017	
Detailed investigation gate	1 Sep 2017	1 Sep 2017	1 Sep 2017	1 Sep 2017	
Development gate	1 Oct 2017	1 Oct 2017	1 Oct 2017	1 Oct 2017	
Trial gate	24 Oct 2017	24 Oct 2017	24 Oct 2017	24 Oct 2017	
Release gate	31 Oct 2017	31 Oct 2017	31 Oct 2017	31 Oct 2017	
launch	1 Dec 2017	1 Dec 2017	18 Dec 2017		Medium
Project completed	2 Jan 2018	15 Jan 2018	8 Feb 2018		High

5. Key issues

Describe the key issues requiring escalation for resolution. For each give:

- the nature and impact of the issue;
- action being taken to resolve the issue and who is accountable.

These are not necessarily the "top issues", but those that you want to draw to the project sponsor's attention at this point in time.

6. Key risks – threats and opportunities

Summarize the significant threats and major opportunities which have arisen. For each give:

- the nature and impact of the threat or opportunity;
- action being taken to manage the threat or opportunity and who is accountable.

These are not necessarily the "top risks", but those that you want to draw the project sponsor's attention to at this point in time.

7. Changes

List all outstanding changes beyond the project manager's authority to approve. For each give:

- the reason for the change;
- impact of the change;
- who is accountable for authorizing the change;
- the change status.

8. Attachments or references

It might be convenient to attach or cross-reference the sources of the above:

- cost report;
- progress bar chart;
- issues log;

- risks log;
- opportunities log;
- change log.

A report from a team manager to a project manager would be similar, but would focus only on the delivery of the work package(s) the team manager is accountable for:

1. Progress summary and outlook;
2. Costs;
3. Milestones;
4. Key issues;
5. Key risks – threats and opportunities;
6. Changes.

Under a bushel

Don't be modest; if you don't acknowledge the achievements made by you and your team on the project, don't be surprised if the stakeholders don't either. It has been said that the definition of an easy project is one which is successful. If it wasn't easy, it would have failed. The project managers and teams of successful projects are, therefore, in danger of becoming "invisible" or having their achievements undervalued even if it was their own hard work, excellent planning and adherence to best practice which got them there. DON'T BE INVISIBLE!

Change control

Once the project has been authorized, its scope, cost, benefits, and timescale are baselined and used as the basis on which to monitor progress. Under certain circumstances it is, however, legitimate (and often desirable and/or unavoidable) to change these baselines. Who authorizes such changes depends very much on the impact. It is, therefore, essential that the extent of the authority given to the project manager and project sponsor is defined. (Chapter 25 describes this more fully.)

Document who has accountability for authorizing changes in Section 3.3 of the business case.

Gates and review points

The management framework comprises a staged approach to projects with the "gates" defining the key points when a formal project review is undertaken related to

As a guide, a project should have a formal review every three months or when a major commitment is to be made. The occurrence of such reviews should be formally documented, as they comprise an essential part in managing the risks on an organization-wide basis.

a decision to start the next stage. If, however, the time lapse in a stage is very long, which can happen, particularly in the develop and test stage, it is essential to build a sufficient number of additional review points into the plan to check that:

- the project still meets a real business need and is achievable;
- the quality of the deliverables is adequate;
- the plans are in place;
- the project organization is working.

As a guide, a project should have a formal review every three months or when a major commitment is to be made. The occurrence of such reviews should be formally documented, as they comprise an essential part in managing the risks on an organization-wide basis.

Reviews are often regarded as taking up valuable time and hampering progress on the project. It is, however, in the project sponsor's interest that reviews take place. (Chapter 27 discusses reviews more fully.)

Document the additional reviews in Section 3.4 of the business case.

Workout 17.4 – Project organization checklist

Use this checklist to audit any projects currently in progress. Remember the following are an aspect of "governance", so make sure you are familiar with the theory from Chapter 16.

Criteria

- Does the project's organization structure and role reflect reality?
- Have progress reporting formats and timing been defined?
- Have progress reporting lines been agreed (who sends which report to whom)?
- Has a system for capturing and managing risks been set up?
- Has a system for capturing and managing issues been set up?
- Has a system for recording and approving changes been set up?
- Is it clear who has the authority to make go/no go decisions at each gate and who should be consulted?
- Are there enough reviews in the project plan and is it clear what purpose each review fulfils, and who are the reviewers?

Define how you will manage your project

Just a reminder: if your organization has an enterprise-wide project management method and you are following it, then there is no need to define your management plan in any detail; it would simply repeat the standard approach, which would be a pointless waste of time. You would only need to say how you have tailored any standard method.

Benefits, risks, issues, and change control

Each of the topics under this section are covered in the respective chapters in this part of *The Project Workout*, together with the associated workouts to help you.

Project administration – document and information management

This is something you will have to define and set up, otherwise your project will soon degenerate into chaos. Projects can generate a considerable volume of information, correspondence, and reports, most of which needs to be accessible and some of which needs to be archived for operational, regulatory, or legal reasons. It is essential for the project manager to set up the administration of the project as soon as practical and ensure all team members and support staff understand what is required and available. The format and media for storing such documentation can vary from being paper-based to a full electronic "groupware" platform accessed via an intranet. Tools such as Microsoft's SharePoint and OpenText's Livelink are commonly used as many organizations already have these deployed. All the major project management tools also include features to aid information management; used well and across the whole organization, they can be very effective: used badly, and inconsistently they can be as bad as any poor, paper-based system.

In many cases, different types of information can be held in different formats thus harnessing the capabilities of any support tools and avoiding duplication. Regardless of how you choose to store the information, its content will be similar. The following comprises a checklist on which to base your own project administration requirements. Benchmarking shows many organizations have a prescribed structure, such as the following, to ensure that records are kept in a consistent way, enabling newcomers to the project, as well as current team members, to know where to start looking for the information they require. By having a consistent structure, project assurance and auditors will be able to access the information needed to undertake their work without having to divert the project team from their duties.

Chapter 28 covers document management.

Project management tools will be looked at in more detail in *The Programme and Portfolio Workout*.

Contents of a project file

1. Project summary details

This should comprise a short description of the project and the names of those holding the key accountabilities.

2. Contact list

A list of all the team members, their roles and how they can be contacted.

3. Project log or diary

A chronological record, owned by the project manager, of significant meetings, events and commitments. This should refer to detail in other sections of the file where appropriate.

4. Business case and change log

This section contains the fundamental definition of and case for your project. The change log is an amendment record, listing any changes to the business case which are under consideration or which have already been approved or authorized. By having a change log as a supplement to the business case, you avoid the need for updating the main document for every change. You need only reissue it when the number of changes becomes too unwieldy to keep in separate documents.

5. Progress reports

All regular and special progress reports should be retained. If a number of different reports are to be prepared for particular audiences, this section should be subdivided accordingly.

6. Project logs

- Issues log
- Risk log
- Lessons learned log.

7. Schedule

This section contains a copy of the most recent schedule showing achievement and forecast against the agreed plan.

8. Finances

This section contains the most recent cost and benefit position showing achievement and forecast against the agreed plan.

9. Meetings

All meetings should either be minuted or notes produced to promote clear communication. This should include:

- agreements: record any agreements made (even agreements to disagree!);
- actions: be clear who has the accountability for any actions, when they have to be done by and who the recipients are for outputs from those actions.

10. Key deliverables

This section comprises a listing of the key deliverables (with accountabilities for preparation, review, and approval). Copies of the documents themselves must be held for team use and archive purposes. Table 17.4 gives some examples.

PLUS any others that are required, as defined in the project, such as detailed specifications, requirements, documents, tender documents, etc.

Table 17.4 Sample list of key deliverables

For gate decisions	Other deliverables
1. Proposal	Output Description
2. Ready for Trial Report	Feasibility Report
3. Ready for Service Report	Test Plan
4. Project Closure Report	Test Results
5. Post-Implementation Review Report	Trial Plan
	Trial Results

11. Correspondence

Record of all incoming and outgoing correspondence.

12. Reviews

Copies of any additional project reviews, other than the mandatory gate reviews (held in Section 10), should be kept.

For complex projects, individual subprojects and work packages should follow a similar structure to that held for the overall project.

Workout 17.5 – Management plan

As already stated, the content of Section 4 of the business case and definition is very much dependent on whether or not the organization hosting your project has an enterprise method. If it has, then Section 4 may be very slim. However, regardless of this, it must cover the topics.

1. Use the following to check whether you and your project team understand how to manage each aspect:

    •   Benefits realization management
    •   Reporting
    •   Planning
    •   Risks and issues
    •   Change control
    •   Document and information management
    •   Configuration management

2. Go back to your output from Workout 16.1 and check that your project organization, definition, plan and management plan adequately deal with each aspect of governance.

Identify and engage your stakeholders

Ignore stakeholders at your peril

Every project will create some change in the organization, otherwise there would be no point in undertaking it! Some changes, however, are "easier" to effect than others as they align with the status quo and do not cross any politically sensitive boundaries. In essence, most of the people carry on as they always have done. Other changes are fundamental and result in shifts in power bases internal to the organization or even external, such as unions, suppliers, or customers.

Stakeholders are those affected by the project. All those involved in the project are, therefore, stakeholders. There are also those who take no direct part in the project as team members, but whose activities will, in some way, be changed as a result. These could be users of new systems, people in new departments resulting from reorganizations (or those made redundant), those taking roles in new processes as managers, supervisors, and workers. Often the project is of little importance to them but they are of great consequence to the project if their consent is critical to success. It is essential to identify them because it is critical to enrol them at an early stage in the project to ensure their power does not cause the project to fail later. Never under-estimate stakeholders' ability to ruin your best- laid plans!

Never underestimate stakeholders' ability to ruin your best laid plans!

It is both the project manager's and project sponsor's role to ensure all stakeholders are identified and adequately briefed on the project. Too much communication will drown them – they won't read it or bother listening. Not enough will mean your project will be lower down their priority list than you want it to be.

Engaging stakeholders and keeping them enrolled is a taxing but essential task. It is accomplished both by a formal communication plan and by "enrolling behaviour" on behalf of all the project team on both a planned and opportunistic basis.

Sources of power

All organizations are "political" to some extent and the greater your project's scope to change the status quo, the more you will need to be tuned in. You will need to identify the power bases you and others are operating from. These include:

*   **Position**, which results from rank and formal authority. This can be actual or "reflected" (when a person uses the position of their boss to enhance their own standing).

- **Status**, which results from how people perceive an individual, often related to their charisma and leadership qualities and may bear no relationship to facts of any particular project.
- **Resource**, where a person has direct authority over resources and can therefore smooth the way for, or block, any initiative requiring those resources. This can be directors, managers, or unions.
- **Expertise**, where the knowledge or skill of an individual is such that others listen to and follow them.
- **Legal and regulatory**, where a group or body has authority over the "rules of engagement" for your industry.

Chapter 26 discusses stakeholder management more fully.

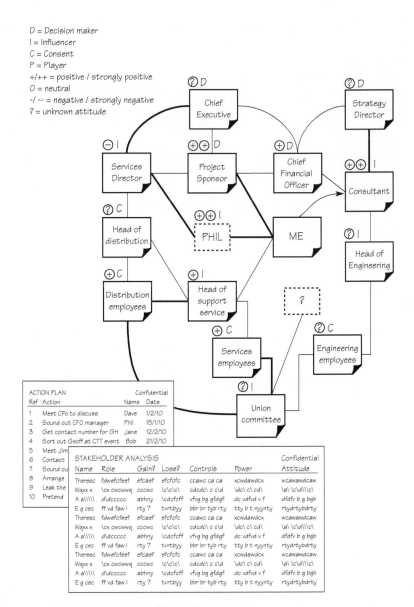

Figure 17.5 A typical stakeholder influence map

The typical output from stakeholder analysis. Key individuals have been identified and a list of their characteristics drawn up. Relationships are shown by lines between the individuals – thick lines represent strong relationships. A number of key individuals have unknown attitudes to the project. Use existing relationships or develop new relationships to address these. Don't rely on the hierarchy. Finally, agree an action plan and be very careful who you allow to see these documents!

Workout 17.6 – Stakeholder influence mapping

To be done in project team mode.

1 Brainstorm who your stakeholders are. Write each on a Post-It® Note and stick them onto a white board or flip chart. Stakeholders may be individuals or groups.
2 Cluster the stakeholders into groups based on similar need or impact from the project. Rationalize the stakeholder list if possible, but don't worry if you can't.
3 Define the role of each stakeholder (Figure 17.5). Stakeholder roles are defined as:

- **Decision maker** – this stakeholder is required to make a decision regarding the project.
- **Influencer** – this stakeholder has influence over the project and/or over the decision makers.
- **Player** – this stakeholder is required to play a part in the project, perhaps providing resources, facilities, or review time.
- **Consent** – the consent of this stakeholder is required if the project is to be a success (e.g., computer system users, customers).

4 Take each stakeholder in turn and, using one flip chart per stakeholder, answer the following questions:

- What is this person or group's stake in the project?
- What is their role in the organization?
- What will they gain as a result of the project?
- What will they lose as a result of the project?
- What do they control, which the project needs?
- What is their source of power now (see above)?
- What will be their source of power after the project (see above)?
- What is their attitude to the project? (strong/weak/positive/neutral/negative)?
- How are they likely to be influenced (e.g. emotional or logic)?

It may be convenient to capture this information in a template for future reference.

5 Write "ME" in a bubble in the centre of a white board. Write those stakeholders you have direct access to around "ME" and join them to "ME" with a line. Use a thin line for a weak link and a thick line for a strong link. Use + or –, or 0, to indicate if they are positive, negative, or neutral to the project. Use **?** if you don't know. This map indicates the stakeholders you have direct access to.
6 Write the remainder of the stakeholders in boxes around the edges of the white board. Using + , – , 0, to indicate if they are positive, negative, or neutral to the project. Use ? if you don't know.

7 Write on the white board the names of others you have access to but who also have access to one or more of your stakeholders. You now have a "stakeholder influence diagram". You can use this to decide your action plan to enrol a particular stakeholder. You may do it yourself or it may be more effective to have others do it on your behalf.

Regarding stakeholders who are negative or neutral. You need to address them.

- For those stakeholders where the line of influence is missing or very long. You must aim to shorten it to gain access to that person.
- As for those whose attitudes are unknown, you must find out what they are.
- Monitor the neutral ones, to ensure they do not become antagonistic.

18

Monitoring, controlling, and reporting

Who, what and when?

Making reporting work for you

Projects must be, and be seen to be, under control; no one is likely to invest money in an enterprise perceived as poorly managed and out of control.

"An unwatched pot boils immediately"

H F ELLIS

- **Only collect information that will be used to control the work.**
- **Check what you are being told – go and see for yourself.**
- **Keep reports timely, simple and relevant to the recipient.**
- **Don't forget to monitor what is happening outside the project.**
- **Act on deviations, once verified – change the plan if needed!**

Who, what and when?

Why monitor, control and report?

The aims of monitoring, controlling and reporting are to ensure you know what is happening and give confidence to the sponsor and stakeholders that the project is being managed well. In particular, you should:

- make sure the project's business objectives are still likely to be met;
- ensure important milestones are met;
- control the allocation and use of resources and funds;
- manage threats to the project's benefits, schedule, cost, resources and deliverables;
- identify opportunities to reduce the cost and timescales or increase the benefits;
- control changes to the project.

Projects must be, and be seen to be, under control; no one is likely to invest money, whether their own or corporate funds, in an enterprise perceived as poorly managed and out of control. Monitoring and control is about making sure the project will be successful or terminating it if it is longer viable. If you can deal with threats, exploit opportunities, minimize costs, reduce the time taken whilst increasing the quality of the delivered product or service, you are more likely to achieve your objectives.

Monitoring and control is also about setting realistic expectations of project performance. Projects do not always go well, even with the best sponsor, project manager, and project team. By having an effective monitoring, control, and reporting regime, you should be able to spot any problems and alert the right stakeholders.

- **Monitoring** project work involves measuring and comparing achievement against the plan.
- **Controlling** is about taking proactive corrective and preventative actions to rectify deviations from the plan and to respond to changes in the project's context. Such measures should be forward looking, keeping the work on course to meet the business objectives, whilst taking advantage of beneficial changes and reducing the effect of negative changes.

Q • **Reporting** lets those who need to know what is happening and likely to happen, so that they can take the appropriate action.

Figure 18.1 shows the key aspects of monitoring, control and reporting in relation to the project control cycle.

Who monitors, controls, and reports?

Monitoring, control and reporting should be done at all levels in a project, using the work breakdown structure as the key; Chapter 16 (Governance) looked at this.

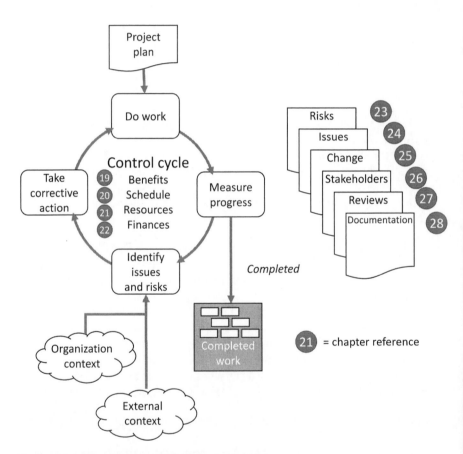

Figure 18.1 Monitoring, control, and reporting

The control cycle is at the heart of monitoring, controlling and reporting and is used to make sure the project is on track to deliver the outcomes needed. Project work, however, is not the only focus, as it is essential to ensure the project still makes sense in the context of what else is happening in the organization and in the external environment within which the organization operates.

Monitoring, controlling, and reporting is undertaken by the project sponsor, project manager, and team managers. The aspects monitored are the same no matter the position in the hierarchy of a person but the focus and degree of detail tends to increase at lower levels in the work breakdown structure. A sponsor should be focused on the project's external context and expected benefits, whilst a team manager will be concerned with the outputs or outcomes they are accountable for.

Not all activities need the same level of monitoring and control; concentrate on those activities which:

- are on the critical paths (but remember that critical paths can change);
- other project teams depend on;
- are due to start soon;
- cost a lot;
- take a long time (but try to split them into shorter activities);
- are difficult to measure progress on;
- are uncertain, in terms of output, timescale, or cost.

Each manager is responsible for setting up, in agreement with the higher-level manager, a way of monitoring the progress against the baselined plan. Their specific responsibilities include:

- identifying and solving problems before they affect the work and its outcomes;
- identifying opportunities for improvement;
- reporting progress;
- adding the results of decisions to the plans and telling their team members about the revised plans.

The project manager should design the most appropriate approach and agree this with the project sponsor. Having set the direction needed for monitoring the project as a whole, the project manager should ensure the team managers understand and agree with the approach. It is important to have "just enough" reporting for each person's need, balancing the effort taken with the value of the information obtained. This is easy to say but may take some trial and error to achieve.

What is monitored, controlled and reported on?

Having a baselined plan is fundamental to effective monitoring and control. Without a baseline, words such as "late", "early", "under-spent" have no meaning.

Having established this, important facets of the plan to monitor and control are:

- actual progress toward realizing your benefits;
- risks and issues;
- progress of any change requests;
- timescale, costs, and the resources needed;

- quality of the deliverables;
- robustness of the outcomes;
- benefits (expected and actual) against the business case;
- upstream external work (inter dependencies);
- outside influences.

Don't ignore this last point; because a project's context is always changing, the project sponsor should continually update the project manager with their view on how this context is evolving and the way this may affect the project's aims and how it is run. This will include what else is happening within the organization, as well as in the wider external context of that organization, in terms of political, economic, and competitive forces. This is why it is vital for a project sponsor and project manager to have an ongoing dialogue and positive relationship. A project manager is far more useful to a sponsor if they are seen as a junior partner rather than a subordinate. The more the project manager understands about the business context the project is delivering into, the better they can undertake their role.

Each of the chapters in Part III focuses on an aspect of project management and describes how each is achieved in terms of approach, techniques, and tools.

Monitoring and controlling specialist work

The heart of a project, however, is not its management; it is the specialist work which is undertaken and this varies depending on the type of project. A project is likely to involve many disciplines, each of which contributes to the overall solution. For example:

- system engineers to ensure every aspect of the overall solution will work as whole, fulfilling the business need;
- software specialists to produce applications;
- infrastructure specialists to design the hardware and equipment needed for the users of the application;
- building specialists to design and construct the facilities needed to house equipment and provide a working environment for the staff;
- training specialists to recommend how best to educate people in the use of the applications;
- change management specialists to determine how best to manage the resulting organization changes;
- communications specialists to deal with external stakeholders.

Each project's scope will be different, and different people will be part of the team, and how progress and the quality of the specialist deliverables are assessed will differ. If the work is able to be seen physically, as in construction, you can actually see the deliverables growing and measure progress against drawings and volumes of material used. If the work is invisible or less tangible, however, as in software development or business change, progress may not be so obvious. Each discipline will have its own ways of measuring progress and quality and it is essential you understand the approaches and metrics to build these into your control regime. Don't be afraid to challenge any such methods and don't take anything for granted until you are confident the approaches used by the specialist teams are sound and telling the right story. Seek alternative views from other specialists in the same discipline if necessary.

When to monitor, control and report

Monitoring, control, and reporting should begin as soon as the project starts. Even in the early part of the first project stage, when no baselined plans are available, you need to have a feel for how things are going. Having your own "plan for developing the plan" is useful, as you can set expectations and a start promoting a sense of discipline, rather than letting the work drift.

When you have finished the plan to the required level of detail and the "doing" starts, whether further investigative work or actual development, the rate of activity and, consequently, the rate of spending will increase. A fully effective monitoring and control regime must be in place before this really ramps up. Plans need to be prepared to reflect the monitoring regime to be used. For example, if agile delivery techniques are used, a plan takes a different form to one where the scope is fixed.

Different levels in a project and different types of work require different frequencies of reporting, as shown in the control cycle in Figure 18.1. The appropriate frequency for the cycle depends on the nature of the project, its stage of development and inherent risk. Completion of activities is evidence of progress but not sufficient to predict milestones will continue to be met. The manager should be continually checking that the plan is still fit for purpose and likely to realize the business benefits on time; the future is more important than the past as that is what you are trying to influence.

Often the control frequency is driven by regular reporting calendars set organizationally, but at other times, reporting may need to be "ad-hoc", such as for high-priority issues and exception reporting. For regular reporting, the frequency may range from daily, which is used in agile techniques and also the roll-out or provisioning of some services to quarterly, as for some high-level boards. Reporting frequency is usually driven by:

- the stakeholders' actual or perceived needs for information;
- the sponsor or project manager's actual or perceived needs to stay informed and their assessment of risk;
- organizational practice set, say, by a programme management office or other overseeing body.

The frequency of the control cycle can change through the life of a project and need not be consistent across a project. For instance, daily or weekly reporting on one work package may be necessary, whist two-weekly on others may be adequate.

Making reporting more convenient – getting the timing right

A large organization, which operated across the world, had the practice of requiring the project manager for each of over 2,000 projects to report on the project in a central system by 5 pm, every Friday, UK time. The assumption was, to be useful, all project reports had to be synchronized or there may be mismatches. Being an international organization meant staff in the Middle East were having their weekend break and staff in the Americas were either still in bed or just starting the working day. Staff in the Far East had just woken up to the start of their weekend. The reporting time did not fit global working patterns and time zone and so relaxations were allowed. That left, however, a large number of people in the UK and Europe still having to submit their reports right at the end of the week and all at the same time. The information systems, mostly unused throughout the week, suddenly had to take on peak load for just one hour every week. Consequently, people were often locked out of the system and had to wait into the evening to submit their reports. In most cases, nobody looked at the reports until they returned to work after the weekend. The attitude to reporting was starting to degrade into being mere "lip service" with the quality of the reports suffering as a result.

The company solved this problem by challenging their own assumption that reporting needed to be synchronized. They had already delinked reporting from the "due time" everywhere outside Europe and then asked themselves, why not do this for every project, everywhere? This is exactly what they did. They allowed each project manager to decide when it was best to report on their project (in agreement with the sponsor or, if in a programme, programme manager), simply insisting that at any point in time no project report should be more than eight days old. They even allowed people to change when they reported and encouraged major issues to be reported as soon as they arose.

Overall control was kept as the central management office ran a report every week listing any project outside the eight-day window (there were very few). This approach was like a breath of fresh air. Reporting quality improved and those people involved could make best use of their time . . . and the information systems people didn't have to upgrade the performance of their servers to deal with the peak load.

Making reporting work for you

How formal should reporting be?

The level of formality for reporting should reflect the project or work package being reported on and risks associated it. You also need to take into account the capabilities of the people you are asking to provide the reports. Reporting is often looked at as a bureaucratic overhead and as a result the quality of reports can suffer. Review and approval of a report may be undertaken informally where a reporting error would not pose a major risk and may be done as part of normal day-to-day management, in which case a manager may approve their own reports. The exception to this is for reports which are being sent outside the organization, say to a customer, when commercial oversight would be prudent so as to avoid accidental commitments or compromising the contract.

Analysing the information from reports that you receive

Analysing the progress information and using forecasting techniques will give you some idea of the likely future cost, timescale and quality of deliverables. How far you can go with analysing and forecasting depends on the type and scale of the project. Earned value management techniques will give you a valuable insight into performance on the schedule and the cost. The techniques also give indicators to help you forecast any remaining work and expenditure. It is, however, a technique that requires good information flow, which many organizations simply do not have. See Chapter 22 for more on earned value management.

You should check carefully forecasts provided by suppliers or team managers to make sure they are realistic. An activity which has been consistently behind schedule is unlikely to completed on time without affecting costs or the quality of project deliverables. Remember, the last 20 per cent can take as long as the first 80 per cent. Don't just rely on the formal reports you are given, whether submitted in writing or verbally at meetings. Where possible, look for yourself; get into the habit of walking about and being approachable; often people will tell you things they are reluctant to put in writing if they meet you informally.

Sending your reports out

When you have finished the analysis, you must then tell the right people about the current state of the project and the likely outcome. A set of well-thought-out reports meeting the needs of the various stakeholders will make this much easier.

Most sponsors and customers insist on regular reports and you should agree the style, content, and timing of these reports when the project is being set up; as the project progresses, continue to check that what you agreed is still valid. The reports should be brief and assure the recipients that objectives are being met and benefits will be achieved. Where necessary, you should say what action you have taken to put any problem area back under control.

Timeliness of reports is also essential. Generally a report which is "approximately right" now is preferable to one which is perfect but three weeks old. Sometimes this can be difficult to balance, especially when reporting to customers as there may be unforeseen commercial implications of a report which is "mostly right". Further, some people take delight in finding faults and errors and can sour what could be good working relationships.

"Cleaning up" report to look good

The practice in one organization was for the line managers of project managers to review the project reports before they were sent out. Similarly, the line managers of the specialist team managers also reviewed their reports. They argued that as these people were their staff, they, as line managers, were accountable for the quality of the work and it was essential they review all reports and amend them if necessary. This not only took time, often days, but also led to the reports being diluted. No line manager wanted to declare that things may not be going so well in their department. The line managers' line managers took the same view and also wanted to review what was being said. The project managers became frustrated as their reports were often changed, hiding uncomfortable truths, and the project sponsors and stakeholders were annoyed at having to wait so long to actually receive a report. They started to realize the report sometimes omitted important information. Projects seemed to stay on "green" status for months and then suddenly turn "red" just before they were due to deliver.

The chief executive of the company was very keen on "flat structures" to speed up information flow around the company, so he sanctioned a radical change to reporting. Under the new regime, a project manager, no matter at what level in the organization, submitted his or her report via a new centralized system directly, with no review by their line manager. The report was available to the project sponsor and line manager at the same time immediately it was submitted. This speeded up information flow dramatically. It also improved the quality of reports. Through coaching and experience, as well as seeing everyone else's reports, the project managers learnt to write more accurately and concisely, keeping the reports to facts and recommendations and avoiding personalities. It also promoted a direct dialogue between the project sponsors and project managers, building trust and this helped circumvent those line managers who still wanted to exert pressure to make the reports "look good", rather than tell the truth.

Reporting templates

Chapter 17 gives you an outline for a project report, detailing the most important information. Often enterprise project management methods include a number of templates for reports, which you can use as a starting point to tailor to meet your particular needs. Remember, the focus of reporting may change over time. For example, requirements metrics may be more important at the start of a project, with testing metrics taking higher attention towards the end, so the report content will need to change. The report should always reflect the way the work is being undertaken; for example, if agile techniques are used, "burn-down charts" are essential. If necessary, develop specific reports for specific target audiences, designed to show particular aspects of the project but do try to minimize the number of reports. The organization in the case study on the timing of reports had just one project report internally with only board level and customer reporting being specially designed. You may not manage to do this, but it's worth trying.

Finally, don't assume all reports have to be written. Verbal reporting, say at a team meeting, can be adequate in many cases but the topics covered are likely to be the same as for a written report, so have a standard agenda. The advantage of covering reporting at a meeting, regardless of whether the report is written or not, is that it gives those present an opportunity to query and challenge the report and so adds to the quality of any resulting actions. Face-to-face reporting can also avoid misunderstandings.

Red RAG to a bull!

"RAG" is a simple status reporting method, enabling the reader of a report to grasp very quickly whether a project is likely to achieve its objectives or understand the status of a particular aspect of the report. RAG stands for Red–Amber–Green:

- red means there are significant issues with the project that the project team and project sponsor are unable to address;
- amber means there are problems with the project but the team has them under control;
- green means the project is going well with no significant issues, although it may be late or forecast to overspend.

Different people will define these in different way, but on the whole, they follow the intention given above. Some organizations use "BRAG", where the "B" is blue and denotes "completed".

The RAG status works best if based on the project manager's own assessment of the situation and is useful for highlighting those projects which may have difficulties. Some organizations have the RAG status set automatically by systems, e.g. when a project is forecast to overspend. Such systems often trigger automated notifications or emails to key stakeholders to alert them of the problem. That sounds very logical as reports should be acted upon and if no report is sent, then no action can follow. Unfortunitey, logic isn't always the best driver on management as the case study shows.

Drowning in RAG notifications

I saw one part of an organization implement an automated "RAG" system and the stakeholders were drowned in notifications, receiving so many that they often missed those that really mattered. Most commonly, a project would be automatically set to "red" if a milestone was forecast to be late. In most cases, the project manager and team were working on solutions and needed no help; this was, after all, why they were there. Alerting the sponsor was unnecessary as they could do nothing at that point in time to help. The automated system was switched off and the overall project status was set manually by the project manager. They did, however, retain the automated flags against the different parts of the report as this helped the project manager spot variance quickly and ensured the current view of "the truth" was not hidden.

Workout 18.1 – Setting up your reporting regime

Use the following prompts to help you define your reporting regime:

1   Reporting should reflect the information needs of the stakeholders, especially those with responsibilities for some aspect of governance.
2   The "weight" of the reporting regime should be appropriate to the work being undertaken and the people undertaking it.
3   For customer projects, the reporting regime should protect your commercial position and collateral.
4   The basic planning elements should be in place to collect the level and detail of reporting required (for example, if project costs are to be tracked, the cost codes need to be created to capture this).
5   A repository should be set up where reports should be available for recipients and archived.
6   A permissions structure should be defined for the reporting repository enabling those who need to publish and see reports can do so.

Workout 18.2 – Is your reporting regime working?

Use the following prompts to check how well your reporting regime is working:

1   Is reporting being undertaken in a timely manner?
2   Is the "weight" of the reporting regime appropriate to the work being undertaken?
3   Is the level of accuracy of the reports appropriate to the needs of the report recipients and the time allocated for preparing the report?
4   Is there evidence that reports are being read and, where necessary, being acted on?
5   Is there information known or being discussed which is should have been included on the reports but hasn't been?
6   Is confidentiality being respected in the reports?

If you answered "No" to any of the questions, adjust your reporting regime accordingly; involve the sponsor and your team in getting this right.

Workout 18.3 – Is each report adequate?

Some people are great at writing reports; others aren't. Unfortunately, the skill of a person in writing a report may not match their skill in their specialist discipline; great technicians may be poor report writers! Use the following prompts to check the quality of each report:

1   Is the report focused on the future and likely outcome for the work covered by the report?
2   Is the content of the report relevant for the readers of the report?
3   Is the style and language used in the report acceptable?
4   Is it clear on why the report recipients would want to read what has been written?
5   Is it clear what, if any, action is expected as a result of the report?
6   Does the report indicate the level of confidence of the manager in any forecasts?
7   Are risks and issues worded clearly and unambiguously?
8   Do the data on the report match those on any subsidiary reports or data?

The best way to handle a "no" on any of the above is to work with the report author and coach them towards writing succinct and valued-added reports. If you don't provide any feedback, don't expect reporting to improve. If you are the author, ask a "peer" to look at it and coach you. This may sound like a lot of time to invest but good information is at the heart of good management and reporting that can be trusted will save far more time than it costs. Don't be tempted to rewrite reports for people; they will become demoralized and simply stop trying and leave it up to you.

If you cannot achieve a good-quality report from your team managers, start by having verbal updates and write up your report; by doing this with the team, they will understand your needs and may soon find it easier to provide a short report in advance the speed the meeting up.

Don't ignore what is happening around the project

19

Managing benefits

Benefits and drivers

Needs, benefits, outcomes, and outputs – mapping

Forecasting benefits

Timing of benefits

Business cases

In short, benefits are about making more money, about using existing resources and assets more efficiently and about staying in business.

"What is a man profited, if he shall gain the whole world and lose his own soul?"

ST MATTHEW 16:26

- **Be clear what drives your business' bottom line.**
- **Understand the outcomes you need to generate the benefits.**
- **Always measure benefits against a known baseline.**
- **Place benefits in the wider business context.**
- **Make benefits tangible, whenever possible.**
- **Look out for unwanted side effects from your project.**

Benefits and drivers

Legitimate projects

Realizing benefits is the sole reason for undertaking a project. If there are no benefits, there should be no project. It is for this reason that the role of project sponsor is vital. He or she is the person in the organization who requires the benefits to fill a particular need in pursuit of a defined business strategy.

To be "legitimate", a project must satisfy at least one of the following conditions:

- Condition 1 – maintain or increase profitable revenue to the business, now or in the future;
- Condition 2 – maintain or reduce the operating costs of the business, now or in the future;
- Condition 3 – maintain or reduce the amount of money tied up within the business, now or in the future;
- Condition 4 – support or provide a solution to a necessary or externally imposed constraint (e.g. a legal or regulatory requirement).

In short, benefits are about making more money, about using existing resources and assets more efficiently and about staying in business. You'll frequently hear words such as "growth", "efficiency", "protection", "demand" reflecting an organization's focus at any point in time. The value of a company is determined by its ability to consistently maximize its risk-adjusted cash flow generation. It follows then, that companies should focus on those factors that help them generate more cash, for longer periods of time and with the least risk possible. These are called value drivers.

The first three conditions relate to the net cash flow into the organization. Money is the organization's key measure of commercial performance in the private sector and value for money in the public sector. It includes measurement of revenue, investments and the cost of running the organization.

The fourth condition is often referred to as a "must do" project, such as ensuring compliance with a legal or regulatory requirement. It is, nevertheless, essential for such projects to be fully costed in order to determine the least cost, highest value approach to fulfilling the need. This cost can then be placed in the context of the organization as a whole and helps the organization's leadership team to establish whether the organization, or the impacted part of the organization, can afford the change and remain a viable business.

Value drivers

There are three broad types of business value drivers: operational, financial, and sustainability drivers.

- **Operational drivers** include all those variables that impact the cash generation capacity of the company either by boosting growth or increasing efficiency. At their most basic level, these drivers include revenues and costs and in turn all those variables that increase the former and reduce the latter (e.g. volume, price, etc.).
- **Financial drivers** include all those variables that minimize the cost of capital incurred by the company to finance its operations. By optimizing the cost (i.e. finding the cheapest source of financing), structure (i.e. finding the best mix of instruments and terms) and allocation of its capital (i.e. using it in the most productive and efficient way), a company can significantly increase its value in the medium and long term.
- **Sustainability drivers** refer to all those variables that enable a business to keep on operating consistently and optimally for long periods of time. Their focus is to find ways to capture synergies with external forces that operate in the company's environment.

Value drivers – why they are useful?

If you have worked in mergers and acquisitions, you may be familiar with how due diligence is carried out to assess the value and the liabilities of the target company. Managers in acquiring companies look at the variables of the target company which drive its costs, revenues, and asset value. This approach is also useful when aiming for greater efficiency and effectiveness in your own organization. The objective is to identify the set of value drivers specific to the organization which can be checked off against the organization's chart of accounts. Of course, the chart of accounts would need to be straightforward; one organization I know of has more than 11,000 account headings, possibly reflecting a poor state of financial management than any deep structural need. Examples of value drivers are as follows but you may have more or different ones in your organization:

1   Reduced personnel costs

- Reduced head count;
- Reduced/avoided recruitment;
- Reduced employment overheads.

2 Reduced cost of ownership of assets

- Reduced maintenance costs;
- Reduced security costs (including losses).

3 Reduced cost of rectification

- Reduced effort per error on investigation and recovery;
- Reduced volume of re-supply per error.

4 Profitable acquisition

- Profitable acquisition of valuable estate;
- Profitable acquisition of valuable IT systems;
- Profitable acquisition of valuable production assets/plant.

5 Improved profitable sales infrastructure

- Enhancement of profitable new sales personnel skills and relationships;
- Acquisition of profitable improvements to sales processes;
- Acquisition of new company data and knowledge that are put to profitable use in sales.

If you know what drives your organization's costs down and its revenues and asset values up, you can compare these against the business changes your project will enable and see exactly how your project drives benefits realization. This technique is the part of Isochron's Dimension Four® method which enables a project sponsor to identify extended benefits, just as projects normally identify their extended costs. These benefits usually go far beyond those envisaged when working within imposed, budget-cutting targets. Dimension Four® recognizes six categories of benefits, supplementing the four "legitimate projects" mentioned earlier, namely:

1 bottom-line savings in the cost of what is being spent now, in this financial year;
2 avoided costs of future committed spend;
3 future revenue increases;
4 new valuable assets;
5 "real options" – assets the project will build which creates options to generate more cash benefits in the future;
6 value for money – benefits with no cash value to the organization but stakeholders want and have been promised.

One of the useful spin-offs of value drivers is how the analysis can increase the project team's understanding of where an organization's money comes from. It can also turn up unexpected drivers which may enhance or devalue the benefits. In one large commercial organization I worked in, the post-implementation reviews showed how many of our projects did not realize the benefits we expected but were still worthwhile as there were unexpected benefits which more than compensated. Alan Fowler, the managing director of Isochron, told me wryly that we obviously didn't have a grasp on our value drivers; if we had, we would have predicted many of these "windfall" benefits. He was right in that we could not explicitly make the connections; I am not so sure, however, it was just luck that our projects proved positive. We gained these windfall benefits very frequently; perhaps it was more about the experience of the project sponsors, truly knowing their business and implicitly taking that into account in their decision making but, at the same time, ensuring there was a formal business case to justify the project. Notwithstanding that, if we had understood where the benefits were derived from, perhaps we could have managed those aspects of the project better and reaped even greater rewards.

 ## Beware of efficiency "savings"

When looking for efficiencies, be very careful not to waste time and energy sub-optimizing aspects of your business. What counts is the throughput of your business, not the individual efficiencies or asset utilization of the different parts. Partially finished goods are not the aim, finished goods are. The trap people fall into is assuming that by increasing the efficiency of every part of a business, the whole business will become more efficient. This is not the case as efficiencies are not additive. This can be demonstrated very simply.

Consider a factory with a five-step process, machines A, B, C, D and E, with a required throughput of 100 units/day. In an ideal world, each machine would be sized for 100 units/day. But we live in a world of breakdowns and unexpected events. If each machine operated with 90 per cent reliability, the chances of actually obtaining 100 units/day are only 60 per cent. Machines therefore need to be over-sized to protect the throughput by ensuring that each machine has a stockpile in front of it to protect against a breakdown further up the chain. Much of the time individual machines won't break down and if you are aiming for each machine to operate as near as possible to its limit (i.e. peak efficiency) you will find that stockpiles of partially finished goods will swamp the downstream machines. The net effect will be decreased efficiency downstream because it simply cannot cope with corresponding increase in throughput.

Eli Goldratt likens this to a chain in his Theory of Constraints. A chain's strength is determined by the weakest link and the chain cannot strengthen by adding weight to any other link. In fact, the chain would be weakened, as the weak link now has an even greater load to bear.

Business objectives and benefits

Whilst the conditions in the previous sections may make a project "legitimate," they are not, on their own, sufficient to define the business objectives for the project, nor indeed the wide range of possible benefits. Business objectives need to include not only the financial figures, but also statements on market positioning, service/product mix, target markets, service quality and such like; these are sometimes called outcomes. Organizations which focus purely on "making the numbers" often resort to "making up the numbers". A finance plan is not a business plan; it is a subset of a business plan. You must always ensure the benefits from each project really are moving the organization toward its business objectives and the price paid in human and financial terms, and risks taken are acceptable.

> *Organizations which focus purely on "making the numbers" often end up by "making up the numbers".*

Project sponsors have different ways of expressing their vision of the organization. Some have no trouble envisaging the end state of the business (outcomes) after the transformational changes. Ask them what their objectives are and their eyes light up and they talk with certainty and precision about how the organization will operate in the future. For a project manager, these people are great to work with as they have clarity of purpose and understand the implications.

Other sponsors will also become animated but will talk in terms of the future being "exciting", "exhilarating" or "challenging", with little or no information as to how the future organization will function. These types of sponsor can also be good to work with but the project manager and team will have to make more effort in the investigative stages of the project to define exactly what "exciting" means. The team will need to be supplemented with people who have the capability to define the practicalities behind the sponsor's woolly vision.

Another group of sponsors will look blank and talk only about what is going wrong, what the risks are and "We need to fix it", by which they mean, "You need to fix it." Sometimes they can be very despairing about the present and fearful of the future and need help in turning such a negative outlook into something positive and workable. Isochron has developed a technique for this "doomsday" scenario called "Transfiguration". Transfiguration enables groups of people to move from a position where everything appears impossible to a position where everything is proved possible and looks perfect. The approach taken is to list all the complaints and grievances during a workshop and then look for outcomes to negate these by rephrasing the complaint in a positive way. This approach is described more fully in Workout 19.2.

Tangible and intangible benefits

Benefits can be:

- **tangible** – those which can be stated in quantitative terms;
- **intangible** – those which should be described as far as is possible.

Wherever possible, benefits should be tangible and clearly articulated. Tangible benefits may be measured either in financial or non-financial terms. **Financial benefits** describe the business objectives in terms of:

- revenue
- contribution
- profit enhancement
- savings in operating costs or working capital

Non-financial benefits describe the value added to a business that is directly attributable to the project but cannot be described in financial terms. Again, these benefits should be tangible and measurable, such as:

- increased compliance with mandatory policy or legal requirements;
- quality of service – benefits to customers, such as shorter queuing times;
- internal management – benefits to the internal organization, such as improved decision making processes;
- personnel or HR management – benefits relating to a more motivated workforce, can lead to other benefits, such as increased productivity;
- revenue enhancement – benefits increasing revenue or provide the same revenue more quickly;
- process improvement – benefits enabling the organization to improve productivity or efficiency by doing the same job with fewer resources, or to do more with the same resources.

Care should be taken, however, to query why money should be spent, addressing any particular measure or indicator; if it doesn't eventually help you achieve any of the four conditions given at the start of this chapter, you should seriously consider terminating the project. You may argue that increasing service quality could help retain customers, or attract new customers, in which case a financial benefit should result; increasing service quality may enable you to expand your business if good service is what your customers value and pay for. You should be able to justify any such assumptions even if the calculation of financial effect is somewhat tenuous or you could apply more rigour and use the value driver approach discussed earlier.

Intangible benefits are frequently the most problematic to deal with. Whilst it is difficult to link tangible benefits back to a project output, the problem is far more difficult when dealing with benefits which are almost impossible to describe and measure numerically. Some people take the view that *all* benefits should be measurable and if a project has no benefits, it should not be undertaken. Such people often live by the maxim, "if you can't measure it, you can't manage it". This is an extreme approach and not one that fits every management circumstance. Take, for instance, a project to implement an accounting system. We all know that any but the smallest organization needs one and intuitively, justifying its cost through financial measures alone is "missing the point". I suggest you treat this as a "must do" project in the first instance. Determine the most efficient and effective way of meeting the need and see, in the context of your overall business plan, whether you *can* afford this and *want* to afford it, bearing in mind everything else you are doing or want to do. Portfolio management techniques are extremely useful in this context. (See *The Programme and Portfolio Workout*.) Examples of intangible benefits you will often see in business cases are strategic positioning, competitive positioning (proactive and reactive) and the provision of management information.

Isochron's Dimension Four

ISOCHRON®, a specialist "think tank", has developed a set of techniques and tools for benefit realization, collected in a method called Dimension Four®. Put together, they reduce the uncertainty of the outcome of a project, but the techniques can be used separately to deal with awkward project difficulties. The method doesn't have to replace other approaches and complements the approaches taken in this book. Parts can be used to together with Managing Successful Programmes (MSP®) and PRINCE2® methods; it also endorses and backs up LEAN approaches and Goldratt's Theory of Constraints.

Like this book, ISOCHRON®, takes a business-centric view of projects, proposing projects should be done "by the business for the business". It asserts that, short of external and market changes, any alteration in the cash flows of an organization can only come about by changes in how the organization operates and, therefore, all benefits must be connected to observable changes in how the organization works. In the private sector, it advocates connecting every change to a cash benefit, even mandatory and regulatory ones, and it has a means to do this. It calls the observable changes "Recognition Events®" and the start of observable changes in cash flow "Value Flashpoints®".

The name of the method – Dimension Four® – is a hint that time is regarded as fundamental in the operation of an organization. The main processes in the method work right to left – from the future back to the present, from the intended benefit to the cause. Uncertainty is transferred from the outcome to the process – the benefits are treated as non-negotiable but the project plan and solutions are seen as negotiable.

Needs, benefits, outcomes, and outputs – mapping

Frequently, the needs which initiated a project can become divorced from the outputs a project produces. It is essential to maintain the linkage. When push comes to shove and you need to trim the project back due to overspends, slippage or budget cuts, having a clear view of this will ensure the right things are trimmed, with no unforeseen side effects. Always remember, benefits do not come from projects but from outcomes resulting from using the deliverables produced by the project. Key questions are:

- What are the overriding business objectives for the organization?
- What benefits do you need in order to meet these objectives?
- What are the outcomes (business changes) needed to generate the benefits?
- What enablers, deliverables or outputs, do you need to enable the outcomes?

Conditions of satisfaction – outcomes

Although quantitative benefits can be measured at corporate level, they cannot always be measured directly for an individual project. You might need to take alternative approaches as illustrated in the following examples.

Example 1 – using a surrogate measure: it is not always possible to measure profit for products. In such cases, an alternative measure should be chosen which can be quantified and has a known relationship to profit. Revenue and margin might be such measures. You may also use measures such as numbers of customers, churn, or percentage utilization.

Example 2 – measuring at a higher level: it is not always possible to relate an increase in demand for a service directly to a recent enhancement to that service. The increase might, for instance, be the result of other dynamics in the market. In such cases, the project should be tied to a higher-level programme or portfolio where the benefits can be measured. For example, an enhancement to a service may be bundled with the overall service which is tracked at product level, rather than by the individual projects and initiatives comprising the product plan.

Despite difficulties with measurement, every project should have a recognizable way of showing whether it has been a success. **Conditions of satisfaction** (introduced in Chapter 17) are the conditions which, if met, enable you to declare the project a success. They need to be chosen such that they are indicative of both the business changes needed and realizing the benefits. In other words, the conditions of satisfaction represent the **outcomes** for the project. There are a number of mapping techniques which can be used help analyse and visualize the link from a project's output to the benefits.

Conditions of satisfaction are the conditions which, if met, enable you to declare the project a success.

True business led project management ensures that outcomes are part of the project scope and not something you expect the "business to do" after you've given them some outputs!

Critical Success Factors (CSFs)

Some organizations refer to "Critical Success Factors". These are factors to ensure achievement of the success criteria for the project – they are not the success criteria. The idea is, if you identify and focus on these success factors, you will directly influence success. The logic is theoretically sound but, in my experience, CSFs are seldom described effectively. Often, they are mere platitudes and statements of the obvious, e.g. "IT to provide resources" or "Regular written communications to stakeholders are vital". There is little point in repeating such generalities in project documents. In practice, they often represent risks (and as such should appear on the risk log), or are used to define what are better described as "dependencies" (deliverables required from other projects). My advice is not to use them but, if you do, make them very specific to the project. Concentrate instead on the conditions of satisfaction (see text above) and use your other controls to capture the factors.

Net benefits

When talking of benefits, always think in terms of net benefits, that is to say, what's left after you've counted the cost.

Benefit mapping

Developing a benefits map is a popular technique in benefits management. A benefits map explains how the outputs from a project will lead to outcomes (business changes), which in turn lead to specific business benefits supporting strategic objectives. It is a flexible tool and can be used in a number of other business planning situations. Benefit maps come in various "flavours", using slightly different terminology, but essentially do the same job.

An output (sometimes called an enabler) is any device, technology or means that gives the organization a new capability. An example is video conferencing technology for the company's major offices across the world. It gives the organization the capability to hold face-to-face meetings between remote workers without incurring travel costs. In Figure 19.1, the expected outcome is a huge reduction in the number of face-to-face management meetings – say 70 to 80 per cent – consuming unproductive travel time and costs. To make this work, other outputs (enablers) are essential, such as dedicated video conferencing suites, a policy to underpin the change of practice, a booking system, training for users and high-bandwidth links between the major offices. All these need to be included in the project's scope.

The benefits of the project will be the reduced expenses claims and a saving of managers' time. The latter may be classified as second-order benefits, because there is no certainty as to how such savings would transfer to the bottom line. In fact, the managers' time saving would only be a financial benefit if the overall bill for managers' posts were to be reduced in some way.

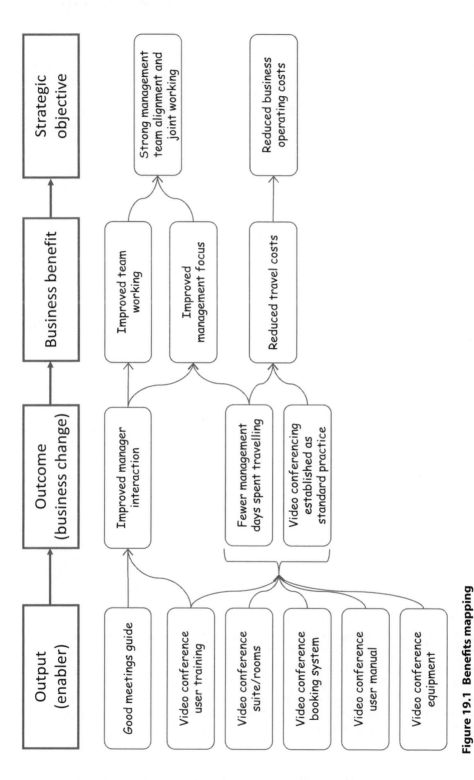

Figure 19.1 Benefits mapping

A benefits map explains how the outputs from a project will lead to outcomes (business changes), which in turn lead to specific business benefits that support strategic objectives.

The benefits map in the video conferencing example shows the outputs leading to the outcomes which, in turn, lead to the savings. It also illustrates how the project ultimately contributes to strategic objectives. Clearly, cost reduction is a valid answer, but posing the question may also reveal the sponsor also wants a change in the management culture of flying around the world and being out of the office for two or three days a week, which he believes is a huge dilution of management attention. The sponsor wants the management team to meet more frequently, for shorter durations, thereby increasing the team cohesion and regards the cost savings to be little more than "window dressing" for the change. The benefits map, therefore, also shows the improved management interaction as a primary business objective, supported by a benefit of better management and team communication (not easily quantifiable), in turn, supported by the outcome of better management availability. This leads to the question of what other enablers are required beyond the video conferencing facilities to induce the change in behaviours and improve the quality of communications and joint working amongst the management team; in this case it is training to encourage the managers to change to a new way of working with each other.

The point of this example is to emphasize the usefulness of the benefit map as a tool to discover the full scope of a project through a better understanding of the desired outcomes and expected benefits. Each horizontal path through the map tells a benefits "story", e.g. implementing video conferencing facilities frees up managers' unproductive time spent travelling, thereby reducing travel costs and supporting the strategic objective of operating cost reduction.

One of the biggest advantages of including a picture such as this in a business case is it sums up the project's intentions in one picture. It is really helpful for those assessing the business case, often very busy senior executives, who have not been involved in its development. The value of the diagrams is the power to summarize a complex situation on a single page, and not as an "engineering drawing" of precision and accuracy, although the system engineering fraternity has now developed "use cases" and frameworks to cover this!

See Workout 19.3 for how to use this method.

FAST mapping

There is another mapping technique called the functional analysis systems technique (FAST). It has been used for a long time in value engineering but its inherent simplicity can also be used to question the benefits a project is being set up to achieve, i.e. the business objectives and the adequacy of any proposel solution. Start by stating what you are trying to achieve and then, by asking a series of **how** questions, you decompose this into increasingly specific statements to show the impact of doing one thing on the next one in line. The technique helps ensure only necessary elements for meeting the objectives are included in the solution. The technique is often called "How–Why" charting and as such, can be used not only in creative thinking (working left to right – **how**) but also to analyse a current situation (working right to left – **why**). See Workout 19.4 for how to use this method.

Dimension Four® mapping

Isochron's Dimension Four Recognition Events® and Value Flashpoints® are types of "condition of satisfaction". Since the value flashpoints each have an estimated monetary value (together with the sources, assumptions, and calculations used), they enable finance and business managers to see how much each business change is worth and where its impact can be looked for in the cash flows. The problem of measurement at a higher level resolves itself because both the recognition events and value flashpoints are almost always found to be duplicated across projects – they all belong to one business level and reflect the viewpoint of the project sponsor. Deduplication often results in simplification and re-scoping of the projects around the project sponsor's business needs, as opposed to around the chosen solutions. We therefore maintain a direct link from "action" to "benefit".

If you use Isochron's approach the project sponsor and stakeholders will have defined, from the outset, precisely what their conditions of satisfaction and hence outcomes are, using the recognition events. In the same method, the completion of the value streams triggered by the value flashpoints will be the conditions of satisfaction for the financial benefit goals enabled by the project. Isochron, solves the "measurement problem" in its methodology by using three spreadsheets:

- one lists the business changes or outcomes – the Recognition Events®.
- the next lists the specific changes to cash flows caused by the recognition events– the Value Flashpoints®.
- the third connects the recognition events to the value flashpoints, to show indicatively how much the achievement of each change in the business will contribute to each value flashpoint.

Forecasting benefits

An initial estimate of the benefits and costs must be prepared during the initial investigation stage. During the detailed investigation stage the estimates must be turned into firm forecasts and be agreed by the project sponsor.

Forecasts serve two purposes:

- to enable evaluation of the project;
- to provide information against which the post launch performance of the project can be measured.

There are four guiding principles for forecasting revenues and benefits:

1 Forecasts must be realistic.
2 Benefits must be matched by the costs of achieving the benefits.

3 Benefits (prices, sales volume, etc.) and costs must be based on the same assumptions.

4 Costs and benefits must be forecast for the worst, best and most likely outcome (scenarios).

Profit (or contribution) forecasting needs to take account of three factors:

1 volume/demand
2 pricing
3 costs.

The overall financial contribution to an organization is the product of demand and price, less costs. This is the basis for justifying any number of projects whether they are for a new product, a marketing campaign, or increasing efficiency. It is important to keep the total picture in mind to make sure projects are not created which merely sub-optimize a part of the business, creating little overall benefit. For example, there is little point in installing a highly efficient new platform for a service for which demand is decreasing because the volumes required to achieve the efficiency will never be realized.

> *Keep the total picture in mind to make sure that projects are not created which merely suboptimize a part of the business, creating little overall benefit.*

Timing of benefits

When looking at benefits, always consider the timing. The earlier benefits are realized, the better it is for your business and the quicker you will recover your investment. Discounted cash flow calculations are designed to ensure the time value of money is taken into consideration when comparing different projects and deciding whether to invest. This is also why it is necessary to look for opportunities to plan projects to ensure early benefits delivery.

Just as early benefits are a good, so delayed benefits are bad. The cost of delays can far outweigh any investment costs and turn a viable project into a financial embarrassment.

Figure 19.2 shows the cash flow for a project over a four-year period. The organization is looking for a 30 per cent return on investment and this meets it adequately. If this project were to slip two quarters, the benefits would also slip, reducing the present value of the project by about 30 per cent. It would actually be worth overspending on the project by up to 50 per cent in order to stem this delay in benefits. This is not to say project overspends should be encouraged, especially in a situation when you cannot be sure that injecting money will actually improve anything. It all comes down to risk. What is important is to understand how sensitive a particular project is to slippage, then plan accordingly. (Sensitivity analysis is dealt with in Chapter 22.)

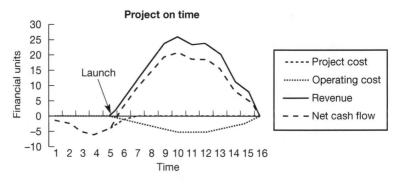

Figure 19.2 Cash flow for a project "on time"

A two-quarter delay to this project would turn it from being a good investment to a financial embarrassment.

Business cases

The business case was introduced in Chapter 17. Section 1 deals with the financial aspects; business cases and benefits management are closely related to each other. The business case justifies why a project is being undertaken and will need to be updated to reflect changes in the business environment of the project and information gathered as the project advances, stage by stage, through it life cycle.

The business case should show, in a compelling and concise format, what the organization gets for the money/effort invested, summarizing the benefits, outcomes and costs together with the associated risks. The business case should include the information decision makers need to decide whether to authorize a project. It provides the answer to, "Why are we doing this project?", and states the specific business objectives and outcomes to be achieved. The level of detail and expected accuracy of any figures should be appropriate to the point reached in the project life cycle; in the early stages, the case may be in outline with a wide range of possible outcomes. By the time the develop and test stage is reached, the case should be much tighter.

A business case does not, however, stand or fall on its own merits. There is always strong competition for investment within a business and any individual business case needs to pass the test of comparison or competition with others. So, from the viewpoint of those developing a business case, there can be no guarantee of creating a winner, even if on its own, it makes sense. For this reason, it may be tempting to "over-egg" the benefits in a business case. This does, however, add a greater risk of failure and may also serve to de-motivate the project team when they realize what targets they have to achieve; it can result in the rejection of the project by key stakeholders who may challenge or reject any exaggerated benefits claims.

The UK government promotes a widely adopted convention that looks at the business case through five individual but related lenses:

1 Strategic lens – how does the project fit the strategy?
2 Economic lens – what other options were considered?
3 Financial lens – can we afford to do this?
4 Commercial lens – does it represent value for money?
5 Management lens – can we actually do this? Is it feasible?

Each lens is described more fully below, and Workout 19.5 uses these lenses to help you challenge a project's business case in a positive way. The document outline in Chapter 17 covers these five aspects.

Strategic lens: the main aim is to explain the business reason for the project, and its urgency, in the context of the organization's primary drivers, imperatives and/or strategic direction. The strategic case should indicate how, and to what extent, the project will contribute to these imperatives. Benefits mapping helps derive this case.

Economic lens: the economic case describes the options for meeting the business aims – not, as you might expect, the investment analysis – see the Financial Case, below. The options should be a feasible range of possible ways of achieving the outcomes needed, explaining their key distinguishing features in terms of approach and levels of benefit. Options considered typically include "do nothing", "do the minimum", "do it faster or slower" and "best value for money", although, ideally, the options are differentiated by how they generate benefits and incur costs.

Financial lens: this tests the affordability of the project through a balanced representation of the quantified costs and cashable benefits over the investment period (e.g. five years) in the form of an investment analysis, such as a discounted cash flow or calculated net present value (NPV). People often think of the investment analysis when they use the term "business case". It should include sensitivity and risk analysis, based on likelihood of the out-turn costs and risks to benefit realization. For instance, it could show how much confidence can be placed on the headline outcome. The requirement for capital expenditure and operating / revenue expenditure needs to be distinguished and the total cost of ownership should be taken into account.

Commercial lens: the commercial case sets out the proposed commercial arrangements with suppliers and demonstrates realistic (if not contracted) prices for the necessary services and equipment. This shows the efficiencies that can be achieved through market leverage etc., value for money, and possibly the recommended spread of commercial risk.

Management lens: the management case addresses the ability of the business to deliver the project outcomes successfully. This typically includes the management team arrangements and leadership responsibilities. It should also address the ability of the organization to cope with proposed changes and how operational management will be tasked with driving the implementation, business changes, and deployment plans, risks, and benefit realization.

Strategic misrepresentation

Strategic misrepresentation is the planned, systematic distortion or misstatement of fact – lying – in response to incentives in the budget process. Jones and Euske applied it to public budgeting in a paper they wrote in 1991. They argued that strategic misrepresentation is a predictable response to a system of rewards in a highly competitive "game" where resource constraints are present. They found it is used both by budget advocates and controllers and at times by both sides of the left–right political spectrum. The study concluded that no amount of moral handwringing over the evils of strategic misrepresentation is likely to lessen the practice. Rather, the system of incentives that triggers strategic misrepresentation requires reform if the behaviour is to be discouraged.

In 2013, The UK's National Audit Office published a report, "Over-Optimism in Government Projects" in which it says how "optimism bias" and other dysfunctions can distort key investment decisions; it investigates the causes of "strategic misrepresentation" and provides some case studies that illustrate the effect. Like Jones and Euske twenty-two years earlier, the report found the incentives in many organizations "to be over-optimistic are very strong, and disincentives relatively weak". The report also points out that "decision-makers seek short-term recognition and rewards, and are often not in the same role when the project is under way and issues emerge". Although written from the perspective of government projects, these findings are also relevant in the private sector, for which a number of studies have also been done.

As I have a said a few times in this book, success is more than having good processes and trained people. Having the right environment and behaviours is vital.

Workout 19.1 – Why are you doing this project now?

You will need the most recent version of the business case and definition document. Based on this, write on a flip chart:

- Why you are undertaking the project; what are its desired outcomes and expected benefits?
- Why it is being done now, rather than later? What in the business plan is driving the timing?
- Are any other projects relying on this project? What strategic or business imperative is driving any dependent projects?
- Does this project rely on any other projects? What strategic or business imperative is driving these precursor projects?

Always link your answers back to your business plan or business strategy. Are the internal projects being done in priority order or is there something else driving their timing? For external projects (i.e. those for customers/clients), test whether that work is targeted at a chosen market segment. If the target is outside the target market, ask why it is being done, what is happening, that the business needs as a result?

If you find gaps, maybe the project should be terminated. Alternatively, perhaps the business case and definition document is incomplete but the project does fill an implicit need. In which case, use the mapping techniques in Workouts 19.3 or 19.4 to check the project scope, its outputs, desired outcomes and benefits, making changes where necessary.

Workout 19.2 – Transfiguration

This workout should be undertaken by a prospective project sponsor with the key stake-holders, prior to the formal start of a project. It is aimed at determining the business objectives for the project in a "turn-round" situation. By capturing people's fears and grievances, you demonstrate you have listened to them and then you concentrate on solving those issues. This approach can be supplemented by working through Workout 24.1.

1 Bring together the people who are unhappy about the current position or antagonistic to what is about to happen. Ask them to tell you all their problems and concerns; write them down on a flip chart. On no account disagree with them – use "brainstorming rules"! Take an active interest and help them to remember all the bad things they can.

2 When they have had a good moan, ask them to pick the worst half-dozen of the complaints.

3 Write the chosen complaints in the top half of a new flip chart – one sheet per complaint.

4 For each complaint develop a positive statement which is the opposite of the complaint. Write this on the lower half of each respective sheet.

5 Hide away the complaints, by folding over the sheets to show them just the positive outcomes. Ask them:

   • when they'd like the world to be like that,
   • whether they think it is possible. See what answers you get.

6 Ask them what they will hear/see/feel happening to show them the world has changed. Their answers help to frame their objectives and help build your conditions of satisfaction.

Caution – objectives gained in this way are only the mirror images of current failures. You should still try to find objectives from visionary people. Published Company Accounts, publicized vision documents and manifesto promises are also good sources for business objectives.

Workout 19.3 – Benefits mapping

This workout is best done early in the project with the project sponsor, project manager and a selection of key stakeholders, comprising those likely to benefit and those who will produce the deliverables. You will need a large paper-covered wall and a supply of Post-It® Notes. Along the top write the words "Output", "Outcome", "Business benefit", and "Strategic objective", just like in Figure 19.1.

1   Write the strategic objective the project supports on a Post-It® Note. Place it towards the right of the wall. If there is more than one need, record each of these on separate notes.
2   Discuss what business benefits you believe you need. Write your answers, one per Post-It®, and place them under the "Business benefit" heading. Link each to one or more of the strategic objective Post-It® Notes.
3   Discuss what business outcomes would ensure the business benefits would be realized. What needs to change? What will be different? Write each on a Post-It® Note and place them under the "Outcome" heading. Link each to one or more of the business benefits Post-It® Notes.
4   Discuss what outputs would enable the outcomes you need. Make sure you cover everything that's needed. Write each on a Post-It® Note and place them under the "Outputs" heading at the right of the wall. Link each to one or more of the outcomes Post-It® Notes.
5   Finally, stand back and check this makes sense. Does it cover everything needed? Could different outputs create the same outcomes? If so, you have some options to be covered in the investigative stages. Make any adjustments necessary to gain consensus and ensure understanding.

Remember, this is not an exact science but a good way for the team to really understand the need for the project and draw out any implicit assumptions. It also helps ensure the scope for the project is complete.

Timing is often critical to success

Copyright © 1997 Robert Buttrick

Workout 19.4 – Linking objectives and needs to deliverables – FAST mapping

This workout is best done early in the project with the project sponsor, project manager and a selection of key stakeholders comprising those likely to benefit and those who will produce the deliverables. You will need a large paper-covered wall and a supply of Post-It® Notes. At the top left write the word "How," with an arrow pointing right. At the top right, write the word "Why", with an arrow pointing left.

1   Write the need/opportunity to be filled on a Post-It® Note. Place it toward the left of the wall. If there is more than one need, record each of these on separate notes.
2   Test these initial needs statements by asking "Why do this?" against each. Write your answer on a Post-It® Note and place it to the left of the original note, linking it with an arrow.
3   Continue this until you are satisfied with the resultant core needs. They should match your overall organization's business objectives.
4   Go back to your original Post-Its® and then for each one, ask the question, "How do we do this?"
5   Write your answer on a note, place it to the right and link it with an arrow. Keep doing this until you have derived a set of "create deliverable" notes, which are sufficient to define the scope of the project.

Notes

- Describe each note using an "active verb + noun" combination. Ensure the verbs are as direct and descriptive as possible, describing an "effect" (e.g. "provide" is not a good word, be more precise). Ultimately the nouns on the right of the chart will be the deliverables.
- Take time to resolve any disagreements over descriptions and placing of notes. These discussions are critical in reaching a common understanding.
- This technique can be used, as above, for overall needs analysis but can also be used on discrete parts of the project as part of detailed design for specific deliverables.
- A variant of the approach is to put the "noun" in the Post-It® Note box and the "active verb" on the arrow.

Workout 19.5 – Six questions to challenge your business case

This workout can be done at any point in the project, but the earlier the better. These are good questions for auditors, project assurance as well for the project team to "test" themselves.

1   Does the project fit your organization's business strategy?
2   Have alternative options for realizing the benefits been investigated. Why were they rejected?
3   Is the project affordable? Will the organization have the funds available when needed? If the project generates some or all of its own funds, what are the risks associated with this?
4   Does the solution represent value for money, whether produced internally or by suppliers?
5   Is the project feasible in all respects? Consider cultural, technical, financial, commercial aspects.
6   Consider also the impact of the project on staff, customers, and suppliers; can they take on the project and its outcomes, bearing in mind what else they are doing?

20

Managing the schedule

The management of the project schedule is one of the most important and fundamental of project management techniques; so much so that many people (wrongly) think that schedule management is project management.

"There can't be a crisis next week. My schedule is full."

HENRY KISSINGER

- **Plan in outline for the full project.**
- **Break the project down into manageable pieces (work packages).**
- **Plan in detail before you start any work.**
- **State what milestone your critical path relates to.**
- **Once a plan is agreed, baseline it.**
- **Measure progress against the baseline.**
- **Keep your eye on the future – forecast, forecast, forecast.**

The project schedule

You will find the management of the project schedule is one of the most important and fundamental of project management techniques; so much so, many people (wrongly) think that schedule management is project management. At a simple level, the schedule tells you how long the project, or any part of it, will take. In addition to giving dates, a well-produced project schedule also tells you:

- who is accountable for every aspect of the project;
- the approach being taken;
- the major deliverables and outcomes from the project;
- the timing of key review and decision points.

Schedule or programme?

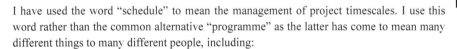

I have used the word "schedule" to mean the management of project timescales. I use this word rather than the common alternative "programme" as the latter has come to mean many different things to many different people, including:

- a very large project;
- a set of interrelated projects;
- a sequence of phased projects;
- a portfolio of projects bundled for management reporting;
- a portfolio of projects bundled by management accountability;
- a series of training courses;
- something you watch on television;
- a chronology, like a theatre programme.

In this book "programme" is defined as a tightly aligned and tightly coupled set of projects and other related work (see Chapter 14).

As you saw in Chapter 17, the schedule is just one part of a project plan but is integral to how benefit, cost, and resource plans are constructed. Unlike costs and resources, which are seen by only a few people observing a project, key dates are often very noticeable. A well-publicized delivery date for a project is, when missed, very hard to hide. While "time" may not be the most important aspect for some of your projects, an observer may develop their own perception of "success" or "failure", purely from the performance of your project against the publicized target dates; just think of all those reports in the news about delayed road improvements, late government IT systems and non-delivery of new military hardware.

Planning is far too important for you to delegate to junior team members, especially in the early stages of the project when the overall strategy and approach are being developed.

The ability to build and manage the schedule plan is one of the essential skills all project managers should have. Planning is far too important to delegate to junior team members, especially in the early stages of the project when the overall strategy and approach are being developed. The plan sets the course for the remainder of the project. Once agreed and set (at the development gate), it is difficult to change or improve. All the decisions with the most leverage on time, costs, and benefits will have been made.

Done effectively, the schedule plan will help you and the team by providing:

- a baseline against which to measure progress (without a plan, words such as "early" or "late" are meaningless);
- a common understanding of the approach you are taking to achieve your objectives;
- a breakdown of the project workload into manageable pieces (work packages), based on the deliverables, outputs, and outcomes, wherever possible;
- a clear way of showing dependencies between activities and work packages within the project and to/from other external projects;
- a listing of accountabilities for different activities and work packages;
- a tool for evaluating if corrective action is needed.

Further, as already discussed in Chapter 17, the actual activity of creating a plan by using the full team, serves to forge a team spirit and a high level of common commitment and understanding.

All projects are undertaken within an environment of risk. Good planning is done in the full knowledge of those risks. You should therefore:

- prevent avoidable risks by planning the project in a different way;
- have a contingency plan for the unavoidable risks.

 Think in ranges, not absolutes

Beware when planning, that your initial "ball park" estimate doesn't become "set in stone" as the target for the remainder of the project. For this reason, it is better, in the investigative stages, to provide ranges of dates and costs, making clear to senior management that your plan still has many unknowns and risks.

"The only way to be sure of catching a train is to miss the one before it"

G K CHESTERTON

Summary and detailed schedule plan

You need to consider your plan on two levels:

* summary (or outline);
* detail.

The former is used to map out the entire project, while the latter shows the detail for the current stage. For work packages done by others (for example, by a contractor), the person or group doing the work will usually prepare the detail but you need to be satisfied that their plan is workable and includes sufficient checkpoints for you to monitor progress. Developing a schedule plan is an evolutionary activity, starting with a statement of key objectives, outcomes, scope, and outputs; the benefits mapping techniques discussed in Chapter 19 relate to this. Planning then continues with the preparation of a summary plan. This comprises:

* the scope, based on the approach to be adopted (or alternatives from which the preferred option will be chosen during the detailed investigation);
* the breakdown of the project into stages and work packages relating to project deliverables (note these same packages should also be used for resource and cost management);
* the key dates, milestones, and time constraints relating to the project;
* review or decision points;
* interdependencies with other projects.

From this, you should be able to estimate:

* the resources required (see Chapter 21);
* the cost of the project (see Chapter 22).

Before beginning work on any stage of the project, you should ensure detailed plans are prepared. The criteria for all the entry gates in the staged framework, from the detailed investigation gate onward, include a detailed plan as a prerequisite. Detailed planning involves work undertaken within your own organization and checking that third parties (such as contractors and suppliers) have planned in sufficient detail, with adequate checkpoints for control purposes. The detailed planning process is similar to the outline process, except that you will be working in more detail, on perhaps one aspect of the project at a time. This includes:

* breaking down each work package into activities to represent the work required for each project deliverable;
* identifying dependencies between activities (predecessors and successors);

- agreeing completion dates for each activity with those accountable for each activity;
- checking the key milestones and overall project completion date can still be achieved;
- ensuring there are appropriate check and review points;
- ensuring time and resources are allocated for planning the next stage.

Figure 20.1 shows the main activities for creating a schedule plan.

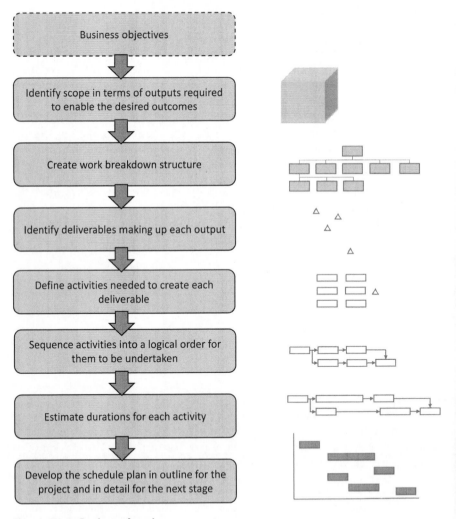

Figure 20.1 Project planning

Project planning starts with the business objectives and ends with detail plans, including schedules, resources, and costs. (See Project Workout 20.1.)

Workout 20.1 – Starting the plan off – introducing backcasting

I said earlier that planning is too important to delegate to junior team members. "But", argue many people, "I do not know how to use these sophisticated planning packages we have on our PCs," or, "I haven't any planning software on my PC," or even, "I haven't got a PC!"

Such excuses do not make sense. Projects have been with us for centuries and certainly well before computers. All you need to start planning is:

*   your brain;
*   your team;
*   a set of Post-It® Notes;
*   flip chart markers;
*   a very big wall covered in paper or a large white board to stick your Post-It® Notes on.

You should do this exercise as soon as possible. In the early stages of a project, getting the feel of the task ahead is more important than worrying about "correctness" and detail.

With the same team, take the project definition output from Project Workouts 17.2 and 19.3 and in workshop format, using flip charts, white boards and Post-It® Notes:

1 Display the flip charts from Workouts 17.2 and 19.3 on the walls for the team to see the project's objectives and outcomes.
2 List each outcome on a Post-It® Note and place these at the right of the wall.
3 Pointing at the one of the outcomes, ask the question: "What smart moves did we make to create this success?" This should lead you to identify milestones and deliverables; add them to the board to the left of the outcome, with an arrow leading to the outcome. For example:

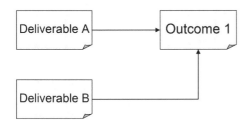

4 Take each deliverable in turn and ask the same question: "What smart moves did we make to create this?" This will be either:

*   more deliverables;
*   activities you need to do and want to capture.

If you "invent" an activity, label it with "A" in the top left. Add Post-It® Notes to the board to the left of xyz deliverable with an arrow leading to it. For example:

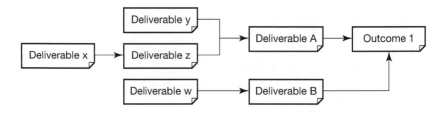

5 Continue on the deliverables, milestones, and activities until you are satisfied you have identified the starting point for the project. Don't be worried if you do not know in what order some deliverables need to be created, or do not know the exact sequence of activities in all areas. If you did know this, your project would be relatively simple. Make a note of the "problem areas", as they are issues which must be planned into your work schedule as problems to investigate and solve. Once you have finished, stand back and look at the pattern. Relocate some stickers to simplify if necessary. You may also notice that some deliverable or actions lead to a number of outcomes. This is good news as it reflects a fundamental of life: one solution can remove many problems. (Look at Chapter 24 on issues, where you will notice the same effect.) It also indicates which of your activities and deliverables are really valuable and important to invest in. Finally, it may indicate your project may be somewhat simpler than you first realized. Concentrating on planning towards outcomes, rather by defining departmental "workstreams" always leads to simpler projects!

6 Look at the plan again and make broad estimates of how long each activity will take. Don't worry if you are wrong; it may depend on the resources you have available: Workout 21.1 will help with this. Note down those activities for which you have very little confidence in your estimate on your list of "problems to solve later".

7 You should notice several tranches of notes, each leading to a particular outcome. These are clues to whether your work breakdown structure (WBS) is right and the key packages of work within each stage of your project are the right ones. Where possible, adjust your WBS to have as few interdependencies between work packages as possible.

Relocate some of the Post-It® Notes to simplify the appearance if necessary. Rationalize any long sequences if they do not add value to the overall plan. (Remember, at the start, this is a summary plan only.)

8 Consider alternative ways of approaching the project, perhaps by brainstorming or discussion. Start again using an alternative approach.

9   Repeat the above for each outcome.

10   You should have created one or two summary plans. You will have discussed different options, identified areas of uncertainty or ignorance and started to reach a common understanding. You should also have been able to add some flesh to the bones of your project definition and be well on the way to creating a realistic, achievable plan.

This may be sufficient at this point in time or you may need more sessions. Assuming you have made as much progress as you can, the work packages should be allocated to key team members to start working on as part of the initial investigation. By starting "in the future" and working back to the present, you ensure only those deliverables and activities necessary to achieve the outcomes are within the plan. This means you have no excessive, non-value-added work in the plan. This "from the future" planning approach is often called "backcast" planning.

Use of project management planning software packages

There are many commercially available software packages for schedule planning and management which also have the capability for handling resources and costs. Using planning packages can be of great assistance to project managers, particularly for projects with more than 50 to 100 activities. The point when using a software package is worthwhile depends on how well a person can use it. Experienced users will find project-planning packages more beneficial for smaller projects than those who are less able. The examples shown in this book were prepared using Microsoft Project, upgraded with a special set of views to ensure they represent good planning practice; you can find these on the book's web site. Similar layouts and reports can be achieved with other software packages (such as Primavera, PlanView, Asta, ChangePoint).

Remember, planning software is a tool, and not an end in its own right. It is not magic and will only give you a short cut to calculating and reporting on schedules. It cannot tell you if your fundamental approach is wrong, or a major task is missing. Like all tools, you must take the time to learn how to use it!

One danger of planning software is that a "planner" might work in isolation to construct a plan for the team. Computer screens are small and do not make good work sheets for teams. In addition, most tools work counter-intuitively by assuming planning should start with concentrating on activities, rather than deliverables. The Post-It Notes method in Workout 20.1 will test your basic approach and ensure your team members are in agreement and aligned. When that has been done, by all means "computerize it".

Factory floor planning

I was given the task of looking at a project plan for a complex change project for a manufacturing organization. I was told that there were six projects and about 400 activities. The complexity was due to over fifty interdependencies between the projects.

I printed out a network chart of the project (the equivalent of the Post-It® Note plan) and laid it out on the factory floor like a carpet. A half-day of study and marking up resulted in a much simpler schedule. There were still six projects, but now only five interdependencies. The original project scopes had been defined largely on departmental lines. By focusing on deliverables, I was able to create relatively independent projects, giving each project manager greater degrees of freedom to plan and manage his or her projects without the need to involve the others.

Critical path, float, slack, and other jargon

There are some concepts and jargon in schedule planning that you need to understand, all relating to whether you can allow an activity to be done at a different time to when you planned to do it. In Workout 20.1 you defined the sequence of deliverables and activities which need to be done in a network diagram. You then estimated how long each would take to do and from this, you knew how long the project would take.

The **critical path** is the route through a series of activities, taking into account the late completion of dependencies which would delay the end date. An activity on the critical path cannot be done later than planned as it will delay the end of the project. It cannot start earlier than planned as the preceding activities haven't been completed. In other words, a critical path activity has no freedom to "float". Float is usually defined as the amount of time an activity may be delayed from its early start date without holding back the project finish date. Float is a mathematical calculation and can change as the project progresses and alterations are made to the project plan. As float is measured in units of time, an activity on the critical path has zero float. If an activity has some float, however, you can do it later.

- **Free float** measures the time an activity can be delayed without affecting any succeeding activity.
- **Total float** measures the amount of time an activity can be delayed without affecting the end of a project.

You need to be aware of this when planning a project, especially if using scheduling software, which can display both the critical path and float without much effort on your part. Remember, scheduling software works from the last date you have in your plan. This may be when your project ends or even when the post-implementation Review is completed. In either case, it is hardly likely to be the most significant date in your schedule. The most important date is one to which you are either publicly committed or triggers the flow of benefits. This is likely to be either the Ready for Service Gate in the project framework in Part II, or the launch/release date. You will need to decide which date is important, then work out your critical path and float based on this constraint. In planning software you do this by "fixing" the date. After checking you are working back from the right date, you then need to consider the critical path carefully. Always state what milestone your critical path relates to. Assuming you have verified the critical path is sensible and there are no obvious logic errors in the sequencing, you need to ask whether each activity might, in practice, take longer. We'll do a workout on this in the risk chapter (Workout 23.2). Building a plan which has a lot of activities on the critical path might slip is a certain way of ensuring the project will be late. Also, don't look at just the critical path, where the activity float is zero; look for all those activities where the float is, say between one and five days. Such activities are very near the critical path, making it likely that the difference between these and your critical activities is not significant within your level of estimating. As you increase the trawl to look for critical or near-critical activities, you may see many critical (and near-critical) paths appearing, indicating just how risky your plan might be. What can you do about this? You'll need to replan your project to relieve the schedule risk you have created, either by adding resources (see Chapter 21), renegotiating the key dates or taking a different approach. You can also look at using risk simulation techniques, as described in Chapter 23, to really get under the skin of your plan to find out where it is solid and where it is soft. In either case, I would never recommend a plan has zero float, and would seek to protect the critical path or paths from unforeseen delays; we'll look at this in relation to critical chain thinking towards the end of this chapter.

Always state what milestone your critical path relates to.

Good planning pays dividends

Tracking progress toward your objectives

"Nothing is inevitable until it happens"

A J P TAYLOR

Tracking progress toward your objective is essential. If you don't, you simply won't know when you are going to arrive. The control cycle is shown in Figure 20.2: once a plan has been agreed, it is necessary to measure progress against the plan, reforecast to the end, note any variances and take steps to bring the project back on schedule if necessary.

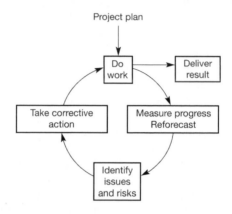

Figure 20.2 Schedule control cycle

There are many ways to measure progress, the commonest being:

- assessing percentage complete;
- assessing the remaining duration for an activity;
- estimating the date when a task will be completed.

It is not unusual to find an activity is 90 per cent complete for 90 per cent of its duration!

Many people use the "percentage complete" method. This method, however, has potential problems if a realistic estimate of percentage complete cannot be determined (such as measuring hours worked); it is not unusual to find an activity is 90 per cent complete for 90 per cent of its duration! A simpler method is to estimate the date when a task will be completed.

An activity is either:

- completed (i.e. 100 per cent complete);
- not started (i.e. 0 per cent complete);
- or started, but not complete (treat this as 0 per cent complete).

Activities which are started, but not finished, are assumed to be 0 per cent complete, but a current best estimate of the expected finish date is made. A special form (Figure 20.8) can be designed to record this information.

The schedule should be updated at least monthly but for faster moving projects, weekly or fortnightly would be more appropriate. This update cycle should tie in with the regular progress reporting on the project as it is the most concise method of showing what has been achieved and what is to happen next. Summary reports should be used for reporting upward and detailed reports should be used for reporting within the project team.

Do not concentrate only on what has been completed. Look at the future and what is coming up next. Consider, based on your experience to date, whether the timescales allocated are adequate; if they aren't, you may need to take corrective action. Anticipating problems is good practice and gives you more time to find solutions. If problems are ignored, they don't go away, they grow and the time available to solve them shrinks. Keep in mind your main focus: to reach the RFS Gate, when benefits start to flow. You do not need to have every activity completed on time. Each duration in your plan is basically a guess. Some will be good guesses, some will be appalling and others will be the unfortunate victims of Murphy's Law, which states "Anything that can go wrong, will go wrong." As a project manager, too much concentration on the wrong detail will divert your attention from the real issues.

Keep in mind your main focus: to reach the RFS Gate, when benefits start to flow. You do not need to have every activity completed on time.

Reforecasting the schedule is not a change to the plan. It is an assessment of how the project is likely to proceed compared to the plan.

Plan instability

When starting work and monitoring against a plan you will often have difficulty assessing progress. This may happen because the work is, in fact, being undertaken in a different way from that planned. In most cases this is not a problem, providing the key milestones, dates and interdependencies are not affected. It can be symptomatic of "microplanning", i.e. planning done at too detailed a level.

At other times, the reason is simply because the plan has not been fully thought through. In this case, it needs to be revised to reflect the actual work to be done (using the change control guidelines from Chapter 25, of course). Changes of this nature often occur in the early part of a project as a result of uncertainty. The plan should become stable quite soon if you apply yourself and your team to it. You may also find a particular work package is unstable. This could indicate that the manager in question has not planned it properly and is not in control, or that it is inherently risky. Both reasons need your attention.

Schedule reports

Consistent format and layout

You must have a clear and consistent legend for the family of reports you will produce. Figure 20.3 is a typical example. Bar charts can be confusing to the uninitiated and difficult to read and so it is good practice to use consistent formats and styles, which people can become used to reading.

The following points should be noted:

- The numbering used for activities clearly shows their level in the project hierarchy. The list is ordered such that each activity is shown within its relevant work package, within the relevant life cycle stage.
- Activities are best described using an active verb, e.g. "Prepare data". Milestones or targets are activities of zero duration and are best described using a passive verb, e.g. "Phase 1 completed". The dates on the activity list should be updated to reflect progress and current expectations of finish dates.
- The accountability column has the name of the single point of accountability for every activity at every level.
- Show both the plan and the actual/forecast on the graphical section of the chart. In this way progress is very obvious.

When reading any of the project reports, it must be clear where the report came from and what it refers to. It is, therefore, good practice to have "quality" headers and footers on each page to ensure the reader is absolutely certain of the source and status of the report.

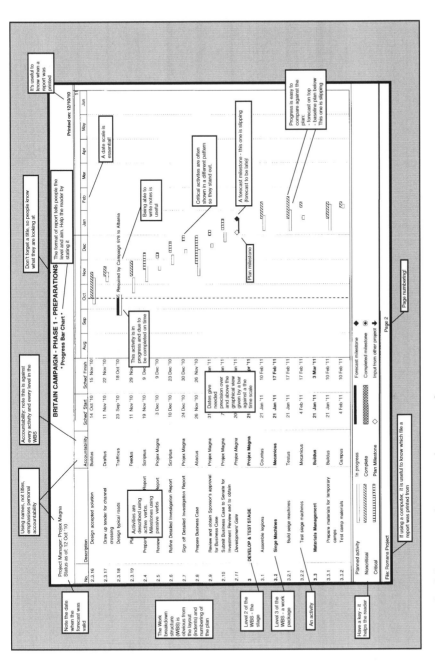

Figure 20.3 Schedule report – best practice example

Inter-project dependencies

Many projects require deliverables from other projects as a prerequisite to completion. For example, a software project may require another project to deliver a particular hardware configuration before it can be tested.

The plan for a project should show only those activities for which the project manager is accountable. Activities done by others in other projects should not be shown in detail. Such linkages should, however, be explicit.

It is very important to ensure the scope of each project is well defined, particularly when different departments in an organization are involved. If the full scope of each project is not clear, then accountability for delivery becomes vague and threatens project success. Often, senior management and line management who are not intimately involved in a project or series of projects will have different perceptions of the scope of a project and may even view a package within a project as a "project" in its own right.

The breakdown of a project into discrete work packages, related to specific deliverables, is essential if confusion is to be avoided. The plan for a project should show only those activities for which the project manager is accountable. Activities done by others in other projects should not be shown in detail. Such linkages should, however, be explicit and the example reports shown later in this chapter have been designed with this in mind. The reports show a **down arrow** on the date when the deliverable is due to be completed and ready for use by the receiving project.

When considering dependencies between projects, the following question should be asked: "What do I (in Project A) require from other projects in order that I may complete the defined scope of work?"

This may result in a list of one or more specific deliverables which should be identified in the other project plan(s). The project manager(s) of the other project(s) should be aware of your requirements and by when. Two projects cannot be accountable for delivering the same deliverable!

Two projects cannot be accountable for delivering the same deliverable!

Report formats

The following section contains examples of schedule reports, presented in the order in which they will normally be used (Figure 20.4).

The examples were prepared using Microsoft Project, but similar layouts can be prepared using other tools. They are all derived from the same basic data and are simply different ways of viewing those data.

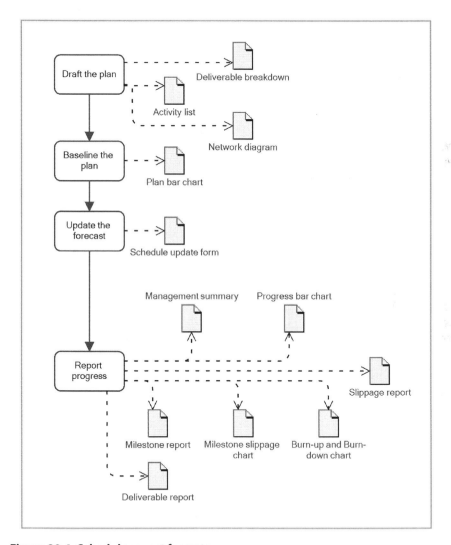

Figure 20.4 Schedule report formats

Different reports are used for different purposes. You will not find a single one which will suit everyone's needs.

Reports used when drafting a plan

Deliverable/product breakdown structure

Purpose

The deliverable (or product) breakdown structure provides a summary listing of each deliverable created by the project team, together with its components. In addition, information such as who is accountable for it, who will review it, who will approve it, dates and format can be added (Figure 20.5).

When to use it

The breakdown structure is used to show a structured view of all the deliverables from the project (or stage of a project). As such, it is created whilst undertaking the planning but is also useful as a tracking tool throughout the project in the form of a deliverable log (see later in this chapter).

Completion

The breakdown structure is derived whilst undertaking the planning, often in tandem with the network diagram (sometimes called a product flow diagram in this context). By concentrating solely on the physical deliverables, those doing the planning are able to visualize the output of the project, starting with a few key deliverables and then breaking each of these in turn into smaller and smaller components (or sub-deliverables). This helps ensure the outputs from the project will be sufficient to meet the business objectives. Strictly, this should be shown as a tree diagram, with rectangles representing each deliverable. It is far more convenient and useful, however, to use a tabular format, with the breakdown represented by the numbering system and indentation of progressively lower levels of the breakdown. Project Workout 20.1 gives you a step-by-step approach to planning.

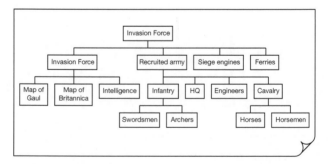

Figure 20.5 A deliverable (or product) breakdown structure in tabular and tree formats

Activity list

Purpose

The activity list records all activities associated with the project, i.e. what needs to be done, who is accountable, how long it will take and by when it should be completed. The list is used to identify activities and milestones and to give information on outline plans (Figure 20.6).

When to use it

The activity list is best used when drawing up a plan, to aid thinking through the key activities, milestones and their dependencies. It is a simple and useful way of communicating a plan if bar charts or other graphic presentations cannot be prepared.

Completion

This report is for people who love lists! it is simply a list of the activities and milestones, together with the names of those accountable, activity durations and dates.

ACTIVITY LIST   BRITAIN CAMPAIGN

WBS	Description	Accountable	Dur'	Plan start	Plan finish	Sched' Start	Sched' Finish	Number	Preceded by?	Summary?	Comment	Sign-off?
1	INITIAL INVESTIGATION	Projex Magna	27d	1 Aug '10	6 Sep '10	1 Aug '10	6 Sep '10	1		Yes		
2	DETAILED INVESTIGATION STAGE	Projex Magna	96d	9 Sep '10	3 Jan '11	9 Sep '10	20 Jan '11	12	11	Yes		
2.1	Assemble Team	Projex Magna	10d	9 Sep '10	20 Sep '10	9 Sep '10	20 Sep '10	13		No		
2.2	Prepare Development Definition	Publius	16d	23 Sep '10	25 Oct '10	23 Sep '10	14 Oct '10	14	13	No		Sponsus
2.3	Undertake Detailed Investigation	Projex Magna	51d	23 Sep '10	15 Nov '10	20 Sep '10	29 Nov '10	15	13	No		
2.3.1	Locate mapping of Gaul	Surveyus	10d	23 Sep '10	4 Oct '10	23 Sep '10	4 Oct '10	16		No		
2.3.2	Maps of Gaul available	Surveyus	0d	4 Oct '10	4 Oct '10	4 Oct '10	4 Oct '10	17	16	Yes		Cartus
2.3.3	Do reconnaisance	Surveyus	20d	23 Sep '10	18 Oct '10	14 Oct '10	8 Nov '10	18	16 FS-10d	No		
2.3.4	Estimate enemy troop numbers	Countus	15d	7 Oct '10	25 Oct '10	28 Oct '10	15 Nov '10	19	18 FS-10d	No		
2.3.5	Define number of legions required	Countus	10d	14 Oct '10	25 Oct '10	4 Nov '10	15 Nov '10	20	19 FS-10d	No		Claudius
2.3.6	Prepare recruitment plan	Countus	5d	28 Oct '10	1 Nov '10	18 Nov '10	22 Nov '10	21	20	No		
2.3.7	Investigate possible routes	Surveyus	20d	7 Oct '10	1 Nov '10	7 Oct '10	1 Nov '10	22	16	No		
2.3.8	Design siege machines	Mechanicus	30d	23 Sep '10	1 Nov '10	20 Sep '10	31 Oct '10	23		No		Marcus
2.3.9	Draw up tender for siege machines	Draftus	10d	4 Nov '10	15 Nov '10	1 Nov '10	14 Nov '10	24	23	No		Hadrian
2.3.10	Design temporary camps	Buildus	30d	23 Sep '10	1 Nov '10	26 Sep '10	6 Nov '10	25		No		
2.3.11	Draw up tender for siege machines	Draftus	10d	4 Nov '10	15 Nov '10	7 Nov '10	20 Nov '10	26	25	No		
2.3.12	Design river bridges	Buildus	25d	23 Sep '10	1 Nov '10	14 Oct '10	15 Nov '10	27	16 FS-20d	No		Neptune
2.3.13	Draw up tender for river bridge parts	Draftus	10d	4 Nov '10	15 Nov '10	18 Nov '10	29 Nov '10	28	27	No		
2.3.14	Receive tunnel designs	Buildus	0d	23 Sep '10	23 Sep '10	14 Oct '10	14 Oct '10	29		Yes	From Campaign 321 - Gibraltar	Orpheus
2.3.15	Decide how to cross English channel	Buildus	10d	23 Sep '10	4 Oct '10	23 Sep '10	4 Oct '10	30		No		
2.3.16	Design accepted solution	Buildus	25d	7 Oct '10	8 Nov '10	14 Oct '10	15 Nov '10	31	30	No		
2.3.17	Draw up tender for channel crossing	Draftus	10d	4 Nov '10	15 Nov '10	11 Nov '10	22 Nov '10	32	31 FS-5d	No		
2.3.18	Design typical roads	Trafficus	20d	23 Sep '10	18 Oct '10	23 Sep '10	18 Oct '10	33		No		
2.3.19	Plan catering logistics	Feedus	15d	21 Oct '10	8 Nov '10	11 Nov '10	29 Nov '10	34	18	No	Required by Campaign 978 to Alba	
2.4	Prepare Detailed Investigation Report	Scriptus	15d	4 Nov '10	22 Nov '10	19 Nov '10	9 Dec '10	35	15 FS-10d	No		
2.5	Review Detailed Investigation Report	Projex Magna	5d	18 Nov '10	22 Nov '10	3 Dec '10	9 Dec '10	36	35 FS-5d	No		
2.6	Refine Detailed Investigation Report	Scriptus	10d	25 Nov '10	6 Dec '10	10 Dec '10	23 Dec '10	37	36	No		
2.7	Sign off Detailed Investigation Report	Projex Magna	5d	9 Dec '10	13 Dec '10	24 Dec '10	30 Dec '10	38	37	No		Sponsus
2.8	Prepare Business Case	Abacus	25d	11 Nov '10	13 Dec '10	26 Nov '10	30 Dec '10	39	35 FS-10d	No		
2.9	Review and obtain Sponsor's approval for	Projex Magna	5d	16 Dec '10	20 Dec '10	31 Dec '10	6 Jan '11	40	39, 38	No		Sponsus
2.1	Submit Business Case to Senate for Inves	Projex Magna	10d	23 Dec '10	3 Jan '11	7 Jan '11	20 Jan '11	41	40	No		
2.11	Development Gate	Projex Magna	0d	3 Jan '11	3 Jan '11	20 Jan '11	20 Jan '11	42	41	Yes		

Figure 20.6 A typical activity list

Network diagram

Purpose

The network diagram is probably the most useful but least used way of depicting a project. It shows the logical relationship (dependencies) between different deliverables, activities and work. Network diagrams can be used for identifying natural checkpoints in the project as the network will show where various strands come together. They are invaluable for calculating project float and determining the critical path (Figure 20.7).

When to use

A network should be used whenever a complex sequence of events needs to be shown clearly. This is particularly useful when first drawing up a plan when it is not always obvious what the logical dependencies are. It is also a useful format to use at planning workshops to determine dependencies between activities before any idea of timescale/duration has been gained.

The network diagram is probably the most useful and least used way of depicting a project.

Completion

The plan is developed by mapping out those activities which can be performed in parallel and those which must be carried out sequentially. Activities or milestones are represented in boxes and their relationships with preceding and succeeding activities are shown using arrows. An activity may not start until its predecessor has been finished. This is called a "precedence network" and is the most versatile method for depicting the logical sequence within a project. For complex projects, this is best prepared using project-planning software.

For planning workshops the activities, milestones and deliverables may be written on Post-It Notes®. Then, starting at the end of the project with the final deliverable, you need to ask yourself: "What would I need to have in place in order to achieve this?" This sequence is repeated until the start point in the project is reached (see Workout 20.1).

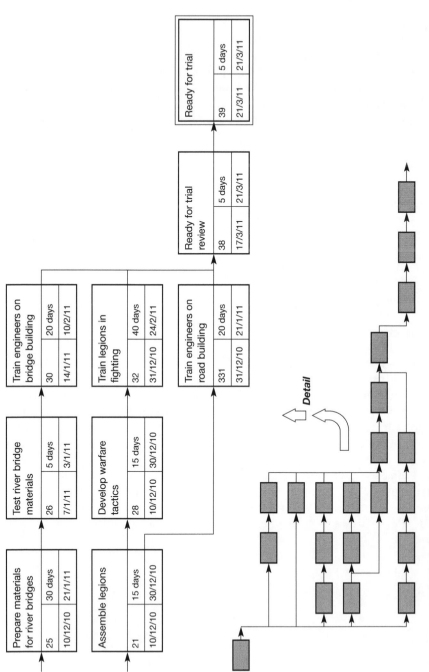

Figure 20.7 A typical network diagram

Plan bar chart

Purpose

The bar chart (or Gantt chart) is a representation of the schedule plan in graph form. It shows the duration of activities against a timescale. It also defines who is accountable for each activity and work package and the place of each activity in the work breakdown structure (Figure 20.8).

When to use

The bar chart is probably the most effective way of communicating a schedule. For this reason, it is highly recommended for inclusion in the project plan and, whenever possible, for use when communicating plans.

Completion

Bar charts can be produced manually or by using computer software, at summary and detailed levels. They are produced from the activity list (see Figure 20.6) once the start and end dates of each activity have been calculated. The left-hand portion contains a reference number, description, duration, the name of the person accountable, and the start and finish dates. The right-hand part shows a bar against a timescale which spans from the start to the finish of the activity. Milestones (dates for key events) are shown as diamonds. Dependencies from outside the project are shown as down arrows.

BRITAIN CAMPAIGN - PHASE 1 - PREPARATIONS
*** Bar Chart ***

Project Manager: Projex Magna
Status as of: 12 Oct '10

Printed on: 12/10/10

No.	Description	Accountability	Start	Finish
1	**INITIAL INVESTIGATION**	**Projex Magna**	**1 Aug '10**	**6 Sep '10**
2	**DETAILED INVESTIGATION STAGE**	**Projex Magna**	**9 Sep '10**	**20 Jan '11**
2.1	Assemble Team	Projex Magna	9 Sep '10	20 Sep '10
2.2	Prepare Development Definition	Publius	23 Sep '10	25 Oct '10
2.3	**Undertake Detailed Investigation**	**Projex Magna**	**20 Sep '10**	**29 Nov '10**
2.3.1	Locate mapping of Gaul	Surveyus	23 Sep '10	4 Oct '10
2.3.2	*Maps of Gaul available*	*Surveyus*	*4 Oct '10*	*4 Oct '10*
2.3.3	Do reconnaisance	Surveyus	14 Oct '10	8 Nov '10
2.3.4	Estimate enemy troop numbers	Countus	28 Oct '10	15 Nov '10
2.3.5	Define number of legions required	Countus	4 Nov '10	15 Nov '10
2.3.6	Prepare recruitment plan	Countus	18 Nov '10	22 Nov '10
2.3.7	Investigate possible routes	Surveyus	7 Oct '10	1 Nov '10
2.3.8	Design siege machines	Mechanicus	20 Sep '10	31 Oct '10
2.3.9	Draw up tender for siege machines	Draftus	1 Nov '10	14 Nov '10
2.3.10	Design temporary camps	Buildus	26 Sep '10	6 Nov '10
2.3.11	Draw up tender for siege machines	Draftus	7 Nov '10	20 Nov '10
2.3.12	Design river bridges	Buildus	14 Oct '10	15 Nov '10
2.3.13	Draw up tender for river bridge parts	Draftus	18 Nov '10	29 Nov '10
2.3.14	*Receive tunnel designs*	*Buildus*	*14 Oct '10*	*14 Oct '10*
2.3.15	Decide how to cross English Channel	Buildus	23 Sep '10	4 Oct '10

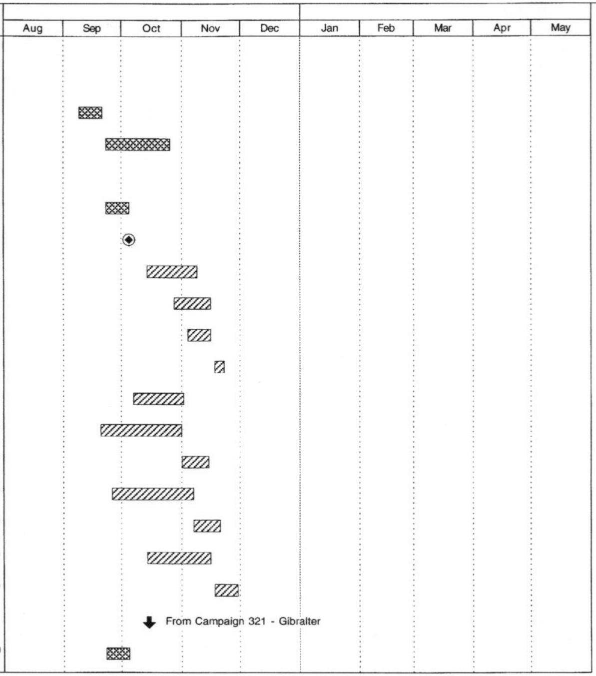
Aug
Sep
Oct
Nov
Dec
Jan
Feb
Mar
Apr
May
From Campaign 321 - Gibralter

Activity — Actual — Milestone ◆ — Completed milestone — Input

File: Romans Project — Page 1 — Product Programmes

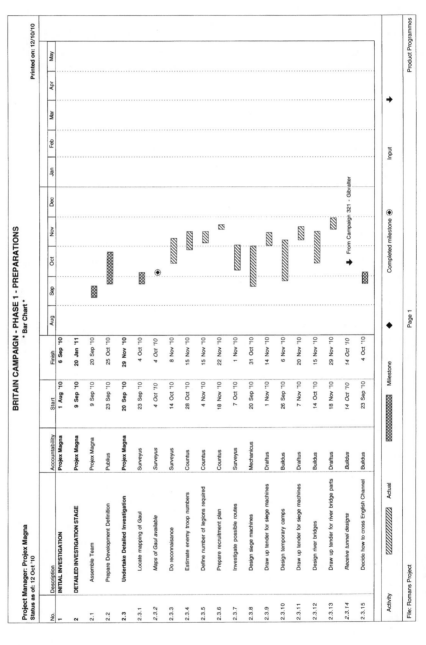

Figure 20.8 A typical plan bar chart

Report used to update the forecast

Update form

Purpose

The update form is used to collect data for tracking progress on the project (Figure 20.9).

When to use

The form is used every time the project manager wishes to check on progress. This should be at least monthly, at month-end, but for many projects it is desirable to update the project weekly or fortnightly.

Completion

The form comprises a filtered selection of unstarted and incomplete activities within a given date range. It has the following columns:

- the reference number of each activity;
- activity description;
- C (complete) and S column (started);
- the actual start and finish dates;
- the expected finish date (for started activities);
- the forecast start and finish dates calculated the last time the project was updated;
- the baseline planned finish date (as a reminder);
- a comment column to record pertinent notes.

The person responsible for reporting progress:

- enters S for all started activities in the "S" column and the actual start date and expected finish date in the relevant columns;
- enters C for all completed activities in the "C" column, giving actual start and actual finish dates.

If it is apparent forecast dates for future activities are wrong, sufficient information should be given to enable rescheduling. Those activities which should have started, but have not, should be slipped forward to start on the update date – their finish date will also slip unless the duration is changed.

Project Manager: Projex Magna
Status as of: 12 Oct '10

Printed on: 12/10/10

No.	Description	Accountability	C or S	Dur	Actual Start	Actual Finish	Expected Finish	F'cast Start	F'cast Finish	Plan Finish	Comments
2	DETAILED INVESTIGATION STAGE	Projex Magna									
2.3	Undertake Detailed Investigation	Projex Magna		96d	9 Sep '10	NA	NA	9 Sep '10	29 Jan '11	3 Jan '11	
2.3.3	Do reconnaissance	Surveyus		51d	20 Sep '10	NA	NA	20 Sep '10	29 Nov '10	15 Nov '10	
2.3.4	Estimate enemy troop numbers	Countus		20d	NA	NA	NA	14 Oct '10	8 Nov '10	18 Oct '10	
2.3.5	Define number of legions required	Countus		15d	NA	NA	NA	28 Oct '10	15 Nov '10	25 Oct '10	
2.3.7	Investigate possible routes	Surveyus	S	10d	7 Oct '10	NA	NA	4 Nov '10	15 Nov '10	25 Oct '10	
2.3.8	Design siege machines	Mechanicus	S	20d	20 Sep '10	NA	NA	7 Oct '10	1 Nov '10	1 Nov '10	
2.3.9	Draw up tender for siege machines	Draftus		30d	NA	NA	NA	20 Sep '10	31 Oct '10	1 Nov '10	
2.3.10	Design temporary camps	Buildus	S	30d	26 Sep '10	NA	NA	1 Nov '10	14 Nov '10	15 Nov '10	
2.3.11	Draw up tender for siege machines	Draftus		10d	NA	NA	NA	26 Sep '10	6 Nov '10	1 Nov '10	
2.3.12	Design river bridges	Buildus		25d	NA	NA	NA	7 Nov '10	20 Nov '10	15 Nov '10	
2.3.14	Receive tunnel designs	Buildus		0d	NA	NA	NA	14 Oct '10	15 Nov '10	23 Sep '10	From Campaign 321 - Gibraltar
2.3.16	Design accepted solution	Buildus		25d	NA	NA	NA	14 Oct '10	14 Oct '10	8 Nov '10	
2.3.17	Draw up tender for channel crossing	Draftus		10d	NA	NA	NA	11 Nov '10	22 Nov '10	15 Nov '10	
2.3.18	Design typical roads	Trafficus	S	20d	23 Sep '10	NA	NA	23 Sep '10	18 Oct '10	18 Oct '10	Required by Campaign 978 to Albania
2.3.19	Plan catering logistics	Feedus		15d	NA	NA	NA	11 Nov '10	29 Nov '10	8 Nov '10	

Figure 20.9 A typical schedule update form

Reports used for progress reporting

Management summary

Purpose

The management summary is a concise presentation of the progress bar chart (Figure 20.10), aimed at providing a summary report on project progress.

When to use

This format is best used for reporting to project boards, project sponsors and other stakeholders.

Completion

The report contains only the specific lines of information (summary, detail, or milestone) you wish to present. The report should be kept as short as possible, concentrating on the project life cycle stages, key work packages, and milestones.

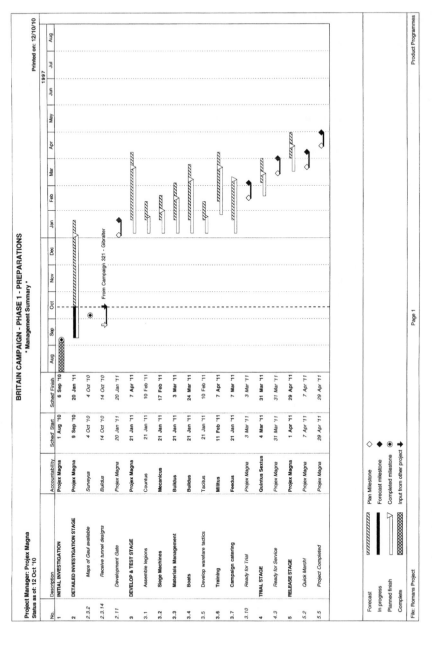

Figure 20.10 A typical management summary

Progress bar chart

Purpose

The progress bar chart is a more complex version of Figure 20.8 which is used to compare forecasts against the agreed plan and hence highlight variances (Figure 20.11).

The progress bar chart shows the current forecast dates for each activity and milestones compared with the baseline plan. The dates given are the actual or current forecast dates. Comments from the progress "update form" (see Figure 20.9) may be included against any item.

When to use

The bar chart is probably the most effective way of communicating a schedule. Progress reports can be made more concise if a bar chart is used to detail progress, rather than progress being described in text.

Completion

Bar charts can be produced manually or by using computer software at summary/ outline and detailed levels. They are produced from the activity list once the start and end times of each activity have been calculated. The left-hand portion contains a reference number, description, duration, initials of the person accountable, and the start and finish dates. The right-hand part shows a bar against a timescale which spans from the start to the finish of the activity. Milestones (dates for key events) are shown as diamonds. The plan dates are shown as a line below the current forecast so that a visual appreciation of slippage is readily apparent. Figure 20.3 and the accompanying text describe how to read a bar chart.

More complex but informative versions of the progress bar chart can be developed which show the "float" available for each activity and dependencies between activities.

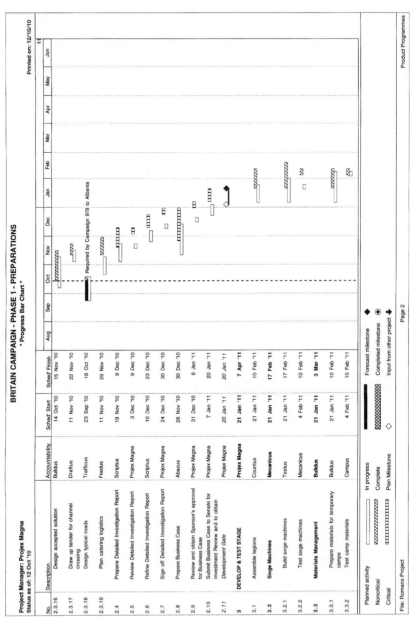

Figure 20.11 A typical progress bar chart

Slippage report

Purpose

This report is used to focus attention on activities likely to be late. This enables the project manager to take whatever action is necessary to bring the project back on schedule. The objective is not to use the report as a tool to "punish" those accountable for slippage, but rather to focus attention on putting things right. With this in mind, the slippage report details only incomplete activities (Figure 20.12).

When to use

This report is useful for identifying those current and future activities forecast as slipping and hence focus attention on remedying the situation. It is best used for plans of more than fifty activities when a software package can extract the "offending" activities automatically. If you are using critical chain schedule management, this report will be replaced by a buffer report (see Figure 20.17).

Completion

The report is compiled by extracting the late (and unfinished) activities from the updated activity list. Most computer project-planning packages have routines for preparing this type of report.

BRITAIN CAMPAIGN - PHASE 1 - PREPARATIONS

Project Manager: Projex Magna * Slippage Report *

Status as of: 12 Oct '10   Report printed on: 12/10/10

WBS	Description	Accountability	Planned Finish	Scheduled Finish	Slippage (days)
2	DETAILED INVESTIGATION STAGE	Projex Magna	3 Jan '11	20 Jan '11	11d
2.3	Undertake Detailed Investigation	Projex Magna	15 Nov '10	29 Nov '10	10d
2.3.3	Do reconnaisance	Surveyus	18 Oct '10	8 Nov '10	15d
2.3.4	Estimate enemy troop numbers	Countus	25 Oct '10	15 Nov '10	15d
2.3.5	Define number of legions required	Countus	25 Oct '10	15 Nov '10	15d
2.3.6	Prepare recruitment plan	Countus	1 Nov '10	22 Nov '10	15d
2.3.10	Design temporary camps	Buildus	1 Nov '10	6 Nov '10	3d
2.3.11	Draw up tender for siege machines	Draftus	15 Nov '10	20 Nov '10	3d
2.3.12	Design river bridges	Buildus	1 Nov '10	15 Nov '10	10d
2.3.13	Draw up tender for river bridge parts	Draftus	15 Nov '10	29 Nov '10	10d
2.3.14	Receive tunnel designs	Buildus	23 Sep '10	14 Oct '10	15d
2.3.16	Design accepted solution	Buildus	8 Nov '10	15 Nov '10	5d
2.3.17	Draw up tender for channel crossing	Draftus	15 Nov '10	22 Nov '10	5d
2.3.19	Plan catering logistics	Feedus	8 Nov '10	29 Nov '10	15d

File: Romans Project	Page 1	Product Programmes

Figure 20.12 A typical slippage report

Milestone report

Purpose

The milestone report shows progress against the key targets for the project. These are items which should be specifically mentioned in the project documentation (Figure 20.13).

When to use

This format is an excellent, non-graphical way for communicating progress and expectations on the timing of key milestones such as the delivery dates for products, or interface dates with other projects.

Completion

The report is presented in tabular form, showing the milestone description, the planned date, the current forecast of the date and the actual date achieved. The final column indicates the slippage (how late) of a milestone compared to the plan. The report is made up of all those activities of zero duration from the activity list which the project manager wishes to highlight. Most computer project-planning packages have routines for preparing this type of report.

BRITAIN CAMPAIGN - PHASE 1 - PREPARATIONS

Project Manager: Projex Magna   *Milestone Report*

Status as of: 12 Oct '10   Printed on: 12/10/10

WBS	Description	Planned Finish	Forecast Finish	Actual Finish	Slippage	Comment
2	DETAILED INVESTIGATION STAGE	3 Jan '11	20 Jan '11	NA	11d	
2.3	Undertake Detailed Investigation	15 Nov '10	29 Nov '10	NA	10d	
2.3.2	Maps of Gaul available	4 Oct '10	4 Oct '10	4 Oct '10	0d	
2.3.14	Receive tunnel designs	23 Sep '10	14 Oct '10	NA	15d	From Campaign 321 - Gibraltar
2.11	Development Gate	3 Jan '11	20 Jan '11	NA	11d	
3	DEVELOP & TEST STAGE	21 Mar '11	7 Apr '11	NA	11d	
3.3	Materials Management	14 Feb '11	3 Mar '11	NA	11d	
3.3.5	Material test certificates ready	7 Feb '11	24 Feb '11	NA	11d	
3.7	Campaign catering	7 Mar '11	7 Mar '11	NA	0d	
3.7.3	Place contract for food supplies	17 Jan '11	3 Feb '11	NA	11d	
3.10	Ready for Trial	14 Feb '11	3 Mar '11	NA	11d	
4	TRIAL STAGE	14 Mar '11	31 Mar '11	NA	11d	
4.3	Ready for Service	14 Mar '11	31 Mar '11	NA	11d	
5	RELEASE STAGE	14 Apr '11	29 Apr '11	NA	11d	
5.2	Quick March!	21 Mar '11	7 Apr '11	NA	11d	
5.5	Project Completed	14 Apr '11	29 Apr '11	NA	11d	

File: Romans Project   Page 1   Product Programmes

Figure 20.13 A typical milestone report

Burn-down report

Purpose

Burn charts show visibility into progress; they are simple and astonishingly powerful. Visibility allows us to show progress against predictions and facilitates the difficult discussions of how to proceed. Burn charts, like other reports, may provide bad news, but at least it will be "bad news detected early", not "bad news detected too late to do anything about it"! They are good for showing progress at any breakdown level in a project stage or work package. Each activity contains the amount of work remaining and is is updated continuously. The chart displays a plot of the amount of work remaining across time. Even though you might think work remaining should always go down, new tasks are always being discovered as work proceeds (in both agile and non-agile environments), so you should expect the work remaining to go up and down.

There are two types of burn chart: Burn-Up charts and Burn-Down charts. The Burn-Down chart is used when you have a good non-expanding unit of measure. Since the team will be aiming to hit the number zero, the Burn-Down chart is emotionally powerful and people get excited about completing their work and seeing the chart tend toward zero. The Burn-Up chart is the opposite and shows progress upward.

The choice of what to count depends on the work being undertaken. In an agile delivery, this refers to story points. In other situations, such as system engineering, this could represent peer reviews. At its simplest, it may be a count of documents or milestones (Figure 20.14).

When to use

This format is used when you have a large number of milestones to track and want to show how progress is being made (or not!) against the plan.

Completion

The report is an extract from the milestone plan or deliverable report. The plan line is plotted by showing:

- for Burn-Up charts the cumulative number of milestones planned to be achieved;
- for Burn-Down charts the number of milestones planned to be remaining.

Against this plot, on each reporting cycle, the actual number of milestone achieved (Burn-Up) or remaining (Burn-Down).

A burn-up chart

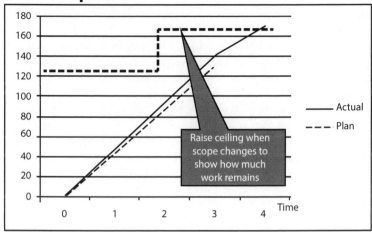

A burn-down chart

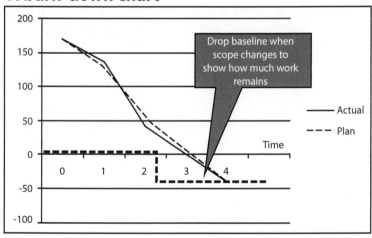

Figure 20.14 A typical Burn-Down and Burn-Up chart

Deliverable report

Purpose

The deliverable report lists all the key deliverables from the project, stating who is accountable for preparing, reviewing, and finally signing them off. These items should be mentioned specifically in the project documentation (Figure 20.15).

When to use

This format is used when the project manager wants to focus on the deliverables and be explicit about who is accountable for the quality aspects for each.

Unless we know who is to review a deliverable and sign it off, we cannot be certain that what is being produced is really fit for purpose.

Completion

The report is an extract from the full project plan, with those activities and milestones relating to deliverables filtered out to produce a listing. Most computer software packages can be customized to do this.

BRITAIN CAMPAIGN - PHASE 1 - PREPARATIONS
* Deliverable Report *

Project Manager: Projex Magna
Status as of: 12 Oct '10

WBS	Description	Accountable	Planned Finish	Forecast Finish	Review by:	Sign off by:	Comment
2	DETAILED INVESTIGATION STAGE	Projex Magna	3 Jan '11	20 Jan '11			
2.2	Prepare Development Definition	Publius	25 Oct '10	14 Oct '10	Project Team	Sponsus	
2.3	Undertake Detailed Investigation	Projex Magna	15 Nov '10	29 Nov '10			
2.3.2	Maps of Gaul available	Surveyus	4 Oct '10	4 Oct '10	Vercingetorix, Flavius, Antonio	Cartus	
2.3.6	Prepare recruitment plan	Countus	1 Nov '10	22 Nov '10	Lucretia, Vespasian	Claudius	
2.3.8	Design siege machines	Mechanicus	1 Nov '10	31 Oct '10	Hannibal Minor, Romulus	Marcus	
2.3.10	Design temporary camps	Buildus	1 Nov '10	6 Nov '10	Flavia, Sextus	Hadrian	
2.3.12	Design river bridges	Buildus	1 Nov '10	15 Nov '10	Hannibal Minor, Romulus	Neptune	
2.3.14	Receive tunnel designs	Buildus	23 Sep '10	14 Oct '10	Vercingetorix, Flavius, Antonio	Orpheus	From Campaign 321 - Gibraltar
2.3.18	Design typical roads	Trafficus	18 Oct '10	18 Oct '10	Vercingetorix, Flavius, Antonio	Mercury	Required by Campaign 978 to Albania
2.7	Sign off Detailed Investigation Report	Projex Magna	13 Dec '10	30 Dec '10	Project Team	Sponsus	
2.9	Review and obtain Sponsor's approval for Business Case	Projex Magna	20 Dec '10	6 Jan '11	Project Team, the Senate, Abacus	Sponsus	
3	DEVELOP & TEST STAGE	Projex Magna	21 Mar '11	7 Apr '11			
3.2	Siege Machines	Mecanicus	31 Jan '11	17 Feb '11			
3.2.1	Build siege machines	Testus	31 Jan '11	17 Feb '11	Hannibal Minor, Romulus	Marcus	
3.3	Materials Management	Buildus	14 Feb '11	3 Mar '11			
3.3.5	Material test certificates ready	Buildus	7 Feb '11	24 Feb '11	Hannibal Minor, Romulus	Neptune	
3.4	Boats	Buildus	7 Mar '11	24 Mar '11			
3.4.1	Build boats	Floata	7 Mar '11	24 Mar '11	Hannibal Minor, Romulus	Neptune	
3.5	Develop warfare tactics	Tacitus	24 Jan '11	10 Feb '11	Mark Anthony, Octavian	Julius Caesar (retired)	
3.7	Campaign catering	Feedus	7 Mar '11	7 Mar '11			
3.7.4	Obtain for food for troops	Feedus	7 Mar '11	7 Mar '11	Hannibal, Quintus, Septimus	Remus	
3.9	Ready for Trial Review	Projex Magna	14 Feb '11	3 Mar '11	Project Team	Sponsus	
4	TRIAL STAGE	Quintus Sextus	14 Mar '11	31 Mar '11			

Figure 20.15 A typical deliverable report

Milestone slippage chart

Purpose

The milestone slippage report shows the milestones dates as forecast at the start of the project or stage of a project and that forecast date at each reporting date time since (Figure 20.16).

When to use

This format is used when the project manager wants to focus attention on the degree of slippage of milestones. It is a good way to demonstrate gradual, month on month slippage.

Completion

This report is an extract from the full milestone report, which includes the milestones the project manager wishes to highlight. For each milestone, plot the date the forecast was made against the date that was forecast. For each milestone, join up the dates to show any "drift".

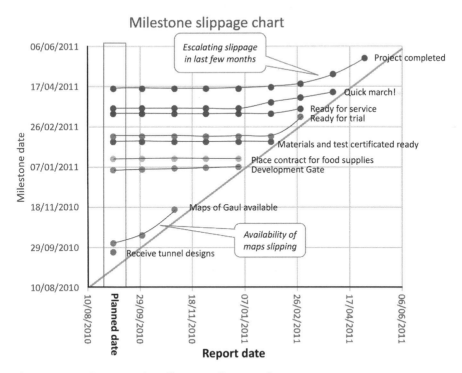

Figure 20.16 An example milestone slippage chart

So why are we nearly always late?

"How does a project get to be late? ... one day at a time"

F BROOKS

Despite decades of project management experience, backed up by ever more sophisticated technology, projects are still late ... unless, of course, the timescales set were so generous that a donkey could have brought it in on time. When really questioned about project timescales, most people admit that speed is not necessarily the most important aspect but *predictability* is. If you are developing a new product, most marketing and sales people would rather have it in four months' time, if promised in four months' time (and working) than have it in three months' time when promised it in two. Once you have achieved predictability, you can concentrate on reducing the overall time taken.

We have seen how a project's duration is basically the sum of the guesses of the durations of those activities on the critical path. This is the definition of critical path. We decide the project approach using network planning and guess (some guesses are very sophisticated) how long each activity will take, bearing in mind the resources needed to work on it. It's all very logical. From here on, human behaviour takes over. If I am a project team member, what should I ask the project manager to put in the plan:

- a short duration I am unlikely to meet;
- a medium duration I might meet if I'm lucky;
- a prudent (longer) duration I'll probably meet.

Most people will choose the last of these – they like to be considered reliable. What then happens is they:

- start work on the activity as late as possible as more "urgent work" is needed first (it's just as well they put in a prudent estimate);
- work on other projects at the same time, juggling between the frantic exhortations of the different project managers and their line manager;
- have a meeting cancelled, actually start work and finish it EARLY. But they don't tell anyone, just in case they are expected to be so fortunate next time, i.e. late hand-offs.

It doesn't matter whether a particular activity is late or not. What matters is when the project as a whole delivers and benefits start to flow.

In short, this one activity is protected by a safety margin which the team member's experience shows is needed. In fact, all activities have their in-built safety. The major drawback is, from an organization viewpoint, it doesn't matter whether a particular activity is late or not. What matters is when the project as a whole delivers and benefits start to flow. Conceivably, a project could be 95 per cent on time and grossly late. Safety is not additive if it is wasted. Statistically, projects plans built this way are more likely to be late than on time. They will hardly ever be early!

The critical chain – a solution?

In his book *Critical Chain*, Eli Goldratt proposes a solution to this problem. Rather than add safety into each activity, as described here, he proposes it should be added in a single lump at the end of the project (Figure 20.17). In practical terms he says:

- cut the durations given by the team in half;
- at the end of the project, add a safety time equal to half the sum of the safety times you trimmed.

In this way you can place the safety in a position where it really counts, at the end of the project, where you can use it.

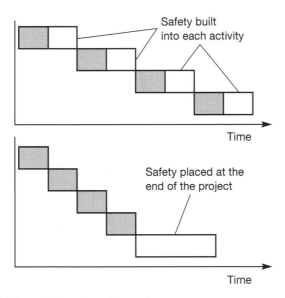

Figure 20.17 Putting safety where it counts

Removing the safety from each activity and placing it at the end of the project enables you to use it when you need to rather than have it wasted by the student syndrome (i.e. doing work at last minute), multi-tasking, or late hand-offs.

You will, however, still have a number of challenges:

*   Why should anyone accept you trimming their time estimates? Be very clear you are adding half of it back at the end of the project.
*   You'll need to be very used to activities being "late". In fact, "late" may no longer be a useful word and this may have implications on reporting.
*   You will need to become used to tracking projects by measuring how much safety is consumed rather than by activity completion alone.
*   You will need to resist senior managers cutting the safety from the end, thus dooming you to certain failure.

You will also need to encourage three behaviours:

*   stop the student syndrome (i.e. doing work at the last minute);
*   end multi-tasking;
*   encourage hand-over as soon as you have finished the activity.

The critical chain method relies on you producing a good network diagram and resourcing the schedule in a similar way to critical path methods. It differs, however, in:

*   choosing a critical route through the project which includes activities which are either on the critical path or which form a constraint due to resource contention;
*   the choice made for activity duration and where any safety is placed.

As we have seen, safety is placed towards the end of the project. This is called a **project buffer**. If a project has a network with several feeders, you will need to protect the critical chain from delays in incoming activities. **Feeder buffers** are used for this. A project buffer protects the entire project from any delay in the critical chain activities. The feeder buffers protect the critical chain from delays on non-critical chain activities (Figure 20.18). The project manager uses a buffer report as the key monitoring tool (Figure 20.19).

End of the project?

The safety should not actually be put at the end of the project. It should be placed prior to the point in the project when you start earning benefits. For most projects following the project framework in Part Two, this is at the RFS Gate. The work beyond this, while essential, is not critical to immediate benefit realization.

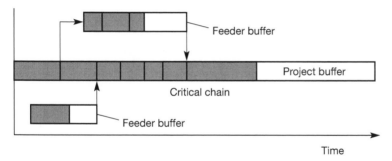

Figure 20.18 Project and feeder buffers

A project buffer protects the entire project from any delay in the critical chain activities. The feeder buffers protect the critical chain from delays on non-critical chain activities.

Buffer report

Ref	Buffer name	Buffer end	Buffer length	% Buffer used	RAG
56	FB| Training agreed	2 Feb 2018	6 days	100%	Red
62	FB| Unit test 5	27 Feb 2018	8 days	73%	Red
109	PB| Ready for Service	21 May 2018	22 days	36%	Amber
87	FB| Acceptance	24 Apr 2018	12 days	31%	Green
48	FB| Roll out hardware	15 Jan 2018	6 days	0%	Green
91	FB| Integration test	13 Mar 2018	10 days	0%	Green

Figure 20.19 A typical report using critical chain schedule management

Rather than concentrate on activity dates, the report shows each buffer by type (FB = feeder buffer; PB = project buffer), its length and how much has been used. From this, the project manager can pinpoint the parts of the schedule which require attention. A simple RAG status helps summarize the status, e.g. Green more than 66 per cent of buffer remaining, Red less than 33 per cent of buffer remaining, Amber 33–66 per cent remaining.

Steps in the critical chain

1 Identify the constraint

The critical chain is the sequence of dependent events preventing the project from being completed in a shorter interval, given finite resources. For a project, the critical chain is the constraint. Plan the network, resource the network, ensure that the activities have safety built in. Schedule the network with everything as late as possible.

2 Exploit the constraint

You need to ensure those activities on the critical chain have the most effort applied to them and people hand over their work to the next person as soon as they are finished. Also, those taking over need to be warned to be ready to accept the hand-off (this is called a resource buffer or flag). You also need to protect the entire critical chain with a safety margin (the project buffer) towards the end of the project.

3 Subordinate every other activity

Where other activities join the critical chain, protect them from delays by introducing feeder buffers.

4 Elevate the constraint

Apply more of the right resources so that key activities within the critical chain can be undertaken in parallel or in a shorter time.

5 Begin again?

Having elevated the constraint, it is probable the critical chain will have moved. You could therefore start the process again. In practice this will not usually create major gains for you unless you have created a very significant change. Generally, it is better to stick to the plan; the inefficiencies in realigning the project team to understand the new plan will far outweigh most other gains. The exception to this is when approaching the RED zone in your project buffer – you will need to take action and this could be one option to investigate.

The steps outlined are a central part of applying the Theory of Constraints (TOC). A full explanation of critical chain schedule management in both single and multiproject environments is to be found in *The Critical Chain* by Eli Goldratt.

Arguments against critical chain planning

Critical chain planning is still not widely practised, so clearly it hasn't been the great solution to planning issues some people expected. This could be inertia in adoption or simply general apathy; for example, how many people actually plan their projects well using critical path techniques, let alone adopt critical chain? That said, one of the biggest difficulties with the method is the lack of solid interim milestones within the plan. If there are no interim milestones, how can you coordinate with suppliers or manage dependencies between projects? How can you plan training, which needs people and facilities to be booked in advance? How can you plan decision making meetings if you don't know when they are needed? How can you reserve time in people's diaries? I am sure you can think of a few more examples where having solid dates to plan from makes sense. If you were to "buffer" all events, your plan would become very complicated and lose the inherent simplicity promoted by the technique.

My answer would be that critical chain planning should not be used in isolation, but rather as one more technique available to help us solve certain problems. There is nothing wrong with planning a project using critical path methods, then doing the detailed planning for some work packages using critical chain techniques. The challenges set on people's behaviours in critical chain are transferable to any discussion you may have with team managers on estimating and reporting. Similarly, the concept of a buffer is very powerful when considered as part of your response to risks. When planning, why shouldn't you consider introducing buffers into your conventional critical path plans where you believe the knock on effects of overruns would be seriously damaging? The idea of making your "safety margin" (the buffers) visible and tracking it in progress reports is innovative and informative. Certainly, if Oded Cohen had not introduced me to critical chain, I would not have had a language in which to apply some of its ideas more widely and thereby make project plans more robust.

21

Managing resources

Resources – the toughest constraint?

Different types of resources

Planning your resources

Reports used when managing your resources

Resource planning is iterative, often time consuming and even after all that work, there is unlikely to be a single answer. There will be many possible project plans, all of which will be feasible, but each carrying a different level of risk.

"You've got a goal, I've got a goal. Now all we need is a football team."

GROUCHO MARX

- Determine if your project is resource or time constrained.
- Think of resources as reusable, replenishable or exhaustible and manage them accordingly.
- Load your resources onto a network driven schedule.
- Level your resources, to remove peaks and troughs.
- Protect your critical and near-critical path.
- Ensure your risks are at an acceptable level; if not, change the plan.

Resources – the toughest constraint?

All projects are managed to constraints. A project needs to be completed within a defined timescale, has to "do the job" and be accomplished within the budget, otherwise it simply won't be viable. Chapter 20 on schedule planning showed how to construct an achievable and robust plan with activities in the right sequence, taking the risks into account. Fundamental to a plan being achievable, however, is having the resources to undertake the work; it's obvious, if there is no one to do the work, nothing will be done. A plan's overall timescale may be driven by the deadlines which need to be met or it may be driven by the resources needed to complete it.

A time-constrained project is one for which the dates need to be met. Obvious examples are sporting events, such as the Olympic Games or FIFA World Cup. For these projects, the resources have to be found to prepare for and run the event; no slippage is allowable. The budget, however, is seldom limitless, often requiring the scope of the project to be reduced accordingly.

A resource-constrained project is one where the date is driven by the availability of the resources for undertaking the work. This particularly applies if the resource needed is very specialist, whether this is people with specific skills, or equipment which is unique.

In practice, you'll rarely find a clear distinction. Truly time constrained-projects are relatively rare, except for the types of example I have given, namely major events of such prestige and high profile they cannot be postponed and cancellation is unthinkable.

Complying with legislation is another area where time constraints can be very marked and set the timescale. For example, in the telecommunications sector in the UK, legislation was enacted to stem the flow of unsolicited sales and nuisance calls to private houses. All telecommunications companies had to be able to register customers who did not want unsolicited calls for the "Telephone Preference Service" starting in May 1999. It is a legal requirement in the UK that all organizations (including companies, charities, voluntary organizations and political parties) should not make unsolicited calls to numbers registered on the service. There was clearly a fixed deadline, by when all projects aimed at ensuring the organization complied with the legislation had to be completed. The case study shows how one organization achieved this within a few months but demonstrates also that such deadlines are often missed and the sanctions are not strong enough to ensure compliance. A company asks, "If I am late by a week (or a month or a year), am I likely to be fined and if so how much? Will it really damage my reputation?" This assessment of the risks of late compliance means such a project is not truly time-driven. Even governments are not immune, for example in the case of European Community countries which often do not comply with new European directives on time.

Dealing with "impossible" deadlines

A telecommunications company's management team found they had missed the regulatory need to comply with the UK's Telephone Preference Service, which was due to come into force in less than three months. This service enabled telephone users to register their number to prevent unsolicited sales calls from UK based organizations. The IT director raised this point at a board meeting and said that, as this was very urgent, they had already looked into the issue and estimated it would take six months and cost £500,000 to build a register. At that time, all their IT projects were overrunning and overspending against initial plan estimates. Despite the clear need for action, the board deferred making any decision to start a project while they sought new information and agreed to convene in a week's time.

The board met and found two crucial pieces of information:

- Market research showed subscribers were unaware of the service and so the number of requests received was likely to be very low;
- the regulation stated customers had to be registered, not that the company had to have a register.

This led to a very cheap and swift response. All the company's customers were also customers of the main national carrier, who had already established a register. If a request to register came in, the company simply registered it on the national carrier's database. Implementation time was only a few weeks, enabling customer service staff training, while the capital cost was zero; full compliance achieved.

Notice, in this case study, no one director had the right answer. Only by working together as a team was an efficient and workable approach to meet the need achieved.

Within an organization, deciding whether a project is time- or resource-constrained can be problematic. If a chief executive says he or she wants a particular facility open or a system in use on a given date, does that constitute a time-constrained project? The answer depends on who you are. For a project manager, such a directive should be treated as time-constrained and the project should be planned to meet the required deadline, but the risks of missing that deadline should be made plain. For the project sponsor, however, it may be less clear. If the costs of meeting the deadline are so high the project ceases to be viable, then if slipping the project dates brings it back into viability, the project is not rigidly time-constrained. I would have hoped, however, that during the investigative stages of the project, different deadline dates had been investigated with the pros and cons of each analysed to decide a target date which was achievable and represented good value. Not all executives work like this and frequently edicts are issued without proper investigation: it's often called "setting a stretch target".

Different types of resources

So what resources are relevant? Resources are often split into three types:

- reusable
- replenishable
- exhaustible

Reusable resources are basically people and equipment. People and equipment can be moved from job to job as and when needed. For example, a test environment for an IT system may be needed for a number of projects, or an excavator could be moved from one construction site to another.

Replenishable resources are those which can be "topped-up" if they start to run out. The most obvious is fuel. A construction site in a remote location is likely to have its own fuel depot but the manager will need to ensure it always contains sufficient fuel for work to continue by planning appropriate deliveries.

Exhaustible resources are those that once they have run out, that is it.

Today's global supply chains are such that you can usually obtain what you need from somewhere. The more localized your operations, the more likely you are to come across an exhaustible resource constraint. Another example, from remote construction sites, is sourcing aggregate for making concrete. Having identified a source of aggregate, it is up to the geologists to ensure the source is large enough to meet the need. A project I was involved in used river gravels as the source, which soon ran out as the grading, or sizes, became unsuitable for use in concrete. The problem was solved by adding a rock crushing plant to create the range of aggregate sizes needed; this was considered less risky than locating another source of naturally graded gravels.

This chapter concentrates on the reusable resources as these are most relevant to project planning. Dealing with replenishable resources is more about logistics and working with exhaustible resources makes risk management essential. Don't get into arguments about definitions; for example, I have classified fuel as replenishable, but some may argue fossil fuels are exhaustible; so what if you use bio-fuel? Similarly, you may consider people as exhaustible if you work them too hard.

Planning your resources

Chapter 17 showed that a plan has to include scope, timescale, resources, and cost. Changing one of these may mean the others need to change. The plan also needs to be constructed to ensure the project is viable, making the consideration of benefits and risk important. By following the schedule planning steps in Chapter 20, you will have determined the sequence of activities and a possible schedule. You then need to check that you have the people and equipment you need to undertake the work. If you haven't enough people, your timescale may be extended; if you have a surplus of people you might even be able to shorten the timescale by using more people. Some activities lend themselves to this but other types of work can actually suffer if too many people work on them. Figure 21.1 draws this together, showing how resource planning sits in relation to overall project planning and schedule planning.

Sometimes there is a physical constraint to the number of resources that can be used. I could dig a 200m trench faster using ten people, if each person has a 20m length to work on, but if I am digging a hole, the size of the hole will limit the number

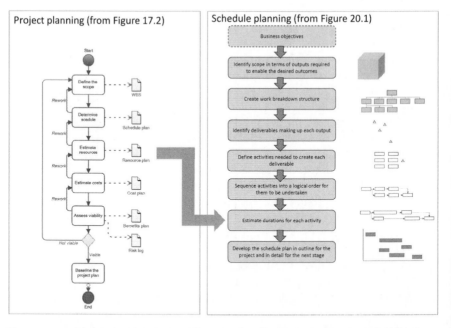

Figure 21.1 Resource planning in the context of project and schedule planning

This figure shows how resource planning sits in relation to overall project planning and schedule planning. Having determined a possible project schedule, you then need to check that you have the resources to complete the work within the required time slot. If you can't, you need to plan your resource allocation to create a workable plan.

of people who can work in it at any one time. The amount of time people or equipment can work is also important. Equipment operations may be restricted in order to limit noise levels. Working time on a building in a city is likely to be more restricted than within a tunnel under the city. Further, different people might work different time patterns: five-day week, three-shift days and public holidays all affect when a person is available for work. For global projects, taking account of time zones is often crucial as the "interactive" periods of the day between a globally dispersed team can be very short; working patterns and workflow need to reflect this. For example, if a team works a standard "nine to five" day, then those in London are unlikely to be at work at the same time as their colleagues in Los Angeles or Tokyo.

All these factors make resource planning more complicated, adding multiple restrictions which need to be taken into account; how the schedule plan is resourced will influence the length of the project.

Resource loading

Resource loading is when you assign resources to the activities in a plan and then determine whether they are under used, overloaded or "just right". Figures 21.2 and 21.3 show a very simple example. For more complex situations, use a planning tool. Resources may be assigned by name or "class"; examples of a class would be "designers", "business analysts", "steel fabricator". On larger projects, most resources would be planned by class initially but, eventually, the name of the people (or equipment) would have to be known when the actual work is allocated.

	Jan	Feb	Mar	Apr	May	Jun	Jul	Aug	Sep	Oct	
A	Chris	Chris									
B		Chris	Chris	Chris							
C			Jo								
D			Jo	Jo							
E					Jo						
F					Jo						
G						Chris					
H							Jo				
	Jan	Feb	Mar	Apr	May	Jun	Jul	Aug	Sep	Oct	Total
Chris	1	2	1	1	0	1	0	0	0	0	6
Jo	0	0	2	1	2	0	1	0	0	0	6

Figure 21.2 Resource loading

This is a simple example of resources being applied to activities. Having determined a possible schedule plan, based on the network diagram, the work (activities A to H) is assigned to Chris and Jo on a full-time basis. On checking the resource loading, it is found that Chris is over-allocated in February and Jo in both March and May. In addition, notice that Chris has a break from work in May and Jo in June.

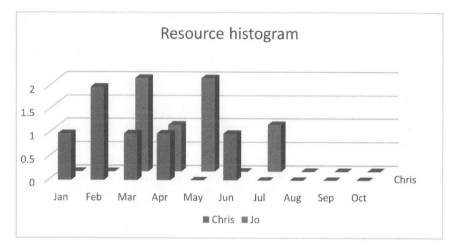

Figure 21.3 Resource loading histogram

These are the same data as shown in Figure 21.2, but shown as a resource histogram.

You need to do resource loading for the most important resources and decide:

- what calendar should be used, such as one with a five-day week, or a seven-day week, with or without public holidays;
- what unit of measurement to use, such as man-days, man-hours or other measurements of "effort".

If the team members are time-recording, the plan should usually be on the same basis as time records are collected. I say "usually", as some companies configure their time recording systems so that they do not reflect the real number of hours worked because they exclude, for example, unpaid overtime. They often do this in order to keep the finance costs correct and as finance departments usually own such systems, they tend to put their own needs above those of the other departments' management needs. Yes, it can become messy.

Resource levelling

We can see in Figure 21.2 that for some of the time, some of the resources are underused and at other times there are simply not enough to undertake the work, when required. Clearly, the work will not be completed in accordance with the plan. What is needed is to change the schedule plan, enabling the resources to be used more evenly; this is called **resource levelling** and is shown in Figure 21.4. It is a lot easier to understand in theory than to do in practice, where there may be many resources to be dealt with, shared across a number of projects or "business as usual" activities. Predicting the timing of activities and milestones, together with resource availability with so many variables, is fraught. One person, catching a cold and taking the day

	Jan	Feb	Mar	Apr	May	Jun	Jul	Aug	Sep	Oct	Total
A	Chris	Chris									
B			Chris	Chris	Chris						
C			Jo								
D				Jo	Jo						
E						Jo					
F							Jo				
G						Chris					
H								Jo			
	Jan	Feb	Mar	Apr	May	Jun	Jul	Aug	Sep	Oct	Total
Chris	1	1	1	1	1	1	0	0	0	0	6
Jo	0	0	1	1	1	1	1	1	0	0	6

Figure 21.4 Resource levelling

This is the same set of activities shown in Figures 21.2 and 21.3 but after resource levelling. Activities B to H have all been slipped and rescheduled, such that Chris and Jo are no longer over assigned and have an unbroken period of work.

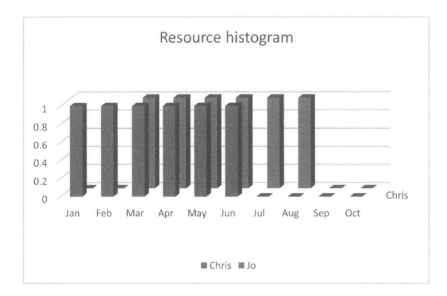

Figure 21.5 Resource levelling histogram

These are the same data as shown in Figure 21.4, but shown as a resource histogram.

off work can have a ripple effect throughout. It is for this reason, resource levelling is often an exercise where approximately right is usually good enough. Do, however, make sure the critical resources, those in most demand and which will cause delays if not available, are planned with particular care. The lessons you learned when reading about critical chain planning in Chapter 20 concerning treating these as a "constraint" should be applied here, even if you aren't actually doing critical chain planning.

Using planning software for resource levelling

As soon as the number of activities and resources grows, the use of planning software becomes essential. Many have automatic levelling features with algorithms to determine which activities are moved or even split. Beware of using these features until you are certain how they work. There is no point in creating a plan if you do not understand the basis on which it is constructed; you have more knowledge of risks and the context for the plan than any planning software and it is vital you use this knowledge to construct a robust plan, rather than trust an algorithm designed by someone who has no knowledge of your situation.

Resource planning

Having understood the terms "loading" and "levelling", let's look at how to create a resource plan. Resource planning is the third step in creating an overall plan (see the left-hand diagram in Figure 21.1). The network analysis carried out as part of developing the schedule plan is fundamental; the network will have determined the first draft of the schedule and hence the critical path and the float; float is the amount by which an activity can be late without affecting the end date.

You can now load the resources onto the schedule and check they are being used efficiently and you have enough:

- if the resources are not being used efficiently, you may want to consider collapsing the schedule but if there is other work (multi-tasking!), then it might not be a problem;
- if you haven't enough resources, you'll either need to acquire more OR re-schedule (resource level) OR do it differently.

When resource levelling, protect the activities on the critical paths as far as possible. Notice I wrote "critical paths" (plural!); there may be more than one. Also, protect the activities which are "near-critical", those with least float. As long as you can protect these, the schedule is maintained, although you may be adding risk. The more activities on or near the critical path, the riskier the schedule plan becomes. A small delay in just one activity would ripple through the plan and impact the end date unless you could take contingency action. Resource levelling causes a similar ripple effect as, by levelling, float is inevitably reduced on more and more activities. If using planning software, you might even find there are some activities with negative float; negative float means the activity is "beyond critical" and lateness is guaranteed. It happens when a date has been "fixed" in the schedule and there is simply not enough time to complete the required work leading up to it. You need to deal with this either through applying more resources or by constructing the plan in a different way, changing the overall strategy and hence network diagram. In some circumstances, it may be necessary to "split" an activity. Splitting an activity means dividing it into two or more activities which do not run one into the other; there is a time gap, when the resources are working on something else.

If resources are devoted to a single project, such as those working on a construction project in an isolated part of the world, then maximizing the use of resources is a good aim. If there is alter- *You should now understand why project planning is too important to be delegated to junior planners!*
native work for the team members, then keeping them gainfully employed may not be an issue. Beware, however, focusing solely only on resource efficiency can be dangerous, as it may threaten the overall success of the project. The aim in any project is to achieve the business objectives and maintain the project's viability; resource efficiency is not an aim in itself, simply one factor which may affect the project's viability.

Resource planning is iterative, often time-consuming and even after all that work, there is likely to be no single "right answer". There will be many possible project plans, all feasible but each with a different level of risk. Start "top-down" by creating a summary project plan and then work up the detailed plans as needed. Often the final allocation of work will be done on a weekly basis, taking into account the ever-changing availability of resources and progress on other activities. Trying to create an accurate and detailed plan from the start is usually a waste of time; spurious accuracy is no substitute for developing a robust plan, which can flex to meet the risks, whether it be for a 48 hour oil production platform shut down for maintenance, weekend working on railway infrastructure, implementation of healthcare systems, development of a new product, or the development of a new missile system.

You should now understand why project planning is too important to be delegated to junior planners!

Real life is not obvious

Project management methods, books, and training courses are divided neatly into different topics: "Yesterday we looked at schedule management, today we'll look at resource management and tomorrow at risk management." This chapter shows "real life" is not so simple. You do not manage a project "a topic at a time" but rather as an ongoing interactive between all the topics: schedule planning requires resources to be verified, which may increase the risk and hence lead to a different schedule plan with amended scope and benefits. Each technique is used as and when needed, often iteratively and in an unpredictable way. You cannot create a scope, schedule, resource, and cost plan in a simple sequence; they must be done together until an overall project plan is created which is viable and for which the risks are acceptable.

Reports used when managing your resources

Tracking resource usage is essential. If you don't, you simply won't know if you will have the people to undertake the remaining work. The control cycle, introduced in Chapter 2 and used for schedule management in Chapter 20, is also at the heart of resource management: once a plan has been agreed, you need to measure progress against the plan, reforecast to the end, note any variances and take steps to adjust the resource plan and bring the project back on schedule if need be; see Figure 21.6. Note, however, resourcing is simply one way of dealing with scheduling issues but the two are inextricably linked.

You need all your resources in place to succeed

Copyright © 1997 Robert Buttrick

Resources – rolling forecast report

Purpose

The purpose of this report is to show, for a project or a work package, the resources which are planned to work on it. This may be for manpower or equipment (Figure 21.6).

When to use it

This report should be used when you need to know who (or what equipment) is planned to be working when. This may be for individual people or items of equipment or for classes or categories of people (skills) or equipment.

Completion

This type of report can be time-consuming to complete manually. It is far better that it is driven by automated feeds from systems such as time recording. On the left it shows the hours worked to date for each item of resource; for example, these could be the actual hours booked to working time on any equipment's log. The main part of the report is the forecast of what work is needed to complete the work package or stage of the project. On the far right is the estimated number of hours for the work, calculated by adding the forecast hours (in the middle) to the actual hours (on the left). The example is from a professional services company and includes, along the top line, the maximum hours that should be forecast in any period, in this case four- or five-week accounting months. This is not the total number of hours in a working month but rather one that has been reduced to 85 per cent capacity to take account of unavoidable "down-time", such as a person being sick or required urgently on another job. If you were to forecast people at 100 per cent, your plan would soon unravel.

MANPOWER - ROLLING FORECAST (HOURLY)

Project: YT2Z/Triton 2000
Detailed Investigation Stage

Period: 4 wks to 28 Sept 2011

Resources	F'cast Month	ACTUAL TO DATE			Oct	Nov	Dec 2010	Jan 2011	Feb	Mar	Apr	May	Jun			FORECAST	Q3	Q4	Q5	Q6	Beyond	F'cast Outturn
		Month	Year	Life																		
					134	134	157	127	134	172	119	119	172	134	127	172	432	425	425	432		
Category 1	70	70	280	560	56	70	70	70	84	112	28											1050
Category 2	75	75	300	600	60	75	75	75	90	120	30											1125
Category 3	30	30	120	240	24	30	30	30	36	48	12											450
Category 4	95	95	380	760	76	95	95	95	114	152	38											1425
Mann. J P	130	130	520	1040	104	130	130	130	156	208	52											1950
Fuller, W	100	100	400	800	80	100	100	100	120	160	40											1500
TOTAL HOURS	500	500	2000	4000	400	500	500	500	600	800	200						432	425	425	432		7500
CUMULATIVE					4400	4900	5400	5900	6500	7300	7500	7500	7500	7500	7500	7500	7500	7500	7500	7500	7500	

This is the guide to the maximum hours per month

This number of hours are forecast by the Project Manager to complete this stage

Forecast may be by resource category or by individual

Figure 21.6 Resources – rolling forecast

Resource usage and capacity report

Purpose

The purpose of the usage and capacity report is to show, for each resource, the number of units assigned to work against the number of units available for work and, by inference, where resources are over- or under-allocated (see Figure 21.7).

When to use it

This report should be used when you suspect a particular resource is over- or under-stretched and action is needed to correct this.

Completion

The report can be in a tabular or graphical format, both of which display the same information. For each time period, show how many units of resource are available and how many have been assigned. This can be done on a white board, in a spreadsheet or as part of a planning package. Any good planning packages will have a range of different reports you can use for this.

Development Function KLO
Function Manager: Perry, TM

MANPOWER - ROLLING FORECAST BY FUNCTION (HOURLY)

Period: 4 wks to 28 Sept 2011

Name/Number	Gd	Disc	Project Code	Managed by	Oct	Nov	Dec 2011	Jan 2012	Feb	Mar	Apr	May	Jun	Jul	Aug	Sep	Q3	Q4	Q5	Q6
					134	134	157	127	134	172	119	119	172	134	127	172	432	425	425	432
Brown, HJ/00345	B	KT	Y4RT	KLO	120	100	70	50	20	10	20	60	60	20	5					
			Y5FT	KLO		25	25	50	50	60	50	20	20							
			Zf5H	HNY	23	9	20	20	8	16	5	5								
			Total		147	134	115	120	78	86	75	80	80	20	5					
			% available		-10%	0%	27%	6%	42%	50%	37%	33%	53%	85%	96%	100%	100%	100%	100%	100%
Green, HJ/00346	C	KT	Y4RT	KLO	20	10		10	20	10	10	5								
			HJUI	HNY	110	80	20		10											
			Total		130	90	20	10	30	10	10	5								
			% available		3%	33%	87%	92%	78%	94%	92%	96%	100%	100%	100%	100%	100%	100%	100%	100%
Unassigned	D	KT	Y4RT	KLO	9	20	70	50	5	5	5	5	5							
			YTDD	FE	120	45	20	20	30	30	20									
			KRG	HNY																
			Total		129		90	70	35	35	25	5								
			% available		4%	33%	92%	80%	96%	96%	96%	100%	100%	100%	100%	100%	100%	100%	100%	100%
TOTAL HOURS COMMITTED					4603	4987	4976	3426	3467	3479	2156	1087	432	210	25					
TOTAL % AVAILABLE					-1%	-9%	7%	21%	24%	41%	47%	73%	93%	95%	99%	100%	100%	100%	100%	100%

Annotations shown on the figure:

- Each person or employee category in the function is listed here
- Hours committed
- % availability
- The total committed hours for the function is shown here. The availability is White Space
- The projects the person is assigned to are shown against their name. The cost centre with management accountability is also given
- Grade
- Discipline

Figure 21.7 Manpower – rolling forecast by function

Once all the project manpower forecasts have been collated, they can be sorted to give each line manager a listing of the people in his/her department or function, stating to which projects each is committed. (Adapted by kind permission of Professional Applications Ltd, UK.)

Workout 21.1 – Planning your resources

You should do this exercise if resources are a limiting constraint on your project's times-cales. You will need the network diagram and schedule plan outputs from Workout 19.1; if you haven't got them, you will need to complete Workout 20.1. Work with the same team in a similar workshop format, using flip charts, white boards and Post-It® Notes.

1   Take the network diagram and initial schedule plan you produced in Workout 20.1 and place them on the wall next to your working area. You should have the duration for each activity noted on the sheet.

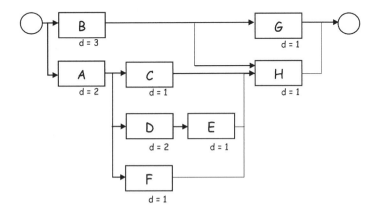

2   On a large sheet of paper or whiteboard, create a calendar to cover the expected period of the project. Using the network diagram from step 1 as a reference, create a time based network diagram.

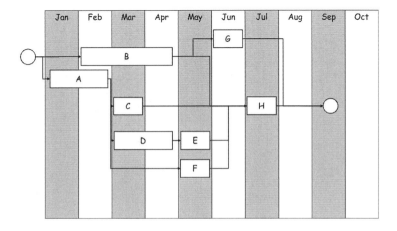

3 Load the resources onto the plan: mark up the diagram to show who will be undertaking which activities, then total up the amount of effort for each person (or resource) needed in each time period. If a person is over-allocated, ring the total.

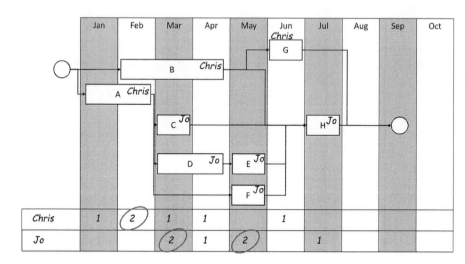

4 On a separate sheet of paper, create a schedule plan. Use the time-based network diagram from step 3, to determine the "free float" on each activity. This is the amount of time an activity can slip without moving any succeeding activities. Keep this on one side as your reference starting point. This is your unconstrained plan.

Resource	Jan	Feb	Mar	Apr	May	Jun	Jul	Aug	Sep	Oct
Chris		A								
Chris			B							
Jo			C							
Jo			D							
Jo					E					
Jo					F					
Chris						G				
Jo							H			

5   Level the resources: return to the network chart from step 3 and look at what activities you can move, within the free float you worked out in step 4. For example, Chris is over-allocated in February; you can slip Activity B to relieve this, as Activity B has a month's free float. For Jo, it's a bit tricky. Jo is over-allocated in March. You could slip Activity C to June but that still leaves Activities E and F in May as a problem; you'll need to slip one of these, but cannot relieve this over-allocation unless Activity H is also slipped one month. In effect we "steal" some float off Activity H and use it for Activity F. Having moved the activities, add up the resource allocation to check no one is over-assigned.

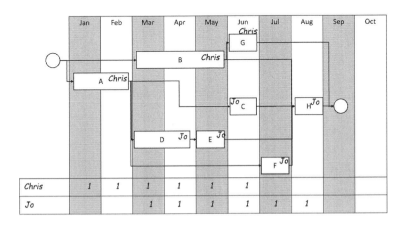

6   Redraw the schedule plan, adding the free float. For example, notice, by reference to the initial schedule plan in step 4, the total float for the project has reduced from two months to one month: this represents contingency.

Resource	Jan	Feb	Mar	Apr	May	Jun	Jul	Aug	Sep	Oct
Chris	◇	A								
Chris				B						
Jo						C				
Jo			D							
Jo					E					
Jo							F			
Chris						G				
Jo								H	◇	
Chris	1	1	1	1	1	1				
Jo			1	1	1	1	1	1		

7   Assess the overall risk of the levelled schedule and change it if necessary. For example, notice, in the worked example, the free float on Activity C has reduced from three months (in step 4) to one month. This may not be a problem, but if your estimate of Activity C is uncertain (i.e. the activity is risky), then you may want to revise the plan to reflect this, as shown below.

Resource	Jan	Feb	Mar	Apr	May	Jun	Jul	Aug	Sep	Oct
Chris	◇	A								
Chris			B							
Jo			C							
Jo				D						
Jo						E				
Jo							F			
Chris						G				
Jo								H		◇
Chris	1	1	1	1	1	1				
Jo			1	1	1	1	1	1		

In order to prevent the charts being too congested, I have recommended you show the float on a separate schedule plan. If you find it easier, you could add the float to the network diagram and simply work from that.

The two key aspects to look out for when levelling are:

- the impact on the risk – some solutions may be less risky than others, but always give risky activities the most float;
- the continuity in the use of resources – sometimes continuous use is preferable to a "stop-start" approach, but sometimes it is not achievable and some activities may even need to be split to keep to a deadline. **You need all your resources in place to succeed**

22

Managing the finances

The financial plan

Financial management controls

Estimating the costs

Authorization to spend funds

Recording actual costs and committed costs

Financial reporting

Earned value

Just as a schedule plan is used as the baseline for measuring progress in terms of "time", the financial plan is the basis for measuring costs and financial benefits.

"We haven't the money, so we've got to think"

LORD RUTHERFORD, 1871–1937

- **Plan in summary for the full project.**
- **Base your costs on the same work breakdown as your schedule.**
- **Estimate in detail before you start work on the next stage.**
- **Once a budget is agreed, baseline it.**
- **Keep your eye on the future – forecast benefits and costs regularly.**
- **Keep your eye on cash flow – the lifeblood of any organization.**

The financial plan

After managing the schedule, management of the finances is the next most important and fundamental aspect of project management. Without a good resourced, schedule plan, it is impossible to have a reliable financial plan. While the schedule is the aspect of a project most apparent to outsiders, cost is often the most visible to insiders, such as the management team – sometimes it is the only aspect they see (or want to see!), especially in organizations which are driven by their finance departments.

At a simple level, a project's financial plan will tell you:

- what each stage and work package in the project costs;
- who is accountable for those costs;
- the financial benefits deriving from the project;
- who is accountable for the realization of those benefits;
- financial commitments made;
- cash flow;
- financial authorization given.

In addition, some organizations also derive the net effect of the project on their balance sheet and profit and loss account.

Just as the schedule plan is used as the baseline for measuring progress in terms of "time", the financial plan is the basis for measuring costs and financial benefits. Many of the principles I have already explained on schedule management are also applicable to the management of finances as schedule and cost plans should share the same work breakdown structure (WBS). By doing this you ensure:

- accountability for both the schedule and cost resides with the same person;
- there is no overlap, hence double counting of costs;
- there is no "gap", i.e. missing costs.

In practice, you will develop the financial plan to a lesser level of work breakdown than the schedule plan.

The financial plan, like the schedule plan, is developed in summary for the full project and in detail for the next stage. There is little point in developing an "accurate" and detailed financial plan on the back of an unstable schedule plan. No matter to what level of granularity of detail you take the calculations, they will be fundamentally inaccurate. You should take the level of accuracy and confidence forward, with the schedule and related costs matching.

The costs are influenced by the following and you must take these into account when drawing up your plan:

- the scope of the project;
- the approach you take to the project;
- the timescale to complete the project;
- the risks associated with the project.

Financial management controls

Financial management of a project comprises:

- estimating the costs and benefits (preparing the financial plan);
- obtaining authorization to spend funds;
- recording actual costs and committed costs;
- forecasting future costs and cash flow;
- reporting.

As illustrated in Figure 22.1, you should plan and track your costs on a stage-by-stage basis, authorizing the funding for each stage at the preceding (or entry) gate. In this way, you limit your commitments to a stage at a time, thereby preventing the full project budget being consumed on the early stages. I am still amazed at the number of organizations which allocate the full funding for the project "upfront", then are surprised when it is spent with little to show for it. Cost tracking is done in the context of the project control cycle. Tracking spend (and any financial benefits) toward your objective is essential. If you don't do it, you simply won't know how much the project will cost. The control cycle is exactly the same as that used for schedule management and is repeated in Figure 22.2: once a financial plan has been agreed, it is necessary to measure progress against the plan, reforecast to the end, note any variances, and take steps to bring the project back within budget if need be.

Bookkeeping!

You should distinguish between the management of costs from a management accounting perspective and from a financial perspective The latter relates to "bookkeeping" where the transactions appear in the formal accounts and include accruals, provisions, depreciation, and other treatments. In the management of projects, this is of little direct use. Managing the actual spend and cash flow is simpler and provides far greater control.

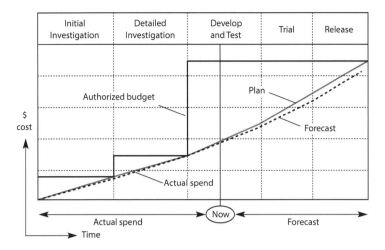

Figure 22.1 Project costs

This figure shows cumulative spend for a typical project, which includes the sum actually spent plus the forecast to completion. This can be compared against the plan (or budget). In the example, the project is forecast to be completed slightly below budget. Also shown is the authorized budget. This goes up in steps. At first a small amount of funding is given to undertake the initial investigation only. This is then increased, based on the results of the initial investigation, to cover the cost of the detailed investigation. Finally, a full business case provides the basis to authorize the remaining funds to complete the development and test, trial and release stages.

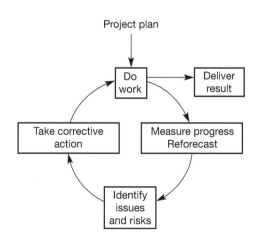

Figure 22.2 Project control cycle

The project control cycle comprises doing the work as set out in your plan, identifying any risks, opportunities, or issues and taking corrective action to keep the project on track. From time to time, results, in the form of deliverables, are generated. (Copyright © PA Consulting Group, London.)

Estimating the costs

"A little inaccuracy sometimes saves tons of explanation"

SAKI

Your cost estimates should be based on the work scope and schedule plan defined in the project definition. You should use the same work breakdown structure as the schedule plan and estimate to the same level of accuracy (summary versus detail).

Your estimate should at least be made up of:

- the cost of using your own employees and equipment;
- the cost of external purchases made as a result of the project.

The overall cost plan should be built up from three elements:

- the base estimate;
- scope reserve;
- contingency.

The **base estimate** is the total of costs for all the activities you have identified, including the cost of your own employees' time and all external purchases.

The **scope reserve** is an estimate of what else your experience and common sense tells you needs to be done, but has not yet been explicitly identified.

Scope reserve can be very large: for example, in the early stages of a project, the scope reserve required in software development stages can be as high as 50 per cent of the base estimate.

The authority to use "scope reserve" is normally, but not necessarily, delegated to the project manager who should use formal change control (see Chapter 25) to move funds from "scope reserve" to "base estimate".

Contingency is included in the estimate to take account of the unexpected, i.e. risks. It is *not* there to compensate for poor estimating. If a risk does not occur, the money put aside as contingency should not be spent. For this reason, the authorization for spending contingency usually rests with the project sponsor. Again, formal change control should be used to move the costs from "contingency" to "base estimate" as you are formally changing the plan. This should be done under the same change request as that for including the contingency plan (schedule, resources, etc.) and its impacts on other aspects of the plan, such as the schedule and scope.

The proportion of your estimate divided between these elements will alter as the project moves through its life cycle stages. You should expect a higher proportion of scope reserve and contingency in the early stages than in the later stages. The accuracy of estimates also alters, depending on the life cycle stage of the project. Figure 22.3 shows in the earlier stages you expect the bulk of the cost to be "soft" except for the next stage; the next stage should be a "hard" estimate. This matches the principle of outline and detail planning. Outline plans tend to be soft; detail plans are hard.

A **soft estimate** is one in which only a low level of confidence can be placed.

A **hard estimate** is one in which you have high confidence.

Regardless of whether your estimates are soft or hard, it is important to state any assumptions, constraints, or qualifications you have. These should be recorded in Part 1 of your business case.

	Initial Investigation	Detailed Investigation	Develop and Test	Trial	Release
At Initial Investigation Gate	Soft	None	None	None	None
At Detailed Investigation Gate	ACTUAL	Hard	Soft	Soft	Soft
At Development Gate	ACTUAL	ACTUAL	Hard	Hard	Hard
At Trial Gate	ACTUAL	ACTUAL	ACTUAL	Hard	Hard
At Ready for Service Gate	ACTUAL	ACTUAL	ACTUAL	ACTUAL	Hard

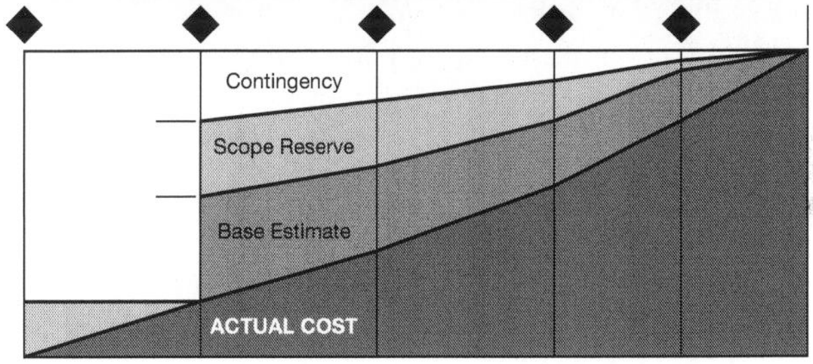

Figure 22.3 Estimating accuracy

In the earlier stages, you should expect the bulk of the cost to be "soft" except for the next stage. The next stage should always be a "hard" estimate. This then alters as you roll through the life cycle stages of the project until you reach the start of the develop and test stage, when your full estimate should be hard. The proportion of estimate distributed between contingency, scope reserve and base estimate also alters as you progress through the project. Toward the start, you should expect a greater proportion of contingency and scope reserve than you would toward the end of the project.

Authorization to spend funds

All organizations have rules which mandate the authority to spend money. If you are a subsidiary, such rules may be imposed on you by your parent organization and can be onerous and time-consuming if not matched to the project process you are using. As a minimum, you should ensure the timing of financial authorization, as laid out in your finance processes, matches the gates in your project framework.

Each of the gates in the project framework provides the opportunity to allocate funds to the project. You should allocate a limited amount of money at the very start of the project (initial investigation gate) to investigate the proposal, enabling an informed decision to be made later at the detailed investigation gate on whether to proceed further. Subsequently, further funds can be allocated on a stage-by-stage basis until the project is completed.

Alternatively, if risks are acceptable, it may be better to allocate funds for more than one stage, thus avoiding the need to obtain authorization from a senior body a number of times and saving time on your projects. If this is done, it is still part of the project sponsor's accountabilities to undertake the gate reviews to check on the on-going viability of the project and make the decision. Just because you've been given the money, it doesn't mean that you continue on blindly.

Just because you've been given the money, it doesn't mean that you continue on blindly.

For long stages, it may be prudent to hold back full authorization and introduce intermediate review points when the project is reassessed prior to further funding being authorized. Such points may conveniently be prior to major commitments, such as letting a contract.

The project framework will work for whichever way you choose to arrange fund authorization. The key is to ensure that such authorization processes:

- are consistent with the principles of the project framework;
- concentrate only on substantive issues;
- are not too lengthy;
- do not duplicate other reviews or approvals.

The decision-making approach outlined in Chapter 4 (Figure 4.5) poses three questions:

- Question 1: Is the project viable in its own right?
- Question 2: What is its priority relative to other projects?
- Question 3: Is funding available?

The control document (business case) used at the detailed investigation gate and at the development gate provides the information needed to answer each question – you should not need to provide a different document for each question. This has two advantages:

- you do not need to write a number of different but similar documents;
- you can be sure the answer to each question is based on compatible (the same!) information.

In certain circumstances, you will be able to delegate all the decisions, based on these questions, to the same person or group. This all depends on how you are organized but distinguishing between the key questions will help you make the decision in a rational way. For example, there is no point in prioritizing a project (Question 2) which cannot stand up in its own right (Question 1).

Throughout this book, I have distinguished between approval and authorization. **Approval** is used when an individual accepts a deliverable as fit for purpose such that the project can continue. **Authorization** is used for allocating the funding and resources needed to carry on the project, giving the project sponsor and project manager the authority to direct and manage the project.

Approval in some form is always required before any funding is authorized, although the converse is not true; just because authorization of funding has been given, it does not mean that *approval* has been given to complete the project. For example, you may have been given, at the detailed investigation gate, full funding to complete a simple project. Work during any of the subsequent stages may uncover issues which cannot be resolved. In this case, approval at subsequent gates might not be forthcoming and the project should be terminated. In such circumstances, the unused project funds should be returned to their source.

Authorization of funds is usually based on some form of investment appraisal. I do not intend to go into this in any detail as there are many books dealing with the plethora of possible methods. While each organization will have its preferred approach, the following key points should be considered:

- investment appraisal should be based on cash flow;
- discounted cash flow techniques are the most favoured;
- use least cost development (lowest net present value (NPV)) if you must do the project;
- use internal rate of return (IRR) for other projects;
- concentrate on substantive elements only – if a figure is wrong and has no significant impact on the appraisal, don't waste time changing it;
- use sensitivity analyses liberally – they give you more feel for the project than spurious accuracy in estimates;
- use scenario analysis to check possible outcomes;
- do not consider financial criteria as sacrosanct: many projects are worth doing for non-financial reasons because they support your basic strategic direction;
- some things can't be reduced to solely financial terms: just because you can't count something, it doesn't mean it doesn't count!
- always consider the risks involved in any decision you make.

Recording actual costs and committed costs

Some things can't be reduced to financial terms. Just because you can't count them doesn't mean they don't count!

If you are to have any visibility over the cost of your project, you will need to have a system of capturing the costs, from wherever they originate in your organization and allocating them to the project. Similarly, you will need to have a method of capturing commitments relating to each project. **Commitments** are orders placed and hence the money, although not yet spent, is committed as part of an agreed contract. If this is to have any meaning costs should be split into:

- money that stays within the organization (e.g. cost of staff and equipment, drawing on internal stores);
- money that leaves the organization (e.g. paid to contractors, consultants, suppliers).

In cash flow terms this distinction is critical as the former have already been "bought", but you have not yet decided what project or activity to apply them to. The latter are not spent at all if the project does not proceed.

In addition, it is essential to have the costs captured for each stage of the project so you can confidently manage actual spend against authorized budget on a stage-by-stage basis. Most mature organizations also capture costs at lower levels in the work breakdown structure, known as a work packages.

 What if I cannot measure costs as you suggest?

A good project or matrix accounting system is vital if you are to reap the full benefits of business-driven project management. If you are unable to account for costs on a project-by-project basis, you will have to rely on conventional cost centre-based accounting or manual processes to maintain control: you have no alternative. This will mean the balance of power remains firmly with the functions that own those cost centres and away from the project (see Figure 2.10).

It is still well worth using the tools, techniques and guidance given in this book but you will be limited in the depth to which they can be applied and ingrained in your culture. No matter what you, as project sponsors or managers, say concerning the importance of projects, line managers will pay more attention to their cost centre accounts simply because they are visible and what their performance is based on.

Financial reporting

The future is more important than the past. Any money you have already spent is lost (sunk) and cannot be recovered. For this reason you must not only record what you have actually spent but also forecast what is yet to be spent. The important figure to concentrate on is the cost at completion or "what the project will have cost by the time it is completed".

To arrive at this figure, you simply add any costs incurred to date to any cost you have yet to incur. The forecast is simply an estimate of what figures are going to appear on your project account during any particular period. So your forecasts must:

- use the same costing methods as actuals are measured;
- be forecast on at least a stage-by-stage basis;
- be timed to match the actuals (usually a monthly cut-off is used).

Figure 22.4 on page 356 shows a typical report for building up the forecast.

Organizations, by means of their accounting and operational systems, collect a considerable volume of data. Unless these data are converted into meaningful information, they are useless. Any reports you produce must be aimed at providing useful information and prompting for action. This implies the reports should be targeted at specific roles within your organization. As the reports seek to promote action they should be:

- timely;
- as accurate as possible within those time constraints;
- forward-looking.

Further, unless individuals involved in collecting the data gain some benefits themselves, the quality of the data will erode and the reporting become useless.

Don't be driven solely by bookkeeping

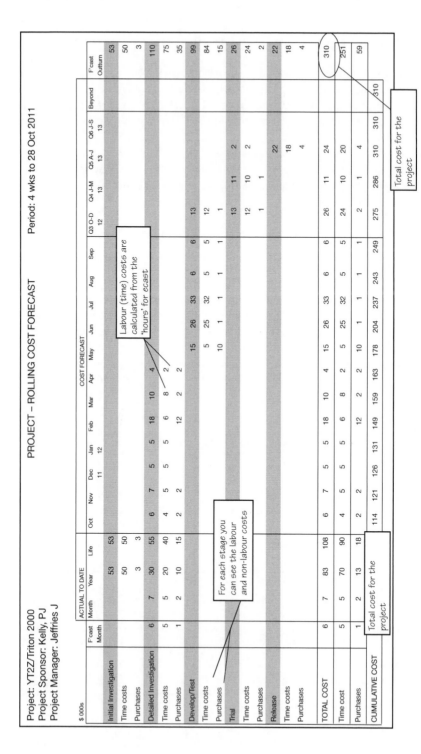

Figure 22.4 A typical report for building the forecast

This report gives a stage-by-stage summary of the total costs for a project and is ideally suited for building the forecast. For example, the time cost line could be derived from a manpower forecast such as that given in Figure 16.2.

Figure 22.5 overleaf is a typical financial report and tells you, in financial terms:

- what has been spent to date;
- the expected cost outcome for the project;
- the impact on the current financial year;
- the cost of work yet to be done.

In addition, you should have detailed reports to:

- list every transaction/purchase made on the project;
- detail time booked to the project for people.

It's not my fault – blame the project manager!

The financial director of a company wanted the project managers to pay more attention to their projects costs. There had been a number of serious cost over-runs, which if the trend continued would impact the bottom line. It sounded very sensible. Unfortunately, real cost information took six weeks to be collated and made available to the project managers, by which time any corrective action they could take was limited. The project managers did not argue with the aim, which was to get the project costs under control, nor that it was part of their job. What they did argue with was having to keep their own "shadow" accounts in order to keep abreast of the costs as the finance department provided such a slow service . . . in fact, the finance department didn't even think it was its job to provide "a service".

Contrast that with another organization, in a similar situation: in this case, the Chief Financial Officer saw it as his role to provide managers with timely informa-tion to help them manage their work. As a result he quickly implemented simple "on-line, real-time reporting" for the project managers as part of the finance sys-tem upgrades.

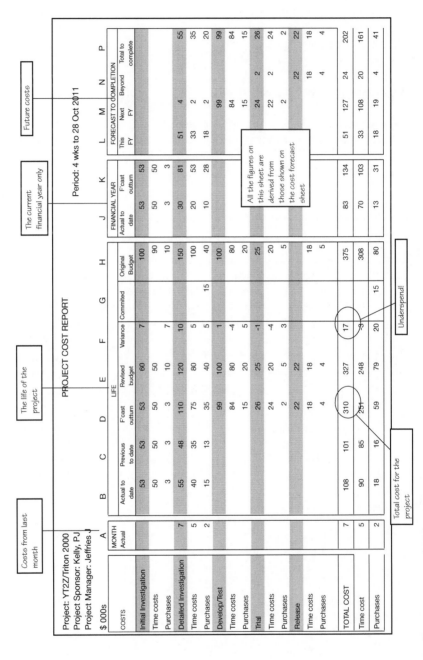

PROJECT COST REPORT

Project: YT2Z/Triton 2000
Project Sponsor: Kelly, PJ
Project Manager: Jeffries J

Period: 4 wks to 28 Oct 2011

$ 000s

Callout labels: Costs from last month · The life of the project · The current financial year only · Future costs · Total cost for the project · Underspend! · All the figures on this sheet are derived from those shown on the cost forecast sheet.

	A	B	C	D	E	F	G	H		J	K		L	M	N	P
COSTS	MONTH Actual	Actual to date	Previous to date	F'cast outturn	Revised budget	Variance	Committed	Original Budget		Actual to date	F'cast outturn		This FY	Next FY	Beyond	Total to complete
					LIFE					FINANCIAL YEAR			FORECAST TO COMPLETION			
Initial Investigation		53	53	53	60	7		100		53	53					55
Time costs		50	50	50	50			90		50	50					35
Purchases		3	3	3	10	7		10		3	3					20
Detailed Investigation	7	55	48	110	120	10		150		30	81		51	4		55
Time costs	5	40	35	75	80	5		100		20	53		33	2		35
Purchases	2	15	13	35	40	5	15	40		10	28		18	2		20
Develop/Test				99	100	1		100						99		99
Time costs				84	80	-4		80						84		84
Purchases				15	20	5		20						15		15
Trial				26	25	-1		25						24	2	26
Time costs				24	20	-4		20						22	2	24
Purchases				2	5	3		5						2		2
Release				22	22										22	22
Time costs				18	18			18							18	18
Purchases				4	4			5							4	4
TOTAL COST	7	108	101	310	327	17	17	375		83	134		51	127	24	202
Time cost	5	90	85	251	248	-3		308		70	103		33	108	20	161
Purchases	2	18	16	59	79	20	15	80		13	31		18	19	4	41

Figure 22.5 The financial report

A report such as this gives you, on a stage-by-stage basis, all the key financial information you should require: actual costs, forecast costs, commitments

Earned value

Integrating cost and time reporting

One of the difficulties with measuring project costs against planned costs is, on its own, you can gain very little information from a fact such as: "At this point in the project we planned to have spent £340,000 but have only spent £250,000." What does this apparent £90,000 underspend mean?

- Have we underspent and the project is going very well?
- Are we running late, but spending at the correct rate?
- Are we overspending and running late?

From the basic facts I have given you, you cannot tell. Earned value analysis (now called earned value management) was created by the US Department of Defense in the 1960s to help solve this problem and bring greater clarity to measuring the performance of their contractors. It is an method advocated by many people, including the College of Performance Management, and exists in a number of different forms. The use of this approach is often mandated by government agencies and some multinational organizations when letting contracts and it is in this context you are most likely to find it. It is less apparent in other situations and rarely seen practised on an enterprise-wide basis on all projects within an organization.

The Project Management Institute's glossary defines earned value management (EVM) as: "A method for integrating scope, schedule and resources and for measuring project performance. It compares the amount of work which was planned with what was actually earned with what was actually spent to determine if cost and schedule performance are as planned."

I doubt if many people can understand that in one reading! Perhaps this apparent complexity is what makes its use rare except in mandated circumstances and what has led the PMI® to replace a plethora of abbreviations (such as BCWS, BCWP, ACWP) with simpler equivalents.

Before we look at earned value in more detail, here's a word of warning: the term "value" has much wider uses than that described in this section. You therefore need to be clear what this method doesn't give you. Earned value does not tell you:

- the residual "financial value" of the project at a point in time if it were to be terminated;
- the benefit gained from the project to date;
- the financial value of any assets produced by the project;
- the usefulness of the project's outputs to the sponsoring organization.

Nor does it have anything to do with another discipline – value management – aimed at choosing the most cost-effective

A word of warning: the term "value" has much wider uses than that described in this section.

solution to meet a particular business need or set of requirements. It is simply a way of looking at performance in terms of schedule and cost in a combined way.

Project S-curves

For many organizations, the simple two line "S-curve" ("planned cost" and "actual cost + forecast") shown in Figure 22.1, supplemented by milestone tracking, is sufficient for project tracking purposes. Nevertheless, as more organizations automate their project management environments, it is possible that earned value techniques could become more common. Whilst Figure 22.1 uses only two lines for cost tracking, EVM adds a third line, showing the "earned value of work completed to date". The earned value line is costed using the same basis as in the plan. Thus, if work package A is planned to cost £25,000, once it is completed, the earned value is £25,000 *regardless of how much it actually cost*, rather like standard costing. It follows, if a project produces all its deliverables at the point in time they were planned to be delivered, the earned value and planned lines is coincident. Figure 22.6 shows this in the form of S-curves. You can calculate two specific variances from these three lines which are shown in Table 22.1.

Looking at Figure 22.6, we can now see the answer to the question I posed at the start of this section. Progress on the project is mixed: it is underspent but running late. So far, what has been completed has been delivered £50,000 cheaper than planned (cost variance = +50) but £40,000 less work has been completed than should have been (schedule variance = –40). On the other hand, the project is forecast to be completed £100,000 under plan and almost one period early. You may wonder what is behind such an optimistic forecast; perhaps all the difficult work has been completed already, thereby forming a better basis for undertaking the remainder of the project.

Performance indices

Estimating the cost of the project at completion is where one of the more controversial calculations for the method comes in. A factor called the cost performance index (CPI) is widely used to forecast the total cost of the project at completion. If a work

Table 22.1 Specific variance calculations

Cost variance	earned value – actual cost	The difference between what has been delivered (based on planned cost) and what it actually cost.	+ve = underspent −ve = overspent
Schedule variance	earned value – planned value	The difference between what has been delivered (based on planned cost) and what it was planned to have cost.	+ve = early −ve = late

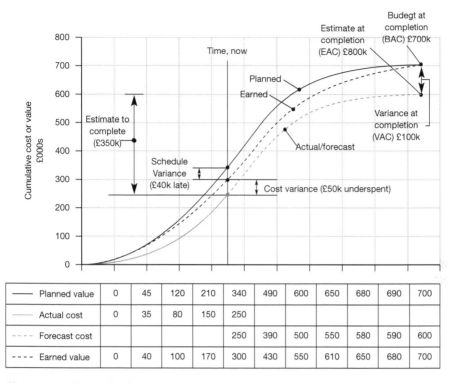

——— Planned value	0	45	120	210	340	490	600	650	680	690	700
········ Actual cost	0	35	80	150	250						
– – – Forecast cost					250	390	500	550	580	590	600
- - - - Earned value	0	40	100	170	300	430	550	610	650	680	700

Figure 22.6 Earned value management – typical project

The three lines used in the method are shown – Planned, Earned, and Actual – each of which shows the typical S-curve shape. If the project ran exactly as planned, these lines would be coincident. In our example, we were planned to have spent £340k but in fact have only spent £250k. Are we late? By referring to the "earned value" line we can see that progress on the project is mixed: it is underspent but running late. So far, what has been completed has been delivered £50k cheaper than planned (cost variance = +50) but £40k less work has been completed than should have been (schedule variance = –40). On the other hand, the project is forecast to be completed £100k under plan and almost one period early.

package within a project is in progress and over-budget, the calculation assumes the final cost will exceed the planned cost by the same margin. This assumption implies the situation will neither improve nor deteriorate further. In our example, the method would indicate a cost at completion of £583,000, somewhat less than the £600,000 forecast by the project manager. See Table 22.2.

Experts in the use of this method will spot the problem immediately. In the example, the project has been treated as a single entity, whereas proper use of the method requires the project to be divided into a large number of work packages, with the earned value analysis performed discretely on each. They are then summed to provide the overall status for the project.

Table 22.2 Cost of project at completion

CPI (£)	Cost performance index	earned value/ actual cost	120%	> 100% = underspent
SPI (£)	Schedule performance index	earned value/ planned cost	88%	< 100% = late
EAC	Estimate at completion (Project manager estimate)	Total estimated cost for the project	£600k	
BAC	Budget at completion	Total planned cost for the project	£700k	
VAC	Variance at completion	EAC – BAC	£100k	+ = underspent

Earned schedule

One of the drawbacks of using earned value management is due to the way the performance indices are calculated. By definition, the schedule variance must converge to 0.0 at project completion, whilst the schedule performance index is at 1.0, regardless of how late or early the project is. At a point, about two-thirds of the way through the project, these become meaningless. A solution to this, developed by Walt Lipke and validated by Kym Henderson, is the "earned schedule" method. In this, rather than using cost as a measure for schedule performance it looks at when the work was to have been completed; the earned schedule measure identifies when the amount of earned value achieved so far, should have been earned. As shown in Figure 22.7, this is the point on the plan line where the planned value equals the earned value accrued. The vertical line from the point on the plan line to the time axis determines the "earned" portion of the schedule. The duration from the beginning of the project to the intersection of the time axis is the amount of earned schedule (ES). The schedule performance indicator, when measured in time, would be the earned schedule/actual time or in the example, $15/18 = 0.83$. As it is less than 1.0, this shows the project is late. The planned duration (PD) is simply the original duration of the project, in our case PD = 42 weeks. The estimated final duration is simply the planned duration divided by the SPI(t). At month 18 of our project our SPI(t) was 0.83. So at that time we would have estimated the final duration as 42/0.83 or 51 weeks. In fact, in our example in Figure 22.6, the project came in on time and £100k below budget; clearly this must have been a "must meet the deadline" project and a lot of scope was discarded . . . perhaps they left the roof off the stadium?

How useful is the earned value method?

The usefulness of earned value management as a method is controversial. The greatest critics see it as a waste of time, whilst there are enthusiastic advocates claiming it is "the only way". In the middle are those who recognize the information gained

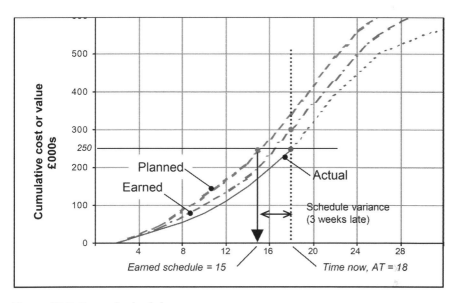

Figure 22.7 Earned schedule

The three lines used in the method are shown, but instead of reporting the costs, as shown on the "y" axis, we use the "x" axis to show the schedule effect.

is potentially useful but are sceptical as to whether the effort needed to collate the data is worth it. As stated earlier, the method was primarily designed for the contracting environment and, as such, is more applicable to the post-investigative stages (develop and test, trial, release); some contracts even have a requirement for the contractors to use the method. The uncertainty around the investigative stages makes it very difficult for the method to add any additional information for the data collection and analysis effort required.

Its usefulness is dependent on having:

- a detailed plan covering cost, resources, and schedule, with appropriate WBS;
- accurate and timely cost information and supporting systems;
- realistic schedule progress reporting;
- effective change control;
- documented requirements leading to stable scope;
- project managers skilled in the method.

If any one of these is deficient, the benefit of using the method will be significantly devalued. For enterprise-wide project management, it is unlikely to prove useful simply because of the wide range of project management competencies such an environment encompasses. Simplicity and ease of data collation are key if the method is to gain a strong foothold outside its traditional "large contract" environment. In such cases, however, the results from earned value management, when used in conjunction with other information, can provide an early indication of the performance of a project, provoking action to resolve problems sooner rather than later.

 Cost? Schedule? Value?

Why are we suddenly talking about "schedule" in a chapter on finances? I would hope that by now you'll know the answer to that question! However, just to emphasize it, the answer is very simple. A project plan comprises schedule, resources, scope, costs, and benefits. Each aspect of the plan changes whenever one of the other aspects shifts; they are intrinsically bound together. As a text book, it is useful to separate the different aspects of planning into its constituent part but that is purely to help understanding. In real life they all happen together and so sometimes the answer to a problem of one aspect is found in a different aspect of the plan.

Workout 22.1 – Project finances

1 Choose one of your projects, preferably one which is in the develop and test stage or beyond.

2 Ask the finance manager, the project sponsor, and the project manager questions (a) to (e):

    a For both time costs and purchases, provide, for the project as a whole, as at the close of the last month's accounting period:

- costs spent to date;
- costs spent this financial year;
- estimated cost at completion;
- agreed budget, when the project was authorized.

    b Answer question (a) for the current work stage.

    c How are "time costs" calculated?

    d Where were these data obtained from?

    e State how easy or how difficult the information was to obtain.

Consider the replies. How long did it take for them to be compiled? Do they give the same information? What parts are missing? Were the same sources for the data used? If there is great consistency, fine. If not, look behind the replies. For example, if it takes a long while to compile the information or some is missing, can you reasonably be expected to work within your budget? Is it acceptable to "fly blind" without adequate instruments? If you are in this situation you should now possess the facts to have a conversation with your project sponsor (or other manager) about being held accountable for something you cannot measure in a timely way. Take the stance that it should be the finance function's job to provide cost information as they own the financial systems.

23

Managing what might go wrong (or right)

Risks

Considering possible threats and opportunities

Addressing threats at the start of the project

Addressing opportunities at the start of the project

Monitoring risks once the project is in progress

Tips on using the risk log

More sophisticated risk evaluation techniques

Taking active steps to reduce the possible effects of risks is not indicative of pessimism, but a positive indication of good project management.

"It is certain because it is impossible"

TERTULLIAN, c AD160–225

- **Risk management starts when the project starts.**
- **Reduce the likelihood of threats materializing.**
- **Contingency plan in the event that threats do materialize.**
- **Focus on the "big ones", but don't lose sight of the others.**
- **Look for opportunities to increase benefits, but not at the cost of increasing risk.**
- **Plan for the most likely opportunities.**

Considering possible threat and opportunities

Risk is the effect of uncertainty on the objectives. Their effect can be positive (**opportunity**) or negative (**threat**); they could impact the realization of benefits. Risks can be event-based or shocks – events that may or may not happen, like accidents. Alternatively, they could be information-based, where we just don't know the facts, for example where costs are underestimated or based on false assumptions, such as interest rates, inflation, exchange rates, or even the weather. All projects are exposed to risk in some form but the extent will vary considerably.

Figure 23.1 shows how risk management sits within the context of other project controls; a risk will become an issue if the event occurs or assumption proved false.

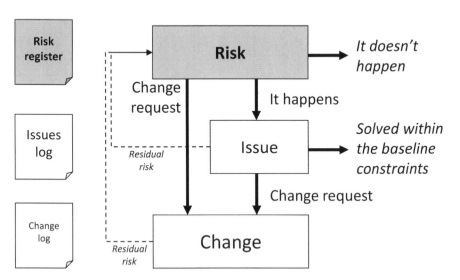

Figure 23.1 Risks, issues, and change control

A **risk** will become an **issue** if the event or occurrence occurs. Issues can be resolved either within the scope of the project as currently defined or via a **change** to the project.

Issues can be resolved either within the scope of the project as currently defined or via a change to the project. Figure 23.2 shows that, once the project is well under way, the threats, or "downside risk", are usually bigger than any "up-side" opportunities due to people having a bias towards being optimistic, as well as wanting to play down the threats in order to get the project authorized!

The purpose of risk management is to ensure:

- threats and opportunities on projects are identified and evaluated in a consistent way;
- threats to the project's success are recognized and addressed, and significant opportunities are exploited without undue delay.

You cannot use risk management to eliminate threats altogether but by careful planning, you might be able to avoid them in some instances or minimize the disruption in others. What if identified threats do not materialize? What if a new approach (opportunity!) comes about which will further your business objectives better than planned? You have two options:

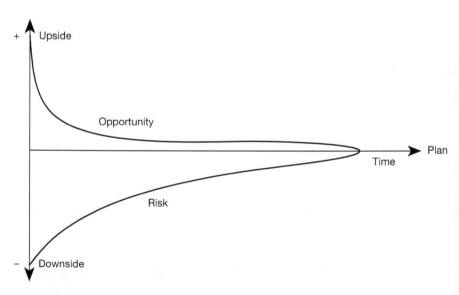

Figure 23.2 Upside and downsides to a project

Once the project is well under way, the risk, or "downside", is usually bigger than any upside opportunities. This is because people are often too optimistic regarding what their project may achieve.

- keep to the original plan, as something quite unexpected may still go wrong and eat into the time and money you've saved; or
- build the new found opportunity into the project and "mine it" for all it's worth.

Traditionally, the former approach is the more prudent but does not necessarily make the most business sense in all cases.

Addressing threats at the start of the project

You should address risk when the project is being set up, during the initial investigation stage. Risk is an important section within the project definition; when a project sponsor approves a project he/she does so in full knowledge of the stated risks, accepting the consequences should things go wrong. It is important the project sponsor accepts the risks as the person undertaking this role is the primary risk taker. For this reason, I suggest you start by addressing the "threats" as these are what will cause your project to fail if they are not managed.

Sometimes, it is easier to identify what might go wrong in terms of creating the deliverables than assessing what may go wrong in terms of outcomes or benefits realization. If your projects are truly business led, you must

When a project sponsor approves a project he/she does so in full knowledge of the stated risks, accepting the consequences should things go wrong.

consider both. To ensure you remember this, it can be helpful to think of your risks in terms of *delivery risks* and *business risks*. Delivery risks impact delivery during the project, whereas business risks impact the outcomes and benefits realization. Naturally, a delivery risk – e.g. significant delay to the project deliverable – may also have an adverse effect on benefits. Don't be too purist! The key is to recognize how some risks (often uncertainties), such as changes in exchange rate or competitor action, clearly not associated with project delivery, but affect benefits (i.e. a business risk). Once you have a "business-led project" mind-set, you won't need to distinguish between delivery and business risks as you will intuitively identify the risks which really matter; the way a risk is described will be sufficient to manage it.

The steps for addressing risk are:

1 brainstorm all the risks that may jeopardize the success of the project. Remember to include those under the control of the project team (e.g. completeness of project scope, quality of technical solutions, competence of project team) as well as those which are largely outside the control of the team (e.g. legislative changes, competitor activity, economic climate). Use checklists to supplement the list after the brainstorm is complete;

2 review each risk in turn;

3 assess the likelihood of the risk occurring;

4 assess the severity of the impact on the project if it occurs;

5　use a risk matrix such as the one that in Table 23.1 to determine the "risk category" (high, medium, low);

6　for high risks, consider ways of preventing or avoiding the event, reducing the impact, or transferring the risk to someone else. Contingency planning is a last resort but as the risk is high, consider making your "contingency plan" the mainstream plan;

7　for medium risks, take preventative, reduction, or transfer measures. Failing that, prepare a contingency plan;

8　for low risks, continue to monitor them as they may become more significant. Decide whether other actions should be taken, based on individual circumstances.

Taking active steps to reduce the possible effects of risks is a positive indication of good project management, rather than indicative of pessimism.

Many possible options exist for addressing risk, including:

Accept – the sponsor decides to go ahead without further changes and accepts the possibility the risk might occur. Sometimes, potential rewards or our inability to mitigate the risk means we do accept risks, but it is not the "norm". More important is that if we do accept risks, we do it consciously and for the right reasons.

Transfer – share this risk with a third party, such as an insurance company. This approach can be used to reduce the total amount of funds held in contingency. Another form of transfer is to place the risk with a third party, such as a supplier, through the use of a contract clause. Do remember that an organization cannot transfer all risks – reputation, for instance, could still be affected if the third party fails in its obligations.

Treat – this is a decision to reduce a risk's negative impact and/or the likelihood of it happening by doing something about it. The better you define the risk, the easier it'll be to decide on the best treatment.

Risk prevention – apply preventative controls to reduce the likelihood of a risk.

Loss reduction – apply loss-limiting controls to reduce the impact of the risk if it occurs. For example, a tested contingency plan.

Avoid – this is a decision to stop, redesign or replan this part of the project to eliminate the risk.

Consider also:

· bringing risky activities forward in the schedule to reduce the impact on the project outcome if causing delays;

· modifying the project requirement to reduce aspects with inherently high risk, e.g. new, leading-edge technologies;

· allowing appropriate time and cost contingencies;

· using prototypes and pilots to test the viability of new approaches.

Table 23.1 Risk matrix

Severity of impact	Likelihood of event occurring			
	Very unlikely <5%	Unlikely	Likely >50%	Very likely >75%
1. Minor impact on project schedule or cost. No impact on benefits	Low	Low	Medium	Medium
2. Major impact on project schedule or cost. Minor impact on benefits	Medium	Medium	Medium	High
3. Major impact on project schedule or cost. Major impact on benefits	Medium	Medium	High	High

Once past the Development Gate, a project should not usually contain any high risks. If it does, the project plan should be reconsidered to lower the overall risk by using an alternative approach, or by introducing ways of reducing the likely impact.

Once past the Development Gate, a project should not usually contain any high risks. If it does, the project plan should be reconsidered to lower the overall risk.

A convenient way of recording risk is in the form of a "log" shown in Figure 23.3.

Ref No	Description of Risk	Date Raised	Probability of occurrence	Severity	Risk Category	Risk Management: Action	by/date
1	Seigathon may launch a new product at the same target market.	2/3/18	Unlikely	3	Medium	Monitor Seigathon market activity.	G Smith 1/5/18
2	The product launch relies on Project X being delivered. There is a risk that this will be delayed.	13/4/18	Unlikely	2	Medium	Monitor Project X progress.	F Kent 1/7/18
3	The contractor for the project is unable to deliver on time due to lack of resources and other commercial commitments.	20/6/18	Very Likely	2	Medium	Build relationship with contractor. Find alternative supplier. Build contingency time into schedule	G Smith 1/8/18
4	The warehouse management system release will be delayed beyond the planned start of testing.	29/6/18	Certain	2	High	Provide paper based system and procedures during initial testing (see issue log).	J Arnold 1/7/18
5	The credit control system release will be delayed beyond the planned start of testing.	29/6/18	Very likely	2	High	Build 3 months contingency into the schedule	F Kent 1/8/18

Figure 23.3 A typical risk log

A risk log is used to record the risk, the date it was recognized, its category, and risk management action (with accountability).

Beware the difficulties of "risk conversations"

To raise the subject of risk is not admitting failure. If the culture in your organization is to see the discussion of risk as a failure, you must change it fast. Driving risk "underground" is not the way to deal with it. If you are truly in control, there is every benefit in sharing risks and understanding the measures you can take to manage them. Research shows addressing risk with your "eyes wide open" is a significant factor in ensuring a successful project outcome.

Things still go wrong

Risk management is not infallible. Something may still happen which will destroy your project. For instance, irrational behaviour by individuals in your organization, from competitors, or government cannot be predicted. Emotional actions and behaviours are often the most difficult to deal with.

Workout 23.1 – Identifying threats 1

"If a man begin with certainties, he shall end in doubt; but if he will be content to begin with doubts, he shall end in certainties"

FRANCIS BACON, 1561–1626

This workout should be done with the project team.

1   Use brainstorming, or other creative methods, to generate as many possible risks as you can. You should include anything and everything anyone wishes to raise. By involving the team, you will start to develop an idea of where their concerns lie and the degree of confidence they have in other team members or departments. In addition, group members will hear one another's concerns and this also helps to form the team. Do not let anyone criticize or comment on any risk raised – just capture thoughts. Hint: look at any assumptions made and at any constraints (as listed in the project definition).

2   Write each threat on a Post-It® Note as it is called out; ask for clarification if it is not understood but otherwise do not allow comments.

3   Put each Post-It® Note on a board where everyone can see them. Carry on generating threats until the team have no more to offer.

4   By inspection, cluster the threats into similar groups. This may be around technologies, people, legal, employee relations, funding, etc. Choose any clusters that "fit" the situation.

5   Rationalize the threats, combining some, clarifying or restating others; number each sequentially.

6   Evaluate each threat using the matrix in Table 23.1 and plot all medium and high risks onto a flip chart.

7   Take time for the team to review the output so far. Are there any themes noticeable in the risks or in the way they are clustered. Are there any particular aspects of the project which appear to be problematic?

8   Begin with the high risks: start generating possible ways of dealing with them. Allow all options to be raised. Do not evaluate, just capture the possible risk-management actions for later evaluation.

9   Evaluate and agree which risk-management option should be followed and who is accountable for managing each particular risk.

Task – strive to eliminate any high risks.

•   Avoid those risks you can by using a different approach to the project for example.
•   Build investigative work into your plan to drive out risks which result from having insufficient information.
•   Capture your threats in a log (similar to Figure 23.3).

Workout 23.2 – Identifying threats 2

This workout should be done with the project team.

1   Take the output from Workout 20.1 (the Post-It Notes network diagram) and display it on a wall.
2   Start at the first Post-It® Note and ask:

- What can go wrong with this?
- How likely is that to happen?
- What effect will that have on the timescale?

3   Use the risk matrix (such as in Table 23.1) to evaluate the risk category. With a different coloured Post-It® Note, mark up the risk and its category adjacent to the relevant part of the network.
4   Repeat this until every Post-It® Note in the network has been evaluated.
5   Take time for the team to review the output so far. Are there any themes or noticeable streams of the project which appear to be problematic?
6   Begin with the high risks: start generating possible ways of dealing with them. Allow all options to be raised. Do not evaluate, just capture the possible risk-management actions for later evaluation.
7   Evaluate and agree which risk-management options should be followed and who is accountable for managing each particular risk.

Task – strive to eliminate any high risks.

- Look for alternative way of approaching the work which avoids sequences of risks, creates contingency time, or brings risky elements forward.
- Replan the project around these risks putting your contingency (safety) where it counts.
- Capture your risks in a risk log (similar to Figure 23.3).

Addressing opportunities at the start of the project

You should address opportunities when the project is first being set up during the initial investigation stage. Like "threats", opportunities may influence your whole project strategy and plan. You should:

- brainstorm all the opportunities with the potential to enhance the success of the project (some of these will be the converse of risks you have already identified);
- review each opportunity in turn;
- assess the likelihood of each occurring;
- assess the impact on the project if it occurs;
- use an opportunity matrix, such as the one in Table 23.2, to determine the "opportunity category" (major, medium, minor).

For major opportunities, consider amending your baseline plan to build the opportunity in from the start. For medium opportunities, prepare an outline contingency plan you could use should it arise. For minor opportunities, take no immediate action; stay with your current plan.

There are many possible options for you to exploit; examples include:

- modifying the project timescale such that it is possible to bring the release date, and hence benefits, forward should a risky aspect of the project proceed without undue problems;
- using time and money saved to incorporate outputs which originally had to be discarded (but make sure these really add benefit rather than are "nice to have").

Opportunities should be recorded in the same log as the threats – the risk log (see Figure 23.3).

Table 23.2 Opportunity matrix

Impact	Likelihood of event occurring			
	Very Unlikely <5%	Unlikely	Likely >50%	Very likely >75%
1. Minor impact on project schedule or cost. No impact on benefits.	Minor	Minor	Medium	Medium
2. Major impact on project schedule or cost. Minor impact on benefits.	Medium	Medium	Medium	Major
3. Major impact on project schedule or cost. Major impact on benefits.	Medium	Medium	Major	Major

Workout 23.3 – Opportunity 1

"Probable impossibilities are to be preferred to improbable possibilities"

ARISTOTLE, 384–322BC

This workout should be done with the project team. Perhaps do this after Workout 23.1 to put a more positive light on the project.

Follow the instructions for Workout 23.1, but instead of concentrating on threats, look for opportunities. If you want, you can do this workout at the same session as Workout 23.1, but be careful, as separating them generates a different (and richer) set of risks than doing them at the same time. In most cases, people are naturally more optimistic at the start of a project and such optimism bias can mean that some threats might not be identified.

Task – build all major opportunities into the base plan.

- Set yourself up to exploit opportunities by designing the project strategy and approach accordingly without compromising your risk-management strategy!
- Build investigative work into your plan to convert medium opportunities into major ones.
- Capture your opportunities in a log (see Figure 23.3).

Workout 23.4 – Opportunity 2

This workout should be done with the project team. Follow the instructions for Workout 23.2, but instead of concentrating on threats, look for opportunities. Rather than run opportunity generation as a separate workout, you can do this workout at the same session as Workout 23.2, but the same issues of optimum bias discussed in Workout 23.3 may exist.

Task – strive to exploit major opportunities.

- Look for alternative sequencing of the work which allows you to exploit opportunities, should they arise, without compromising your risk-management strategy!
- Replan the project around these opportunities.
- Capture your opportunities in a log (similar to Figure 23.3).

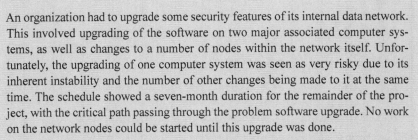

Teams get better results than individuals

An organization had to upgrade some security features of its internal data network. This involved upgrading of the software on two major associated computer systems, as well as changes to a number of nodes within the network itself. Unfortunately, the upgrading of one computer system was seen as very risky due to its inherent instability and the number of other changes being made to it at the same time. The schedule showed a seven-month duration for the remainder of the project, with the critical path passing through the problem software upgrade. No work on the network nodes could be started until this upgrade was done.

By following a sequence such as in Project Workouts 23.1 and 23.2, the project team identified they could delink the network node work from the problematic software upgrade and allow it to proceed immediately (this involved a change to the upgrade specification in the second computer system). This simple change in the project approach resulted in the schedule plan of seven months having three months float; ample time to investigate and solve any problems on the computer system or to implement a manual alternative.

This exercise showed how team working produced a better result than any individual could – there was no one person who had the technical knowledge to devise the adopted solution. Further, the team formed a bond of understanding that stayed with them throughout the remainder of the project.

Monitoring risks once the project is in progress

Once the project has started, you should:

- maintain a log of the risks similar to the example given in Figure 23.3.
- regularly monitor them with the team and reassess the likelihood of occurrence and seriousness of impact;
- log, categorize, and report new risks together with the action being taken to deal with them;
- report new, high risks in the regular project progress report (see Chapter 17) and highlight potential, significant opportunities.

During the course of a project, either of the following can happen:

1 A risk "event" occurs – this should be noted in the "action" column in the risk log and a corresponding entry made on the issues log.
2 A risk "event" is passed, i.e. the project proceeds and the event does not occur. The category should be recorded as "none".

In both cases, the risk log entry is "closed" and the line in the log should be shaded to show that the event no longer requires management attention.

Tips on using the risk log

- Phrase each to fit the sentence "There is a risk on this project that . . . caused by . . . resulting in . . ."
- Make sure your threats are truly "risks" and not merely "worries" and that your opportunities are not just unfounded dreams.
- Only one threat or opportunity per "line" – grouping can make managing them difficult.
- Do not add to existing entries, except to provide clarification.
- Cross-reference to the issues log when an event "happens".
- Keep all risks visible, even those which have happened. This acts as a check in case others' perception is different. Shading closed risks makes it clear which are live and which are not.

Expect some things to go better than you expected

Copyright © 1997 Robert Buttrick

Making your own luck

A major change project undertaken by an organization relied on completing a contract with a third party for outsourcing a part of their operations. The risk of being unable to sign a mutually beneficial contract was considered highly unlikely but it was anticipated that negotiations could be very long, at least four to six months.

The preparatory work for handover to the outsource organization was expected to take two months and could take place in parallel with negotiations. Rather than delay starting this preparatory work, it was decided to proceed immediately, so in the event of the contract being signed early, the organization would be in a position to bring forward the implementation date (Figure 23.4).

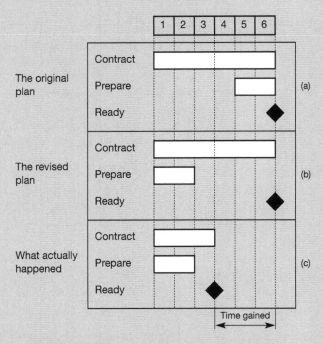

Figure 23.4 The effect of planning to create your own luck

In the original plan, (a), work would not start on preparation until the latest possible time in order to meet the required date. However, there was a possibility that the contract could be signed early and there was little risk of failing to sign. In plan (b) the preparatory work started as soon as possible. In fact, the situation that happened is represented by (c). The contract was signed early and the organization was in a position to reap the rewards earlier.

Threats? Opportunities? Issues? But what do I do first?

In managing a project, you will always have to make choices about where to apply your time. Frequently, there is not enough time or resources to manage every aspect of the project as fully or as rigorously as the "theory" demands or the benefit of hindsight gives.

Having a framework within which you can deal with these aspects of project management helps ensure they all have visibility and are not forgotten. When under time pressure, you should concentrate on the "issues" as they are now, "facts on the ground" that have to be dealt with. Delegate as many as you can, leaving the most critical for your own attention.

Next, apply yourself to the threats. Your mission is to deliver the project according to the plan, keeping your eye on the future. Pre-empting future issues is part of that. Remember, some threats may be potentially more dangerous than issues. They are definitely more dangerous than opportunities.

Finally, look for the opportunities.

If, as part of the initial and detailed investigation stages, you have promoted an open dialogue on threats and opportunities within your team (for example, by doing the workout exercises). The team itself will intuitively scan the environment for risks outside their own immediate accountabilities (acting responsibly – see p. 180) on your behalf, thus sharing the workload. After all, what is a team for?

More sophisticated risk evaluation techniques

The basic approach to risk described so far in this chapter can be used by any person on any project. It requires no special tools, technical or statistical knowledge. In many cases, it is the most powerful and effective approach, relying on the creativity and common sense of the team.

Nevertheless, there are occasions where other tools and techniques are very valuable for supplementing intuitive analyses.

Sensitivity and scenario analysis

So far, we have looked at risk as a black and white occurrence. Either it happens or it doesn't. In practice, however, there may be a range of outcomes, with impacts ranging from the disastrously negative to the unbelievably positive. You can identify such items easily; these are your assumptions. All assumptions are risks and should be treated as such. Examples are market rates, customer usage, plant efficiency, inflation, customer demand, cost forecasts, and timing. For most projects, uncertainty will have a greater impact on the benefits than on project cost and schedule.

Sensitivity analysis is used to review the impact on the project of the possible range of values for each assumption. In this way, you will be able to decide which assumptions are substantive to the case and need to be addressed further. The steps are:

1 identify your assumptions;
2 decide on a range of values for each assumption;
3 rework your calculations (business model), using these values to see the effect on project viability on variations to that particular assumption;
4 identify those assumptions which have most impact and log them as risks;
5 decide on your response to these risks.

For example, in Table 23.3, we see that project viability is more sensitive to percentage moves in tariff than costs.

Scenario analysis takes sensitivity analysis a step further by looking at alternative futures. A scenario comprises a set of compatible assumptions, chosen from the risk and sensitivity analysis, which describe the future. This often requires a model to be built so the different assumptions can be used consistently. e.g. fewer customers may lead not only to less revenue, but also less cost of sales, while fixed costs may remain the same. Three scenarios should be investigated:

1 optimistic
2 most likely
3 pessimistic.

Thus, for a pessimistic scenario you may assume a late project completion date with a cost overrun, slower customer take-up and usage and more severe downward price pressures than anticipated. This can be tabulated, as shown in Table 23.4.

Table 23.3 Project viability – sensitivity

Assumption		−20%	−10%	+10%	+20%
Change in cost	NPV ($)	215k	416k	764k	987k
	IRR	14%	32%	52%	67%
Change in tariff	NPV ($)	10k	234k	865k	1234k
	IRR	9%	17%	16%	102%

Table 23.4 Scenario prediction

Parameter	Pessimistic	Most likely	Optimistic
Timing of RFS	2 months late	On time	2 weeks early
IT cost	$450k	$340k	$320k
Customer take-up	+5%	+12%	+15%
Usage	35 minutes/day	50 minutes/day	65 minutes/day
Tariff erosion	−15% annual	−5% annual	−5% annual
IRR %	−6%	40%	87%
NPV ($k)	−1767	2990	3875
Payback	No payback	3 years	2 years

As for sensitivity analysis, the aim is to provide decision makers with an objective view of what may be the consequences of continuing the project, enabling them to balance the possible opportunities (upside) with the associated threats (down side).

Getting your assumptions wrong

At the end of the 1990s, a famous American hamburger restaurant chain decided to celebrate its birthday by providing cut-price offers on its leading product. The PR behind the event was superb. Not only did the advertising reach its target, but also many news and magazine channels on radio and television as well as the press, covered the forthcoming event. On the day, consumer demand far outstripped supply to such an extent that many restaurants closed early and thousands of people had to be turned away. The event was dubbed by the press as "McBungle". Was this a success? True, the advertising was effective, but what was the real cost to the organization as its supply chain failed and its customers became angry? What of the financial cost in having to provide about four times as many cut-price meals as expected? What of the cost in lost revenue as the irate customers chose to use a competitor in future?

- How do you think the marketing executives viewed this campaign?
- How do you think the operations executives viewed the campaign?
- How did the hourly paid shop staff feel having worked harder and then had their day (and pay) cut short?
- What actions could have been taken to avoid the situation?

And remember, before you look at this with the benefit of hindsight, maybe they did do all the right things but Murphy's Law proved too strong an adversary!

Risk simulation

Risk simulation can be used to help analyse a project with respect to its most sensitive parameters and likely scenarios. It relies on the application of a range of durations, costs, and benefits associated with a particular element in a project. This is input as:

- the lowest likely value;
- the most likely value;
- the highest probable value.

The simulation software will then analyse the network and calculate a range of likely costs and durations with a set of probabilities. The results are plotted on a chart such as that shown in Figure 23.5.

Software for critical chain scheduling (see Chapter 20) also includes risk and probability distributions to enable a rigorous plan to be built, tested, and rolled out.

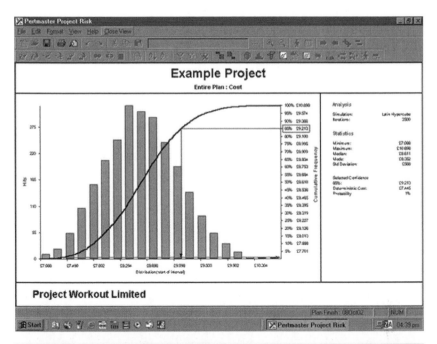

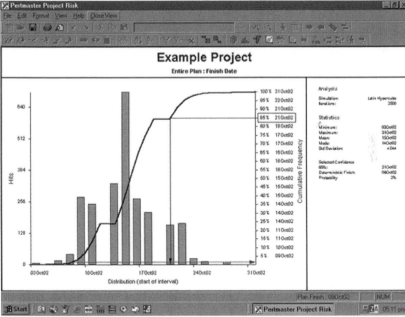

Figure 23.5 A typical output from a Monte Carlo analysis

The figure (created using Oracle Risk Manager®) shows typical outputs you can expect from a Monte Carlo analysis. At the top is a histogram for costs, so you can place a percentage confidence measure on completing the project within a stated cost. The bottom screen is the same project, but shows the variation in schedule for a range of confidence percentages. In this example, we can be 85 per cent confident the project will be completed by 21 October and for less than £9,200.

A mature approach to risk

A systems supplier to a health provider was running late on the delivery of its first release. Three representatives of the client visited the offices to understand the problems and decide what action to take. This was of concern to them as they had to plan the staff training and roll-out within the clinics, which required adequate notice to back-fill for staff absences. The supplier had run a number of simulations and identified the activities within the schedule most likely to lead to further delays. The supplier explained the reasoning and gave the customer three dates with associated probabilities, as follows:

Go Live, 1 June – 63 per cent. This was the contracted date.
Go Live, 5 July – 80 per cent.
Go Live, 13 July – 95 per cent.

One person on the client's team asserted that 1 June was the contracted date and the contractor *must* meet it, "or else" face the consequences defined in the contract. The other two representatives took the view that the supplier was being as honest as possible and providing a set of scenarios or potential outcomes; if the contractor was late the work of the clinics would be severely disrupted, patient visits cancelled, and the training reorganized. The client therefore took the view that as there was only a week's difference between the 80 per cent and 95 per cent dates, they would plan for an even later "Go Live" of 20 July, requesting the contractor to deliver as soon as they could within that deadline.

In the end, the contractor delivered on 8 July, enabling the deployment to go smoothly. Had the client insisted on the contractor meeting the 1 June date, that deadline would have been missed. Yes, the client could have demanded liquidated damages but it would have been their clinics, clinicians, and patients who would have been disrupted, showing that some risk cannot be fully transferred.

Ignore risks at your peril

Copyright © 1997 Robert Buttrick

24

Managing what has gone wrong (or right!)

Issues

What do we mean by "issues?"

When an issue is identified

Tips on using the issues log

An issue is something that has happened and either threatens or enhances the success of the project. Compare this to a risk which is something that might happen.

"There are no hopeless situations: there are only men who have grown hopeless about them"

CLAIRE BOOTH LUCE

- **Be open about issues within your team – declare them.**
- **Never "sit" on an issue – if you can't deal with it, escalate it.**
- **Use the team to resolve the tricky issues.**

What do we mean by "issues"?

Issues management is the process for recording and handling any event which either threatens the success of a project or represents an opportunity to be exploited. It could be a problem, query, concern, or risk that has occurred. Figure 24.1 shows the context: an issue occurs, either as a result of an identified risk event, or as a result of something unexpected. An issue can either be dealt with within the project, as defined, or require a change to keep the project viable. Examples of issues are:

Problem issues:

- the late delivery of a critical deliverable;
- a reported lack of confidence by users;
- a lack of resources to carry out the work;
- the late approval of a critical document or deliverable;
- a reported deviation of a deliverable from its specification;
- a request for additional functionality;
- a recognized omission from the project scope;
- an assumption being breached, say an exchange rate or inflation rate, or a lower than expected response to a sales campaign;
- a competitor launches a similar service or product.

Opportunity issues:

- a contract negotiation is concluded early;
- a breakthrough on a new technology cuts months off the development time;
- a new, cheaper source of raw materials is located;
- the enrolment of key stakeholders happens sooner than planned;
- a contract tender comes in significantly less than the pre-tender estimate;
- a competitor announces it has to delay its next major product launch.

An issue is something that *has* happened and either threatens or enhances the success of the project. Compare this to a risk which is something that *might* happen.

When talking to the team or any stakeholders, be careful, as "issue" can also mean a "topic" or an "important point": unless you are all tuned to the same definition, you may find your conversations confusing!

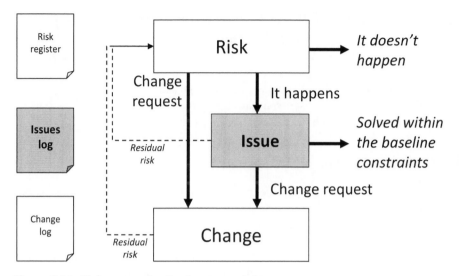

Figure 24.1 Risks, opportunity, issues, and change

An issue occurs either as a result of an identified risk or opportunity event occurring, or as a result of some other unexpected event. An issue can either be dealt with within the project, as defined, or will require a change in order to keep the project viable.

When an issue is identified

When an issue is identified, you should:

1   Record in the issues log any issue which has been drawn to your attention for resolution. (An example issues log is shown in Figure 24.2 on page 392.) You should:

   - describe the issue;
   - record who brought it up and when (date);
   - rate the issue priority (1 (critical) to 4 (minor impact)).

2   Decide and agree who will be accountable for managing the issue's resolution. If the issue cannot be dealt with by the project team, refer it outside the team to a person with the necessary level of knowledge and/or authority (the project sponsor or project board for example). You should record in the log:

   - the name of the person accountable for managing the resolution of the issue;
   - the date by which resolution of the issue is expected.

3   Regularly update the progress commentary on the log.
4   Once the issue has been resolved, record the method and date of resolution in the log. The line can then be shaded to show the issue no longer requires attention.

If the issue resolution requires an amendment to the project scope (deliverables), cost, timescales or benefits, it should be handled through the change control process (Chapter 25).

5   Report new, significant issues in the regular project progress report (see Chapter 19).

Expect a large number of issues to be raised at the start of the project, or at the start of a new stage within the project. These will be mainly from people seeking clarification that aspects of the project they are concerned with have been covered. This is a rich source of feedback on stakeholder concerns as well as a check on completeness of the project plan and scope.

> *Make sure you record issues, even if you have no time to address them or cannot yet find a person to manage the resolution. Just making them visible is sometimes enough to start resolving them.*

Make sure you record issues, even if you have no time to address them, or cannot yet find a person to manage the resolution. Just making them visible is sometimes enough to start resolving them (see case study). Many issues cannot be resolved on their own simply because they do not reach the core problem; they are merely symptoms. As soon as other "symptoms" appear as issues, it is possible to start making connections which can help identify the core problem. Once this is solved, a number of issues can be struck off in one go.

The power of the issues log is related to its accessibility. If it is kept secret, no one will know what the problems are and, obviously, not be able to help. This openness does, however, carry its own dangers. If seen by an uninformed stakeholder, an issues log can look like a negative and damning list. You should, therefore, be very careful how you write up the issues and how you circulate or communicate them. Avoid being personal and concentrate on problems: the old saying "be tough on the problem, not on the people" is very pertinent here.

> *You should, therefore, be very careful how you write up the issues and how you circulate or communicate it.*

"I know that's a secret for it's whispered everywhere"

WILLIAM CONGREVE, 1670–1729

Issues Log

Ref	Description of issue	Date raised	Raised by (name)	Issue owner	Resolution date	Priority (1,2,3,4)	Comment: progress: resolution
1	The mobilisation of the 24th Legion has been delayed and it will not be ready for the start of the campaign. How can we ensure the campaign progresses on time and victory is not delayed?	1/4/10	Marcus	Lucius	2/6/10	2	From Risk 4: delay demobilisation of the 19th Legion veterans
2	No time has been allocated for training recruits. How can we ensure the campaign is launched and there are sufficient legionnaires trained to take part?	5/4/10	Flavius	Keaso	15/7/10	1	
3	There is a general lack of awareness of what this campaign will do for the Roman Empire. How can we address this?	5/4/10	Trajan	Lucius	15/4/10	3	Provide an 'update' in the Senate and bribe senators to vote additional funds to the campaign
4							

Priority
1: Critical – needs escalation
2: Major impact – can be handled by team
3: Medium impact
4: Minor impact

Figure 24.2 Typical issues log

The issues log contains the list of all the "happenings" which either threaten the success of the project or which may lead to an opportunity. It comprises a description of the issue, the date raised, who it was raised by, the name of the person accountable for resolving it, and a target date for resolution. The final column contains notes to help the reader understand the current situation or record how the issue was resolved.

Use your "magic list"

A project manager was heard to say to another, after running an issues log for some months:

"This is my magic list. All I do is list the problems on it, share them with my team and . . . magic! They get resolved!"

"I don't believe you; it looks like a load of bureaucratic nonsense to me."

"Honestly, I have to work on some of the key ones quite hard myself, but many others have been sorted out by the team without me. They see them written there and just act on them if they can. It's all a matter of creating your own luck."

Murphy's law will strike, so learn how to handle it!

Copyright © 1997 Robert Buttrick

Tips on using the issues log

- Phrase the issue as a question; this is more powerful in helping to focus on a solution.
- Have only one issue per "line". Grouping a number of issues together (even if related) makes identification of a solution difficult.
- Do not add to existing issues or they will never be resolved; record a new issue if a different facet becomes apparent; they may be symptoms and the more you collect, the more likely you are to find the core problem.
- Make cross-references between issues or refer back to the risk log (by a note in the "comment" column) if this is helpful.
- Keep all issues visible, even those which have been resolved, as this shows achievement in overcoming problems and exploiting opportunities. It also acts as a check in case the same issue resurfaces later. Shading completed issues makes it clear which are live and which are resolved.
- If the resolution of the issue requires a project "change", put a cross-reference to the change log in the resolution column.
- Be open with your issues log within your core team and share it "with care" with others on whom the project will have an impact.

Phrasing an issue well helps resolve it

A manufacturing organization was relocating its works. It was intended that the existing plant would be moved and operated in the new location. After the site was acquired and construction almost complete, an issue was raised which stated that under European legislation the old plant would not be allowed to run in the new location. It was deemed to be a new site and hence all plant had to conform to new emission restrictions immediately.

An issue was logged and immediately escalated to the project sponsor as the project manager had no knowledge or power to deal with this. The project sponsor quickly circulated the problem among various contacts within the organization. Soon a specialist unit was identified in the head office that was able to review the issue. It found that the issue was a misinterpretation of the legislation and not valid. The issue was potentially a "killer" for the project. By identifying the problem and describing it accurately, the issue was able to be circulated and resolved (or in this case dissolved). A potentially very expensive change to the project was thus avoided.

Remember, an issue can be raised at any time by anyone and is the means of making a problem visible and having it escalated to the level where it can be resolved.

Workout 24.1 – Resolving issues – from breakdown to breakthrough

The following steps, if used in full, are an effective and powerful was of resolving issues. Followed rigorously, it will enable you to "breakthrough" an issue blocking your project. The toughest part is to declare that you do, in fact, have a problem. Doing this puts you in a position of responsibility and enables you to proceed. Be careful, however; the natural tendency will be to dwell on what's wrong: what's wrong with you, or with the project, or with "them". Steps 3 to 8 should be done in a facilitated workshop, with those who have a stake in the issue, recording the input from the group on flip charts. Follow all the steps and do them in the right order. Do not jump ahead.

1   **Declare that you have an issue!**
    Tell everyone who could possibly have an impact on resolving the issue, even those you do not want to know about it. Don't hide the issue. Merely putting it in your issues log is not enough. Actively tell people!

2   **Stop the action**
    Call everything around the issue to a halt. Don't react. Don't try to fix it. Relax.

3   **What, precisely is the issue?**
    Exactly what did or didn't happen? When? Distinguish between fact, gossip, and rumour. Then, describe the issue in one sentence. This is the sentence you should write in the issues log.

4   **What commitments are being thwarted?**
    Which of your commitments is being thwarted, stopped, or hindered by the issue? Remind yourself of the reasons for the project in the first place and the drivers for action.

5   **What would a breakthrough make possible?**
    What would the resolution of the issue, under these circumstances, look like? What would it make possible? Are you really committed to resolving this and furthering these possibilities? If so, continue. If solving the issue will achieve nothing, then stop now.

6   **What's missing? What's present and in the way?**
    Take stock of the entire project. What's the situation now (stick to facts!)? What's missing, that if present, would allow the action to move forward quickly and effectively? What's present and standing in the way of progress?

7   **What possible actions could you take to further your commitments?**
    Leave the facts of the current situation and what is missing in the background. Stand in the future, with a breakthrough having been accomplished and create an array of possible actions that brought you to this point. Look outside your paradigm. Think from the future, back to the present. Think laterally.

8   What actions will you take?

Next, narrow down the possibilities to those with the greatest opportunity and leverage, not necessarily the safest and most predictable! Then, choose a direction and get back into action. Make requests of people and agree the actions needed. Hold them to account on those actions.

(Adapted, with kind permission of the London Peret Roche Group, from their "Breakdown to Breakthrough" technology. Copyright © 1992, N J.)

Let's do it differently

Change control

Controlling change

The change control process

Accountabilities for change decisions

The change request form

Changes are an inevitable fact of project life. Unless you manage these changes effectively, you will soon lose sight of the objectives and scope and thereafter lose total control of the project.

"Change is certain. Progress is not."

E H CARR

- **Change is inevitable – control it.**
- **Have a clear, simple process for introducing changes.**
- **Assess the impact of proposed changes.**
- **Beneficial changes enable good business results.**

Controlling change

Changes are an inevitable fact of project life; seldom do things go exactly to plan. Unless these changes are controlled effectively, you will soon lose sight of the objectives and scope and thereafter lose total control of the project. A survey undertaken by Wellingtone and the Association for Project Management found, after benefits management, change control was the most difficult practice to embed into an organization.

Change, in the context of a project, is any modification to the approved benefit, scope, time, or cost plans. Consequently, there can only be a "change" if there is an approved standard or "baseline". The baseline is provided by the business case and definition, which sets out the:

- benefits and outcomes to be realized by the project;
- scope of work and detail for each deliverable;
- project timescale and intermediate milestone dates;
- project cost;
- contractual agreements.

Change control is the means by which changes to a project (approach, cost, schedule, scope, or benefits) are introduced and evaluated, prior to their adoption or rejection. Central to this is a **change log**, which lists proposed and actual changes.

Controlling change does not mean preventing change, but rather allowing only beneficial or necessary changes to your plan to be adopted. Effective change control provides the following benefits:

- enables stakeholders to get the deliverables necessary for the desired outcomes to be delivered;
- enables plans (including schedules and budgets) to be kept up to date and relevant;
- enables a meaningful assessment of changes;

- discourages the acceptance of commercially unsound changes, through rigorous review and impact assessment;
- identifies and allocates responsibility to the change owner;
- leads to a common understanding of changes being introduced;
- helps develop the ability of programme staff to assess changes holistically;
- focuses project management attention on the real and most important changes.

Change control is related to risk, opportunity, and issue management; a risk or opportunity becomes an issue if the event occurs. Issues can be dealt with either within the work scope as currently defined, or via a change. If this "issue" is to be resolved by a change to the defined work, the impact of this change should be assessed, particularly with respect to the expected benefits. The change itself might not eliminate all risks, and any residual risks resulting from the change should be logged as risks (see Figure 25.1). For this reason, always consider the risk to the project, both with and without the change. Sometimes the risks associated with not implementing a change far outweigh the risks of rejecting it, even if the schedule slips and costs increase. Remember, change control is not simply about keeping to your cost, time, and scope baselines, it is primarily about ensuring you have a viable project and the benefits can be realized.

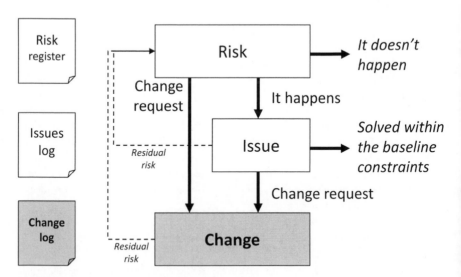

Figure 25.1 Risks, issues, and change

A **risk** will become an **issue** if the event occurs. Issues can be resolved either within the scope of the project as currently defined or via a **change** to the project. If this "issue" is to be resolved by a change to the defined project, the impact of this change should be assessed, particularly with respect to the expected benefits.

Change may result from a number of sources:

- changes in business needs/requirements driven by the project sponsor or other stakeholders;
- changes in the business environment (e.g. economics, social factors, competitor action);
- problems or opportunities which occur during the course of the project;
- modifications or enhancements identified by the project team (beware of these!);
- faults detected by the project team or users (these must be addressed).

Do not confuse "change control" with the management of transformational change, covered in *The Programme and Portfolio Workout*, or with change management with respect to changes to operational systems (as defined in ITIL®). I have witnessed many arguments about what is and what is not "change" simply because people from different disciplines have a different viewpoint; again, they are not usually wrong, simply "differently right". The key, on your project, is to ensure project change is controlled and for your team to understand why this is important.

When planning a project, consider the risks associated with the work and the possible impact of a change on the way the work is undertaken. Generally, the later changes are introduced into a project, the more costly they are to implement. For example, adding a new feature to software at the design stage may be comparatively cheap, whilst adding it later, after the software has gone into production after training and supporting collateral has been completed, may be very costly.

"Scope creep" is a phenomenon where a project overruns the agreed timescale and budget due to many extra (often minor) "requirements" being added in an uncontrolled manner. By using change control, and bundling a number of such small changes together, assessing them as a whole, choosing to implement only those which will further the objectives of the project, you will prevent the project from going out of control, whilst still introducing necessary and beneficial changes. At the other end of the scale, it is sometimes wise to consider delaying the addition of a major change until after the project is completed and introduce it as a second phase project.

Remember, the primary aim of a project manager is to fulfil a stated business need. As long as this need is satisfied, fine tuning, enhancing, or embellishing the outputs is a potential waste of resources and time.

Inevitably, a time will come when an issue will arise on a project which cannot be resolved while still keeping the project viable. Perhaps a time window will be missed or the additional costs will be so high even a marginal cost analysis concludes it is not worth continuing, as shown in Figure 25.2. In these cases, the impact assessment will result in a recommendation to terminate the project. Such an outcome should be treated as a success, as there is little point in continuing with a project which is not viable in business terms (for more on termination, see Chapter 29).

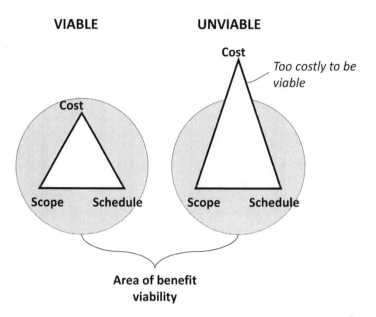

VIABLE   **UNVIABLE**

Figure 25.2 Project viability

The left-hand project is viable as the benefits can be achieved within the scope, time, and cost constraints. However, in the project on the right, the costs have escalated to the extent that the project is no longer viable. If, through replanning and change control, the project cannot be made viable, it should be terminated.

 Scope creep

"Scope creep" is a phenomenon where a project overruns its agreed timescale and budget due to many extra (often minor) "requirements" being added in an uncontrolled manner. For this reason it is often easier to bundle a number of small changes together and assess them as a whole, choosing to implement only those which will further the objectives of the project.

Don't make decisions on changing the project without assessing the impact

Copyright © 1997 Robert Buttrick

Accountabilities for change decisions

All proposed changes need to be reviewed and their impact assessed before they are accepted or rejected. A project may have several levels for the review and authorization of changes, depending on how serious or far-reaching the impact of the change will be. Table 25.1 suggests such levels.

Notice the first two levels of authority lie within the project itself as the impacts do not affect other projects. Once other projects are affected, it is necessary to have the change reviewed and authorized by a higher authority who can balance the conflicting needs of different projects and sponsors.

The impact levels should be defined and agreed when the project is authorized. Often an organization has a standard set as part of its project authorization process. This should be documented in the initial or full business case.

Table 25.1 Change decisions

Impact of change	Approval required by
No impact on overall schedule, cost or benefits. Allocation of scope reserve.	Project manager (record in change log).
Minor impact. Change affecting schedule or costs which can be accommodated without affecting other projects and are within the authority (tolerance) delegated to the project sponsor. Allocation of contingency.	Project sponsor (use change request form and record in change log).
Major impact. Change affecting scope, objectives, benefits, schedule, or costs which cannot be accommodated within the authority (tolerance) delegated to the project sponsor or which affects other projects.	Project review group (use change request form and record in change log). In some cases a business programme board may have delegated authority which would normally be at project review group level.

The change control process

As change has the potential to reduce projects to chaos, it is essential to adopt a formal approach to assessing and authorizing change right from the start of what? (Figure 25.3):

- Note the proposed change in the change request form and change log (see Figures 25.4 and 25.5, for examples).
- Assess the impact of the change on the project and any interdependent projects. (See Figure 25.6 for a summary impact assessment form.)
- If within the project manager's authority, reject or accept the change proposal.
- If it is outside the project manager's authority, refer the decision (with a recommendation) to the appropriate level for review and decision.

The change proposal may be:

- accepted for immediate implementation;
- accepted, subject to certain conditions being met, such as with amendments or deferred to a later date;
- rejected (with/without recommendation to include in a later project).

Once the decision is made, the project manager should:

- obtain further financial authorization (if needed);
- record the result in the change log.

If the change was accepted:

- implement the change;
- update the project documentation;
- inform all interested parties about the change; inform the originator of the result and, if rejected or amended, give the reason for the decision.

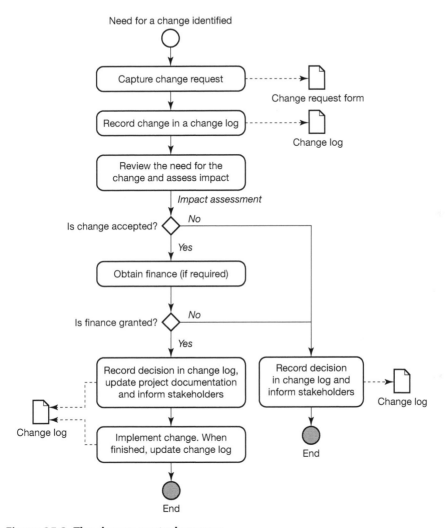

Figure 25.3 The change control process

The change control process comprises capturing the proposed changes, assessing the impact on time, costs, benefits, and scope, making a decision on whether to approve the change and obtaining further funding, if required.

Project change log

Ref No	Description	Originator	Date raised	Impact assessment by (name)	Approval by	Approved Yes/No	Date approved	Date authorized	Comments
1	Extend scope of tracking system to include all customers.	A Cronin	3/8/18	G Holdom	G Large	Yes	3/10/18	5/10/18	No impact on timescale Extra $12K required. Funded from contingency.
2	Change the approach for communicating to customers.	M Mclellan	1/10/18	D Allen	K Mason (Project manager)	Not required			Required as a result of legal and regulatory issues which were not taken into account at the start of the project. Extra $2K cost. Funded from scope reserve.
3									

Figure 25.4 A typical change log

The change log supplements the initial or full business case by recording all potential and approved changes to the project.

The change request form

If a change is minor in nature and can be approved by the project manager, this may be noted directly in the change log – why waste time "filling in yet another form"? If approval is required by higher authority, a change request form should be used to ensure the relevant information is captured prior to completing the log and to present the information in a standard way.

A change request form is used to:

- document requested changes;
- summarize the impact of the change and any recommendations;
- formally record the decision regarding the change.

An example is given in Figures 25.5 and 25.6. While this is a "paper-based" example, the logic lends itself to electronic-based workflow systems.

The project manager should:

- enter the relevant data into the change log (change reference number, description, originator, date raised, impact assessment by, assessment due);
- complete Part A of the change request form. See Figure 25.5;
- assess (with the help of others) the impact of the change and complete Part B (impact) of the form. See Figure 25.6;
- pass the form (with any supporting information) to the higher authority as appropriate for approval. Any necessary financial authorization documents should also be prepared.

The "approver" should:

- review the proposed change and complete Part C as appropriate. See Figure 25.5;
- return the form to the project manager.
- The project manager should complete the entry in the change log.

Change Request Form	
Project number:	
Project title:	
Change number:	

PART A Proposed change (to be completed by the Project Manager)

Description of change requested

Reason for/benefits of the proposed change

Approval required from:	By (date)

PART C Decision (to be completed by the "Approver")

The change is accepted for immediate implementation* The change is accepted subject to the comments noted below * The change is rejected * *Delete as appropriate	Name Date

Action required/Comments

Figure 25.5 A change request form (page 1)

This sheet describes the change, reason for it and records approval.

PART B Summary of impact

Quantifiable benefits

Estimated incremental cost of change

Effect on timescales/schedule

Additional resources required

Effect of scope

Effect on other projects/activities

Risks if this change is approved and if it is not approved

Recommendation and reasoning
Change should be accepted*
Change should be rejected*
*Delete as appropriate

Assessment done by	
Date	

Figure 25.6 A change request form (page 2)

This sheet summarizes the impact of the change on the project.

Workout 25.1 – Do you control change on your projects?

1   Take any one of your longer-running projects which is in the develop and test stage or beyond. From the authorized documentation, extract the following data:

- total budgeted cost;
- baseline completion date (or other identifiable milestone);
- scope;
- expected benefits.

2   From the most recent project progress report, extract the following data:

- total forecast cost;
- forecast completion date (or other identifiable milestone);
- the current scope;
- current expected benefits.

3   Compare your answers from 1 and 2. If there are differences, are they due to time slippage or cost overruns? Or are they due to a deliberate decision to change one of the four key control aspects of a project? If the latter, how do you know?

Harnessing information technology (IT) for risk, issues, and change

Now many organizations have IT capabilities on virtually every desktop, the opportunity exists to streamline the project control logs. Many organizations are building database tools to integrate the risk, opportunity, issue, and change logs into a single tool. In addition, meeting notes, action, and lessons learned are also often included. Such tools can greatly simplify administration. Always remember, however, you do need to communicate these logs/reports and unless all your team members and stakeholders are equipped, you risk "cutting them off".

26

Keeping your stakeholders engaged

Why stakeholder management?

Identification, analysis, and planning

Engagement and monitoring

Signs of resistance

Why communications?

Right audience, right message, right time, right media

*On a person-to-person basis, nothing replaces
maintaining personal contact and gauging
attitudes on an ongoing and informal
basis. Do not underestimate the benefits of
walking around and talking to people.*

"The single biggest problem in communication is the illusion that it has taken place"
GEORGE BERNARD SHAW, 1856–1950

- **Understand your stakeholders, their needs and interests.**
- **Decide what you need to communicate.**
- **Plan the timing of your communications.**
- **Choose the most appropriate way of delivering your communications.**
- **Check how effective your communications are and change your plan if necessary.**

Why stakeholder management?

A stakeholder is any person or group of people who are affected by the outcome or undertaking of a project. For the project to be successful you either need the stakeholders' commitment or at least know they won't get in the way. **Stakeholder management** is the set of activities relating to the identification, analysis, planning, and engagement of stakeholders.

Project success does not only rely on effective technical management and planning, but frequently on managing the politics. This is particularly the case for internal major change projects or where you are supporting your customer through a significant change. You ignore your stakeholders at your peril; they have the power to turn even the best planned project to chaos if their interests are not understood and managed. The aim of stakeholder management is to lead stakeholders to behave in a way beneficial, or at least neutral, to the aims of the project.

Stakeholder management falls into four broad activities:

- **Identification and analysis**: in this activity you should identify your stakeholders and determine what their attitude is towards the project and the impact this may have on the outcome. Chapter 17, Project setup, looked at this but you will also need to do this throughout the project as new stakeholders appear.
- **Planning**: through this activity you decide which of the stakeholders you need to engage to ensure the project objectives will not be compromised and then decide what actions to take.
- **Engagement**: this is the real work when you carry out the actions you have planned. This will involve meeting people (formally and informally), as groups or individuals, presenting at meetings, writing personal emails or letters and generally using whatever media available to influence the support you need. I tend to think of stakeholder engagement as the more personal activities, whilst regarding "communications", covered later in this chapter, as addressing large numbers of people.

- **Monitoring**: you should monitor the actions resulting from your engagement plan and determine to what extent they have been successful. If they are not working, you may need to change your approach. You will also find new stakeholders are identified and some existing ones will "disappear" and become irrelevant.

Identification, analysis, and planning

Identify your stakeholders and analyse their needs

The identification and analysis of stakeholders requires a number of activities to be undertaken. First, identify your possible stakeholders, capturing any personal information, such as their role and contact details. You also need to understand the interest they may have in the project outcome, often called "WIFM" or "What's in it for me?" The idea is to gain an understanding of each stakeholder and determine their importance in achieving the project objectives. Think of them as:

- **advocates**, who proactively back the aims of the project; you can call on whenever needed;
- **supporters**, who support the aims of the project and will help the project team, if asked;
- **neutral**, who are ambivalent about the project and will let the project happen. Beware of the neutral ones, they may be just hiding negative views; do not lose sight of them;
- **critics**, who are against the project and take every opportunity to speak or act against the project team;
- **blockers**, who work to ensure the project does not proceed, or fails.

Try to discover what motivates each of your stakeholders and understand their source of power, which may be:

- **position**, resulting from rank, formal authority and whatever decision rights they have;
- **status**, resulting from how an individual is perceived, often related to charisma and leadership qualities but may bear no relationship to facts of any particular project. Status can also be "reflected" (when a person uses the position of their boss to enhance their own standing);
- **resource**, where a person has direct authority over resources and can thereby smooth the way, or block, any initiative requiring those resources. They can be directors, managers, or unions or even be the person with the key to the stationery cupboard;
- **expertise**, where the knowledge or skill of an individual is such that others listen to and follow them;
- **legal and regulatory**, where a group or body has authority over the "rules of engagement" for an industry.

Determine what you require from each stakeholder; for example, do they hold resources you need? Look at the relationships between the stakeholders and not just the formal company reporting lines and hierarchy; look at personal friendships or animosities. In modern organizations, people change jobs frequently and the formal hierarchy is not always representative of who knows whom. In one organization I worked in, many of the senior managers were from the armed forces and often knew each other well before they joined the organization. If your project extends outside your organization, relationships can be even more important. Work out who has power or influence over others which may be valuable to you and whom you have no access to. This is particularly useful if you have a vital but particularly difficult stakeholder you want to become an advocate. This may sound Machiavellian, but it can be done ethically and with integrity. The same techniques and tools can be used for good as well as darker purposes; what matters is the motivation of the person using the tools.

For all stakeholders, you need to consider what they stand to gain or lose from the change you are attempting to make and the extent they are vital. What do they control that can affect your ability to implement the change and what can they provide? Determine what part they play; are they a:

- **decision maker**: are they required to make a decision?
- **influencer**: can this person sway the decision makers toward or away from your objectives?
- **player**: are they required to play an active part in making the change happen?
- **consenter**: are they on the fringes but, without their agreement, success is impossible (for example unions)?

This analysis can become overwhelming, especially as the number of stakeholders rises. For this reason, stakeholder mapping tools are useful to help visualize the relative positions, relationships, and interests of stakeholders so you can start making judgements and choices on who matters and why. If you did Workout 17.6, you have already started to use mapping. There are more tools and variants of tools being developed all the time, but Figures 26.1 to 26.4 show a number of commonly used mapping techniques, each looking at stakeholders from different points of view.

Stakeholder landscape

The stakeholder landscape is used to check you have a good spread of stakeholders across the organizations impacted by the project (Figure 26.1).

Divide the map into sectors, one for each "domain" you want to look at. The commonest would be the divisions or departments in an organization. Next, place each of your stakeholders in the appropriate sector, positioning the most powerful towards the centre. You can then see, at a glance, if each sector is covered and the position of each stakeholder.

In the following example I have shown eight sectors, representing major parts of the organization. We can now see that Jim in Finance is the main blocker for this

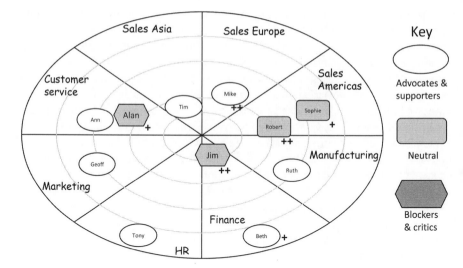

Figure 26.1 Stakeholder landscape

The stakeholder landscape is used to check you have a good spread of stakeholders across the organizations impacted by the project.

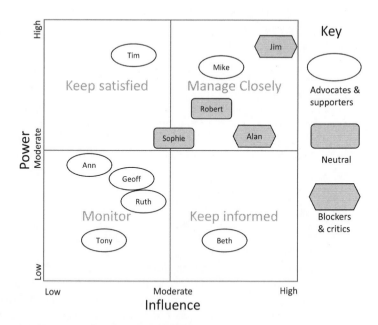

Figure 26.2 Power-influence stakeholder map

The power-influence map shows each stakeholder, either individual or group, and their relative power and influence over the project and its outcomes.

project. Beth is also in Finance but appears to have little power to help. Sales Americas doesn't seem to care one way or another, so perhaps they see the project as being irrelevant; the other two Sales are positive. You are also able to see where any gaps are; for example, do you need a power figure in HR? If so, Tony may not be adequate for your needs.

You can have variants of this map, by plotting influence or level of support, instead of power. You could also use different markers on the plot icons to provide additional information, such as adding a "++" to those with high influence or "+" for moderate influence. I have also shown this in Figure 26.1.

Power-influence map

The power-influence map shows each stakeholder, either individual or groups, and their relative power and influence (Figure 26.2 opposite).

On a scale of 1 to 10 (10 = high), assess how much power an individual or group has; think in terms of their formal authority and resources they can mobilize.

On a scale of 1 to 10 (10 = high), assess how much influence the person or group has; think in terms of their informal power, rather than the authority they have. For example, a trusted consultant may have very high influence but relatively low power.

You can then plot each stakeholder on the grid and gain a visual appreciation of where the balance of stakeholder positions lie. Those with both high power and influence need to be managed closely in order to retain momentum and turn around any detractors. Those with high power and low influence should be kept satisfied. Those with high influence and low power need to be kept informed, and not feel neglected. Remember, these people can sway others' opinions for the better or worse in their day-to-day interactions with other stakeholders. Finally, those in the lower left quadrant need to be monitored, in case their role changes.

Figure 26.2 shows a problematic stakeholder situation. Most of the advocates and supporters have low power and influence, but the two main detractors, Jim and Alan, have both high power and influence. Unless these two can have their views changed, the project is likely to founder. Mike is the only positive stakeholder who could influence the detractors but that would depend on his relationship with them. Robert and Sophie are not likely get involved as they have no position on the project, unless you can convert them into advocates.

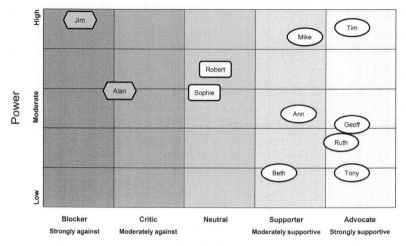

Figure 26.3 Power-support stakeholder map

The power-support shows each stakeholder's stance on the project, plotting their level of support against their power.

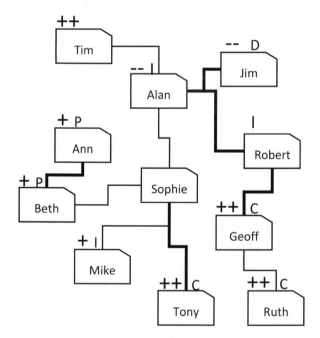

Figure 26.4 A stakeholder relationships map

This map shows the relationships between individuals and group, and can therefore help you identify different routes to engaging each stakeholder.

Power-support map

The power-support map is an alternative way of viewing the data to that shown in the power-influence map. Plot each stakeholder's stance on the project, showing their level of support against their power (Figure 26.3).

I have plotted this for the same project as we used in the other two maps. The marked difference between the two detractors, Jim and Alan, and the backers, becomes obvious. This project certainly has a groundswell of support from the less powerful stakeholders, but they also have Mike and Tim on their side. Would this be enough to ensure the success of this project? Without understanding the project, its aims and the interests of each stakeholder, it is impossible to determine.

Stakeholder relationships map

This map shows the relationships between individuals and groups and can, therefore, as shown in Chapter 17, help identify different routes to engaging stakeholders.

For instance, if the example project is to succeed, Jim and Alan's attitude needs to be changed. Jim and Alan have a close relationship, with Jim, as decision maker, being influenced by Alan. Perhaps, if Alan could be persuaded of the merits of the project, he would deal with Jim. As it happens, Tim, Sophie, and Robert all have access to Alan. Robert's relationship is stronger, but he doesn't seem to care about the project. Tim cares a great deal but his relationship with Alan is more remote. You could, therefore, try to influence Robert, so that both he and Tim could take on Alan, who, in turn, could deal with Jim. You might also look at why Robert and Sophie are neutral to the project. They both have a relationship with Alan, so they might really want the project but do not want to jeopardize the relationship with Alan, whom they both know to be antagonistic towards the project.

You can tailor this map in a number of ways to show other aspects by adding "qualifier" tags to the named boxes.

Plan how you will engage them

Having determined who your stakeholders are, both as individuals and groups, plan how to approach them. The stakeholders will fall into two broad groups:

- positive stakeholders, who are well disposed to the changes you intend to make;
- negative stakeholders, who are antagonistic to the project outcomes and may work to undermine your objectives.

There may also be others who appear to be neutral to your project's aims. They need to be watched with care, as apparent neutrality can often hide real negative feelings. They could also be persuaded either way, for or against.

For each stakeholder, determine how to approach them, either to neutralize their negative feelings or harness their positive attitudes. For the groups, tie this in with your communications plan. Identify the activities, resources, funding and time required for this work and build it into your project plan. Such work is not cost-free but if you are looking for success, it is not optional. Think how much time politicians spend on stakeholder management when seeking election or a higher office in government. Like politicians, use quantitative measures to determine how well your stakeholders are engaged. These metrics can be very simple, for example the level of attendance at user group or stakeholder forums, or more sophisticated, relying on statistical sampling in the form of well-designed surveys.

Nothing, however, can replace maintaining personal contact and gauging attitudes on an ongoing and informal basis. Do not underestimate the benefits of walking around and talking to people to assess what their feelings are and how their colleagues are disposed. People are far more open in an informal setting; I can't count the number "unexpected!" meetings I have engineered near a water cooler, in the company café or at a favourite pub.

Engagement and monitoring

Checking the mind-set of stakeholders throughout a project is essential if you are to achieve your aims. As time passes, attitudes will change. Some who were positively disposed may become antagonistic and vice versa. Unless you keep up to date, your engagement plan and activities may be misplaced or even detrimental. Having identified any issues, take action to put your plan back on course. Don't forget to use supporting processes, such as risks or issues management to highlight particular problems but be careful how you phrase those connected to individuals or groups of stakeholders.

Not only attitudes will change, but the stakeholders list itself will also alter over time. New people will appear and old ones will become less relevant. Review the completeness of your stakeholder list at frequent intervals and then analyse and plan for any new stakeholders or changes in attitude. Stakeholder engagement activities will only end after the outcome of the project has become clear. As such, stakeholder management is required throughout the project life cycle, starting when the proposal is formed, running through the investigative and "doing" stages, right to the end of the project.

Signs of resistance

When working with your stakeholders, look for signs of resistance, some of which are listed in Table 26.1.

Be careful, as these signs can be misread. Sometimes they do not reflect resistance at all, but a genuine concern to "get it right" and I have indicated some of these alternative views in the table. Don't take just one sign of resistance and act on it. Look for clusters of behaviours which reinforce each other. It's no different to reading a person's face rather than just hearing their words. Angry words with a smiling face may simply be a joke. Angry words with an angry face are likely to be the real thing. If you need a person on board, take time to investigate their concerns – they might be right and if they believe you care about their opinions they may turn into your greatest advocate. On the other hand, you might just have the right project at the wrong time. You may know that an organization needs a new capability, facility or whatever which would significantly improve the organization's performance, but if the key stakeholders either don't agree or are distracted, even the best idea will fail. Feedback from stakeholders will tell you if your project is in that situation and if so, it is up to the sponsor and key stakeholders to trim or terminate the project to suit the reality.

Table 26.1 Signs of resistance

Sign of resistance?	Or is it?
Postponing meetings on a regular basis	or they might really be busy
Attacking the detail to find one flaw and use it to discredit the whole concept	or they really could be experts in the area concerned
Promising everything but doing nothing	or they may simply lack the resources
Referring to the "real world" to infer the proposal is an academic pipe dream	or they may see real flaws
Asking for more detail and no matter how much you give, it is never enough	or they really do have a genuine concern
Flooding you with detail to "prove" you do not understand what you are doing	or they are passionate about helping you see another point of view
Silence. If you want people to act, you can never assume silence as meaning consent	or they may be busy on other things
Attacking your methodology They ask so many questions about the method, you never have the chance to discuss the real issues raised by the change	or they may have experience which they wish to share

Why communications?

Whilst engaging some stakeholders face to face and on an individual basis is possible and desirable, you need to address any larger groups in a different way. This is where good communications are essential to project success. A common understanding of what the project is about and how different stakeholders are affected will increase commitment and reduce opposition. Communication is about giving people the information they need so they can do their jobs properly, make decisions, and gain a common understanding. Information must be timely, two-way, open, honest, and fair. It must also be seen in this way by the people receiving it. Both the sent message and the received message must be the same and be understandable. You need to establish:

- who the audience is;
- what the message is;
- when the message is to be delivered;
- how the message is to be delivered; and
- how effective the communications are.

There are many reasons for communicating, the commonest being to inform, influence and instruct (see Table 26.2).

Table 26.2 Reasons for communicating

Purpose	Example
Inform	to publicize success to let them know where to find more information
Instruct	to provide people with enough information to do their jobs properly to tell people to undertake specific, required actions
Influence	to gain commitment through understanding to move opinions

Communications are about informing, instructing, and influencing

You should also differentiate between "communications" and "reporting". In some standards this is not made clear. Reporting happens within the project team and includes reports from the team managers to the project manager and reports from the project manager to the project sponsor. It may include others "in the know", such as user groups or the project board or managers of those employed on the project. Reporting should be regular, routine, and in a consistent format; it is an essential part of a project's information flow and hence governance. On the other hand, communications go to people outside the immediate project team. They can be any in any media as long as it takes the message to the right people. Often multiple approaches are used to gain people's interest. Communications need not be regular, although sometimes a "newsletter", or similar, can be used.

Right audience, right message, right time, right media

There are many audiences to consider, often with different needs. Everyone with an interest in a project, direct or indirect, needs to know what is happening. Effective stakeholder identification and analysis will ensure the audience is identified and what their interests are.

Having identified the audience, consider what kind of information is needed, for example:

- how they, and the way that they work, will be affected;
- how the change will benefit their work and help provide quality service to customers; and
- how this change relates other ongoing changes – remember change on change on change can look like "chaos" to the uninformed observer.

Different groups may need different messages and you may need to tailor what you say to suit their circumstances and even the type of language they use. Be careful to ensure you are consistent across all your messages and not telling different groups contradictory stories. How you time communications is governed by the following considerations.

- is there something important to say?
- is action needed from those you communicate with?
- is the change about to affect the people you communicate with?
- is a significant milestone due?

Remember, communication involves lead times which, in the case of established channels (for example, internal newsletters, internal web casts, business newspapers, magazines, radio and TV), are beyond your control and you need to take this into account when planning to ensure deadlines are captured and tracked within your overall project plan.

Having defined your communication aims, what you want to communicate, when and to whom, you will need to choose the most appropriate way of doing this. Most large organizations have a number of channels you can use and many employ communications specialists to help. On some projects, communications will be a significant work package which may be handled by a specialist contractor or team manager. As project manager, you still have ultimate responsibility for ensuring all communications support the aims of the project.

Communications plans are used to capture this information. They can take many forms but typically include the topics listed in Table 26.3.

Table 26.3 Communications plans

Key audiences	Segmentation of the audiences as defined in the stakeholder analysis.
Key messages	Statement of the key messages to be drawn on throughout all communications, who is the key provider and what the intended impact is of delivering the message.
Channels	Communications channels which are available for use. Include both "transmit" and "receive" channels.
Communications plan	Listing of planned communications events.
Measuring effectiveness	Method of gauging feedback and the success of the communications events.
References	List of the documentation which is referred to in this document.

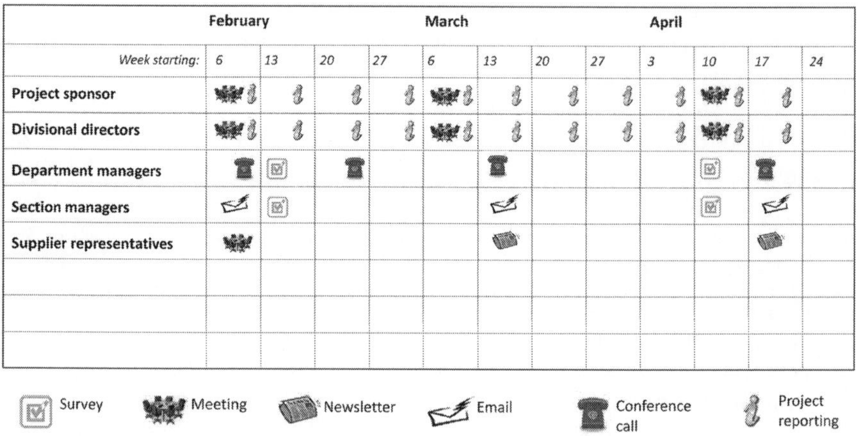

	February				March				April			
Week starting:	6	13	20	27	6	13	20	27	3	10	17	24
Project sponsor	🐝	⌀	⌀	⌀	🐝	⌀	⌀	⌀	⌀	🐝	⌀	
Divisional directors	🐝	⌀	⌀	⌀	🐝	⌀	⌀	⌀	⌀	🐝	⌀	
Department managers	☎	☑	☎		☎					☑	☎	
Section managers	✉	☑			✉					☑	✉	
Supplier representatives	🐝				📰						📰	

☑ Survey 🐝 Meeting 📰 Newsletter ✉ Email ☎ Conference call ⌀ Project reporting

Figure 26.5 A typical communications road-map or plan

A typical communication plan showing the target audiences, timing and the media used. A similar approach can be used to show the timing of key messages to each audience, rather than media.

Presenting the plan in a graphic way is also helpful, as in Figure 26.5 above.

In a similar way, you should plan each communication event, making sure you can answer the questions in Table 26.4 below.

Table 26.4 Communications questions

Area	Prompt questions
Objectives *Driver*	What is the change really about? What is the case for change? What are the key changes being proposed? What are the key milestones?
Specific purpose Why	What do we want to achieve through this communication – Why are we doing it? Inform? . . . why? Instruct? . . . to do what?. . . . why? Influence? . . to do what? . . . . why?
Audience *Who*	Who do we need to communicate with? Who do we need to take action as a result of this communication? Change behaviour, be aware? Which people/groups are critical to success and which aren't?
Internal issues	What is the current culture, behaviours, attitude, or expectation? What else is going on that may affect audiences – do we need to coordinate timetables?
External issues	Will our communication have an external impact? News; PR; City; customers; suppliers, etc.
Messages *What*	What are our messages we need to put across? Do we need to tailor different messages for different audiences for different objectives?
Channel *How*	Where are our audiences? How can we communicate with our audiences?Which channels/media are most suitable and which can we use?
Accountabilities *Who*	How should we allocate tasks and delivery accountability? Do we have the communication skills/resources to achieve our objectives? Have we allocated accountabilities?
Timing *When*	When do we need to communicate to each audience?
Measuring effectiveness and feedback	How do we measure the effectiveness of the communication against the objectives? How do we receive feedback form the targets (if required)? Have our messages been understood? Does what we have learned affect any follow up communication plans?

Were your communications successful?

You may have had the right message, going to the right audience at the right time but was it enough? Did anyone see or hear what you said? Did they understand what you wanted? Did they react in the way you wanted them to? Unless the answer to all these questions is "yes", you may need to start again. If they understood the message but then responded in the way you least wanted, it could be damaging: in the public domain, users of social media can be very explicit and cruel. In a company, people tend to be more polite and might keep a low profile but attack the project quietly over a drink with friends. You must therefore evaluate your communications to understand the effects of what you are saying. There are many ways of soliciting feedback, for example, interviews, questionnaires, surveys, and you should check whether your communications are effective in three general areas:

- What has been learned?
- What was liked or disliked?
- What is still needed?

Table 26.5 Measuring company media

Channel	Measure
Company news sheet	For printed news sheets you will only know how many were sent out, not if any were read. If an on-line newspaper, you can monitor how many people accessed the pages and how long they spent on each page.
Web conference broadcasts	Attendance is the main indicator as a number as a percentage of those invited. How long did people stay on the call? Some facilities have features to survey the participants and gain immediate feedback on content.
Web conference recordings	These are used to record live conference broadcasts, aimed at those who could not attend. You can monitor how many people accessed the recording. I found usually double the number of people accessed a recording than attended the live event.
email	Percentage number of read receipts but some people will not allow read receipts to be sent.
Project specific newsletters	This is something that people may opt to receive or not receive. Measure would be the number of current recipients; number of new recipients; number of lost recipients. Specific feedback and requests for articles.
Events	Number of attendees. Level of satisfaction with the event and the information provided, whether they will attend subsequent events. General comments about presenters, content and style of event or via an exit feedback form.
Podcasts	Number of participants. Number of questions and advice sought, its relevance to the podcast and depth of engagement shown via questions. Number of volunteers for specific tasks.
Web sites and blogs	Number of hits and clicks through. Time spent on each page. Specific information sought and downloaded. Feedback provided on each page/blog.
Meetings	Number and level of attendees. Actions taken as a result of the meeting.

It is difficult to build a complete picture but because something is difficult it doesn't mean it should be ignored. Table 26.5 lists some commonly used company media and how you might measure them.

When designing any media, always consider how people can get in touch if they have something to say or ask. Always provide information on whom they can contact and make sure every web page has a simple "feedback" button, with a form they can complete.

Raising awareness in your chosen audience

I was implementing an enterprise-wide programme and project management method at a major company with over 100,000 people worldwide, of which 5,000 considered themselves "project professionals". One issue raised was the method was designed for the practitioners already in the profession while, in reality, many projects were being run by "accidental project managers" who found the new method a bit daunting. I decided to create a video, "The essence of project management in 15 minutes" which covered all the basic principles. To promote this, we used the profession's internal news channel, but, as the "accidental project managers" weren't in the project management profession, they would not see these news releases. We therefore took a four-week slot on the company's internal web site home page, which simply had a still shot from the video and the title. By combining the promotional media (company web site) with the message media (video) we had over 12,000 viewers; this was a significant proportion of the management staff in the company and almost three times the number in the project profession. In addition, as we encouraged people to feed-back, we received pages of very positive comments and mostly 5* ratings for the video.

Workout 26.1 – Stakeholder communication planning

Work with your project team using the output from Workout 17.6 on stakeholder identification and influence mapping.

1   On a flip chart, brainstorm the following for each stakeholder:

- the messages you need them to receive;
- possible methods/media or people you could use to communicate with them;
- frequency of communication.

2   Consider, if you were them, what you would want to know and when. Aim to see things from their perspective. If possible, ask them!

3   On a large sheet of paper or a white board, list each stakeholder along the top.

4   Decide who should receive the standard regular progress report. Put an asterisk over the relevant stakeholder to indicate this.

5   Brainstorm the possible communications to send out to the stakeholders. Write each on a Post-It® Note. Place these on the chart on the left-hand side, in chronological order.

6   On smaller Post-It® Notes, add a tick to show which stakeholder(s) is/are "hit" with each particular communication.

7   Review how frequently each stakeholder will receive a message. Is it too often? Not frequently enough? Rearrange the Post-It® Notes until you create a plan the team is comfortable with (see Figure 26.5 for an example plan).

8   Focus on your key stakeholders and create a separate sheet, just showing them; make sure the messages and number of communications are right for each of these.

9   Transfer the key communications to your schedule plan and "fix" the plan onto your white board by rewriting directly onto it rather than onto Post-It® Notes.

Do not be concerned if you cannot always see very far into the future. The objective is to make sure you consider whom you need to communicate with, when and how, while you also need to be able to react quickly to any emerging situations.

Workout 26.2 – Stakeholder communication tracking

Using the same white boards from Workout 26.1, simply write the communication made and the date on the left-hand side, ticking the relevant stakeholder columns similar to that shows in Figure 26.6.

You will thus build a listing from which you will easily see who you have missed. You can then work both from your formal plan and add extra communications when you see these as desirable. You will also be confident that they look rational and consecutive to the recipients.

	Date	Sponsor	Chief executive	Strategy director	Finance Director	Divisional presidents
Start-up brief	1/3/19	x	x	x		
Team brief	12/3/19					x
Memo A	14/3/19			x	x	x
Memo B	21/4/19	x	x			
Presentation A	3/6/19	x				x

Figure 26.6 Stakeholder communications tracking

A simple grid can be useful for tracking which stakeholders receive which communications and that each stakeholder is not ignored nor bombarded with too many messages.

Always check your stakeholders continue to support you

Reviews and more reviews

Assurance

Keeping sight of the objectives

Review when a proposal is raised

Review at the detailed investigation gate

Reviews during the project

Project closure review

Post-implementation review

*You should always welcome reviews as
they are the opportunity to correct any
shortcomings or improve those things which
are going well to make them even better.*

"One sees great things from the valley; only small things from the peak"

G K CHESTERTON

- **You, as project sponsor, should initiate the reviews.**
- **Focus on the business objectives and benefits.**
- **If the project is no longer viable – terminate it!**
- **Don't assume performance to date is an indicator of future performance.**
- **Be forward looking; don't dwell on past problems and failures.**
- **Agree an action plan and see it through.**

Keeping sight of the objectives

Your project is underway and may have been running for a long time. The team is immersed in the day-to-day work of building and delivering the required outputs. This is when you are in danger of losing focus on the real business objectives which initiated the project in the first place. It is vital to lift yourself above the day-to-day workload and review whether:

- the project still aligns to your business objectives;
- the outcomes you need will be achieved;
- the conditions of satisfaction are clearly understood and being pursued;
- continuation of your project is still justified before committing to further costs (e.g. signing a major contract);
- your project is being effectively managed and the team is confident the project will be completed.

Such reviews are an indispensable part of good project management, reassuring you, if you are the project sponsor, that the benefits you require will be realized and, if you are the project manager, giving you an independent view on the effectiveness with which you are running the project. You should always welcome reviews as they are the opportunity to correct any shortcomings or improve those things which are going well to make them even better.

> *The team is immersed in the day-to-day work of building and delivering the required ouztputs. This is when you are in danger of losing focus on the real business objectives which initiated the project in the first place.*

If a review is to be welcomed, it must be conducted in an open, honest way with "fault" and "blame" rarely, if ever, used. Witch hunts during the course of a project seldom benefit anyone – be tough on the problem, not on the people. If you can foster an atmosphere of trust, the review will:

- give the project sponsor the confidence that their money is being well spent to provide clear business benefits that will be realized or (conversely) a project which is no longer viable is terminated);
- give the project manager and team confidence in what is being done is really supported by the business.

Witch hunts during the course of a project rarely benefit anyone.

Conversely, a review conducted in an atmosphere of retribution, fear, and blame will not uncover a reliable picture of the status of the project.

It is important to distinguish between a "review", a "decision", and a "progress check". A **review** is when advice and comment, external to the project, is requested. Such advice may or may not be followed. A **decision** follows a review and is a choice between possible futures. Such a decision may draw on the collective "wisdom" of the reviewers but ultimately rests with the person making the choice. The role of the reviewers is to ensure the decision makers make informed choices. A **progress check** differs from a review in that it is conducted by the project manager and focuses on the execution of the project (what, when, how much), rather than its overall objective (why). In summary a review is an essential aspect of project assurance and gives you the opportunity to:

- recall **why** you are doing the project;
- check that **what** you are doing is still appropriate;
- assess **how** you are going about it;
- confirm **when** it is going to be completed;
- confirm **how much** it will cost you;
- and . . . whether you still need it!

When should you have a review?

You should hold a review prior to making any key decisions affecting the future of the project. Typically, these will be:

- at the initial investigation gate, when a proposal has been submitted;
- at the detailed investigation gate, when the initial business case is approved and the project is committed into your project portfolio;
- during the course of the project:
  - leading to the gates prior to starting key stages of the project:
    - development gate;
    - trial gate;
    - ready for service gate;
  - when major contracts are to be let;

- during inherently risky stages;
- when a "critical" issue has been identified;
- when the risks look like they've become unacceptably high;

- at the "close" of the project (whether completed or terminated);
- at an appropriate time after the project completion to check the outcomes are still as expected and to assess the achievement of the benefits (post-implementation review).

Notice, with the exception of those related to an issue of risk, all these reviews are event driven and occur when a particular point in the project is reached. You should plan them into the project schedule in advance.

Who is accountable for ensuring a review happens?

There is little point in the project manager completing a project on time, within budget and to the expected standard, only to find it is no longer needed. Consequently, it is the project sponsor (or higher authority, e.g. programme manager or sponsor, business portfolio manager) who is accountable for ensuring all other reviews take place. The sponsor may undertake a review personally but is more likely to appoint another person, independent of the project manager, to undertake it. This could be project assurance, if the business has such a group, or the manager of another project who has the right experience.

There is little point in the project manager completing a project on time, within budget and to the expected standard, only to find it is no longer needed. Consequently, it is the project sponsor who is accountable for that ensuring all reviews take place.

You must be clear on the purpose of each review and know:

- the scope of the review (total project, subpart, etc.);
- the driver for the review (the event which triggers the review);
- the names of the review manager and team members;
- evaluation criteria to be used (checklists, etc.).

Except for names and actual dates, these are predefined in the staged framework for the gates, project closure review and post-implementation review.

The reviewer is looking for evidence that the project will achieve its business objectives. He/she will therefore investigate the business context within which the project is being undertaken to see if the conditions have changed since the project was approved. If there have been changes, the reviewer will need to understand what, if any, the implications are. For example, if a competitor has launched a product similar to that being developed, there may be serious consequences on the benefits to the gained and how the market may perceive the company; in such circumstances getting a product delivered on time, to costs and with the right features may be irrelevant. The reviewer will also look inwardly at how the project is being managed, at progress to date, status, and trajectory of the project, benefits realized, and the viability of the project approach. The aim is to gain an understanding of the risk, reasonableness, and robustness of the plans and effectiveness of internal controls. The objective is to build confidence that the business need will be satisfied and, where shortfalls are identified, recommend how to put the project back on track.

Sometimes a reviewer will need a team to support them; the experts on such review teams should be independent from the project team so that the review can be both suitably challenging and draw lessons learned from other projects. Unless included in formal gate deliverables, the review manager should record and communicate his or her findings in a brief review report covering:

- details to enable the project and review to be identified (name, sponsor, and manager);
- summary of the project's business objectives;
  - current status and relevant history of the project;
  - why a review is being undertaken (purpose) and the particular focus for the review;
  - how the review was carried out and any relevant circumstances which may impact the review findings;
- findings and recommendations;
- list of people involved;
- documents and information reviewed, with any comments.

The review report should be sent to the project sponsor (and project board if there is one) who should agree with the project manager which recommendations should be incorporated into the project, by when, and by whom. If there are lessons which could usefully benefit other projects or provide useful feedback on the project processes, these should be recorded and sent to the relevant people.

 Terminating projects is not indicative of failure

In some circumstances, it is apparent the project is no longer likely to meet its stated objectives and should be stopped. This may be because:

- the business need no longer exists;
- an issue has arisen which cannot be resolved;
- risks are unacceptably high;
- any prescribed criteria noted in the business case have been encountered.

Such circumstances should always be considered within any review and stopping projects as a result should not be treated as a "failure".

"Almost complete" is often not enough

Review when a proposal is raised

The staged framework prescribes that any proposal for a new project is formally written up, sponsored, and registered at the initial investigation gate. The key question at this point is: is this proposal worth consuming resources and money on undertaking an initial investigation? Is the objective compelling? While information on costs, timescale, and impact may be sketchy, it should be possible to decide if the proposal fits within the current strategy. If this is not possible, the proposal should not proceed.

Review at the detailed investigation gate

One of the key lessons of project management is that if high emphasis is placed on the early stages of a project, the likelihood of project success is increased considerably. A thorough review at the time the project is formally committed into the project portfolio (at the detailed investigation gate) is, therefore, essential as it is at this point that the proposal of "what we **want** to do" becomes a project, i.e. "what we are **going** to do". The project sponsor is, in effect, stating he/she can be held accountable for all subsequent costs and benefits associated with the project, no matter where they are spent or earned within the organization.

The review is intended to ensure all interested parties understand the objectives of the project, their accountabilities during its execution and how it will affect them once implemented. The review should confirm the correct project is being started at the right time; if the review finds otherwise, then the project should be terminated or postponed.

The health check

Project Workout 27.1 comprises a "health check" which may be used to aid any review. This tool is designed to give an overall assessment of the supporting environment, within which the project exists together with an associated "risk" rating.

Reviews during the project

Reviews during the execution of the project provide additional check points when the objectives and general "state of health" of the project can be assessed.

Reviews related to gates

Within the staged framework, these reviews support the decision maker at the gates prior to starting new stages, for example, at the development gate, the trial gate and the ready for service (RFS) gate. In such cases, the review should focus on the decision to proceed with the project (or not) and, if so, check the adequacy of preparation for the next part or stage of the project.

For long stages, intermediate reviews should be planned into the project schedule. These should usually be event driven (i.e. a particular milestone has been reached such as signing a major contract) rather than time driven.

For long stages, intermediate reviews should be planned into the project schedule. These should be event driven (i.e. a particular milestone, such as signing a major contract, has been reached) rather than time driven. It is good practice to plan reviews such that one is due approximately every three to six months. Notwithstanding, it may also be appropriate to review a project prior to the regular quarterly business reviews. These reviews should confirm the project's costs, timescales and targets remain achievable and the expected benefits will be realized by the business.

Finally, the project management practices should always be assessed to confirm they are being implemented effectively. The "health check" tool included in Workout 27.1, later in this chapter, can be used to assist in this.

Reviews related to risks or issues

You cannot predict when reviews relating to risks or issues are needed. They are the most difficult to set up and manage as there is the persistent hope that all will come right in the end, especially if you don't have to waste time doing a review! Realism and honesty are what are called for. The project manager needs to recognize when circumstances are conspiring against the project and the project sponsor needs to be made aware. The project sponsor also needs

There is the persistent hope that all will come right in the end, especially if you don't have to waste time doing a review!

to recognize that perhaps, the benefits he or she seeks may not be realized through this project. In such cases, it is important to focus on **why** the project was started and look at what else could be done to meet those same objectives.

Project closure review

A project can be closed either when it has been completed or if it is terminated. Any review may lead to termination! It is important to close a project in a controlled way and all accountabilities relating to it are discharged and lessons learned. The **closure review** aims to fulfil this and is described more fully in Chapters 11 and 27. It should:

- review the efficiency of the project in terms of meeting the original scope, time, and cost targets;
- assess any benefits realized to date and confirm the benefits have been built into the business forecast;
- record and communicate any lessons which are relevant to future projects.

As far as the project sponsor is concerned, either the project has been completed and he/she can now expect to benefit from it, or the project has been terminated. In the latter case, this may be because the original business need no longer exists, but, if it does, the project sponsor will need to take action to address this unresolved business need.

Post-implementation review

Between three to six months after the project has been completed, the project sponsor should undertake a formal review to assess whether the project has, in fact, met its stated business objectives, or is on course to achieve them. This is called a **Post-implementation review** (see also Chapter 12). It should:

- assess the benefits already achieved and compare them with those planned;
- assess how well the outputs for the project are working in practice;
- assess if the required business changes (outcomes) are still working;
- make recommendations for corrective actions (if any);
- record and communicate any lessons useful for future projects.

It is important that the review is considered from the differing viewpoints of the various stakeholders involved, for example:

- project sponsor;
- benefiting functions and units;
- operational users;
- third parties;
- customers.

Of course, they will all have their own opinions as to whether the project was successful or not!

Workout 27.1 – Project health check

This tool is a useful analytical device to assess the current "health" of a project. It looks at the full project environment and, using a set of key questions, results in an assessment of the overall risk associated with the project. As such it fulfils two roles:

- a checklist;
- a tool to indicate where a project manager's efforts should be directed.

It is recommended that the "health check" is carried out as a part of every project review and at least quarterly. Expect a higher level of risk at the start of the project. An Excel version of this tool is on the web site.

Instructions

1   Score each statement with a grading –4 to +4:

–4	=	strongly disagree or don't know
–2	=	disagree
0	=	neutral
+2	=	agree
+4	=	strongly agree.

2   Enter the total score from each section in the summary section.
3   Add the scores together.
4   Use the key to assess the overall health of your project and hence the risk associated with it.

Project plan	☐	P score
Resources	☐	R score
Ownership	☐	O score
Justifiable case	☐	J score
Expertise	☐	E score
Clear specification	☐	C score
Top level support	☐	T score
Total score	☐	

Key: degree of risk

+14 to +7 = low	+ 7 to 0 = medium
0 to –7 = high	–7 to –14 = impossible

(Adapted with the kind permission of the Strategic Management Group, based on the Project Implementation Profile by Jeffrey K Pinto and Dennis P Slavin.)

Project plan

There is an outline plan for the full project (including benefits, costs, and schedule).

There is a detailed plan for the current stage of the project.

It is clear who is accountable for each work package and activity in the plan.

Slack time and transferable and flexible resources have been identified.

Known risks have been taken into account in the plan.

Total

P score = total/10

Resources

Sufficient manpower exists to complete the project.

The project team has the facilities to undertake their work effectively.

Project tools and systems are suitable and are fully supported.

I am confident that the resource managers will release people to work on the project.

All team members understand their roles.

Total

R score = total/10

Ownership

The project sponsor is fully committed to the project's success.

The project sponsor has the authority to undertake the role effectively.

The project sponsor is responsive to escalations and requests for advice.

The stakeholders are demonstrably positive towards the project.

Stakeholders understand the benefits the project will realize.

Total

O score = total/10

Justifiable case

The project fits the organization's strategy.

The project is financially viable and the source of funding is reliable.

The option chosen for the solution represents the best approach.

All suppliers offer value for money.

I am confident the project's objectives are achievable.

Total

J score = total/10

Expertise

People engaged on the project have the right skills and experience.

Specialist advice is available from experts, when needed.

The method if individual performance evaluation is effective
and understood.

All suppliers are capable of delivering what is required in their contracts.

Adequate training is available and timetabled within the project plan.

Total

E score = total/10

Clear specification

The solution from the project is fit to meet the stated objectives.

Ongoing operational aspects have been included in the project's solution.

The solution is fully defined, documented and configuration controlled.

Future users of the solution are confident it will meet their needs.

Transformation plans reflect the complexity of the change needed.

Total

C score = total/10

Targeted control

Risks and issues are being managed to bring them within acceptable limits.

Defects are being captured, managed, and resolved effectively.

Changes to the defined baseline are being effectively controlled.

Reporting to necessary stakeholders is accurate, timely, and effective.

The right number and types of reviews are planned and taking place.

Total

T score = total/10

28

Coping with all that documentation

Before you skip to the next chapter, read this

What does document management give you?

A bit about document features

Key document management activities

Document management roles

What to look for in a document management solution

In brief, without effective document management you will have confusion, time wastage and cost escalation and the project sponsor will have a failed project on their hands.

"We can lick gravity but sometimes the paperwork is overwhelming"

WERNHER VON BRAUN, 1912–1977
GERMAN ROCKET PIONEER

- **Make sure each document is "good".**
- **Stay legal and secure.**
- **Withdraw documents which are no longer relevant.**
- **Use document management systems extensively and wisely.**
- **Keep an eye on the number of documents you have!**

Before you skip to the next chapter, read this

There is probably no other aspect of management with such a bad reputation or held to be bureaucracy for the sake of it as "document management". The term often conjures up nightmare visions of pedants, surrounded by a huge pile of paperwork, ticking boxes, and filling in forms. What I say is, thank goodness there are those who care enough to take on the role of document manager or at least make sure it is effectively done. When properly implemented, document management is not "bureaucracy for its own sake" but an essential aspect of governance and therefore rigorous and pragmatic. Done well, it protects the organization from expensive errors and can even be a source of competitive advantage. Remember also, what applies to document management also applies to information generally. Much of the information that used to be in document form is now held in information systems, a trend which will continue. For example, engineering designs are as likely to be in "BIM" or CAD systems as in traditional paper documents. If you think document management is a complex bureaucracy, then you have not yet touched the complexities of configuration management and its related disciplines. We'll look into those in *The Programme and Portfolio Workout*.

> *Done well, it protects the organization from expensive errors and can even be a source of competitive advantage.*

Project managers and their teams create a wide range of documents. Some documents are important and need to be stored and maintained to ensure they are not lost and the correct version is available to whoever needs it. You probably do this yourself already at home, a folder in a cabinet for important documents or a folder in your laptop where you copy things just in case. You probably also have a back-up for those really precious files. By doing this, you are already doing "document management". You might even use the same approach at work with a mixture of files in drawers and files in various folders in your laptop. You might be able to find what you need, but what about your team and co-workers? If a document is buried in your personal space, your team won't be able to find it and might each create their own copies, which might be different versions, with different content.

Let's look at an example of how this might affect you. As a project manager, you'll probably understand the need for defined requirements to work to and which form the basis of your whole project. If those requirements keep changing and everyone working on the project isn't working to the same set of requirements you have a recipe for disaster. At any point in time, it must be clear which version everyone should be using; this is document management in action. If you don't do this, your project is doomed to failure. If you don't have effective document management in place:

- people might work on out of date documentation;
- documents will be lost or misdirected and nobody will notice;
- pages which have been taken out of a document cannot be relied on;
- change control will become unmanageable;
- you will have no evidence in the case of a dispute, either within the organization or with a third party;
- you won't be able to comply with any legal requirements; did you know that in many jurisdictions, contract documents have to be archived for a minimum period in case of future disputes?
- you risk breaches of security by sending documents to the wrong people.

In brief, without effective document management you will have confusion, time wastage, and cost escalation, and the project sponsor will have a failed project on their hands.

What does document management give you?

Document management is concerned with managing documents and other information from creation, through to publication, distribution, withdrawal, and disposal. It involves the indexing, storage, and retrieval of documents and other information in an organized way. It also includes the formal receipt and submission of documents from and to third parties, such as suppliers, customers, regulators, and the media.

There is little point in carefully establishing baseline documents at the start of a project if they are not maintained and protected effectively throughout the project (and beyond for the lifetime of the project's outputs in many cases). This is what "document management" is all about; it:

- ensures ownership for content (for new documents and changes to existing documents);
- defines the approach for drafting, reviewing, and approving documents;
- defines the validity of the document (status);
- defines who is allowed to see the document (security rating);
- ensures all approved documents are stored in a secure location, accessible to the right people;

- provides an audit trail for any changes (who's created, amended, accessed, or deleted what?);
- ensures documents are reviewed and updated regularly to ensure they are current or withdrawn when no longer needed.

As the number of documents increases, the benefits accrued from applying formal document management increase. Conversely, the risks and negative impacts of not doing so become more apparent.

A bit about document features

If you take any document you are using at work, you should know exactly what it is, even if pages are missing. Similarly, if you find a page from a document left in the photocopier, you should be able to tell where it came from and even if you should be reading it! Good document design, which should be in every template, makes this easy to achieve. Figure 28.1 shows the document control page from a "good practice" document which has a number of features. It is not important where the features are placed on a page, that is a matter for designers, but every page of the document should have:

- the document's name, document number;
- security rating, denoting who may read it (such as Internal, Confidential, Secret);
- status, so that you know what level of reliability you can place on it (such as Draft, For review, For approval, Approved, Withdrawn, Working document);
- page number, with total number of pages, just in case you lose some from the back if the printer runs out of paper;
- who issued the document, its version number, and issue date.

The document control sheet should include:

- the document owner, author, reviewers, and approvers, so the readers know whom to talk to if they have any queries;
- a change history, showing the dates of each version issued and why it was issued;
- a copyright notice. This is not essential under English law, but it is best to exert this right explicitly;
- a note as to the circumstances which determine if the document is controlled" or "uncontrolled";
- if derived from a template, the version of the template on which the document is based. Lessons learned are often built into the templates and it is good to know that the latest one was used, or for an old document, which version was used and hence what may be missing if a new template was used.

Desktop tools normally have most of this information included in the "meta data" for the files. In Microsoft Office, these are called "document properties" and can be maintained and updated very simply although, as with all software, there are some quirks you may have to work around.

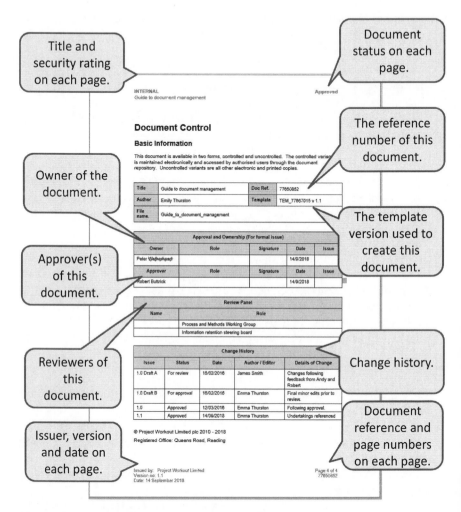

Figure 28.1 Features for good document control

Good practice document management requires a number of features. It is not important where the features are placed on the page, but that the features appear in the document and, where stated, on every page.

Major and minor changes to a document

Having put a document through all the effort of being reviewed and approved, a few weeks later you find some small changes are necessary. Do you need to ask everyone to go through it again? I would hope not. Unfortunately, that is what some organizations' document management processes require and, as a result, people are further disenfranchised by receiving trivial review requests, reaffirming their belief in "bureaucracy gone mad". Sometimes, the author simply ignores the process. If common sense leads people to ignore a process, then the process is wrong. One way around this problem is to have major and minor versions of a document, as illustrated in this example.

Major versions are represented by: 1.0, 2.0, 3.0 etc. A major version is required when, in the judgement of the document owner, the changes have been significant enough to warrant full review and approval.

Minor versions are represented by 1.1, 1.2, 1.3 etc. A minor version is used to make minor changes to a document which, in the opinion of the document owner, do not require a full review and approval cycle and may be limited to a peer review of the changes only.

Drafts are represented by letters: Draft A, Draft B, Draft C, etc. Thus the first draft of a document would be 1.0 Draft A (that is to say, it's Draft A of what will become version 1.0, when approved). The typical sequence of draft, major and minor version would be:

* 1.0 Draft A (this is the first draft)
* 1.0 Draft B (this is the second draft)
* 1.0 (this is the first formally approved document)
* 1.1 Draft A (this is the first draft for a minor update, which will become 1.1)
* 1.1 Draft B
* 1.1 (this is the first formal approval minor version)
* 2.0 Draft A (this is the first draft of the second major version)
* 2.0 Draft B
* 2.0 (this is the second formally approved major version)

This approach can also be used very effectively in a customer–supplier situation. Many contracts require the customer to approve a document. A customer might take so long to do this, the supplier could be using later versions already. In this case, say "Version 1.0 Approved" has been forwarded to the customer, any further changes by the supplier could be designated minor versions. In other words, get an agreement with the customer that they need only approve major versions but are welcome to inspect or be informed of any internally approved minor versions.

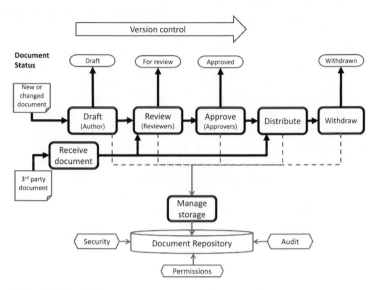

Figure 28.2 A typical document management process

An outline for a complete document management process, which you can either use or adapt to suit your needs.

Review and approval record	
Project number	
Project title	
PART A Request (to be completed by the person making the request)	
Deliverable to be reviewed	
Purpose For informal review* For review* For approval* *Delete as appropriate	
Review criteria	
Reviewers (names):	Review requested by: (name):
Issued to Reviewer on (date):	To be returned to by (date):
PART B Response (to be completed by the reviewer or approver, as appropriate)	
The deliverable is approved* The deliverable is approved subject to inclusion of the comments noted below* The deliverable is rejected for the reasons noted below* *Delete as appropriate	
Comments	
Name	Function
Date	

Figure 28.3 An example of a review and approval form

An outline for a form which can be used to request and respond to review or approval requests. This may in any format, using any tool. For example, it could be built into a work flow tool or embedded in a standard email.

Key document management activities

Most document management processes are similar; they include drafting a document, getting it reviewed and then, when ready, obtaining approval. Unfortunately, that is all many processes contain. You also need to distribute the documents to whoever needs them, withdraw documents which are no longer needed or valid, manage any documents you receive from outside your organization, such as from suppliers or customers, and manage how the documents are stored securely. Figure 28.2 shows an outline for a complete process, which you can use or tailor to suit your needs. Figure 28.3 shows a typical document tracking form for use with the process. This may be in any format, using any tool. It could, for example, be built into a work flow tool or embedded in a standard email.

Draft the document

The producer or author of the document should work on the content, consulting whomever necessary to ensure the document is comprehensive and concise. You need to write the maximum content in the minimum number of words; the more you write, the less will be read. Whilst the draft is being prepared, the document status should be set to "Draft".

The person drafting the document should use a template, if available, so that all documents relating to the project, or even across a whole organization, are consistent in terms of branding, style, and document features. This should include document status, date, title, reference number, author, security classification, review panel, and approval panel. Templates can be:

- **General** and used for any document. Such templates normally have a cover sheet, table of contents, and document control information. If the document is only one or two pages long, then a "short form" template should be used, which has no cover or table of contents as it is pointless to create a document where the peripheral pages outnumber the real content. A short form document template should simply have the control information, which is best placed at the back.
- **Specific**, with a table of contents and guidance already included, such as for a business case, project closure report, feasibility report.

Most enterprise project management methods have templates. You can see examples of some on *The Project Workout* web site.

A template should have guidance on how to complete it; this may be either within the document itself or in a separate guide or product description. Not only should this help when writing a document but it should also include the quality criteria for reviewers and approvers to use when deciding if the document is "good". Guidance may also include who the approvers and reviewers should be, the format the document should take, and tailoring guidelines. The tailoring guidelines

Working document

Document Review Record

Document Title:	Document title	Document Ref	XXX_XXX_NNNN	Version:	X Draft X	Author:	Author

	REVIEWER'S COMMENTS				AUTHOR RESPONSE	
No	**Reviewer Name**	**Date**	**Page/ Section**	**Description or comment with suggested change**	**Criticality**	**Response**	**Response to Comment**
1.		Dd/mmm/yy					
2.							
3.							
4.							
5.							

Note: Insert additional rows above as required

Criticality: M = Minor; S = Significant; C = Critical. Response: A; = Accept; AW = Accept with modification; R = Reject; D = Defer.

Based on Template: 78261874 v2.1

Figure 28.4 A typical document review record

A standard format for gathering comments on documents makes it easy for all comments to be collated and for people to see each other's comments. If done in a spreadsheet, you can sort the information to suit your needs.

are important if the template is going to be used in a wide range of different circumstances. For example, tailoring guidelines may suggest merging a number of documents into a single document, splitting a document up into its constituent parts or applying alternative quality criteria. For example, a possible tailoring of the business case described in Chapter 17 would be to have the same content in four separate documents:

- financial analysis
- project definition
- project plan
- project management plan

Chapter 30 tells you more about tailoring.

Review the document

At this point in time, the document status should be "For review". As the author of a document, you need to make it as easy as possible for reviewers to do their job, whilst making it easy for you to consolidate comments from a number of reviewers. It is therefore best to send a document out for review together with a **document review record**, with the document details, such as document status, date, version, title, and reference number, already completed. A document review record is simply a table, like that in Figure 28.4, in which the reviewer can add their comments. They can also note whether they consider this a critical comment or simply editorial. Always encourage reviewers to propose alternative or new wording so that their intentions are clear. There is not much an author can do with a comment which simply says, "I don't like this paragraph". You might consider holding a meeting to present the document to the reviewers and encourage wider debate as a team, rather than have reviewers working in isolation.

Send the document to the reviewers for formal review; if you have prepared the way, the content should come as no surprise to the reviewers as you should have already engaged them, or their representative, in the development of the document. Ensure it is clear whom any review comments should be returned to and give a deadline. If there is a document guide or product description, include it as this would be the standard against which a reviewer needs to judge the document and make their recommendation on whether it is fit for purpose. If there is no guide, simply add the quality criteria to the review request (Figure 28.3); the vaguer you are, the more wide-ranging and less relevant the review comments are likely to be.

Many people work on the "high jump rule" and assume, for a major deliverable, it will take three review cycles until the document is fit for approval.

Each reviewer, or group, should list their comments in the review record and return it. You then need to ensure all review comments are consolidated. You can respond accordingly and, if necessary, improve the document.

It is unlikely that you will have created a good document from a single draft. Many people work on the "high jump rule" and assume, for a major deliverable, it will take three review cycles until the document is fit for approval.

Approve the document

When the document is ready to be sent for approval, set the document status to "For approval" and send it to the approvers. Include the consolidated review record for an approver to see, first hand, what comments have been made and how the author responded. As with the reviewers, refer to any quality criteria, document guide or product description to help determine whether the document is fit for purpose. Remember to give a deadline and clearly state what responses are needed. The options are:

- **approved**, or
- **not approved**, in which case the approver should give their reasons are and provide direction regarding the improvement needed.

If approved, update the document status to "Approved". If the document is not approved, it should be revised and either a full review required, or if the changes are less trivial, the revised document may be returned directly to the approvers. Some organizations, especially when working with partners or customers, make a distinction in the "approved" status to denote which organization it was approved by. For example, assume I am a supplier, ABC Limited: I may "approve" the document internally (status = ABC Approved), prior to sending it to my customer. As the document is marked "ABC approved", the customer will know it is at a high level of completion, not just an early version for discussion. Once the customer has approved it, the status would be set to "Customer approved".

Distribute the document

Any approved document will need to be sent to the people who need to use it and with a statement as to why it is being sent to them. The document control panel may include the distribution list and also the circumstances under which the document should be distributed. For example, for certain documents, it is only necessary for some people to be told about new documents and major changes to existing ones. For minor changes to existing documents, only those directly affected need be told. Reducing the number of "hits" a person has from document management is a good way to reduce the perception of "bureaucracy". Some systems send out automated emails every time a document changes, regardless of the significance of the change; this can result in some people getting scores of emails a day from different project teams with no way of telling if the notification is significant. The result is that all such emails are ignored, so there was no point in sending them.

The other documents which need to be distributed are those from outside the organization, particularly a supplier or customer. Such communications can have contractual significance and the document needs to be registered as being received and action taken accordingly, such as acknowledging receipt, making informal comments on an early draft, reviewing the document or approving the document.

Ensure all versions of the document and correspondence regarding review and approval cycles are stored in the document store or archive.

Withdraw the document

A document may be withdrawn at any point. It should also be withdrawn in accordance with an organization's information retention policy. First, it should be verified that the document can in fact be withdrawn, by consulting stakeholders and, if available, the document author. The document and the document register can then be set to status: "Withdrawn".

Ensure all document recipients are told that the document has been withdrawn.

Receive document

Documents originating outside the organization, particularly from a supplier or customer, can have contractual significance and need to be registered as being received and action taken accordingly. This usually follows one of two courses:

- the document needs to be distributed to those who need it;
- the document needs to be reviewed, either as part of a formal review, or as a precursor to an approval request.

Make sure all versions of any documents and associated correspondence are kept in the document store or archive; you might need them if a dispute arises.

Manage storage

The document control environment, including structure and permissions should be set up at the start of a project and the project team briefed on how to use it and where to get help, if they need it.

The manager of the solution will need to ensure permissions and access to the document repository are up to date, with new people added and leavers removed.

They will also need to monitor the usage; many systems produce reports which show the effectiveness of the procedure and the state of the document repository, such as outstanding reviews and time to process a document.

When document management is no longer required on a project, all "write" permissions will need to be withdrawn, documentation deleted in accordance with the information retention policy, and any remaining documentation handed over to whoever will continue with its ongoing management. In many industries, especially aerospace, it is not unusual for documentation to be held long after those who created it have retired, just in case of any incidents; these are often called "resurrection documents"!

Which documents are still relevant?

I was reviewing a major defence programme's controls with particular regard to document control. The electronic system they were using was old but they believed it was effective; it currently held over a million documents. As this programme had been underway for almost ten years, I asked how many were still relevant. I was met with blank stares. There was no way of telling because the system did not have a "Withdrawn" status. At least they didn't delete them, otherwise they would have been in breach of their document retention obligations.

Document management roles

The roles involved in a document management process generally focus around those needed for each document and those needed to manage all the documents. The following is a guide but will need to be adapted to suit your particular needs and situations.

For each document

For each document, the following roles are needed. Note these are not jobs, simply a role people undertake which is vital for document management.

The **document author** is accountable to the document owner for:

- producing the draft document, either as an initial draft or a proposed update to an existing document;
- organizing and facilitating reviews as required;
- responding to all comments in a timely manner and revising the document to them into account;
- agreeing who needs to see the completed and approved document.

The same individual may undertake the roles of document owner and document author. The document author should not normally be the document approver.

The **document reviewers** are responsible to the document approver for:

- reviewing the document and providing constructive comments within the required time frame and in accordance with any quality criteria provided;
- indicating agreement that their comments have been considered (if not actually accepted!).

The **document approver** is accountable to the document owner for ensuring the document is formally approved following review and amendment. As a minimum, one formal approver is required but others may be included as needed.

The **document owner** is the person responsible for:

- identifying the document requirements;
- ensuring the document is properly prepared;
- ensuring that the document is reviewed;
- ensuring the approved document is properly controlled and its future review planned undertaken;
- ensuring the document is archived or disposed of (where necessary).

The document owner may be the same person as the document author.

For all the documents

The **document manager** is accountable for:

- defining the document management solution for the project;
- ensuring compliance with the solution.

For a stand-alone project, this role may be done by the project manager or by a support function. If the project is within a portfolio or programme, then the role may be undertaken as part of an enterprise function or programme management office.

The **document controller** is accountable to the document manager for the day-to-day document management operations:

- receiving documents from and sending them to third parties;
- ensuring documents are correctly filed;
- notifying the document owner when a future document review is expected;
- notifying those affected when a document is revised or withdrawn.

Depending on the degree of autonomy given to the authors and the level of automation in the solution, the controller may also support the document author and owner by:

- circulating the document for review, together with the review comments sheets;
- consolidating review comments into a single sheet for submission for the document author;
- reissuing the document for approval once comments have been addressed;
- distributing the documents.

What to look for in a document management solution

A document management solution should define:

- the document and content types that should be managed within an organization;
- a template for each document type, referenced centrally in a document register;

- the metadata each document should contain to enable effective indexing and searching;
- in line with the agreed file structure, the most appropriate place to store documents throughout its life cycle;
- the status of each document as it moves through its life;
- the distribution of documents around the organization including control over how, and if, they should be converted (for example the conversion of Word documents to PDF for publication);
- policies to apply to documents, e.g. auditing, reviewing, retention, and disposal;
- how documents should be treated as corporate records, which must be retained according to legal requirements and corporate guidelines;
- how to handle distribution and access to documents according to their information security classification.

As with any management procedure, it is the pragmatic application of the solution to suit local conditions that defines its successful use.

Your document management approach needs to be established during the project setup. Beforehand, however, you should check if your organization or (if working as a contractor or supplier) your customer has any prescribed methods, approaches, or requirements. The buzz words to look out for are:

- document or information retention;
- information security;
- data protection and control.

As with any management procedure, it is the pragmatic application of the solution to suit local conditions that defines its successful use.

If there any prescribed approaches, make sure to comply with them and if you are a supplier, cost this in – document management is not cheap. As a minimum you should have:

- **a procedure**: provide your team with a clear and simple approach to the "draft – review – approve –withdraw" sequence of a document to ensure a clear understanding of who should do what at each step. See Figure 28.2.
- **templates**: create templates for your team to use, with all the necessary document management features built in. See Figure 28.1.
- **a document repository**: agree and establish a document repository and structure – if everyone knows where master copies are held, consistency will be established, rework will be reduced and people can be sure they are using the correct document. Many tools have features built in to them to make this easier. Even if you use a tool, you'll still need to define the document control approach and IT infrastructure to be used and set the correct permissions.
- **numbering and naming conventions**: use a standard file numbering and naming convention; this provides clear visibility on file types, speeds up access to information and promotes consistency.

- **date convention**: decide what format any dates on your documents should be written in. If you're in doubt of the worth of this, think of the confusion caused by American and English date formats: 2/4 is 2 April in the UK but 4 February in the USA! I usually avoid this problem by only using real names for months.
- **a document register**: set up a document register including, as a minimum, reference, title, author, approver, version, issue date, status, Make this the master index for your document repository. On-line tools have this as a standard feature but you may need to create your own report formats for it to be useful.

You will probably be using an on-line document repository which might be shared across an organization; examples are Microsoft's shared folders and SharePoint and OpenText's Livelink. Most of the enterprise "PPM solution" providers include document management as part of their solutions. Given the huge and growing volumes of data within organizations, ensuring consistency of approach and access becomes virtually impossible without an electronic system. For stand-alone programmes and projects, this also becomes more critical as the size of the programme or project increases.

Key features of an electronic system to look for include:

- the ability to store and retrieve documents effectively; each document must be adequately described to support appropriate retrieval, retention period and security level, status, and classification according to your needs and taxonomy;
- unique referencing. A document and version of a document should have a unique identifier in the system which does not change, even if the document is reclassified or moved. It is likely many documents will need to be referenced from web pages, and having a stable hyperlink, which won't break, is essential;
- permissions management, to ensure only those who need to can edit documents. It also defines who is able to view documents. Do not tie down "read only" access too tightly; this is probably what your security advisors would want on the basis that the only "safe" document is one that no one can see! The benefit of having document management systems is to enable collaboration and ease of visibility, in teams formed of people from any department in the organization. If you restrict access unnecessarily, you will negate these benefits and create a large management overhead maintaining access controls. You must, however, make sure you comply with the security rating; for example, there may be no problem letting everyone in the organization have access to your project management templates, but access to commercial information would need to be limited;
- check in/check out or document locking so that only one person can edit a document at any one time; you need to ensure multiple users do not overwrite each other's contributions;
- version control, so the latest version is always the most visible but previous version are still available, if needed;
- roll back to correct errors;
- audit trail so you can not only see previous versions of documents but also who loaded them, when; some systems also enable you to see who has read a

document, which is useful if you want to see how successful a document is or if the right people are using it;

• an automated back-up and disaster recovery capability.

Make sure you are all working to the same version of the information

Problems with unique document IDs

A large international company with over 100,000 employees used OpenText's Livelink as the document repository, containing many millions of files. The tool allocated a unique reference number to each document (file) which stayed the same, regardless of where the document was in the system. The URL was simply the name of the system's web address, followed by the unique reference number. The reference number stayed the same regardless of the file type and if a template changed from being a text file to a spreadsheet file, this made no difference. Similarly the file name could be changed without any problem. In addition, the different versions of the files were held in a stack, with only the latest visible on top; previous versions could be retrieved and each was held, as an archive, with its own unique number. The system was very stable and did not experience breakage in links.

Then a decision was taken to move to Microsoft SharePoint, which we were assured had all the facilities needed. In the event:

- unique IDs could be duplicated using a simple "copy" command and were only unique within a portion of the system and so not "unique" at all;
- a "unique reference" was tied to a fixed file type, so when text templates were changed from ".doc" to ".docx" a new unique ID needed to be created and all hyperlinks manually revised;
- at one point referencing from unique IDs failed and old style folder/file string references had to be reinstated manually for web sites to connect to the right document.

All in all, it proved to be a very unstable and expensive system to manage with a high risk of links breaking. Perhaps problems have been "fixed" in later systems, but this story shows how these types of problem do occur, despite suppliers' assurances; sometimes it relates to local configuration but often not. The lesson is to make sure you really test this aspect of your proposed document solution to understand its real limitations, before buying or using it.

Workout 28.1 – Document management "must dos"

Take a look at your project and assess whether you are covering the essentials of document management:

1	Repository	Have you established a document repository and folder structure so everyone knows where master copies are held? This will ensure consistency and reassurance that people are using the right document or template.
2	Numbering and naming conventions	Do you use a standard file numbering and naming convention? This provides clear visibility on file types, speeds up access to information, promotes consistency.
3	Stakeholders	Are people's accountabilities clear with respect to each document? it is important to establish who is empowered to make decisions on changes and approvals for each document.
4	Document register	Have you set up a document register, including reference, title, author, approver, version, issue date, status, and security rating?
5	Procedure	Have you provided your people with a clear and simple approach to the "draft–review–approve" life cycle of a document so they have a clear understanding of who should do what?
6	Version control	Has version control been established for each document, together with defined status labels "Draft, For review, Approved", etc.).
7	Security	Have you ensured the security of the files is maintained through effective access control and encryption, where needed? Are people using the security labels on the document correctly?

29

Closing the project

It is the project sponsor's role to approve the closure of a project. However, if a project is to be closed part way through and other projects are affected (the project definition will include inter-project dependencies), approval may need to be given by a higher authority or agreed with other affected parties.

> *"Yes, in the old days that was so, but we have changed all that"*
>
> MOLIÈRE, 1622–1673

- **Closure is the project sponsor's decision.**
- **Check interdependent projects before terminating.**
- **Make project closure explicit.**
- **Communicate closure to the stakeholders.**
- **Learn the lessons and share them.**

Project closure

The objective of project closure is to ensure that:

- a project is closed down in a controlled and organized way;
- all accountabilities relating to it are discharged or handed over to line management or to another project.

Closure is the formal "end-point" of a project, either because it is **completed** or has been terminated. **Termination** may occur if the project is no longer viable or the risks associated with it have become unacceptably high. The closure review should:

- review the efficiency of the project in terms of meeting the original time, cost, and scope;
- confirm the benefits have been built into the business forecast;
- record and communicate any lessons of benefit to future project teams.

As far as the project sponsor is concerned, either the project has been completed and he/she can now expect to benefit from it, or the project has been terminated. In the latter case, this may be because the original business need no longer exists, but if it does, the project sponsor will need to take action to address the unresolved business need which initiated the project in the first place.

There are three key steps to closing a project:

1 Prepare the closure report.
2 Formally close the project.
3 Close down and communicate.

The closure report

It is the project sponsor's role to approve the closure of a project and the project manager's job to prepare for it. If a project is to be closed part way through and other projects are affected (the project definition will include any inter-project dependencies) approval may need to be given by a higher authority, or agreed with other affected parties.

When a project is to be closed, you, as project manager, should:

- check the status and completeness of the business case and definition, the change and issues logs, the most recent progress report and any papers referring to early cancellation of the project (do this using the checklist in Workout 29.1).
- prepare a draft project closure report with the team, including the terms of reference for post-implementation review (PIR).

The purpose of the closure report is to record the reason for closure, the benefits the project expected to achieve and any outstanding accountabilities which need to be handed over. It also documents any lessons learned regarding how the project was conducted and the efficacy of the supporting processes and methods.

The project closure report should include the following sections:

1 Business objectives and scope
2 Closure statement
3 Benefits measurement
4 Outstanding risks, issues, deliverables
5 Project efficiency
6 Lessons learned
7 Acknowledgements

An appendix should give the terms of reference for a post-implementation review, if one is required.

Contents of a project closure report

1 *Business objectives and scope*
Restate the business objectives as given in the business case, including any changes approved since it was authorized (see p. 213). If there have been any major changes, state the reasons.

Summarize the scope of the project and the intended outcomes and outputs.

2 *Closure statement*
State the circumstances under which the project is being closed as one of the following:

- the project has been successfully completed;

- the project has been terminated prior to completion, describing the reasons for termination and indicate the current likelihood of the project being reinstated.

Summarize the outcomes that the project has enabled.

3 Benefits measurement

Restate the tangible benefits (given in the business case; see p. 292) which the project will provide and how these will be measured, together with who will be accountable for measuring them. In addition:

- state whether the current business plan/forecast reflects the project benefits;
- include defined review points for measurements of benefits.

4 Outstanding risks, issues, and deliverables

List any outstanding risks, issues, or key deliverables. For each give:

- the nature of the risk and/or issue or reason for non-acceptance of a deliverable;
- who has agreed to be accountable;
- the proposed resolution (including date).

5 Project efficiency

State the actual cost and resources consumed as well as the actual schedule achieved compared with the plan.

	Project cost (£,000)	Resource (man-days)	Trial gate date	Release gate date	Launch date	Project completed date
Original baseline						
Current baseline						
Actual						
Variance						

6 Lessons learned

Referring to project efficiency and the project team's experiences, (e.g. major issues encountered, changes of strategy), state what could have been done better:

- identify areas where time, money, or resources could have been better used.
- recommend courses of action for future projects to help eliminate any inefficiencies found.
- identify what worked well and recommend methods, processes, procedures, and tools other project teams may find of use in the future.

7 Acknowledgements

Acknowledge all individuals who have made special contributions to the project.

Appendix A: terms of reference for PIR

The post-implementation review (PIR) is designed to measure the benefits realized by the project against the conditions of satisfaction given in the business case.

If a post-implementation review is required, state:

- who is accountable for organizing and leading it;
- when it will occur;
- which functional areas and stakeholders are required to participate.

The closure meeting

You should invite key individuals to a meeting at which the project is formally approved for closure by the project sponsor. By drawing the group together, the project manager has an opportunity to:

- ensure feedback reflects the differing viewpoints of those involved;
- assign accountabilities for outstanding risks, issues, and deliverables;
- acknowledge the team and celebrate.

The quality and sharing of feedback is always greater when done in a group than when conducted in isolation.

A suggested agenda for a closure meeting is detailed in Figure 29.1.

The quality and sharing of feedback is always greater when done in a group than when conducted in isolation.

The draft project closure report, provides the briefing for the attendees and should be circulated prior to the meeting. This will be amended as a result of the discussions and feedback received at the meeting.

Small projects

If the project is small or the project sponsor and project manager do not believe a meeting will add value, formal closure should be agreed by the project sponsor after a review of the closure report by the relevant individuals.

Large projects

For large projects, it may be advisable to hold two meetings; the first to cover agenda items 1 to 6 and the second to cover item 7, lessons learned. This is of particular value when it is known that the project can contribute greatly to the organization's corporate learning.

PROJECT CLOSURE MEETING
AGENDA

1 Deliverables

Confirm that all final deliverables have been approved and accepted by their owners.

2 Outstanding issues

Review outstanding issues; for each issue, obtain agreement from a named person in the line or in another project that they will 'own' the issue and its resolution.

3 Benefits and business plan

Confirm that the benefits have already been built into the business plan or are due to be included in the next forecast.

Accountability for the monitoring of benefits should be agreed together with a timetable of defined review points.

4 Post-Implementation Review

If a PIR is required, the terms of reference should be agreed together with a timetable and named participants. The accountability for the review must be agreed.

5 Acknowledgments

Acknowledge all contributions to the project.

6 Formal closure

Assuming all the preceding business has been conducted, the project sponsor should 'sign-off' closure of the project.

7 Lessons learned

What worked well on the project? What did not? Were all the controls effective and useful? What would we use again? What would we do differently next time?

Suggested attendees:

- Project sponsor.
- Project manager.
- Project board members.
- Key team members.
- Functional line/process managers accountable for signing off key deliverables.
- Functional line/process managers who will accept accountability for outstanding issues.
- Project manager from any related projects who will accept account ability for any outstanding issues.

Figure 29.1 A suggested agenda for a project closure meeting

Like all meetings, the closure meeting should have an agenda. The example above includes all the important points that need to be included. The scope may be covered in a number of meetings. For example, it is not unusual for lessons learned to be dealt with at a separate meeting, preferably before the main closure meeting.

Closure actions

Following approval to close the project from the project sponsor, the project manager should:

- finalize the project closure report;
- prepare a communication, enclosing the approved project closure report to the project sponsor, project team, and stakeholders, confirming the decision to close the project;
- complete any outstanding closure actions;
- feed back any suggested process improvements to the relevant project offices and/or process support group.

A full checklist is included in Workout 29.1.

What happens to the lessons?

Collecting the lessons learnt from each project and focusing on them at project closure will ensure those involved in the project are less likely to fall into the same traps twice. It will not, however, ensure no one else does! If your organization as a whole is to benefit, you need to be able to make these lessons more widely available and they must be somewhere where people will look. The lessons relating to processes, methods, systems and such like should be given to the person who is accountable for them and who will, hopefully, act on them. In large organizations this can be problematic as the volume of information can be daunting and ownership of corporate capabilities is not always clear.

Don't fall into the trap of listing each lesson in a long document; no one will find anything. You must invest some time in making the lessons accessible and relevant. Think of a cookery book. It is not merely a set of recipes that the author has used over the past year. It is carefully divided up and indexed to make it as easy as possible for the reader to find what is needed. Your lessons learnt should be the same.

Make sure you tell them it's over

Copyright © 1997 Robert Buttrick

Workout 29.1 – Project closure checklist

1   Deliverables

☐ Have all project deliverables been approved and handed over to ongoing "owners?"

☐ Has accountability for outstanding deliverables been agreed?

2   Issues and risks

☐ Have all issues been resolved?

☐ Has ownership of each outstanding risk and issue been accepted by a named person in the line or in another project ?

3   Business forecast

☐ Have the functions and business units updated their plans to take into account the operational resources, costs, and benefits relating to the project?

☐ Has the business forecast been updated, or will it be?

☐ Has a person accepted accountability for monitoring the benefits?

☐ Have review points for measuring the benefits been defined?

4   Post-implementation review (PIR)

☐ Has a decision been made to have a PIR?

☐ Have the timing and terms of reference for the PIR been agreed?

☐ Has it been agreed who is accountable for ensuring the PIR takes place?

5   Team and stakeholders

☐ Have all who need to know about the closure of the project been informed?

☐ Have all team members been reassigned to other activities?

☐ Have project team appraisals relating to the project been completed?

☐ Have those who deserve special acknowledgement been acknowledged?

6   Project documentation

☐ Has all documentation pertaining to this project been filed, archived, and referenced?

7   Facilities

☐ Have all project facilities (equipment, desks, computers, office space, etc.) been released?

☐ Have all facilities reserved for the project outputs or contracts raised been cancelled?

8   Project accounting and other systems

☐ Has the project account been closed such that no further expenditure can be attributed to the project?

☐ Have other corporate or functional project tracking systems and registers been updated?

PART IV
MAKING PROJECT MANAGEMENT WORK FOR YOU

"Better be wise by the misfortunes of others than your own"

AESOP

In Parts II and III, I explained how you can plan and run a project, covering the most commonly used project management techniques.

In this part, I will provide you with some advice on how to put this book into practice on your particular project. Each of you reading this book will come from different types of organizations, operating in different sectors and be working on different types of projects. The culture of your organizations will also vary considerably. My experience in a range of different organizations and sectors has shown the techniques in this book are widely applicable but that doesn't mean to say you can follow everything blindly. Some of you may be in organizations with a well-developed project management method; others of you may be working in companies where project management is applied in a very arbitrary way or not at all! As a project manager, you need to adapt your personal style and the detail of how you apply the techniques to suit your project team, senior management team, customers, and stakeholders.

Principles

- Be faithful to the principles underlying project management.
- Adapt your personal style to the culture, but don't compromise your ethics.
- Tailor your approach to project management to suit those around you.
- Be realistic regarding other people's knowledge and capabilities.
- Communicate in plain language; no acronyms or jargon!
- Use "enough" process to gain the consistency your need.
- Use each project as a learning vehicle for the next project.

How to use Part IV

The sections in Part IV are written to open your minds to the challenges you face. Even with the best advice, methods, and tools, things may become tough. You are, after all, dealing with people, each of whom has their own agenda, aspirations, fears and needs. This is what every manager has to deal with on a daily basis and as a project *manager* you are not immune and, because of the transitory and unique features of projects, those challenges can be greater for you than for line managers who have more opportunity to continually tune their operations. Chapter 30 deals with the less tangible aspects of being a project manager and Chapter 31 provides you with ideas on how to define your project method.

Being a project manager

Keep the business objective in mind

Justifiably different – tailoring

Don't forget the people!

Make each project an opportunity to learn

You should not only adapt your project management approach but also your personal style to match the culture and other people's knowledge and capabilities.

"Learn from the mistakes of others, you'll never live long enough to make them all yourself"

RALPH WALDO EMERSON

Keep your business objective in mind

This book has covered a lot of ground, giving you not only the essential techniques for managing a successful project but also stressing the importance of how you act as a manager. Being "right" in the wrong way is seldom a good means of making progress. I have also emphasized the importance of focusing on the business objectives; the reason why a project is being undertaken. Project management is simply a means of organizing a team to achieve those objectives, not an objective in its own right. That said, consistent, best practice does enhance the chances of success. You don't have to make every mistake yourself. This why very large projects and organizations develop their own project management methods and train people in their use. If you do not define something, you cannot expect consistency in approach nor expect performance to improve. Instead, success will rely on the "hero" who achieves the objectives, despite the organization, not because of it and that type of success is not reproducible.

If your project budget can accommodate it and the project is likely to last a long time, it's worth developing your own method. This will enable the project team to become accustomed to a consistent way of working and new members of the team will have a set of good working practices to follow. Further, if you define your method, you can improve on it based on the experience of the team using it. Chapter 31 will give you an outline to help with this.

Justifiably different – tailoring

We are all different

You may have wondered, as you read this book, whether the implied "one size fits all" approach is practical. Can you really direct and manage a small internal project using the same approach as you would for a major multi-million dollar endeavour? Can you take another company's method and use it on your project? Can you simply adopt an off-the-shelf method, such as those discussed in Appendix C, to use on your project? Common sense tells you this cannot be right . . . and usually common sense is right! All projects are different and you need to take account of that . . . but still keep to the principles and lessons from Part I. Before adopting a ready-made method or developing your own methods, whether for a single project or entire organization, this seeming paradox needs to be solved; to do this, you need to understand the concept of "tailoring".

What is tailoring?

Tailoring enables a project manager to decide how to adapt and use methods and standards for a particular project (Figure 30.1). Tailoring is also used to create an enterprise-wide project method, where the owner of the method decides how to adapt methods and standards to create an enterprise method, suited to the business (Figure 30.2). This is dealt with in *The Programme and Portfolio Workout*.

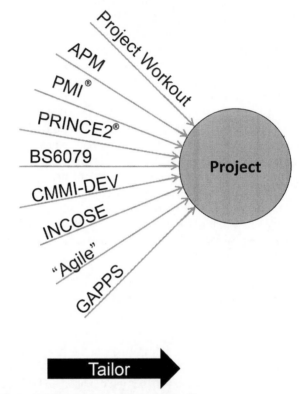

The project manager tailors from international and national best practice, maturity models and standards to suit their own project's circumstances.

Figure 30.1 Tailoring for a single project

The project manager creates the management approach for their project, drawing on a range of different sources and adapting them to suit the project and team.

As an example, Chapter 13 describes how to tailor the standard project framework from Chapter 4 to suit different types of project. Similarly, any aspect of any topic in this book can be tailored. For example, you will decide on your project framework, the design of your risk matrix and log and who will authorize the project at the start of each stage.

Tailoring is not a "licence" to do whatever you want, nor is it a matter of personal preference. Consistency makes life easier for everyone and consistent methods

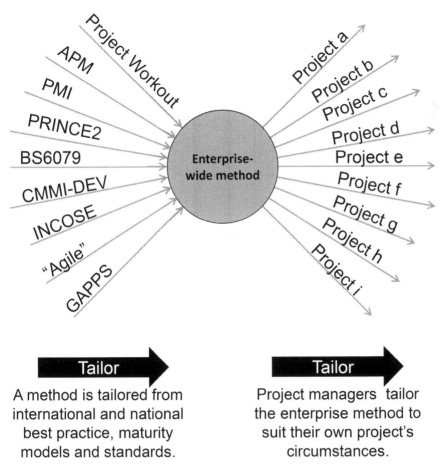

Figure 30.2 Tailoring for an enterprise-wide method

To create an enterprise-wide project management method, draw from a range of standards, methods, and models to create a corporate method. The organization's project managers and teams then use this corporate method, tailoring it to suit their particular project's needs.

should be used whenever consistency adds value. You need to stay true to the lessons and principles in Part I.

Tailoring takes time and costs money; a project manager should only tailor a standard method, whether corporate or proprietary (like PRINCE2®) when the difference adds value. Remember, any local tailoring must be defined and maintained and this adds more overheads.

Tailoring is not for dummies

Project management is more of an art than a science. Like any management discipline, it requires a mix of soft and hard skills, coupled with sound experience. This is why good professional qualifications don't just test knowledge but also look at the experience of the individual and how they apply that knowledge. Tailoring is fundamentally about dealing with a project in a specific context not foreseen by a prescribed standard or method. As such, it is a way of dealing with the unpredictable and cannot be defined in a code or strict set of rules. As a result, effective tailoring requires a certain amount of knowledge and experience. A novice is hardly likely to have the breadth of experience to tailor effectively. On the other hand, you don't need to have experienced everything to be able to make sound judgements regarding how to tailor a project management approach; you should have experienced enough to be able to understand the different approaches others have taken as presented in proprietary methods, standards, text books, case studies, papers and at conferences.

Don't forget the people!

Be adaptable

Projects are undertaken by people and how you manage a project must take into account the members of the team as well as the stakeholders. Chapter 15 focused on the most appropriate ways of managing the project team and Chapter 26 looked at engaging stakeholders. You should not only adapt your project management approach but also your personal style to match the culture and other people's knowledge and capabilities. As different people will be at different levels of skill and knowledge, always talk and write in plain language, avoiding acronyms and jargon; this is especially true when dealing with the sponsor and senior stakeholders. Be realistic regarding how much "project management" they can handle before they switch off. How the project is managed is irrelevant to many stakeholders, even though you may know how important it is. If that person is not blocking progress or undermining governance then it doesn't matter. Above all, how you manage must reflect your values and ethics or you will risk putting yourself under an intolerable level of stress.

Manage up as well as down

Whether you are a team manager, project manager, or project sponsor, you will be accountable to someone (see Figure 30.3). As shown in Chapter 16 on governance, this chain of accountability continues right to the top of the organization. The effective running of a project relies on this chain and from time to time you will need clarification, decisions, direction, or advice from your boss. How do you influence your boss? Before we go into the detail, remember, as a manager, you are also a "boss" and the people reporting to you may have the same frustrations and challenges you have . . . or even worse!

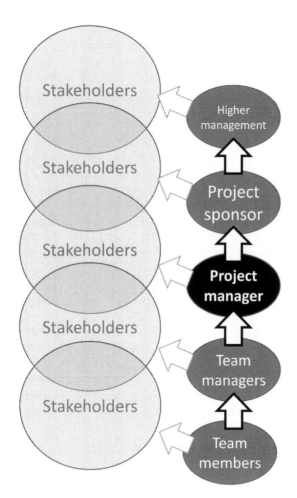

Figure 30.3 Managing upwards

No matter what role you have, you will always need to "manage up", both in terms of the project organization and other stakeholders, such as line managers, external consultants and internal subject matter experts.

Let's look at this from the perspective of the project manager. Firstly, remember the project belongs to the project sponsor; he or she owns the business case and is the primary risk taker. You need to understand their priorities; the project is probably just one of a number of topics they are dealing with. You need to respect their time, use it wisely by being clear on any requests you make; don't waste their time by escalating issues you should deal with yourself. Don't jump decisions on them at short notice or you may be seen as forcing them into a corner; give as much notice as you can and, where appropriate, provide options.

Try to build up a consistent way of working together, establishing ground rules like agreeing times of the day or week they do not want to be disturbed, when to approach them directly and when to go via a personal assistant. Find out how they would prefer to be kept updated on the project and as you get further through the project check if this is still appropriate.

Trust is at the heart of any relationship, whether on a project, in line management or in your personal life. Admit any mistakes you make, don't lie or hide information in the vain hope you can bury it, and follow through on your commitments. Any commitments you make should be authentic. By this, I mean when you make a commitment, you fully intend to carry it out. Authenticity, however, also means that if you find you cannot meet a commitment, you should say so and agree an alternative approach. No one likes bad news, so don't sit on it and then offload it at the last minute, as in the "green-green-green-green-RED" scenario in Chapter 18. Part of maintaining trust is avoiding gossip and inappropriate personal commitments; if you criticize others in a disrespectful way, then your boss may wonder what you say about him to other people. Always stick to facts, filling in the gaps with considered assumptions, if necessary. The old saying "be tough on the problem, not on the people" is as valid today as ever.

Dealing with rumours and gossip

There will always be gossip in your team and amongst stakeholders. Do not ignore it, but do not add to it either! Rumours can damage people's reputations and threaten the success of a project by undermining confidence in the sponsor, manager, and team or in what is trying to be achieved. If there is gossip associated with your project, find the source. Sometimes rumours start from facts which are inadvertently (or maliciously) distorted, especially in a political context. Talk to people directly asking where they heard this and correct their perception if necessary. If there is a germ of truth in the rumour, this should be exposed before dealing with any problem so that you can respond with facts rather than emotions. You may also need to find additional information from alternative, trustworthy sources. Do your homework discretely; perhaps there is a need for improved communications, a change of approach on the project or some unforeseen consequence of the project which might have been overlooked.

Each project is an opportunity to learn

If you work in project management, it is unlikely that you will work on just one project. Most people are first exposed to project management as a specialist within a project team, working on a work package, reporting to a team manager. As you progress, you will become the team manager and accountable for one or more work packages. This is when you really need to understand the basic project management techniques of planning, reporting, risk management, issue management, and change control. A good project manager will act as a coach, to ensure the project team is working together in a consistent way. At some point, you may start to have more of an interest in project management than in the specialism you started your career pursuing and will look for a project manager role. For some organizations, promotion to being a project manager is part of normal progression. This can lead to discussions on the "right career path"; should a person be rewarded for specialist knowledge by promoting them to a management role where they no longer practice their specialism? It sounds a bit odd. Alternative paths are that the "project manager" manages a project based on their core expertise and they undertake not only a management role but a specialist role. This is why project management is often wrongly perceived by people as a "technical" discipline, primarily for engineers.

Regardless of how you first came into project management, you should treat each project as a personal learning experience so that at the end of it you have grown in understanding and confidence, able to take on more complex work, should you choose to do so. Look at the various standards and at the competencies you need and try to gain experience in as many as you can, as fast as you can.

If you are a project manager, put in place a "lessons learned" approach on the project. Encourage your team managers to share lessons as the project proceeds. Make this continuous; don't wait until the end of the project and the more formal "lessons learned review". Act on any improvements suggested and explain why some suggestions are not adopted. This can be run formally, with lessons learned logs being added to when necessary, lessons learned on the agenda at team meetings and reviews at the end of stages and at the end of the project. On the other hand, this can be very informal but just as effective. The golden rule, however, even if not adopting any suggestion, is never to ignore a person who provides feedback; if you ignore them they'll never bother again. Similarly, accept feedback and suggestions in any form and at any time, whether in the staff café, in the corridor, at a meeting or in the street. Make a note and log the idea yourself; a certain way of being perceived as a bureaucrat is to tell them to enter the feedback into "the system". Like as not, they won't bother.

Having received feedback you can then decide if it needs to be acted on and by whom. In my experience, those needing action from outside the project team could prove to be the most difficult to address. For example, most project teams need to buy goods or services as part of the project through the corporate procurement systems. In some organizations, the data required in these systems and the number of sign-offs required by totally uninvolved people is a source of frustration and time slippage. In this case, passing feedback to owners of those systems may help trigger improvements, especially if any other teams express the same opinions.

31

Project management methods

Be aware, however, that the less mature an organization is in project management, the greater the help the project team will need. If the skill and experience of the people is low, they ask for and need more detail and explanation.

"Many things difficult to design prove easy to performance"

SAMUEL JOHNSON, 1709–1784

Designing your project method: teach me to cheat

How to document and organize your project management method or processes can pose a number of problems. If your organization has a standard method, then that is what you will need to work with, tailoring it to suit your project and providing feedback to the owner if you see opportunities to improve it.

If, however, you have no project management method, then you will need to define the approach yourself, specifically for your project. This can be time-consuming and usually only very large projects can afford to develop a complete method. If you are designing your own approach, you will really need to be very focused. This chapter provides you with some ideas on how to define your project management approach.

Think about dividing your documentation into three basic types, procedures or processes, templates and guides. This is shown in Figure 31.1.

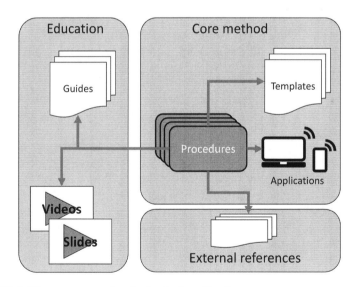

Figure 31.1 The components of a typical method

At a minimum, a method should contain the processes which refer to templates to ensure consistency in frequently used documents and to guides which provide a greater level of education around a topic. Guides may be enhanced by using videos, slide shows or podcasts. The use of the procedures may be enhanced by using tools and applications. Where needed, the procedures should refer to internal materials, such as corporate processes, policies or external references, like standards or proprietary methods.

The procedures (or processes) should be simple tabulations stating the activity, who is accountable, the deliverable, and whom it goes to, referring to any relevant templates or guides. Use flow charts if they add clarity. Keep the text brief and factual, with no explanation. Any guidance or templates should be held external to the procedure, not embedded within it. Figure 31.2 gives an idea of what a tabulation and figure looks like and Figure 31.3 shows an example of a simple, high-level flow chart. Include references to any external materials essential to understanding and undertaking the activities in the procedure. You'll find more on the web site which accompanies this book. Procedures should be very slim documents, easy to use and refer to.

The templates are the skeleton for documents which need to be repeatedly produced. They should not only contain the section titles of each document but also describe what each section is for. Each template could be supplemented by a product description outlining its purpose, the content, quality criteria and who should review and approve it.

The guides are the "education" documents. They should contain the principles, the methods, and best practice. They may be simple one-page summaries or more lengthy documents. The less your project team understand about project management, the more of these and the more detailed they will need to be. As the project manager, you'll need to ensure your team understands enough about project management and its various techniques to enable the project to run smoothly. Only give people the minimum needed but always be open to explaining further, adding to existing guides or writing new ones if needed. Don't be tempted to build this "education" into the processes or procedures and they will become bloated and unwieldly.

An advantage of this approach is that it needs very little administration and lends itself to intranet publication with the process at the core and the guides and templates hyperlinked in the appropriate places.

I have used this approach effectively on a number of projects and even built it into an enterprise-wide method for use on thousands of projects. I have also used additional types of components, as shown in Figure 31.1 – for example, one company I worked in had excellent video-making facilities and I created a number of high-quality training videos to supplement the guides. This may be prohibitively expensive on many projects but for large projects or enterprise-wide project management methods, it can be a cost effective way of engaging people. On the other hand, slide sets and screen capture videos can be quick and cheap to produce and very effective.

Ref	Activity	Deliverables	Roles	Output to (Role)	Guidance
1	Receive notification to initiate a project. Mobilise and brief team managers, communicate initial project codes & WBS structure for cost recording.	Team briefing	Accountable: Project manager	Team manager(s)	Guide to mobilisation Direct & Manage a Project - Video briefing
2	Identify and engage stakeholders; involve them, as needed, in initiation activities. Prepare initial version of communications plan.	Identified stakeholders Communication Plan (Initial version) Stakeholder engagement plan	Accountable: Project manager Consulted: Business change manager	Team manager(s)	Manage stakeholders procedure Guide to stakeholder and communications management
3	Within the context of the overall project plan from the Proposal, plan the first stage of project, with team, undertake review and obtain approval.	First stage plan	Accountable: Project manager Responsible: Team manager(s); Quality manager	Project sponsor	Manage planning procedure Guide to programme and project planning Project plan (template)

Figure 31.2 A typical tabulation for a project procedure

Procedures can be defined in simple tabulations stating the activity, the deliverable, who is accountable, and whom it goes to. In addition, you can have a further column (on the right) which refers to any relevant processes, templates, guides, or briefings.

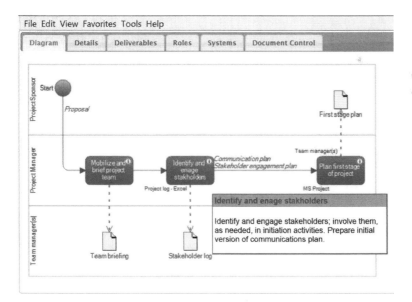

Figure 31.3 A typical flow chart for a project procedure

Procedures can be defined in simple flow charts showing the activity, the deliverable, who is accountable, and whom it goes to. The charts may be on-screen, as shown in the figure, or in printed form.

Deciding how to document your project management method

Before going into the detail of a method and its architecture, you'll need to think carefully about how to document it and keep it up to date. What will suit your users? You have two main options:

- document-based, in which the processes are written up in documents, either read on a screen or printed out as booklets. This may sound old-fashioned but some people still find it easier to read from a paper copy than a screen. Many people also like to make their own notes on a printed document. Documents are transportable and can be shared with third parties if the need arises. Naturally, documents can be accessed via web sites; or
- web-based, in which a process and its activities are displayed on a screen, enabling the user to click and move wherever they want, drilling down for detail or following interfaces to other processes. The advantage of the web-based approach is the users can go to the part they need to and find the references they are looking for, without wading through a complete document.

Frequently, process documents are written in a tool, such as MS Word, with the flow charts drafted in Visio or PowerPoint. Keeping the two aligned is extremely difficult and it is inevitable that mistakes will be made. There are, however, tools available now, such as BusinessOptix, which provide the best of both worlds. The text and diagrams are developed in a single tool with both document style and web outputs, meeting the differing needs and preferences of users. Commonly used aspects of the procedures – such as deliverables, role descriptions, and glossary – can be defined once and used many times in different parts of the method; this creates a consistency not attainable when using conventional MS Word and Visio based approaches. As the documents and web site are derived from the same information, they are always in step, whenever they are updated. or when common elements are updated. For a simple example of this look at the web site which accompanies this book.

 Inexperienced people need more help

Be aware that the less mature an organization is in project management, the greater the help the project team will need and the weightier the method. If the skill and experience of the people is low, they will ask for and need more detail and explanation. Guides, slides, and videos will be needed to fill the knowledge gap; templates may need to be more descriptive and contain more detailed instructions while procedures may need to be taken to a greater level of granularity, explaining each step and activity.

A framework for your project management approach

A suggested project management framework and its component procedures is included in Figures 31.4 to 31.6, which show the main activities and the information which passes between them. In the suggested approach, each major management activity is based on the separate roles introduced throughout the book (see Chapter 5 for project roles). For example, the project sponsor undertakes "Direct a project"; the project manager would undertake "Control a project". The separation of processes by role, for management processes, ensures each process can be targeted at the appropriate users, without burying them in detail which has to be undertaken by others. For example, a team manager won't be very interested in the sponsor's activities and vice versa.

Management procedures are the core of the method. These include all the essential activities the project sponsor, project manager, and team managers need to undertake, as described in Chapters 4 to 29. Within these procedures, all the information is drawn together; for this reason they can also be called integrating procedures. You will notice, however, many of the activities – such as managing risks – are not only to be done on a project, but also for each work package. I have, therefore, grouped these common elements as support procedures and detailed them separately. The advantage of this approach is if, or when, you develop your enterprise-wide programme and business portfolio methods, you can reuse the support procedures on the programmes and portfolios. You wouldn't want individuals on the same team adopting different approaches for undertaking the same activity; that would be wasteful and counter-productive. *The Programme and Portfolio Workout* will pick up this theme.

Method or process?

Whether you call your project management approach a method or a process is your choice. Some companies are very explicit on the difference between processes and methods; processes are very rigid, "must do", and mandatory, whilst methods are looser, leaving the manager to decide the detail with a fair degree of freedom in how it is used (dare I say, tailoring!). I have mixed up the terms "process" and "method" in this book as I have used different terms in different organizations, without any problems. In the USA the word "process" is used in the same way that "activity" is in the UK. Regardless of name, your process or method should have an architecture which defines how each part relates to the other parts in terms of inputs and outputs and you should use your selected terminology consistently. If I were given a choice, I would choose the word "method" over "process" as I prefer the implication of flexibility. I would reserve the word "process" for the "must-do" aspects such as obtaining finance and procurement related activities.

The management activities

The activities are described in the following sections and shown in Figure 31.4.

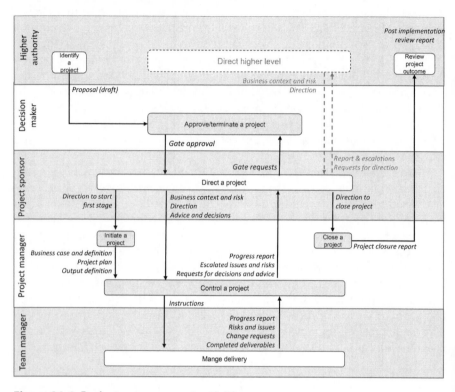

Figure 31.4   Project management activities

The key management activities and their relationships (inputs and outputs) are shown here, with each activity in a swim lane to show which role is accountable. Notice the "higher authority" lane. Who undertakes this depends on the context; this may be a programme manager, business portfolio manager or other corporate role. This is the level to which the project sponsor is accountable.

 Naming your processes and activities

When naming a procedure or describing an activity within a procedure, start with a verb, such as "Control project", "Direct and manage project", "Identify issue", "Approve business case". This makes it clear what the activity is. If you use a noun, such as "Risk", it is not clear what is meant to happen. This approach mirrors the good practice naming convention for schedule plans, looked at in Chapter 20.

Manage "higher level"

The project management approach you create must work within its own context. Chapter 3 discussed how a project may be stand-alone, part of a programme, or part of a business portfolio. This activity represents any of these. It is where the idea for a project comes from and it is here that the post-implementation review is undertaken to verify the outcomes were achieved. The purpose is to ensure the targets for the project are set in terms of expected outcomes and benefits. This will be developed further in *The Programme and Portfolio Workout*, which looks in more detail at programmes and business portfolios.

Approve/terminate a project

The purpose of this activity is to ensure each stage of the project is started in the knowledge that the project is still required, has a viable plan, and the risks are acceptable. In addition, the process is used to suspend (place on hold) a project over which there are doubts as to its viability and, if necessary, terminate it. I have not presumed who the ultimate decision maker should be, although the person undertaking the project sponsor role should, as a minimum, be the person to submit the authorization requests to the decision maker. In practice, most organizations have a table or "scheme of delegation" with a list of criteria, often financially based, stating who has the delegated authority to make a particular decision. This is very organizational and context specific. If the project is stand-alone, then the project sponsor is the decision maker. This is covered in Chapter 16, on governance.

Direct a project

This activity is undertaken by the project sponsor to ensure the business interests of the organization undertaking the project are paramount. You'll find more about this in Chapters 5 and 16.

Initiate a project (Set up)

This activity is undertaken by the project manager, supported by the team, to ensure the project is properly set up and planned (see Chapter 17).

Control a project

This activity is undertaken by the project manager, supported by the team, to ensure each stage of the project is managed throughout its life. It also includes the activities to prepare for the authorization of the next stage. Chapters 16 to 28 deal with different aspects of control.

Close a project

Close a project is undertaken by the project manager, supported by the team, to ensure the project is closed, whether because it is complete or because it has been terminated early (see Chapter 29).

Managing delivery

The purpose of this activity is to ensure the deliverables from the project are developed to the right quality, within in the cost and time constraints and the required outcomes, or business changes, happen. This activity is undertaken by a team manager, supported by the project team members. Specialist processes would be used for undertaking the work itself, so don't confuse these. Team managers would use the same controls as the project manager for controlling their individual work packages.

Don't forget tailoring!

It is possible to assemble the processes in a number of ways to emphasize different approaches or reflect an organization's culture. For example, in Figure 31.4, I have shown the gate requests going from "Direct a project" as I have taken the view that as it is the project sponsor's project, he or she is the person who should make the request. This approach emphasizes the role of the project sponsor as a leader, rather than letting them abdicate the role to the project manager. Alternative approaches may show the gate request going from the project manager, after verifying it with the project sponsor.

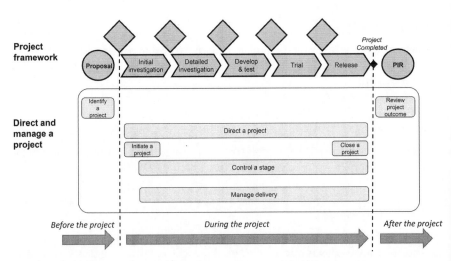

Figure 31.5 The relationship between the project life cycle and the management activities

The management activities and project life cycle should not be confused. This diagram shows the project stages within which each process is typically used.

494

The supporting activities

In addition to the management procedures, there are a number of **supporting activities or procedures**. I have shown a few of the most important activities with the relationships between them in Figure 31.6 overleaf. If you are going to have formal procedures, it is important to define the interface, otherwise accountabilities will become muddled. The supporting activities are there to ensure the techniques essential for effective management are used consistently by all role holders at all levels, be it project or work package. This simplifies reporting and communication dramatically. It also enables you to have a more cost-effective tools strategy and provide the same training. Note that the figure shows just one possible configuration. You could design any number of alternatives which would work as long as each is internally consistent. For example, in the figure the updated plan could pass directly from Manage planning to Manage reporting, rather than shown as going via the central Direct and manage a project activity.

Most of the topics essential to project management are contained in this book but you may wish to add others, to reflect the needs of your organization.

Project frameworks or life cycles

In Chapter 5, I proposed using a single project framework for every type of project, tailored to reflect different work undertaken. The advantage is that, top-down, all projects will look similar to senior management, who will invariably have to sponsor many different types of project.

Don't confuse the project framework or life cycle with the procedures. They are different and necessary. Just to confuse you, many organizations call their project life cycles a "process" as well, so don't be fooled by names alone. Figure 31.5 opposite shows the relationship between the two. A given activity always happens in a procedure but each procedure may be used many times in different stages of the project with the exception of:

- identify a project always happens before a project starts;
- initiate a project always happens at the start of the first stage of the project;
- control a project and manage delivery happen throughout the project;
- close a project always happens at the end of the final stage of a project or if the project is terminated;
- review project outcome always happens after the end of the project.

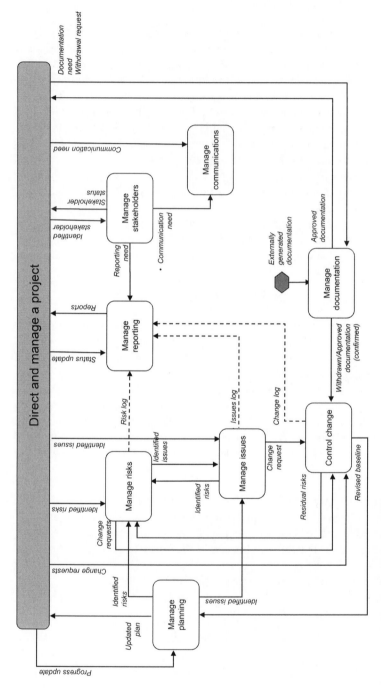

Figure 31.6 The supporting activities

Some of the key support activities and their relationships (inputs and outputs) are shown here. Unless you define an overall architecture, such as this, you will find the interfaces between processes become muddled, which in turn, leads to muddled accountabilities.

Appendix A: Glossary

This appendix provides the definitions for the terms used in *The Project Workout*. It also includes some commonly used alternatives to help you understand the book in the context of your current project management knowledge and so that you can tailor the concepts and terms used in the book to suit your situation. Key cross-references are shown in *italics*.

Accountability What you can count on a person doing. That person and only that person can be called to account if a task they have accountability for is not done or is not done adequately. Note *The Project Workout* distinguishes between "accountability" and *"responsibility"*.

Activity Individual components of work that must be undertaken to complete the stages of the *project*. Each activity should be defined in terms of its start and end dates and the name of the person accountable for its completion. Common alternative: task.

Approval The term used when an individual accepts a deliverable as fit for purpose such that the *project* can continue. Note *The Project Workout* distinguishes between "approval" and *"authorization"*.

Assumption An assumption is made when an unknown is taken to be a fact. Assumptions can be tested using sensitivity analysis and often pose a *risk* to a project. An assumption is used so that work can continue, without the full facts being available.

Assurance Assurance ensures a project remains viable in terms of costs and benefits (business assurance), checking that the users' requirements are being met (user assurance), and that the project is delivering a suitable solution and *outcomes* (specialist or technical assurance). Assurance includes *reviews*, carried out by an independent team on behalf of the *project sponsor*.

Authorization The decision which triggers the allocation of the resources and funding. Authorization is needed to carry on a project and provide the *project sponsor* and *project manager* with the authority to undertake the project or the part of the project which has been authorized. Note *The Project Workout* distinguishes between "authorization" and "*approval*".

Backcasting Using the desired end result (*outcome*) of a project as the principle basis and starting point for planning. This means planning is initially conducted working backwards from project completion.

Bar chart A visual representation of a project's schedule, showing the start and finish dates of the *activities* a project and its stages, work packages and activities. Each activity's duration is shown as a horizontal bar, the ends of which correspond to its start and end dates. *Baseline*, actual and forecast dates can be shown on the same chart. A bar chart is also known as a *Gantt chart*.

Baseline The *project plan* used to track progress. The baseline plan includes start and finish dates of activities, resources, scope, and costs. The baseline cost is often called a *project budget*.

Benefits The quantifiable and measurable improvement resulting from an *outcome* which is perceived as positive by a *stakeholder* and which makes the investment worthwhile. Benefits are normally expressed in monetary or resource terms. Benefits are expected when a change is conceived. Benefits are realized as a result of activities undertaken to effect the change. Examples include quantified increases in revenue, decreases in costs, reductions in working capital, and/or increases in performance which occur directly as a result of a project.

Blueprint A description of the "future business or organization", its working practices and processes, the information required and the technology needed. It is the fundamental sourcebook describing a project's *outcome* and *output* in terms of "feel", technology, commercial, and customer/user needs. It is the document which integrates all the individual system, processes, and platform requirements and specifies how they work together.

Brainstorming A technique for generating ideas in a group. See Appendix E.

Budget Planned, approved cost for the project. See also *baseline*.

Business case A document providing the justification for undertaking (or for continuing) a project, defining the financial and other *benefits* the project is expected to realize, together with the schedule and other constraints within which the project is to operate. This is usually prepared in two stages. The first is the initial business case which is prepared for the detailed investigation gate review. The second is the full business case which is prepared for the development gate review.

Business portfolio A business portfolio comprises current benefit generating business activities, together with a loosely coupled but tightly aligned *portfolio* of programmes, projects and other work, aimed at realizing the benefits of part of a business plan or strategy.

Business portfolio office A *support office*, which supports the roles of the business portfolio sponsor and manager.

Business portfolio plan A part of the organization's business plan which focuses on the targets (*benefits*) and resources of a particular *business portfolio*.

Capabilities Building blocks of systems, processes, and competence which are combined with other capabilities to provide an organization with operational potential.

Capacity buffer A *critical chain* term. Protective time placed between projects within the drum resource.

Change control The formal process through which changes to the *project plan* are introduced and approved. Changes are recorded on a *change log*. (Not to be confused with the *management of change*.)

Change log A list, maintained as part of *change control*, of all proposed and actual changes. Also called change register.

Closure Formal "end-point" of a project, either because it is complete or has been *terminated* early. Closure is formally documented in a closure report.

Commitments Orders placed and hence the money, although not yet spent, committed as part of an agreed contract.

Conditions of satisfaction Conditions which, if met, enable the project to objectively be termed a success. These should be indicative of *benefits* realization. *Recognition Events*™ and *Value Flashpoints*™ are special types of condition, used in the Isochron methodology.

Configuration management A discipline, normally supported by software tools, which gives management precise control over the *deliverables* of a project (or components of an operational environment) and ensures the correct version of each part of a system is known and documented.

Constraint Defined restriction or limitation imposed on a project or operational work. A constraint limits a manager's freedom of action.

Contingency plan An alternative plan of action to be followed in the event of a *risk* occurring.

Cost plan Document detailing items of cost associated with a project, in categories (*work packages*) relating to the schedule plan. See also *budget* and *baseline*.

Critical chain The critical chain of a single project is the sequence of dependent activities that would prevent the project from being completed in a shorter interval, given finite resources.

Critical path The path through a *network* of activities, taking into account dependencies, in which late completion of activities will have an impact on the project end date, or delay a key *milestone*.

Critical success factors Factors to ensure the achievement of *success criteria*.

Culture Culture comprises two elements:

- The norms and behaviours of a group (the way things are done here!);
- Unconscious programming of the mind, leading to a set of similar collective habits, behaviours and mind-sets.

Customer project A project undertaken for a customer or client with the primary benefit gained being the revenue as payment for the services provided. See also *project* and *internal project*.

Deliverable Output produced by the project, e.g. a report, system, or product. Deliverables may be:

- intermediate or temporary, used only during the undertaking of a project;
- final, comprising part of the *outputs* from the project.

Each key deliverable should be defined in the *project definition* section of the *business case* document and represented by a *milestone* on the project plan. Alternatives: product, work product, asset.

Dependency A constraint on the sequence and timing of activities in a project. Activities may be dependent on other activities within the same project (internal dependency), or on activities/deliverables from other projects (*interdependency*).

Detailed investigation stage The second stage within the project framework, when a feasibility study is undertaken to choose the best solution from a range of options and when the chosen solution is defined in sufficient detail for delivery to start.

Detailed plan Developed throughout the project, from the *summary plan*, breaking down the forthcoming stage into manageable work packages and activities.

Duration The amount of time required to complete an *activity*. It is calculated as the finish date – the start date.

Earned value A management technique used to analyse and determine project progress by comparing the amount of work planned with what was actually earned and what was actually spent. Earned value is usually measured in currency units but effort or notional points may also be used; the key is that the actual measure and the plan need to use the same units.

Effective Successful at realizing an objective.

Efficient Providing progress or performance with minimal waste of resources.

Emergency project A project required as a result of a business issue which will severely damage the organization if not addressed without delay. These projects may cause previously committed projects to be allocated a lower priority or to be *terminated* to release resources.

Escalation To increase the awareness and ownership of a problem or *issue* to a level in the organization where the required resources, expertise and/or authority can be applied to resolve that issue.

Estimate An approximate calculation or judgement of the value, number, quantity, or extent of an element of a *plan*. In project management, an estimate may be considered "soft" or "hard":

- a soft estimate is one in which only a low level of confidence can be placed.
- a hard estimate is one in which you have high confidence.

Feeding buffer A feeding buffer protects the start of a *Critical chain activity* from a delay of an upstream dependent non-critical chain activity. A project can have many feeding buffers.

Float The amount of time an activity may be delayed without delaying subsequent activities. Float (also called slack) is a mathematical calculation and can alter as the project progresses and changes are made to the project plan. Float is measured in units of time, so an activity on the critical path has zero float. If an activity has some float, however, it can be done later.

- **free float** measures the time that an activity can be delayed without affecting any succeeding activity.
- **total float** measures the amount of time an activity can be delayed without affecting the end of a project.

Fog project (walking in a fog) Formally known as an open project, this type of project occurs when you are unsure of both what is to be done and how.

Gantt chart See *bar chart*. Henry Laurence Gantt, an American mechanical engineer, is recognized for developing the Gantt chart.

Gate The point, preceding each stage, at which all new information converges and which serves for:

- quality control checks
- prioritization
- a point from which to plan forward
- a go/no go decision point

Health check A tool used in project reviews to help assess the overall risk associated with the project.

Idea A possibility for a new or enhanced capability, system, service, or product. This is written up as a *proposal*.

Impact The marked effect or influence of one action on another.

Impact assessment A study undertaken to determine the effect of an *issue* or *risk* on the project. An impact assessment is required as part of *change control* and as part assessing the advantages of taking one course of action over another (options).

Interdependency If Project B requires a *deliverable* from Project A, in order to achieve its objective, Project B is dependent on Project A. Dependency is when a deliverable is passed from one project to another.

Internal project. A project which an organization is undertaking for its own benefit. For example an internal project may be the development and roll-out of a new billing system. See also *project* and *customer project*.

Internal rate of return (IRR) A method used to determine the value of a project. The discount rate at which the value of the opportunity will be zero. In principle, the higher the IRR the "better" the opportunity, but this guideline should be used with caution as other factors, such as cash flow and risk, may be more important.

Issue A circumstance (event, lack of knowledge, etc.) that has occurred and which will affect the success of a project. They are recorded on an *issues log*. An issue can either be resolved within the project as defined, or a change may be required to accommodate it.

Issues log A list, maintained as part of issue management, of all *issues* and their status. Alternative: issues register.

Late activity An *activity* which is forecast to end later than the *baseline* plan finish date. This is reported on a late activities report.

Life cycle A sequence of defined *stages* over the full duration of a project, i.e. initial investigation, detailed investigation, develop and test, trial, release.

Link A relationship between *dependent* activities.

Management of change A term often used to describe the action of transforming an organization from one state to another. Not to be confused with *change control* which is a technique used on projects to ensure that alterations to the project schedule, scope, *benefits*, and cost are introduced in a regularized way.

Method A collection of practices, rules, tools, and instructions used by teams or individuals to achieve a specific result. A method defines principles and provides documentation and tools. It is the responsibility of users to identify and plan the relevant component to carry out their specific tasks. As such, a method provides flexibility but requires each user to choose and organize the set of activities relevant for the work. A method may comprise one or more procedures, supported by guides and templates.

Milestone A major event (often representing the start of a *stage*) used to monitor progress at a summary level. Milestones are *activities* of zero duration.

Movie project (making a movie) Formally, a semi-open project, where the means are known but not the *output*.

Net present value (NPV) The value calculated by projecting the future cash flow and discounting the value of future years' cash at the discount rate to give its notional value today.

Network chart or diagram A diagram which shows *dependencies* between project *activities*. Activities are represented as boxes or nodes and the activity relationship is shown by arrows connecting the nodes. Often called a PERT chart.

Opportunity An uncertainty that could have a positive impact on objectives or *benefits*. See also *risk*.

Originator The person who conceives an "*idea*" or need for a new development or enhancement and publishes it in the form of a *proposal*. This person can come from any function or level in the organization.

Outcome The way a thing turns out; a consequence. In a programme and project management context, this means the result of change, affecting real-world behaviour or circumstances through a programme, project, or business operation. Outcomes are desired when a change is conceived and are achieved as a result of the activities undertaken, and *outputs* produced to effect the change. Desired outcomes, if achieved, usually produce a benefit for the organization.

Output A specialist product (the tangible or intangible *deliverable* or set of deliverables) is produced, constructed, or created as a result of a planned activity. Outputs, if used, will result in an *outcome* or business change.

Phase A phase is a single project within a phased programme of projects (hence phase 1 project, phase 2 project, etc.). Note the PMI® definition of "phase" equates to *The Project Workout* definition for "*stage*".

Pilot A pilot is the ultimate form of testing a new development and its implementation plan prior to committing to the full release. It is undertaken using a sample of potential customers and users. This would normally take place in the *trial stage* although may, in some cases, be treated as a limited release.

Portfolio A grouping or bundle of programmes and/or projects and other work collected together for management or reporting convenience. See also *business portfolio*.

Post-implementation review (PIR) A review, three to six months after the end of the project, to establish whether:

- the predicted *benefits* were delivered;
- the most effective operational processes were designed;
- the solution really met the business needs, both for users and customers;
- the changes have been sustained and are likely to remain so; sometimes referred to as being "sticky".

The post-implementation review checks the *effectiveness* of a project as opposed its *efficiency* which is reviewed as part of project *closure*. Alternative: Post-project review.

Post-investment review (PIR) A review, three to six months after the end of the project, to assess whether the expected *financial benefits* are being achieved. This checks the financial effectiveness of a project. A post-investment review is included in a *post-implementation review*, but often financed departments insist on the financial aspects being covered in a separate document to the operational aspects.

Process A series of actions or steps taken to achieve a particular end.

Programme Programmes are a tightly coupled and tightly aligned grouping of projects and other related work.

Progress bar chart A bar chart which shows the actual and forecast dates for each *activity* compared with the *baseline* plan dates.

Progress report Regular report from the *project manager* to the *project sponsor* and other *stakeholders* summarizing the progress of a project, including key events, *milestones* not achieved, *risks* and *issues*.

Product A term used in some project methods in place of *deliverable*. Hence the terms "product breakdown structure", which identifies, in a hierarchical way, the deliverable/

products required and "product flow diagram", which identifies each deliverable's derivation and the *dependencies* between them.

Project A project, in a business environment, is:

- a finite piece of work (i.e. it has a beginning and an end) undertaken in *stages*:
- within defined cost and time constraints;
- directed at achieving a stated business *benefit*.

See also *internal project* and *customer project*.

Project board Body established to monitor the project and assist the *project sponsor* in realizing the *benefits* and the project manager in delivering the deliverables. Sometimes called a steering group or steering board.

Project buffer The project buffer protects the project end date from viability in the duration of the tasks in the *critical chain*. For a single project, the size of the buffer depends on the number and duration of the critical chain activities and the degree of risk associated with each. See also *feeding buffers*.

Project definition A section within the initial and full *business case* which summarizes a project in terms of the expected *outcome*, what will be done, how it will be delivered, and what business need the project supports.

Project manager Person accountable for managing a project on a day-to-day basis, from start to finish, to ensure successful implementation within agreed cost, schedule, and quality targets.

Project plan The supporting detail to the *project definition* which details the schedule, resources, and costs for the project. It can be in outline or detail.

Project portfolio A grouping or bundle of projects collected together for management convenience, e.g. the collection of projects sponsored by an individual is his or her sponsorship portfolio; those projects managed by a person is a management portfolio; the full set of projects within a organization is the organization portfolio.

Project review group The term used in this book for the body accountable for the project authorization. There is no industry standard for this.

Project sponsor The person who sees a commercial possibility in an idea and agrees to take ownership of the proposal. Once a project is approved, the project sponsor is accountable for realizing the benefits to the business. Typically, he/she will:

- chair the *project board*;
- appoint the *project manager*;

- represent the business and users in key project decisions;
- approve key *deliverables*;
- resolve *issues* which are outside the project manager's control;
- ensure that the delivered solution matches the business needs;
- be the primary *risk* taker.

Project support office (PSO) A group set up to provide certain administrative and other services to the project manager and team. Sometimes a PSO services several projects in parallel. See also *support office*.

Proposal A short document prepared, by the *originator* for the initial investigation gate review, which outlines the desired *outcome* for the proposed project, its fit with current strategy and, if known, the impact on the organization, broad estimates of benefits, cost, and expected time to completion.

Quality The totality of features and characteristics of a *deliverable* that bear on its ability to satisfy stated and implied needs. Also defined as "fitness for purpose" or "conforms to requirements". Hence, "quality criteria" are the conditions a deliverable must meet to be accepted as fit for purpose.

Quality review A review of a *deliverable* against an established set of quality criteria.

Quest project (going on a quest) Quest projects are formally known as semi-closed projects. You are clear what is to be done but have no idea about how to do it.

RAG (Red-Amber-Green) A simple status reporting method, enabling the reader of a report to grasp very quickly whether a project is likely to achieve its objectives. RAG stands for Red-Amber-Green:

- Red means there are significant issues with the project that the project team and project sponsor are unable to address.
- Amber means there are problems with the project but the team has them under control.
- Green means that the project is going well with no significant issues, although it may be late or forecast to overspend.

The RAG status is usually based on the project manager's own assessment of the situation and is useful for highlighting those projects which may have difficulties. Some organizations also have RAG status set automatically by systems, e.g. when a project is forecast to overspend. Some organizations use "BRAG", where the "B" is blue and denotes completed.

Ready for Service (RFS) The *milestone* prior to the *release stage*, by when all pre-requisite project work, testing, and trials have been completed and full operational support is in place.

Recognition Events™ A real life happening that when it occurs, tells a sponsor and other stakeholders that one particular expectation of the *project plan* has been met. This is a term used in the Isochron method. See also *conditions of satisfaction*.

Release Generic term used to denote when an *output* from a project is put into service, e.g. a product can be used by a customer under standard terms and conditions (i.e. not trial agreement), handover of a customized service for the customer to start using, a system started to be used, new process operational. It must not be confused with *ready for service* which is the point when all capabilities are ready to use but have not yet been put to use.

Release stage The final stage in the staged project *life cycle* or framework during which the final *output* is launched and put into service.

Resource buffer A resource buffer is used in *critical chain* schedule management to provide early warning, from one critical chain activity to another critical chain activity, for an activity to start.

Resource levelling is when the planned assignment of resources is changed to ensure no over or under commitment of the resources. The aim is to be as evenly spread as possible.

Resource loading is when resources are assigned to activities in a plan so that their over- and under-allocation can be determined.

Resource manager A person in each unit and function accountable for knowing the future assignment of resources to processes and projects.

Responsibility What a person is or feels responsible for. It assumes they have a commitment, beyond their own *accountabilities*, to act responsibly to ensure the project objectives are met.

Review A formal assessment of something with the intention of recommending changes if necessary: for a project as whole, a review is to ensure the business objectives will be achieved (project *assurance*); for *deliverables,* a review ensures the deliverable is fit for purpose. Reviewers are contributors to a decision but do not actually make the decisions (see *approval*).

Risk A risk is the effect of uncertainty on the objectives. Their effect can be positive (opportunity) or negative (threat); risks could impact the realization of *benefits*. Risks can be event-based or shocks – events that may or may not happen, like accidents. Or they could be information-based – where the facts are unknown, for example, costs are underestimated or based on false assumptions, such as interest rates, inflation, exchange rates, or the weather. Risks should be recorded on a *risk log*, continuously assessed, and mitigation action taken.

Risk log A list, maintained as part of risk management, to track all *risks* and their status. Alternative: risk register.

Simple project A project where the end point can be seen clearly from the detailed investigation gate. Typically, simple projects consume few resources or have their own separate resources which cannot be allocated to other projects.

Single point accountability The concept that any *activity*, or *work package*, at any level in the *work breakdown structure* has only one named person accountable for it.

Slippage See *late activities*.

Sponsor See *project sponsor*.

Stage The natural high-level breakpoints in the project *life cycle* (e.g. initial investigation, detailed investigation, develop and test, trial and release).

Stakeholder Any person or group with an interest in the project or its *outcome*. Typically some support it, some are neutral and other are antagonists.

Stakeholder influence map A diagram used to depict the influence individual *stakeholders* have on others. The objective is to identify the routes by which key influencers and decision makers can be enrolled in the project's objectives.

Standard A required or agreed level of quality or attainment.

Subproject A tightly aligned and tightly coupled part of a project. Subprojects are usually run to their own staged *life cycle*.

Success A successful project achieves its business objectives and *outcomes*, and realizes the expected *benefits*. Traditionally project success has been seen in terms of a project being completed within the defined time, cost, and quality constraints but in the "real world" that is not always essential. Success is formally measured against the *conditions of satisfaction* and *benefits* stated in the *business case*. Different *stakeholders* will have their own views on whether a project is successful, regardless of what the business case may say.

Success criteria Used for judging if the project is successful (see *conditions of satisfaction*).

Summary plan Initial part of the evolution of the schedule, resource and cost plan, developed at the start of the project, defining the overall targets and key dates.

Support office A group of people providing administrative and/or specialist services to defined roles in the project management environment. Hence *project support office* and business *programme office*.

Tailoring alters or adapts methods or processes for use in a particular situation. At organizational level, a single method will not suit every permutation and combination of situations and needs to be adapted to suit (tailoring). Similarly, for most organizations, one enterprise-wide method or process will not be appropriate for every project in every circumstance. Some adaption is normally needed if the project is to be run both effectively and efficiently, to suit both the type of work and the people involved.

Tailoring guidelines describe what can and cannot be modified in a process or method; they may also provide examples of tailoring.

Termination The premature *closure* of a project due to an *issue* which cannot be addressed or because the *risks* have become too high.

Theory of Constraints The theory expounded by Eli Goldratt which led to the development of *critical chain* schedule management.

Threat An uncertainty that could have a negative impact on objectives or *benefits*. See also *risk*.

Trial stage A trial of a capability in same environment as the customer or user will use it. Often denoted as a beta trial under special trial agreements or a pitot.

Value driver The things which increase revenue or decrease cost or increase asset value in the organization.

Value Flashpoints™ A *recognition event* at which a particular project cash benefit starts to be realized. In the Isochron method, value flashpoints are used to map financial implications of the project to the organization's accounts and ties all project activity and investment to the points where benefits start. See also *conditions of satisfaction*.

Value management A technique used in the investigative stages of a project to ensure *deliverables* are clearly defined and matched to business needs and solutions represent value for money whilst remaining fit for their intended purpose. Do not confuse this with *earned value*.

White space Unassigned resources which are available to work on future projects. White space is required at short notice for initial investigations and at medium notice to resource future projects after the detailed investigation gate. Without white space, organizations are unable to change themselves without taking resource from previously authorized and committed work.

Work breakdown structure (WBS) A structured hierarchy of *work packages*.

Work package Generic term used to describe a grouping of *activities*, *stages*, etc. each of which has a defined scope, timescale, cost, and a single person accountable for it.

Appendix B: Document outlines

Templates for the key control documents described in Part II are given on the following pages:

Proposal
Business Case (Initial and Full)
Feasibility Report
Test Plan
Ready for Trial Review Report
Test Results
Trial Plan
Trial Results
Ready for Service Review Report
Project Closure Report
Post-implementation Review Report

Proposal

The proposal is a very brief document (one to five pages) which outlines the need the project will meet, its intended outcome, likely benefits and how it fits with current strategy. If known, the impact on the organization, and broad estimates of benefits and cost, and required time to completion can also be included.

1 Background
2 Business objectives
3 Scope and interdependencies
4 Benefits
5 Output definition.

Business case

The initial business case contains the business rationale for the project. It is the document which outlines *why* you need the project, *what* options you intend to work on, *how* you will do it, and *who* is needed to make it happen. It also answers the question *how much*? and hence is used to authorize the funding for at least the next stage of the project.

1 Finance

    1.1 Financial appraisal
    1.2 Sensitivity analysis

2 Project definition and plan

    2.1 Background
    2.2 Business objectives and outcomes
    2.3 Benefits
    2.4 Output description
    2.5 Scope, impacts, and interdependencies
    2.6 Deliverables
    2.7 Schedule
    2.8 Costs
    2.9 Risks
    2.10 Prerequisites, assumptions, and constraints
    2.11 Project approach
    2.12 Analysis of options

3 Project organization

    3.1 Organization chart and roles
    3.2 Progress reporting
    3.3 Change control criteria
    3.4 Gating and review points
    3.5 Stakeholders

4 Management plan

    4.1 Benefits realization management
    4.2 Reporting
    4.3 Planning
    4.4 Risks and issues
    4.5 Change control
    4.6 Document and information management
    4.7 Configuration management

Appendices

A   Business commitment
B   Schedule plan
C   Resource plan
D   Financial plan
E   Terms of reference for detailed investigation (Initial business case only)
F   Financial sensitivity (business case only)

Note: the same table of contents is used for both the initial business case and full business case.

Feasibility report

The feasibility report includes the recommendation for which option should be adopted as the solution, and compares it against rejected solutions in financial and non-financial terms.

Executive Summary

1   Background
2   Conclusions and recommendations
3   Prerequisites, assumptions, and constraints
4   Options considered
5   Output definition
6   Benefits

Appendices

A   detailed analysis of options

Test plan

The test plan documents the tests required to verify performance of any outputs from the project both in isolation and working as a complete system.

1   Business objectives
2   Output definition
3   Purpose and approach
4   Customer and user involvement
5   Test prerequisites, assumptions, and constraints
6   The test list
7   Planned timescale, accountabilities, and resources

Appendices

A   List of reviewers
B   Relevant information

Ready for trial review report

The ready for trial review report is a short report which confirms that all deliverables, resources, and prerequisites across all functions required for starting the trial are in place.

1   Business objectives
2   Recommendation
3   Comparison with plan
4   Outstanding issues/activities

Appendices

A   List of reviewers
B   High-level checklist for the trial gate
C   Detailed checklist

Test resuslts

The test results verify that any testing has been completed in accordance with the test plans and acceptance criteria, prior to doing the ready for trial review.

1   Business objectives
2   Output definition
3   Purpose and approach
4   Conclusions
5   Influencing factors
6   The test record
7   Actual time, accountabilities, and resources
8   Issues raised

Appendices

A   List of reviewers
B   Relevant information

Trial plan

The trial plan documents the way in which the output will be piloted and the criteria for determining whether it was successful.

1   Business objectives
2   Output definition
3   Purpose and approach
4   Customer and user involvement
5   Trial prerequisites, assumptions, and constraints
6   The trial list
7   Planned timescale, accountabilities, and resources

Appendices

A   List of reviewers
B   Relevant information

Trial results

The trial results is a summary document which confirms that the trials have been completed in accordance with the trial plan, acceptance criteria validated and the developed solution is now ready to move to the release stage. Any outstanding risks and issues are also noted.

1   Business objectives
2   Output definition
3   Purpose and approach
4   Customer and user involvement
5   Conclusions
6   Influencing factors
7   The trial record
8   Actual timescale, accountabilities, and resources
9   Issues raised

Appendices

A   List of reviewers
B   Relevant information

Ready for service review report

The ready for service (RFS) review is a short report which confirms that all deliverables and prerequisite activities required before starting the release stage have been completed.

1   Business objectives
2   Recommendation
3   Comparison with plan
4   Outstanding issues/activities

Appendices

A List of reviewers
B High-level checklist for the trial gate
C Detailed checklist
D Executive summary from the business case

Project closure report

The project closure report contains the notes of solution handover and project closure, including "lessons learned" from the project in terms of how the processes, organization, systems, and team worked (i.e. the efficiency of the project). A terms of reference for the post-implementation review is also included.

1 Business objectives
2 Achievements
3 Project efficiency (cost and schedule performance)
4 Impact of changes
5 Outstanding risks, issues, and deliverables
6 Lessons learned
7 Acknowledgements

Appendices

A Terms of reference for the Post-implementation review (PIR)

Post-implementation review report

The post-implementation review (PIR) report assesses the success of the project against predefined criteria given in the business case and confirmed in the terms of reference for the review. It assesses how effective the project was in meeting its objectives and includes recommendations for improvements.

1 Business objectives
2 Benefits
3 Project effectiveness (operational and financial)
4 Outstanding risks and issues
5 Lessons learned

Appendix C: Method and standards commentary

What is the difference between a standard and a method?

In the context of project management:

- a **standard**, such as ISO 21500, defines what needs to be done and by whom but not how activities are done;
- a **method**, such as PRINCE2®, provides not only a set of activities to be done, together with roles, but also techniques for undertaking these activities.

As such:

- a standard can be used to help assess the completeness of any method;
- a method is intended for practical use.

Organizational approaches to project management normally fit within the definition of a "method" as they are designed for practical use within a specific organization. They may be derived directly from a method like PRINCE2®, or based on a particular standard. By including techniques, a method is far more prescriptive (and helpful!) about the way a particular activity should be undertaken; for that reason, methods tend to be longer and more detailed.

Like many aspects of project management, organizations may use the same words in different ways. The terms "standard", "method", or "process" may not be always used in the way I have used them in this book, or in the way you use them in your workplace. You'll also find some publications seem to cross over the definitions I have given. Don't worry about it; what is important is that you choose the words that fit your project or organization and then use them consistently.

This appendix is where you are likely to come across the most acronyms and jargon as some authors seem to love them! You will also find the different publications are not easily comparable as they may use different structures and terminology. Don't be too daunted by this. You'll only need to refer to the standards and method if your role requires it.

Standards, methods, and other sources of best practice are simply a consensus amongst the authors of what they believe is important. When searching the Internet, be careful about the provenance of any information you find.

The most trustworthy sources are the official international and national standards, but they tend to lag behind good practice as it can take a long time for the experts involved to reach a consensus. The national professional bodies are also a good source and will have papers on new approaches. Such articles tend have a more practical approach than research papers produced from universities. There is also the International Project Management Association (IPMA), which acts as an umbrella organization for many national bodies, including the UK's APM. IPMA provides a global network that enables its member bodies a large degree of autonomy. It promotes professional growth through its conferences and has a competence-based certification for project managers to which national bodies can align and hence promotes transferability of project professionals across national boundaries.

What is *The Project Workout*?

The Project Workout is neither a method nor a standard. It is a text book explaining how to manage a project. It can, however, be used as a core source to create a practical method. If you do this, then the text book becomes your "training manual". As *The Project Workout* also supports the concepts in many standards and proprietary methods it can also be used to support organizations basing their project management method on them. As "tailoring" is now a feature of all standards, *The Project Workout* gives you a view of what really counts when managing a project to help you understand how all these different approaches can be used together.

Appendix C1 – Project management standards

About project management standards

A standard is an agreed way of doing something, or an agreed quality criteria for a product or service. Standards can cover a wide range of activities and products undertaken and used by organizations and used by their customers. They can be:

- **prescriptive**, such as a specification or a *normative* standard. You'll find the word "shall" used in these. For example, the outer dimensions shall be less than ..."
- **for guidance**, such as a code of practice or *informative* standard. You'll find the word "should" used in these. Project management standards tend to fit into this category. For example, "The project manager should tailor the management processes ..."

The language used in standards is carefully chosen; each standards body has their own usage rules, usually described in the standard! For example British Standards has BS 0, *A standard for standards – Principles of standardization*, together with its accompanying rule book.

In the context of this book, standards improve the effectiveness of project management by drawing attention to the key principles and activities required. The standard becomes a "checklist" against which the management of the project can be assessed. Standards also seek to define the use of words in a particular context.

Once established, standards can promote continuous improvement by being periodically reviewed and updated to ensure the latest consensus on best practice is included and any omissions or clarifications are dealt with. In this way, all users of standards benefit from the collective experience and feedback of other users.

Official standards, with international and national recognition, tend to come from three different sources. The numbering convention usually makes it clear:

- **National standards**, such as BS (British), DIN (German), NF (standard), ANSI (American [USA]), SS (Swedish), JIS (Japan).
- **European standards**, denoted "EN", are used throughout Europe; these are automatically adopted by EU member states.
- **International standards**, denoted "ISO" may be used throughout the world. Adoption by individual countries is optional. For example, in the UK, an adopted international standard is denoted as "BS ISO".

There are complete books devoted to using standards, but I should be able to provide you with sufficient understanding to find your own way and ask the right questions. I'll do this by looking at a comparison of:

- ISO 21500:2012, *Guidance on project management*;
- BS6079 Part 1: 2010, *Project management – Part 1: Principles and guidelines for the management of projects*.

ISO 21500 *Guidance on project management*

ISO 21500:2012 was the first international standard on project management and, as such, represents a major achievement in developing an international consensus on what "project management" comprises. It's a slim volume of only thirty pages plus the appendices, structured around what it calls "Subject groups" and "Process groups". In this respect, it mirrors the way the USA's PMBOK® (see later in this chapter) and Germany's DIN standards are structured. It is almost entirely focused around what a project manager does. Each subject group consists of processes applicable to any project phase or project. These processes are defined in terms of purpose, description and primary inputs and outputs and are interdependent.

The process groups include those activities typically used when:

- **Initiating** a project, to start and define a project phase (stage) or project and approve the start of the work.
- **Planning** a project to develop the plan in sufficient detail to establish a baseline against which performance can be measured and controlled.
- **Implementing** a project to undertake the management activities and support the development of the project's deliverables.
- **Controlling** a project used to monitor, measure, and control project performance against the project plan.
- **Closing** a project to formally verify that the work is finished and to provide lessons learned.

The subject areas are listed in Table C.1 below, with a tick to show which process group the components are reflected in:

Table C.1 ISO 21500 – process and subject groups

		Process groups				
		Initiating	Planning	Implementing	Controlling	Closing
Subject groups	Integration	✓	✓	✓	✓	
	Stakeholder	✓		✓		
	Scope		✓		✓	
	Resources	✓	✓	✓		
	Time		✓		✓	
	Cost		✓		✓	
	Risk		✓	✓	✓	
	Quality		✓	✓	✓	
	Procurement		✓	✓	✓	
	Communication		✓	✓	✓	

So, for example, the "Risk" subject, has four "processes", allocated to three of the process groups as shown in Table C.2.

Table C.2 The processes of "Risk"

	Initiating	Planning	Implementing	Controlling	Closing
Risk	-	Identify risks Assess risks	Treat risks	Control risks	-

The subjects are mostly self-evident, except for "Integration". This is the set of activities, which brings the others together, that is, the activities to identify, define, combine, unify, coordinate, control, and close the various activities and processes related to the project. BS6079 Part 1 deals with these in its "integration activities".

The Project Workout and ISO 21500

The Project Workout covers all the roles and activities required to direct and manage a project, whereas ISO 21500 only covers the activities undertaken by a project manager. As such ISO 21500 has a narrower scope. *The Project Workout* covers all the knowledge area except "Procurement"; this is because most organizations have procurement processes which apply to the whole organization and not just to projects.

Apart from the interpersonal aspects of managing projects, *The Project Workout* includes the following topics which are not covered in ISO 21500:

* Management: identifying the need, directing a project, authorizing a project, managing delivery; reviewing outcome.
* Support: benefits, issues management, document management, reviews.

The Project Workout also provides more information on project life cycles and their use.

The main terminology differences are:

* *The Project Workout* uses "stage", ISO 21550 uses "phase";
* *The Project Workout* describes "management activities", which ISO 21500 calls "Integration activities".

BS6079 Part 1 *Project management – Part 1: Principles and guidelines for the management of projects*

The 2010 edition of the British Standard on project management was a major rewrite of the previous version, taking into account the growing consensus on project management both in the UK and internationally. In particular, it reflects the body of knowledge from the UK's Association for Project Management and the lessons learned from using the PRINCE2® method. There are other standards in the "6079 family", such as for vocabulary (Part 2) and risk (Part 3), but Part 1 is the one you are most likely to need. BS6079 Part 1 takes a systematic view of the key project management roles and activities and, as such, provides a set of practices which can be tailored to suit a particular organization or project. Unlike ISO 21500, the British Standard treats 'project management' in an holistic way, including activities undertaken by the project sponsor, decision makers, project board, project assurance, and the project team managers and the project team, as well as those undertaken by the project manager. Furthermore, it includes a detailed explanation of project life cycles as well as competencies.

BS6079 Part 1's architecture is very different to ISO 21500 in that it has two sets of activities (BS6079 uses the term "activity" where ISO 21500 uses "process"). The **integration activities** deal with the management of the project from the creation of an idea through to the review of project outcomes after the project has been closed. The **support activities** are drawn on from the integration activities and deal with the detail for specific techniques. See Figure C1.

It takes these two sets of activities and then defines inputs and outputs (deliverables) but, unlike ISO 21500, it also states the relationships between the activities.

BS6079 Part 1 is a good basis on which to develop an enterprise project management method as it is holistic and includes sufficient detail to start defining your own processes. The scope of ISO 21500 is wholly encompassed in BS6079. Figure C.2 highlights this.

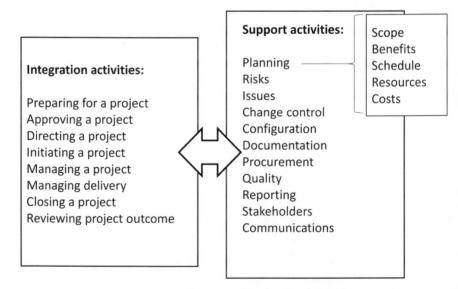

Figure C.1 BS6079 Part 1's integration and support activities

BS6079 Part 1's architecture has two sets of activities: the **integration activities** deal with the management of the project from the creation of an idea through to the review of project outcomes after the project has been closed; the **support activities** are drawn from the integration activities and deal with the detail for specific specialist techniques.

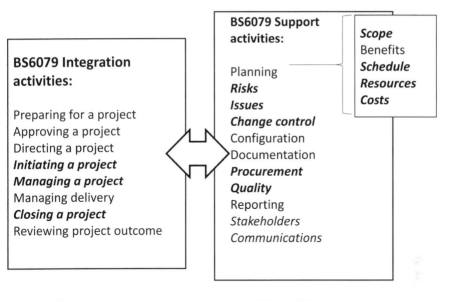

Bold italics represent activities which are in ISO 21500

Figure C.2 A comparison of the scope of ISO 21500 compared with BS6079 Part 1

The scope of ISO 21500 is wholly encompassed in BS6079. This diagram shows BS6079's integration activities and highlights in bold/italics which of them is covered by ISO 21500 processes.

The Project Workout and BS 6079 Part 1

The Project Workout and BS 6079 Part 1 cover all the roles and activities required to direct and manage a project. *The Project Workout* covers all the topics in BS 6079 Part 1 except:

- "Procurement" – this is because most organizations have procurement processes which apply to the whole organization, not just to projects.
- "Configuration management" – this is a specialist discipline in engineering-based organizations and not core to every project. Further, configuration management is only successful if undertaken with the right tooling, which itself defines the processes to be used.
- "Quality" – the concept of quality is embedded in every aspect of *The Project Workout* rather than treated as a separate subject. A defined project managed approach is a quality approach.

The Project Workout and BS6079 Part 1 treat project life cycles and gating in the same way, with gates being key decision point to start a stage.

BS 6079 Part 1 and *The Project Workout* are a good fit with no conflicts. The main terminology differences are:

- *The Project Workout* uses "stage", BS 6079 Part 1 uses "phase";
- *The Project Workout* describes "management activities", which BS 6079 Part 1 calls "Integration activities".

The UK government's project delivery standard

The Project Delivery Standard is one of a set of UK government functional standards which aims to set out expectations for, and align, the most important activities undertaken in all departments of government. The project delivery standard sets expectations for the integrated direction and management of portfolios, programmes and projects, ensuring the successful, timely and cost effective delivery of government policy and departmental objectives. It is a standard, written by government, for government.

The standard describes the "why" and the "what" but does not define "how" anything should be done, leaving it to those who introduce the standard to decide the best way to apply its content in their context. It sets out, in a concise way, the practices that you would expect to find on any government portfolio, programme or project and is intended to be used as a reference to dip into as and when needed. It is a brief document (just eighteen pages of core text) and so doesn't contain the same level of detail that is included in other standards and methods, many of which it refers to. Its terminology mostly draws on the AXELOS publications (PRINCE2®, MSP®, MoP® etc.) as these were initially developed by government and are the foundation for programme and project management training in government. It's scope is wider than any other single document mentioned in this appendix and is compatible with all of them.

Although aimed at UK government promoted project delivery, the majority of this document is applicable to any project, in any sector and is available, as a download, free of charge.

The Project Workout and the UK government's project delivery standard (GovS 002)

The Project Workout and the UK government's project delivery standard share the same principles and architecture. As the project delivery standard covers portfolio, programme and project management is goes beyond the scope of this book, however *The Programme and Portfolio* Workout covers the remaining topics. The topics not covered in *The Project Workout* are:

- programme and portfolio management (except for simple programmes);
- management of change;
- resource, capacity and capability management;
- configuration management;

- requirements, solution design, development and integration, verification and validation;
- procurement and supplier management.

Other standards

Other standards you may come across include:

- ISO 9000 family on quality management
- ISO 31000:2009 *Risk management*
- ISO/IEC/IEEE 15288:2015 *Systems and software engineering – System life cycle processes.*

The ISO 9000 family addresses various aspects of quality management and contains some of ISO's best known standards. These standards provide guidance and tools for companies and organizations who want to ensure their products and services consistently meet customer requirements and quality is consistently improved. In the context of project management, if your organization seeks to be "ISO 9000 certified", then your project management processes and method will need to comply with this.

ISO 31000:2009 can be used by any organization regardless of its size, activity, or sector. Using ISO 31000 can help organizations increase the likelihood of achieving objectives, improve the identification of opportunities and threats, and effectively allocate and use resources for risk treatment. ISO 31000 cannot be used for certification purposes, but does provide guidance for internal or external audit programmes. Organizations using it can compare their risk-management practices with an internationally recognized benchmark, providing sound principles for effective management and corporate governance.

ISO/IEC/IEEE 15288:2015 is very much for those in systems engineering. It covers much of the same ground as the project management standards, but is aimed specifically at systems engineering. I take the view that you can learn from anyone and what works in one industry or situation may be transportable and give you competitive advantage in another context. It defines a set of processes and associated terminology which can be applied at any level in the hierarchy of a system's structure. Selected sets of these processes can be applied throughout the project life cycle for managing and performing the stages of a system's life cycle. It provides processes that support the definition, control, and improvement of the system life cycle processes used within an organization or a project. Organizations and projects can use these processes when acquiring and supplying systems. ISO/IEC/IEEE 15288:2015 concerns those systems that are man-made and may be configured with one or more of the following system elements: hardware, software, data, humans, processes (e.g. processes for providing service to users), procedures (e.g., operator instructions), facilities, materials, and naturally occurring entities, which just about covers everything from a railway network to missiles.

Appendix C2 – Methods

About project management methods

A method is a collection of practices, rules, tools, and instructions used by teams or individuals to achieve a specific result. It defines principles and provides documentation and tools. It is the responsibility of users to identify and plan the relevant component for their specific tasks. As such, a method provides flexibility but requires each user to choose and organize the set of activities relevant for the project.

PRINCE2®

The most commonly available method is PRINCE2®. First published in 1996, PRINCE2® is used not just in the UK but in more than 150 countries worldwide. This growth in use is the result of a number of factors. Expectations for its use have been set by successive UK governments with the aim of seeing that project performance in both the public and private sectors improves to benefit the country as a whole. Consequently, many other countries followed that lead as there is very little alternative "open copyright" material available for organizations to draw on. PRINCE2®'s scope covers all the roles and processes needed to direct, manage, and undertake a project. There is also a growing requirement for "accreditation" to be proven in a supplier/contractor context and PRINCE2® fills that need, being supported by training and examinations.

The scope of PRINCE2® is similar to that covered by BS6079 Part 1. Being a "method", however, it includes far more detail and defines specific techniques: the main ones are:

- Business case. Looked at in detail in PRINCE2®, but the use of the document and its development through the project life cycle are identical in BS6079.
- Exception management, as a technique. This is not prescribed in the British Standard.
- Product-based planning. The British Standard is nonprescriptive, but both documents end up with the same planning components, covering benefits, cost, resources, schedule, and scope.
- Health checks.

PRINCE2® is structured around principles, processes, and themes.
The principles are:

- continued business justification;
- learn from experience;

- defined roles and responsibilities;
- manage by stages;
- manage by exception;
- focus on products;
- tailor to suit the project environment.

The processes are:

- starting up a project;
- directing a project;
- initiating a project;
- managing a stage boundary;
- managing product delivery;
- closing a project.

The themes are:

- business case
- organization
- quality
- plans
- risk
- change
- progress.

PRINCE2® is not a single document but part of a family of publications, including programme and portfolio management. More recently, a guide has been developed which specifically shows how PRINCE2® can be used in the context of agile delivery methods. If you are interested in agile delivery in the context of project management, then also look at Atern, from the Agile Business Consortium, which uses the classic life cycle (staged) approach to project management and demonstrates how this is used to encompass the iterative approaches to development which are core to agile delivery.

Comparing PRINCE2® and the standards

Using PRINCE2® meets the requirements of both BS6079 Part 1 and ISO 21500, provided the following elements are covered by other organizational processes:

- document management;
- procurement;
- skills and competencies.

Referring to Figure C.3, the scope of ISO 21500 is totally contained within the scope of BS 6079 Part 1. BS6079 Part 1 also includes activities relating to the executive/project sponsor role and the team manager/team member roles, as well as configuration

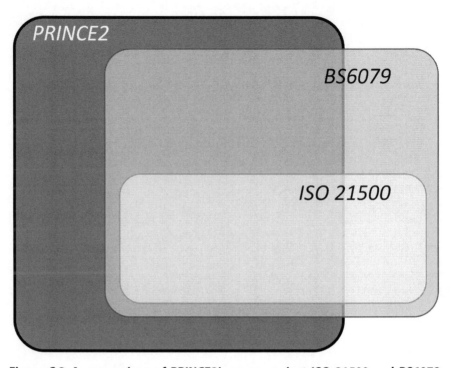

Figure C.3 A comparison of PRINCE2's scope against ISO 21500 and BS6079 Part 1

management; procurement; skills, competencies and document management. The scope of PRINCE2® and the scope of BS 6079 Part 1 are more closely aligned. BS 6079 Part 1 includes procurement and document management, skills, and competencies. PRINCE2® includes detailed techniques for undertaking certain processes; the standards have no prescriptive techniques for these and allow the user to determine their own approaches. AXELOS has produced a white paper which provides more detail.

The Project Workout and PRINCE2®

The Project Workout and PRINCE2® cover all the roles and activities required to direct and manage a project. The principles are aligned, with both documents focusing on the business objectives driving the project.

The Project Workout covers all the topics in PRINCE2® except "Configuration management" as this is a specialist discipline in engineering-based organizations and not core to every project. Further, configuration management is only successful if undertaken with the right tooling, which itself defines the processes to be used.

The processes in PRINCE2® match the management activities in *The Project Workout* except that *The Project Workout* includes an additional activity, after the project is finished to determine to what extent the business objectives were achieved (post-implementation review).

The PRINCE2® themes are represented as the topics in Part 3 of *The Project Workout*. *The Project Workout* has no specific quality topic as the concept of quality is embedded in every aspect of *The Project Workout* rather than treated as a separate subject. A defined project managed approach is a quality approach. PRINCE2®'s "Planning" theme prescribes product-based planning, whereas *The Project Workout* is more flexible, recommending a "product"-based start to planning, back-casting from the desired outcomes, but adding activities as and when you want to capture them.

The Project Workout:

- includes issues management explicitly, whereas PRINCE2® treats issues and change control together;
- focuses more on "outcomes" than "outputs" or "products" as they are termed in PRINCE2®. PRINCE® can, however, be used successfully if you tailor it to widen the term "product" to include outputs and outcomes;
- like BS6079 Part1, treats gates as key decision points, to start new stages and that stages can overlap; PRINCE2® talks of "managing stage boundaries" and implies stages cannot overlap and should be sequential.

PRINCE2® defines a project in the project initiation documents; *The Project Workout* simplifies this in its business case and project definition document. PRINCE2®'s project initiation document is a set of a twelve "parts", which may be sections in a document or documents in their own right. It is one aspect which needs to be tailored to make it appropriate, otherwise it risks becoming a very unwieldy.

PRINCE2® and *The Project Workout* are a good fit; the main conflict relates to stages and gates and can be dealt with through tailoring.

The main terminology differences are:

- *The Project Workout* describes "management activities", which PRINCE2® calls "processes";
- PRINCE2® uses "product", whilst *The Project Workout* uses "deliverable" and "output";
- PRINCE2® uses "Executive", *The Project Workout* uses "project sponsor";
- *The Project Workout* uses "log", PRINCE2® uses "register" (as in risk register) for formal lists and "log" for less formal notes (as in daily log);
- *The Project Workout* uses "proposal", PRINCE2® uses "Project Brief".

Appendix C3 – Other sources of best practice

What are the other sources?

Standards and methods are not the only publications available; there are others from a range of international and national organizations and they can come in many forms, such as knowledge bases, maturity models, and competency frameworks. Some are described below, though this is by no means a comprehensive list:

- APM *Body of Knowledge*, from the UK's Association for Project Management;
- *A Guide to the Project Management Body of Knowledge* (PMBOK®), from the USA's Project Management Institute;
- Capability Maturity Model Integrated (CMMI), from the Software Engineering Institute;
- GAPPS, Global Alliance for Project Performance Standards.

Most professional bodies publish a range of guides, whitepapers and research findings, all of which might help you understand the latest thinking on various topics.

APM Body of Knowledge

The UK's Association for Project Management's *Body of Knowledge* (in its 6th edition at the time of writing) provides the foundation for the successful portfolio, programme and project management, across all sectors and industries. It sets out the areas of knowledge a project manager should have if he or she is to be successful. It covers context, people aspects, delivery, and interfaces.

- **Context** includes governance, sponsorship, life cycle, success factors, and maturity, as well as the project in relation to operations management and strategy.
- **People** aspects cover interpersonal skills, like communication, conflict management, delegation, influencing, leadership, team work, and negotiation, as well as professionalism and ethics.
- **Delivery** covers the classic project management techniques, providing guidance on integrative management, planning (scope, schedule, resource), risk management and quality.
- **Interfaces** includes topics such as accounting, health and safety, law, sustainability, and security.

Whilst it has its own glossary of terms and seeks to be internally consistent, the authors recognize that different terminology will be used and give some of the commonly used alternatives. Each section in the document has references to further reading in terms of relevant standards, books, and papers.

APM's body of knowledge differs from all the other documents mentioned in this chapter in that it is not process-based, recognizing that there can be "many right ways" to undertake the activities associated with project management.

The Project Workout and the APM *Body of Knowledge*

The Project Workout and the APM *Body of Knowledge* both cover all the roles and activities required to direct and manage a project. *The Project Workout* covers all the knowledge area, except "Procurement"; this is because most organizations have procurement processes which apply to the whole organization and not just to projects.

The structures of the two documents are very different as they serve different purposes. The APM *Body of Knowledge* has a wider scope as it reflects a professional organization; it therefore includes topics such as accounting, ethics, sustainability, health and safety and contract law. The APM also includes a numbers of topics which have a basis in system engineering such as requirements management and solutions development.

The APM *Body of Knowledge* is not prescriptive with particular process, methods, or terminology; it is more concerned with good practices.

The Project Workout has a good fit with the APM *Body of Knowledge*.

A Guide to the Project Management Body of Knowledge (PMBOK®)

A Guide to the Project Management Body of Knowledge (PMBOK® Guide) is a publication which presents a set of terminology and guidelines for project management. Note the title; it is a **guide** to the body of knowledge and does not claim to be **the** body of knowledge as that would encompass both explicit and implicit knowledge on the topic, throughout the world. PMI® claims this document to be the "the preeminent global standard for project management". Its development is overseen by the USA's Project Management Institute (PMI®). Earlier versions were recognized as standards by the American National Standards Institute (ANSI/ PMI 99–001–2017) and the Institute of Electrical and Electronics Engineers (IEEE 1490–2011). The current edition (at the time of writing), the 6th edition, has a standard in Part 2 of the PMBOK®. Whilst I have placed this under "other sources of best practice", some may argue the standard section could be mentioned under "standards" above.

The PMBOK® is process-based and its architecture is very similar to ISO 21500, but there are slight differences. ISO 21500 was developed after the PMBOK® and is a consensus of international opinion, not necessarily that espoused by PMI. At the time of writing, the USA had not adopted ISO 21500.

Like ISO 21500, the PMBOK's® processes are focused around what a project manager does. Each knowledge area consists of processes applicable to any project phase or project. These processes are defined in terms of purpose, description, and primary inputs and outputs and are interdependent.

The process groups include those activities which are typically used when:

- **Initiating** a project, to start and define a project phase (stage) or project and approve the start of the work.
- **Planning** a project to develop the plan sufficiently to establish a baseline against which performance can be measured and controlled;
- **Executing** a project to undertake the management activities and support the development of the project's deliverables.
- **Monitoring and controlling** a project used to monitor, measure, and control project performance against the project plan.
- **Closing** a project to formally verify that the work is finished and provide lessons learned.

Each of the ten knowledge areas contains the activities that need to be performed to achieve effective project management, defined by PMI®. The activities also fall into one of the five process groups, creating a matrix structure such that every process can be related to one knowledge area and one process group. The knowledge areas are listed in Table C.3 with a tick to show which process group the component processes are

Table C.3 PMBOK®'S Knowledge areas and subject groups

		Project management process groups				
		Initiating	Planning	Executing	Monitoring and controlling	Closing
Knowledge areas	Project integration management	✓	✓	✓	✓	
	Project scope management		✓		✓	
	Project time management		✓		✓	
	Project cost management		✓		✓	
	Project quality management		✓	✓	✓	
	Project human resource management		✓	✓		
	Project communications management		✓	✓	✓	
	Project risk management		✓		✓	
	Project procurement management		✓	✓	✓	✓
	Project stakeholder management	✓	✓	✓	✓	

reflected in. Notice how similar this looks to the table for ISO 21500 (Table C.1) but also notice the differences. This just emphasizes that there are many different ways to depict the same concepts.

Be careful about how you use the process groups; some users of the PMBOK® manual incorrectly interpret them as representing the stages in a project life cycle. It was not PMI®'s intention to uses these as a life cycle; they are simply groups of process directed towards a particular purpose.

The Project Workout and PMBOK®

The Project Workout covers all the roles and activities required to direct and manage a project, whereas PMBOK® just covers the activities undertaken by a project manager. As such PMBOK® has a narrower scope. *The Project Workout* covers all the knowledge areas except "Procurement"; this is because most organizations have procurement processes which apply to the whole organization and not just to projects.

Apart from the interpersonal aspects of managing projects, *The Project Workout* includes the following topics which are not covered in PMBOK®:

- Management: identifying the need, directing a project, authorizing a project, managing delivery; reviewing outcome.
- Support: benefits, issues management, document management, reviews.

The Project Workout also provides more information on project life cycles and their use. The main terminology differences are:

- *The Project Workout* uses "stage", PMBOK® uses "phase";
- *The Project Workout* describes "management activities", which PMBOK® calls "Integration activities".

Capability Maturity Model Integrated for Development (CMMI-DEV)

CMMI looks at maturity. Whilst skills and competencies are a feature of an individual's capability, maturing refers to the capability of an entire organization. To achieve maturity, the model states your organization has to be able to consistently and repeatedly be able to undertake a number of specified "practices", depending on the maturity level you claim to be at. The term "practice" is used as CMMI assessors are concerned with what people actually do in their day-to-day jobs; how the processes are structure is less relevant. A single CMMI practice may correspond to one or more "processes" or procedures. CMMI can therefore be used to check a project management approach, whether on a single project (CMMI maturity level 2) or on all an organization's projects (CMMI maturity level 3 and above). You'll find CMMI-DEV covers general practices, project management, process management, support and engineering practices.

The general practices cover how to manage your process or method. For example, General Practice 2.3 is to "Provide resources: Provide adequate resources for performing the process, developing the work products and providing the services of the process". In other words, make sure you have the people and other resources needed to do the work you want to do. General Practice, 2.4 is "Assign Responsibility: Assign responsibility and authority for performing the process, developing the work products, and providing the services of the process". In other words, ensure someone is accountable, as in Chapter 15.

CMMI's project management practices are defined under their process groups:

- **Integrated Project Management**; this is about managing a project, involving the stakeholders.
- **Project Monitoring and Control** is concerned with providing an understanding of the project's progress so appropriate corrective actions can be taken.
- **Project Planning** is concerned with establishing and maintaining plans and defining project activities. Notice, like *The Project Workout*, BS6079 Part 1 and PRINCE2®, it treats planning in an holistic way.
- **Quantitative Project Management** is a step up from monitoring and control and takes a metrics-based view on this.
- **Risk Management** is aimed at is identifying potential problems before they occur so risk handling activities can be planned and called on if needed.
- **Supplier Agreement Management** is about buying products and services from suppliers (procurement).

CMMI does not contain information on how to undertake the practices, but leaves that to the manager to decide. By having the engineering activities within its scope, however, it shows how these and project management rely on each other. If you are working in a system engineering-based organization, such as aerospace, automotive and construction, this is a useful perspective.

The Project Workout and CMMI-DEV

The Project Workout and the CMM-DEV are designed for different purposes which is reflected in their structure and content. *The Project Workout* covers all the roles and activities required to direct and manage a business-driven project, whereas CMMI-DEV concentrates more on the control of work. CMMI-DEV does, however, stress in its general practices that there must be a business driver for any work undertaken.

The Project Workout covers all CMMI-DEV's project management process areas except "Supplier agreement management"; this is because most organizations have procurement processes which apply to the whole organization and not just to projects.

CMMI-DEV is not prescriptive on particular process, methods, or terminology; it is more concerned with good practices. *The Project Workout* has a good fit with the CMMI-DEV's project management process group and could be used as the basis of a Maturity Stage 3, CMMI-DEV compliant method.

GAPPS, Global Alliance for Project Performance Standards

The Global Alliance for Project Performance Standards (GAPPS) was formed to provide a neutral platform for all parties interested in the leadership and management of projects, including professional associations, public and private sector organizations, and academic institutions. The primary aim is to promote mutual recognition and transferability of project management standards and qualifications by providing a reliable source of comparative information. Everything GAPPS produces is made available, free of charge, on their web site.

GAPPS has developed an approach to categorizing projects based on management complexity. Their framework uses a tool to differentiate project manager roles based on the complexity of the projects managed. The tool identifies seven factors affecting the management complexity of a project. Each factor is rated from 1 to 4 using a qualitative point scale, and the factors are totalled to produce a management complexity rating for the project. This was used as the basis for the development of two levels of Project Manager Standards: G1 is for a moderately complex project and G2 is for a very complex project. Anything scoring below a G1 is considered to be a simple project. The comparisons of different standards and methods are made against the GAPPS set of project management competencies, from which an overall percentage coverage for each standard is derived. For example, Table C.4 shows the IPMA's competency standard (ICB3) and PRINCE2® have the greatest coverage. A detailed look at the results on their web site will show you where the differences lie. Beware, however; all these standards and methods are updated, and be sure to check editions or versions you are working from are current.

Table C.4 Comparison of different standards against the GAPPS framework

	AIPM 2008 (Australia)	ANCSPM 2011 (Australia)	ICB3 (IPMA)	ISO 21500	P2M (Japan)	PMBOK 2008 (PMI)	PRINCE2 2009 (Axelos)
Very complex project % coverage	65	70	98	54	73	70	92
Moderately complex % coverage	69	74	99	58	81	79	93

Source: GAPPS, Comparison of project management standards, 27 Feb 2014.

Appendix D:
Good meetings

Meetings take up a considerable amount of time, drawing on people, often from a number of different organizations. Ensuring time is spent wisely and all the right people are engaged is a challenge anyone who calls a meeting must face. To help with this, I have produced a set of checklists to help your meetings run efficiently and effectively.

Before the meeting

The person calling the meeting should:

- decide who will chair the meetings;
- fix the objective, venue, date, time, and attendance well in advance; keep numbers to a minimum;
- ensure all required parties are invited and have authority/knowledge to take decisions and/or make a valid contribution;
- set accountability and time limits for each agenda item, taking into account the participants' different interest levels for each item;
- send out agenda and written submissions in time to allow participants to prepare.

Those invited should accept the invitation, decline, or provide a substitute attendee, as appropriate.

At the meeting

The chair should:

- confirm who the note-taker is;
- confirm the objective of the meeting;
- start and finish the meeting on time: censure late arrivals;
- stick to the agenda and timetable;
- ensure there is an agreed approach for undertaking each agenda item;
- keep the meeting focused;
- ensure full, participative discussion takes place;
- guillotine "knotty" issues for resolution outside the meeting;
- summarize each agenda item at the end and ensure agreements and actions are recorded;
- agree and fix the date for next meeting, if needed;
- seek meeting participants' feedback on the effectiveness of the meeting.

The note-taker should:

- act as the chair's right-hand person;
- ensure all decisions and agreements are noted;
- take brief, relevant, action-oriented notes.

Meeting participants should:

- keep to the point and be brief;
- listen to others and not hold private meetings;
- be constructive, adopting a "can do" approach;
- agree realistic plans/actions;
- make a note of their own actions (including recipient and date).

After the meeting

The chair should review the effectiveness of the meeting and note improvement points for the next meeting.

The note-taker should publish the notes or minutes to the participants and those who need them within two days.

Participants should:

- assess their own effectiveness at the meeting and note areas for improvement; make suggestions to the chair if appropriate;
- read the minutes and address all actions and note those actions where they are the "recipient".

Making it easier for yourself

Do not hold a meeting at all if there is a better way of achieving the objective. The time taken during the meeting should typically represent only 10 per cent to 20 per cent of the total time needed to prepare for and follow up the meeting.

Set up a specific area in your collaboration system (such as Livelink or Share-Point) for the meeting collateral, including agenda, notes, and any supporting papers required. Ensure all attendees have access.

If available, use an electronic task list to record the meeting's actions. In this way, no actions are lost and those accountable for each action can readily find them.

Place "Review of Previous Minutes" towards the end of the meeting agenda, rather than at the beginning. This will encourage the meeting to go forward rather than starting by dwelling on what happened last time. If important, many of these items will be dealt with in the main agenda items.

If the notes are not for a formal meeting then consider the use of handwritten notes or a photocopied page in your work book:

- record actions, in handwriting, at the meeting;
- photocopy the sheet(s) just before the end of the meeting;
- distribute to participants before they leave;
- scan and file the handwritten note if you need a record.

Good behaviours

If all else fails, ask your meeting participants to:

- START ON TIME
- Switch off or silence mobile devices
- Keep to the agenda – Stick to the point
- No private meetings
- No interruptions or walk-outs
- LISTEN!
- Speak out during the meeting – not afterwards
- Be constructive
- Be polite
- Agree conclusions and actions
- FINISH ON TIME.

Appendix E: Brainstorming

"He objected to ideas only when others had them"

A J P TAYLOR

Brainstorming is a very popular technique for generating ideas in a group, but despite its popularity it is often poorly practised. In a project management context it can be used when planning, identifying risks, planning a response to a risk, resolving issues, and agreeing lessons learned.

Principles for brainstorming

Brainstorming was developed by Alex Osborn in the 1930s and had five basic principles.

1 **Defer judgement**. Do not criticize any ideas generated as part of a brainstorm. If each idea is analysed as it is created, few ideas will actually surface and many will be suppressed. This will either be because you will run out of time or because a proposer of an idea may not want to appear "silly". It is exactly the "silly" ideas which trigger unique and creative solutions. Never mix idea-generation and analysis.
2 **Quantity breeds quality**. By deferring judgement, you will increase the quantity of ideas. This in turn leads to an increase in the probability of delivering more creative solutions.
3 **The wilder the idea, the better**. Divergent thinking requires a certain amount of risk taking. Breakthrough ideas are hardly likely to come from "safe" propositions.

Remember at this stage you are hardly taking a risk by calling out something which may make you look foolish. The bigger risk is that you are quiet and the killer solution never sees the light of day.

4 **Combine and improve ideas**. Build on what has gone before. Most ideas are not new; they are built on what went before by modifying and evolving.

5 **Take a break from the problem**. Idea generation is tiring. Tired people do not perform well. Keep each idea generation session to about 10 to 15 minutes.

A blueprint for a brainstorming session

1 Choose a facilitator. This person will not take part in the idea-generation session. He or she should start by reminding everyone of the principles and should ensure these principles are upheld and act as the scribe. The facilitator may only contribute if the flow has stopped and the group needs reinvigorating.

2 Define the subject; write it on a flip chart. Make sure everyone can see it and understands what the problem, issue, or opportunity is.

3 Generate ideas; ask the group to contribute ideas by calling them out. The facilitator should write them on Post-it® Notes and display these prominently, where everyone can see them. No criticizing any ideas!

4 Cluster the ideas into groups (hence the use of Post-it® Notes) to aid the selection and analysis of the ideas. If necessary, try different clustering approaches until you find one that fits.

5 Identify possible options for resolving the problem, issue, or opportunity drawing on the clusters.

6 Evaluate each option in turn and agree which is the best approach in the circumstances. Look at the pros and cons and the risks.

7 Agree the actions and plan going forward.

A facilitator's checklist

As a project manager, you are likely to have to lead creative sessions, so here is a checklist to help you succeed:

1 Explain the brainstorming principles.

2 Encourage any and every idea enthusiastically; nothing is too bizarre.

3 Set approximate timescales for each session (10–15 minutes).

4 Act as scribe on Post-It® Notes; write ideas up in plain English, ensuring everyone understands what is being said.

5 Deflect and discourage criticism of ideas.

6 Tease out full ideas from people who have stalled halfway in the middle of a contribution.

7 Encourage non-contributors to contribute.

8 Only contribute if the flow has stopped and needs starting again.

9 Keep people to the subject on the flip chart.

10 Close the brainstorming session when appropriate.

Alternative approaches

You can also vary your approach to brainstorming to keep the sessions alive, such as by:

- **using Post-It® Notes**: ask people to write their ideas on Post-It Notes® themselves and stick them on the wall (the silent brainstorm);
- **playing pass the parcel**: each person writes their ideas on a sheet and after 5 minutes passes the sheet to the left for the next person to add to. Do as many times needed to create the ideas;
- **using subgroups**: divide the group into subgroups of two or three people. Give each subgroup a flip chart on which they post their ideas. Swap flip charts every few minutes until each group has visited each flip chart twice to add their ideas;
- **drawing rich pictures**: divide the group into subgroups of two or three people and ask them to draw, on a flip chart (or several stuck together), a picture or cartoon of the problem or issue at stake. Pictures can often bring out truths which people are reluctant to put into words.

Index